Cornelius Castoriadis
Political and Social Writings
Volume 1

CORNELIUS CASTORIADIS

POLITICAL

AND SOCIAL

WRITINGS

TRANSLATED AND EDITED BY DAVID AMES CURTIS

Volume 1, 1946-1955: From the Critique of Bureaucracy to the Positive Content of Socialism

University of Minnesota Press, Minneapolis

The Preface, "General Introduction," "On the Regime and against the Defense of the USSR," "The Problem of the USSR and the Possibility of a Third Historical Solution," "The Concentration of the Forces of Production," and "The Exploitation of the Peasantry under Bureaucratic Capitalism." In *La Société bureaucratique, 1: Les Rapports de production en Russie* (1973).

"The Yugoslavian Bureaucracy" and "The Bureaucracy after the Death of Stalin." In *La Société bureaucratique, 2: La Révolution contre la bureaucratie* (1973).

"Stalinism in France" and "The Situation of Imperialism and Proletarian Perspectives." In *Capitalisme moderne et révolution, 1: L'Impérialisme et la guerre* (1979).

"Proletarian Leadership" and "Sartre, Stalinism, and the Workers." In *L'Expérience du mouvement ouvrier, 1: Comment lutter* (1974).

"On the Content of Socialism, I" In *Le Contenu du socialisme* (1979).

Published by the University of Minnesota Press
2037 University Avenue Southeast, Minneapolis, MN 55414.
Published simultaneously in Canada
by Fitzhenry & Whiteside Limited, Markham.
Printed in the United States of America.

Library of Congress Cataloging-in-Publication Data

Castoriadis, Cornelius.
    Cornelius Castoriadis, political and social writings.

    Selected works originally published in French.
    Includes bibliographies and indexes.
    Contents: v. 1. 1946-1955, from the critique of bureaucracy to the positive content of socialism—v. 2. 1955-1960, from the workers' struggle against bureaucracy to revolution in the age of modern capitalism.

    1. Social sciences.   2. Communism.   3. Labor and laboring classes.   4. Bureaucracy.
I. Title.   II. Title: Political and social writings.
H61.C34   1988   300   87-10893

ISBN 0-8166-1614-0 (set)
ISBN 0-8166-1615-9 (pbk. : set)
ISBN 0-8166-1616-7 (vol. 1)
ISBN 0-8166-1617-5 (pbk.: vol. 1)

Contents

Contents
Political and Social Writings
Volume 2

Foreword
David Ames Curtis

> We do not have any Good News to proselytize concerning
> the Promised Land glimmering on the horizon, any Book
> to recommend whose reading would exempt one from
> having to seek the truth for oneself.
> —Cornelius Castoriadis, "General Introduction"

In presenting the first two volumes of translations entitled *Political and Social Writings*, we are offering to the American reader a selection of Cornelius Castoriadis's writings published in the Editions 10/18 series between 1973 and 1979. The majority of these articles, essays, and other documents were originally published in *Socialisme ou Barbarie* (*S. ou B.*, Socialism or barbarism), a journal founded by Castoriadis and Claude Lefort in 1949.[1]

It is not my intention in this brief Foreword to provide a comprehensive overview or analysis of Castoriadis's work and of this journal's significance (Castoriadis provides his own "General Introduction" [*GI*]). Nor do I want to take advantage of my position as the first reader of these writings in English to try to prescribe what one should make of them. It has rather been my intention to make Castoriadis's political and social thought available to the American public (and in particular to the American Left) so that it can benefit from his forty years of reflections upon politics, society, and culture and make use of his distinctive theoretical elaborations, social analyses, and critical responses after its own fashion. Let me instead share my experience of discovering Castoriadis by way of explaining why I believe his writings should be made available and can be of use.

Due to an accident of birth (I have just turned thirty), I was too young to be actively involved with the political upheavals of the 1960s. While others remember the Berkeley Free Speech movement, the Summer of Love, and Chicago, I remember the Boston Red Sox "Impossible Dream" year of 1967. My introduction to sixties' politics came from reading New Left theoretical writings over the next decade and a half and from being involved in the community organizing, civil rights, and labor movements. It is perhaps understandable that I once imagined the student protestors of those turbulent times consulting

Herbert Marcuse's *One-Dimensional Man* at their bedsides after a hard day of demonstrations.

Although later disabused of that notion, it was with great interest that I read about Daniel ("Dany the Red") Cohn-Bendit, the former French student leader (and now a Greens party activist in Germany), in Arthur Hirsh's *The French New Left* (1981).[2] Hirsh tells how Cohn-Bendit, in his book about the May 1968 student and worker rebellion in France, *Obsolete Communism: The Left-Wing Alternative*,[3] had acknowledged his debt to a journal called *Socialisme ou Barbarie*, saying, "I am not, and do not want to be, anything but a plagiarist when it comes to preaching of revolutionary theory" and "the views we have been presenting are those of P. Chaulieu."[4]

This journal, and a group with the same name, I discovered, were small but influential sources for French New Left thought and, as Cohn-Bendit testifies, action. "P(ierre) Chaulieu," along with "Marc Coudray" and "Paul Cardan," I learned, were all pseudonyms[5] for Cornelius Castoriadis, an economist and philosopher of Greek extraction who lived in Paris and edited *Socialisme ou Barbarie*, an "Organ of Revolutionary Criticism and Orientation," as the journal's subtitle proclaimed. The name—and the choice it implied—referred to an issue discussed in both Marx and Rosa Luxemburg, and, more proximately, it strongly alluded to a statement Trotsky made in 1939, soon before his assassination by a Stalinist agent. If the war did not end in revolution, he had said, Stalin's Russia and Nazi Germany would have to be reexamined, for perhaps these two social-economic and political systems were forerunners of a new kind of barbarism, far removed from either socialism or capitalism as traditionally conceived.

Born in Constantinople in 1922, Castoriadis studied law, economics, and philosophy in Athens. Though a member of the Greek Communist Youth in 1937 and, after the German occupation of Greece (1941), cooriginator of a journal attempting to "reform" the Greek Communist party (CP), he had become a Trotskyist by 1942, spending much of the rest of the war avoiding both Stalinist and Gestapo agents. He came to Paris at the war's end, joined the French section of the Trotskyist Fourth International, and agitated from the Left against the Trotskyists' lack of revolutionary theory and action, especially with regard to the Russian question and the Fourth's attempt at a "united front" with the Stalinist CP (in this volume see "On the Regime and against the Defense of the USSR" and "The Problem of the USSR and the Possibility of a Third Historical Solution"). Castoriadis, Claude Lefort (a student of the existentialist philosopher Maurice Merleau-Ponty), and others left the Fourth to form *Socialisme ou Barbarie* in 1949.

At the close of the Second World War, France found itself in an ambiguous strategic and political position. The experience of the war, the German occupation and the Vichy government, the paramount role of the CP in the French Resistance, and France's slow economic recovery in the aftermath of the war all served to provide the pro-Russian Parti communiste français (PCF) with a considerable power base and enormous popular stature. The fact that France was liberated by the *Western* allies, the Red Army having halted its advance two hundred miles to the east, the outbreak of the cold war, and a number of other factors, many of which are explored by Castoriadis in this first volume, served to counterbalance those factors that had brought the PCF to such a position of predominance. The PCF was a powerful, bureaucratically run mass organization that could neither rule France in this political-strategic situation nor be ignored in its consequent role of opposition force.

The Party's exit from the French government in 1947 only exacerbated this state of affairs. The PCF retained a considerable (though dwindling) following among its union supporters and among many other members of society who desired changes in the Fourth Republic. Of equal importance for French society, this pole of opposition attracted large numbers of the French intelligentsia who continued to gravitate toward the Party. Successive generations of these intellectuals, from Sartre to Althusser and beyond, entered the Party's orbit—thus providing it with an air of legitimacy and respectability—before breaking away or being repelled in disappointment, disillusionment, or disgust. These recurrent cycles of mental migration, unabated for over thirty years, were of such predictable periodic frequency that it is surprising—and perhaps revealing—that the precise, rational, and scientific French mind did not chart their course, let alone note their existence.

It is within this context that Cornelius Castoriadis and his small band set out to challenge the assumptions, the practices, and the direction of the entire French Left. At the age of twenty-six, Castoriadis drafted the far-reaching and strikingly comprehensive founding document of his group and journal, also entitled "Socialism or Barbarism" (*SB*, included here). Modeled on the *Communist Manifesto* of 1848, this 1949 antibureaucratic salvo from/at the Left combined his analyses of the bureaucracy in the Soviet Union, the bureaucratic nature of "Communist" parties (see "Stalinism in France"), and a reworking of Lenin's theory of imperialism, updated to take into account the process of worldwide capital concentration that had crystallized into an intransigent conflict between two expansionist superpowers, both of which were characterized by the increasing bureaucratization of their societies as well as their economies (see "The Concentration of the Forces of Production"). The clear and unmistakable conclusion for this revolutionary group was *workers' management*, an idea that became a political and economic demand in Hungary in 1956 and the motto for a social-cultural rebellion in France in May 1968.

Working at first in near obscurity, the group published (unorthodox but faithful) Marxist critiques of "bureaucratic" rule in the "Soviet" Union (see the two classic pieces: "The Relations of Production in Russia" [*RPR*] and "The Exploitation of the Peasantry under Bureaucratic Capitalism") and in the "popular democracies" (see "The Yugoslavian Bureaucracy" for a telling discussion of an early split within the "worldwide communist movement"—made up as it is of conflicting national bureaucracies—that avoided the Trotskyists' temptation to accord a progressive meaning to "workers' management" as imposed from above by Tito). It covered the East German Revolt of 1953 and the Hungarian Revolution from the perspective of the working-class challenge to "communist" rule. And it developed analyses of various phenomena such as the student and women's[6] movements, wildcat strikes in America, and the demand for workers' self-management as manifestations of people's tendency toward the "instauration"[7] of *autonomous* forms of organization and struggle in modern capitalist society.

In the first volume of the present translation one can also read an analysis of the distinctive class structure of Russia in "The Bureaucracy after the Death of Stalin" as well as a discussion of the world situation and of the two expansionist superpowers in "The Situation of Imperialism and Proletarian Perspectives" (*SIPP*), where Castoriadis and the group revise their earlier ideas about the imminence of a third world war while noting the increasing militancy of the working class on both sides of the "Iron Curtain" in combating war and bureaucratic rule in the early 1950s. Also included in this first volume is Castoriadis's contribution to a controversy between Lefort and Jean-Paul Sartre over the latter's "The Communists and the Peace," a series of articles published in *Les Temps Modernes*, which were occasioned by the increasing detachment of the French working class from the PCF and in which Sartre declared "an anticommunist is a dirty rat." (Sartre was later heard to say that Castoriadis was right, but at the wrong time. Castoriadis's reply was that Sartre had the honor of being wrong at presumably the right time.)

Under Castoriadis's guidance, the group became increasingly critical not only of the so-called "Marxist" or "socialist" countries of the Eastern bloc, but also of Marxism itself, with its nineteenth-century scientism and other attitudes that he believed shared more with a capitalist outlook than with socialism. Unlike many former Marxists who found new religion in right-wing and reactionary circles when confronted with "the God that failed," Castoriadis and his group consistently developed and broadened their radical critique of both capitalist and "communist" societies.

During this period Castoriadis was a professional economist for what is now called OECD (the Organization for Economic Cooperation and Development), an international organization of economic analysis and cooperation serving the major industrial countries (his official title at OECD was "Director of the Branch of Statistics, National Accounts and Growth Studies"). Working inside a bureaucracy that was a "bureaucracy for the bureaucracy," Castoriadis was positioned at a useful vantage point to study the workings of the world capitalist economy as well as the internal functioning of a modern bureaucratic apparatus. After translating and reading Castoriadis's writings I find it difficult to imagine him making small talk around the water cooler, though the spectacle of Karl Marx as a cub reporter for the *New York Tribune* is no less baffling. In any case, it provided him with a firsthand opportunity to sharpen and broaden his critique of Marx's and Weber's analyses of capitalist and state-bureaucratic "rationalization," which appears throughout his writings of this period.

The journal itself was only one part of the group's work. A monthly, roneotyped supplement to *S. ou B.*, *Pouvoir Ouvrier* (Workers' power), also was published beginning in 1958. Members were urged to organize where they worked, trying to avoid the Trotskyist practice of "parachuting" "professional revolutionaries" into others' battles, but also offering assistance to workers who wanted to organize their own struggles. Discussion groups were set up in numerous cities and in Paris. Castoriadis would be found at a hall called Mutualité in the Latin Quarter, holding evening meetings on a variety of topics treated in the journal. The group established contacts with similar organizations in other countries,[8] and helped to found what became Solidarity in England, which eventually inspired a like-named group in Philadelphia. *S. ou B.* also experienced a number of internal disagreements and breakups ("scissions").[9]

Two years before May 1968, Castoriadis convinced the group to disband, complaining that readers of the journal had remained mere consumers rather than active participants. He also pointed out, however, that its views already were gaining acceptance in left-wing and student circles.[10] Hirsh says in retrospect that Castoriadis, Lefort, and the collective work of *Socialisme ou Barbarie* together constituted one of the three main influences on the development of a French New Left, along with Henri Lefebvre and Jean-Paul Sartre. And as a recent article in the French left-wing daily, *Liberation* (June 28-29, 1986), put it, "Many are the intellectuals who, in the 70s, have, how should one put it . . . 'boasted' to having signed an article" in *S. ou B.* or "at least to having belonged to the same political territory as the review" (to which Castoriadis responded in jest, "If all these people really had been with us at the time, we would have taken power in France somewhere around 1957").[11]

More important, Castoriadis felt the need to investigate what he calls "the inherited ontology" of Western (which includes "Marxist") thought beyond the confines of a review and a group such as *S. ou B.* This new turn, first signaled in the last five issues of the journal in a series by Castoriadis entitled "Marxism and Revolutionary Theory" (published in 1964-65, but originally drafted at the time of "Modern Capitalism and Revolution" [*MRCM/MCR*] in 1959), has been elaborated in *The Imaginary Institution of Society* (which includes a reprint of these articles), *Crossroads in the Labyrinth*, the recently published *Domaines de l'homme* (Domains of man), and in *De l'écologie à l'autonomie* ("From Ecology to Autonomy"), a transcription of presentations made by Castoriadis and Cohn-Bendit to a gathering of 1,000 environmental activists in Louvain, Belgium in 1980, as well as in a more recent critique of Russia, *Devant la guerre* ("Facing War"), published in 1981.

Castoriadis left his job at OECD in 1970 to study to become a psychoanalyst. He has been practicing in Paris since 1974. (Castoriadis describes himself as a "close collaborator" with the "Fourth Group" in French psychoanalytic circles. The "Fourth Group" split from the Lacanians in 1968. Unlike the other two main groupings of French psychoanalysts, neither the Lacanian [third] group nor the "Fourth Group" maintains ties to the international psychoanalytic establishment.) He also was elected as a *Directeur d'études* at the Ecole des hautes études en sciences sociales, where he has been teaching since 1980. He continues to publish and lecture, and his work is far from complete. A sequel to *Devant la guerre*, examining (Western) "fragmented bureaucratic societies," a philosophical work on the imagination, and other writings are in progress.[12]

Perhaps the most "controversial" aspect of Castoriadis's work for the American public will be his frequent, indeed unrelenting, focus on the Soviet Union. One hopes that his extensive, forty-year theoretical, sociological, and cultural critique of Russia actually will be read and not just dismissed out of hand as "sounding too much like Jeane Kirkpatrick." For this would miss what seems to me the key contribution of Castoriadis's work. If one feels that there are problems on the Left, but that the job of criticizing Russia, "communism," and other aspects of "the Left" should be left to the Right, one will get, not so surprisingly, a right-wing critique of the Left; moreover, one will allow the Right (or what passes for the Left) to define what socialism, social change, and left-wing politics are all about. Castoriadis's main contribution lies in the fact that he starts off from a criticism of what *passes* for "the Left" in order to work out an unabashed and immensely fruitful positive conception of the prospects for a socialist society. This, indeed, is the main movement that can be discerned in this first volume, which develops "from the critique of bureaucracy to the positive content of socialism" and is worked out in ever-more painstaking detail and ever-greater breadth in volume 2 and the proposed third volume.

Of course, there are certain people "on the Left" in America who have discovered the evils of the Soviet Union rather recently, just as the French "new philosophers" (see "The Diversionists," to be included in volume 3) "discovered" the "Gulag" in the 1970s after reading Solzhenitsyn. Susan Sontag's Town Hall speech after the imposition of martial law in Poland comes to mind, in which she stated that the American Left would have done better reading the right-wing *Reader's Digest* instead of most American Left publications over the past few decades—and this from someone who has devoted a fair amount of her time to presenting to the American public what she deemed important in modern French thought! This headline-catching suggestion unconsciously reveals the point I have just made concerning the vacuum on the Left that the Left itself creates when it leaves criticism of itself to the Right, or indulges in belated "self-criticism" such as Sontag's that still ends up referring us to a right-wing publication.

Two other, interrelated aspects of Castoriadis's work deserving brief mention here are (1) what he regards as his success in anticipating political and social trends and (2) his attitude toward the role of revolutionaries and revolutionary groups in aiding the development of people's autonomous struggles. Let us take these two considerations in turn.

Castoriadis is rather unabashed in his self-assessment. Not only were the analyses by *S. ou B.* and himself the only ones to have faithfully pursued Marx's problematic, as he says in the "General Introduction" (though this also entailed its destruction, he adds), but these analyses have been "confirmed by experience" in a large number of cases. The growing importance of workers' demands for self-management and for the elimination of hierarchy, the "proletarian struggle against the bureaucracy" in Eastern Europe (East Germany in 1953, Hungary in 1956, and time after time in Poland—to cite merely some of the overt forms it has taken), the conflicts between national "communist" bureaucracies (first analyzed in relation to Yugoslavia, but applicable to China, Vietnam, and other cases), the generalization and extension of autonomous struggles against bureaucratic capitalist society described at the beginning of the 1960s in "Modern Capitalism and Revolution" and "confirmed" in what he called the "anticipated revolution" (May 1968, though here it was the revolutionary students who did the "anticipating"), and so on, are for him so many instances of correct anticipations of future events. He makes no bones about it

It is not my purpose here to make a case one way or the other for such claims (though I would add that, in my opinion, they can be justified). I wish to point out what may appear as a contradictory or complementary tendency (depending on how one conceives of his "anticipations") that runs through his writings. Even in his earliest articles, written while still a part of the Trotskyist movement, Castoriadis explicitly eschews pretensions to "prediction," which he views as a lamentable tendency of this movement and whose attempts have led nowhere but to being repeatedly rebuffed by reality. In these early texts, we find the beginnings of a characteristic move on Castoriadis's part when he speaks against those who would seek some sort of automatic "guarantee," a "foolproof" theory capable of predicting events or a preordained, scientifically discerned process mandating future success.

We see this already in "The Problem of the USSR and the Possibility of a Third Historical Solution," which, although formulated in an admittedly unsatisfactory way, takes Trotsky's problem of the "degeneration" of a revolution and turns it against itself. Against the idea that the process of revolutionary degeneration is a problem peculiar to a backward and isolated country like Russia (other, more "advanced" countries presumably not having this problem because of the "objective" conditions afforded by a higher development of the productive forces), Castoriadis points out that any revolution can degenerate because any country is backward and isolated . . . when it is isolated and thus rendered backward in relation to the rest of the world economy. It is not some sort of "objective guarantee" one should be looking for, since none exists, but a choice one should make (not that choice is all there is to it) between "socialism or barbarism."

We can see this exploration of such ambiguities, inconsistencies, and incoherencies in his criticism of so-called objective analyses (which supposedly lead to iron-clad guarantees and infallible predictions), including those of Marx. The contradiction between the "law of wages" and Marx's concession that wages are set by "moral and historical factors" is recognized as early as 1949, in *RPR*—although it took him until a decade later, in *MRCM/MCR*, to bring it fully to light. Perhaps this move can best be seen, though, in a section of "On the Content of Socialism, III" (*CS III*), entitled "The Hour of Work." Here he shows that the "hour of work" is an *indeterminate* concept in capitalist society, a concept that not only is necessarily at the center of the capitalist's calculation of wages (unless one switches to the equally indeterminate but just as necessarily central concept of "real output"), but that is also constantly being displaced by the real, but ever-shifting determinant of the hourly wage, the class struggle— which, with its objective *and* subjective aspects, makes a mockery of Marx's

"iron-clad" laws—though, ironically, it was Marx himself who "put class struggle on the map," Castoriadis says.

Of course, one may say that these examples I cite here (there are many more
in the translated texts) are "merely" instances of Castoriadis's more general critique of the Western process of "rationalization" and the "bureaucratic project
of capitalist society," torn as it is by the contradiction between "direction" and
"execution" when the former set of functions become embodied in *separate*, socially instituted apparatuses. As Castoriadis has said, he just picked up a loose
thread of Marxism (the problem of bureaucratization) and kept pulling until the
entire fabric of Marxism as a theoretical and practical method for analysis and
action came apart in his hands. (So *that's* what he was doing beside the water
cooler!)

But does this adequately describe Castoriadis's work, his "method"? Is
Castoriadis a "forerunner" of "deconstructionism," happily decentering away
the entire edifice of Marxism, capitalism, and traditional rational thought
throughout the postwar period? Are these examples I have cited "merely instances of a more general critique," as if we could speak of a "Castoriadian
method" (which other people just haven't gotten the hang of yet for some reason
or another)? Given his self-avowed ability to anticipate events and this on-going
strategy of laying bare the Left's contradictions not by saying that "the Emperor
has no clothes" but by actively pulling the loose thread of a protective garment
woven of ideological mystifications, ought we to conclude that Castoriadis is the
"*Prophet of Indeterminacy*,"[13] just as Marx ended up being the "Scientific
Prophet" of his time (see *GI*)?

I think not, and for several reasons. First of all, sometimes he is just plain
wrong, and he admits it, as in his revision of his initial ideas about the "immediacy of a third world war." (See *GI* and *SIPP*. Yet here we must also recognize
the continuing applicability of his analyses of superpower conflict within the
context of the increasing bureaucratization of world capitalism.) Second, though
unabashed in proclaiming his powers not of prediction but of *anticipation* (the
former being merely the extrapolation of current events and processes), he does
not make this into an occult process. It was rather the very rational, but not rationalistic, effort to elaborate revolutionary ideas, programs, and forms of organization and action capable of remaining *open to* changing events while being engaged in responding to the present situation that has enabled Castoriadis's work
to stand the test of time like that of no other writer of the postwar world.

Like Marx when confronted by the Paris Commune, Castoriadis greeted the
Hungarian Revolution as an autonomous popular *creation*, something *new* that
was not contained in what came before it, even as it confirmed the ideas about
workers' management expressed in his 1949 inaugural text, "Socialism or Barbarism." Both events occasioned and necessitated a reworking of ideas, an overthrowing of old conceptions and a confrontation with new problems and questions at the same time that they also required a defense against those who would
challenge or refuse their meaning or try to push these events back into previous
schemata of interpretation.

To see in such creative events a new meaning implied, however, a choice for a

new interpretation that in no way was guaranteed in advance. And these new interpretations have not all been equally fruitful. To take but two examples found
in these translated texts, the evolution of Eastern European societies has not followed the course of more and more explicit challenges to bureaucratic "communist" rule after the Hungarian Revolution (the Polish Solidarity movement,
though better "organized" on one level, has been more diffuse and less clear
about its objectives than the nearly spontaneous Workers' Councils of Budapest
in 1956), as was implied in "The Proletarian Revolution against the Bureaucracy" (see volume 2; "The Hungarian Source," Castoriadis's twenty-year ret-
rospective on the Hungarian Revolution, is to be included in volume 3). Nor has
the working class in the most advanced capitalist countries adopted the English
example of the shop-steward form of organization described in *MRCM/MCR*,
where Castoriadis said that to study the class struggle in England and America
"today" (1960) was no different than Marx studying England in 1860.

Now, Castoriadis's analyses and his anticipations, although not fulfilled completely or in every instance, retain a compelling power that is not easily denied.
The analyses of bureaucratization, of centralization, of privatization, of the consumer society, of the superpower conflict as well as inter- and intrabureaucratic
conflicts within each bloc; the critique of hierarchy and of the separation between the functions of "direction" and "execution" in modern bureaucratic capitalist society; and the conception of the autonomy of the proletariat and later
the emphasis on the autonomous struggles of women, youth, and others are the
enduring legacy of a thinker who has *challenged tradition*, not for the sake of challenging tradition, but to help people to become aware of what is new, what is being created today, both with respect to the world they live in and with respect to
the possibilities for change that can be effected. And the unabashed effort to extract from these analyses, critiques, and conceptions a *positive content* that can be
taken up and carried further by others distinguishes him from all those critical
thinkers and cautious revolutionaries who have tried in their embarrassment to
hide behind either "the power of negative thinking" or a complacent orthodoxy
in order to disguise their fear or reluctance to engage the present with a view toward an unpredictable future. (See, e.g., how in *RPR* and in *CS I* Castoriadis
attacks the idea that Marx's conception of "bourgeois right" somehow justifies
"Marxist" excuses for continuing exploitation and hierarchy in "socialist" societies. In the latter article especially, he shows how the antagonistic form of production found both in the Eastern and Western types of bureaucratic capitalism
itself raises the issue of the suppression of hierarchy and exploitation and makes
possible the instauration of other forms of cooperation, based upon equality and
the technical and other changes occurring today as well as those changes that can
come about through this very act of suppression.)[14]

One might be tempted to say that Castoriadis's "method" remains true, even
if the overall revolutionary perspective, formulated at a certain point in time,
and some of the prospects it sketched out do not. This attempt to play to
Castoriadis as Lukács played to Marx, however, cannot hold up, even if we were
to accept its premises. For, Castoriadis is very explicit that the attempt to di-
vorce "method" from (an ever-changing) content (while at the same time apply-

ing the former to the latter) is not only absurd, meaningless, and impossible to achieve, but is also what halts the progress of the revolutionary problematic in its tracks. Indeed, this point is what separates what Castoriadis is doing from "structuralism," "deconstructionism," "poststructuralism," or any other movement of thought that has become crystallized into a "method," of one kind or another. Whether one *subsequently* protests that the "label" was not the one they intended, that it was imposed upon them by others, or that they are trying to do something to clarify matters, in the end matters little. Whether one is "discoursing on method," "searching for a method," or even declaring oneself "against method," one is caught up in the same movement of Western rational thought and rationalization that stretches from Descartes to Sartre and beyond, where the importance of *method* predominates. That the triumph of method over practice is a characteristic moment of the process of bureaucratization just makes the irony of the situation that much more telling.[15]

(All this may make Castoriadis a less salable commodity, and less likely to become next year's intellectual superstar, sponsored by today's radical, left-wing readers/consumers of *Reader's Digest*. Not to worry. As Castoriadis points out in his article on Sartre, most academics and intellectuals won't venture beyond the walls of their ivory towers unless they are assured of receiving a few good swift kicks. They need only turn the pages of these volumes to be assured of a plentiful supply that will keep them standing for weeks.)

Castoriadis himself has dealt with the issues I have raised here precisely on this question of the revolutionary problematic. And this brings me to my second point. Two articles that many would be tempted to dismiss as an old-fashioned or uninteresting concern with "the revolutionary party" ("Proletarian Leadership" and "Proletariat and Organization, I"), and which indeed have been surpassed in their specific formulations (the restriction of their concern to the autonomous activity of the *proletariat* already was considerably loosened in *MRCM/MCR*, which appears at the end of volume 2, and was outstripped in such texts as "Recommencing the Revolution" in volume 3), are crucial, I believe, to an understanding of the meaning and import of Castoriadis's work. Castoriadis poses the dilemma as follows: How can one reconcile the goal of revolutionary activity (the autonomous development and unfolding of people's creative activity, the elimination of hierarchy and of any and all *separate* categories of leadership, management, and direction) with the need to organize in the here and now of a bureaucratized, centralized, hierarchized society of exploitation? Why not just give up or sit back ("folding one's arms") if one really believes, as Merleau-Ponty put it, paraphrasing Castoriadis (and attributing this remark merely to "one of my Marxist friends") after his attack on Sartre's "ultra-bolshevism" in *The Adventures of the Dialectic* (1955),[16] "that bolshevism has already ruined the revolution and that it must be replaced with the masses' unpredictable ingenuity"? What point is there in a rational analysis or "planned and organized activity" when the revolution itself will be original and unforeseeable, as well as an enormous expansion of the boundaries of this reason through the "creative activity of tens of millions of people"? One might also ask, what point is there, even, in reading *this* book when, as the quotation we have used to head up this Foreword proclaims, "We do not have any Good News to prosely-tize concerning the Promised Land glimmering on the horizon, any Book to recommend whose reading would exempt one from having to seek the truth for oneself"? How can one reconcile the necessity for acting with the fact that it may appear useless or superfluous to act?

Castoriadis provided a number of answers, in these two articles and in others. It is not my intention to discuss them here. His whole work can be seen as an attempt to answer these questions, especially in the light of the problems posed by the increasing bureaucratization, centralization, and privatization of social life. But in these *provisional* answers he also has stressed that there can be no theoretical answer that serves as a solution any more than there could be a practical solution that purely and simply ignores theoretical concerns.

In America, we see some left-wing "critical" journals placing the emphasis entirely on the necessity of getting theoretical matters settled "first" (when they will get around to anything else is open to question). We also see community, labor, and other social-change organizations whose hierarchy tells you not to think in any but practical terms because "workers" ("community people," etc.) don't worry about such matters, you couldn't communicate to them what you thought anyway, and, if all else fails, you aren't "real people" but (in most cases) "middle-class" (and if you weren't before, you will become so once you get hired as a "professional organizer"—which isn't necessarily a bad thing to be, but ultimately it is beside the point . . . or rather a way of maintaining the dominant viewpoint both hidden and unchallenged).[17] Another American example of getting trapped in this antinomy (the word is philosophical, but so are the attitudes that one is being "just practical" or "just theoretical") whereby one conceives of oneself as both "necessary" and "useless" comes from the end of the 1960s and the breakup of SDS. Having grasped in some fashion that what one is trying to bring about is an outpouring of autonomous, creative activity, the Weathermen (later Weatherpeople) took Bob Dylan's lyric statement that "You don't need a weatherman to know which way the wind blows" (cf. Castoriadis's criticism of Trotskyist "meteorological" *fore*casting) and could find nothing better to do in their necessary uselessness than to build and explode bombs, and occasionally take over a high school in order to lecture students until they had to run out the back door when the cops came (how much one could foster autonomous activity under such circumstances the Weatherpeople probably did not think about too hard in advance, but some people were so hell-bent on following a Leninist path into clandestinity—how convenient for the leadership!—that they would destroy an aboveground organization under the pretext that Richard Milhous Nixon was Czar Nicholas II). Their followers would not have done any worse if they took to heart Dylan's other line from the song "Subterranean Homesick Blues": "Don't follow leaders, watch your parking meters."[18] They might have done *better* by remembering that SDS stood for "Students for a Democratic Society."

The word that recurs in these discussions of Castoriadis's "anticipations" and of his presentation of the revolutionary problematic is "foresight." In some sense,

Castoriadis "foresaw" a number of significant events or trends and subsequently brought out their meaning, though, as he says in his 1974 introduction to *MCR*, this was due not to any objectively guaranteed process of Marxist divination but to a new conception of socialism and the autonomy of people's struggles. There is the tension between a rational anticipation of future events and the very unforeseeableness of the content of these events, which overthrows previous rational determinations.

Now, the term "foresight" is certainly unfortunate in one respect. It borrows from the Greco-Western tradition that theory (from the Greek *theorein*, to look at) is a seeing (of the Ideas, of essences, of "the truth," etc., in short, of something already there) instead of one form of activity that relates to (though it does not univocally determine) something to-be-accomplished. Castoriadis corrects this "view," as we can read in his "General Introduction." But there is another aspect that, though related, is of broader interest as well as specifically applicable to our discussion of Castoriadis.

Strange as it may seem, let me mention, by way of introduction, how Castoriadis spent his late-night hours back in the late forties. After a day at the office analyzing the capitalist system and an evening at Mutualité preparing to overthrow it, Castoriadis and friends retired to the Bal nègre, a hopping joint where he could listen to jazz and dance among an interesting mix of black American ex-patriots, Africans living in Paris, left-wing activists and intellectuals, and "lower-class" whites. I mention this only because, beyond the critique of bureaucracy and "rationalization," there is a positive effort, an attempt to bring out a collective, cooperative, and unfettered kind of activity, an *improvisatory* life of social and cultural creation. We see this in his writings (much more in their content than in their style, I would add),[19] an evocation of a kind of life that does not deny rationality, planning, and organizing, but does not confuse the plan with living nor does it live for the plan.

In a way, the *improvisatory* nature of jazz perfectly expresses what Castoriadis is trying to get at. Although not an explicit topic in his writings, he will talk at length about jazz, telling how C. L. R. James (the Jamaican-born half of the "Johnson-Forest tendency" within the American Trotskyist movement) used to hold forth in Paris delivering revolutionary speeches, playing his vocal chords in the style of Louis Armstrong's trumpet. And he is always quick to point out that jazz is *the* original American art form, created on American shores.

There is an ambiguity, however, in the word that characterizes jazz as an art form and distinguishes it from so-called classical music. The word is "improvisation" and the ambiguity lies in its Latin root. To "im-pro-vise" literally means *not* to "foresee," not to anticipate. As such, it is inadequate and misleading, for it borrows from a Western rationalist tradition that assumes that to act "rationally" is to have everything planned out in advance (the less planned out, the less "rational") *and* that it is really possible to merely react with no foresight at all, this being "improvisation."

Both ideas are wrong. One need not write out all one's notes in advance, nor even "plan" them all, as evidenced precisely by jazz "improvisation." But playing *before* this planning process is "complete" is not a lack of "*fore*sight," a failure to "provide," to make adequate "*provision*" (the root and the prefix are the same), or rather it is, as Castoriadis might say, not *fore*-"sight," but an exemplary instance of creative imagination at work (or: at play) in the mode of autonomy, where the music you will play and the music you have played lives with the music you are playing. And yet jazz improvisation is not "immediacy" either, some sort of "primitive" music somehow evolved by black Americans that inexplicably has its own history, performance principles, and social institutions (as well as, in many cases, "charts" and rehearsals), no matter how much, at one level, the Latin cognate word "improvisation" implies this racist conclusion.

Contrary to the two definitions provided by the *New World Dictionary* (Second College Edition, 1976, p. 707), "to improvise" is neither "(1) to compose, or simultaneously compose and perform, on the spur of the moment and without any preparation; extemporize," nor "(2) to make, provide [*sic*], or do with the tools and materials at hand, usually to fill an unforeseen and immediate need" since the first definition denies the role of preparation (or negates it because this process of preparation is not "complete") while the second definition negates itself in its very act of definition: One "provides" for the "unforeseen" need (i.e., that which was *not* already "provided for") through "improvisation."

In "improvisation" as I conceive it, one does not act in an "immediate," unprepared way lacking all foresight. The reference to "unforeseen needs" fudges the issue, for how can one act or even react if the need is truly unforeseen, and how can one still call one's activity "improvisatory" in the traditionally defined way if one now envisions or makes provision for a need that once was, but no longer is, unforeseen? The word "extemporize" contains the same definitional ambiguity (besides the larger problem of how to de-fine or de-limit truly improvisatory activity) when one is referred merely to "improvisation" and acting "without preparation" (*New World Dictionary*, p. 495). The Latin root, on the other hand, is more helpful here, for it tells of action (usually "speaking") that is *ex tempore* or "from, or coming out of time," but we would have to refer to Castoriadis's later writings on "time and creation" (see the subsection with this same title and subsequent subsections in Chapter 4 of *The Imaginary Institution of Society*) and on the radical imagination as "self-alteration" through time, all of which goes beyond the confines of this brief introduction.

Let us say simply that (jazz) improvisation is not instituted in the (illusory) "once and for all" mode of separation between composition and performance. It is not (and could not be) a type of activity that lacks all preparation, and yet through its *results* (which include the methods and practices it establishes along the way) it *creates* the "unforeseen" and "unforeseeable." This does not mean that we ought to make a fetish of the unforeseen, to value it for its own sake. The very process of "improvisation," when it is not conceived of in a merely privative fashion as lack of foresight, as responding to the need that was not foreseen, involves planning, the making of choices (one of the most elementary being *when* to start "playing" and when to remain silent), and the creation of alternative forms of articulation (*what* to "play"); it also gives birth to that which was not contained in previous activities. It is no mere accident or ethnological curiosity that jazz was created by *black* Americans. But it is no less true that it is a "mulatto" art form that has adopted, reworked, and fashioned anew and in particular ways the instruments, practices, and rules of a different, dominant culture while changing that culture in the process.[20]

The preceding discussion does not "provide" a *definitive* answer to the question of how we should understand Castoriadis's work, nor how it should be applied in an American setting. And there is certainly a difference between improvisatory music and most written prose, at least since composition and "performance" are necessarily tied together more closely in the latter case. Nor I am not trying to make Castoriadis into a Jack Kerouac of revolutionary prose essays (though they were born within twenty-four hours of each other). But I hope to have brought out some of the ways in which his writings can be approached by a culture that is quite capable (some present appearances to the contrary) of fostering autonomous movements and of "improvising" new and creative forms of organization and action (and demands)[21] for achieving social change.

And it is in an "improvised" way that we can and should respond to Castoriadis's work. The specific ways in which he formulated his ideas have in many instances been surpassed in one way or another, as he himself admits in his Introduction. Castoriadis explains, for example, that the nature of hierarchy in bureaucratic societies today is such that the hard-and-fast distinction between "direction" and "execution" no longer encompasses the separations and divisions that still rend these societies. Even "revolution," a word he still held onto when he demolished Marxist theory and practice in "Modern Capitalism and Revolution" and "Marxism and Revolutionary Theory," does not encompass what he is now trying to get at in his more recent work, as he also admits in his Introduction.[22] There is no prescribed doctrine to be preserved (which in no way nullifies the value of the positive content of his previous writings, open as they are to further interpretation and improvisation), nor any set "method" to be applied to the problems America and the world face today. If Castoriadis's thoughts, as set down in these writings, are applic*able* in America today, their applicability is to be found precisely in their resistance to such a separated view of "method" (which is not the same thing as being "against method" or being against programs and organizational structures) and in their refusal to allow his work to lend itself to such an interpretation—which is just the flip side of his (and others') continuing efforts to open up possibilities for imagining and bringing about an autonomous society.

Castoriadis has often been inspired by autonomous challenges to authority that have developed in America, such as the women's and students' movements, the phenomenon of "wildcat strikes," and, as we have said at some length, America's original art form, jazz. Perhaps after his having looked at (and listened to) America for the past forty-plus years, America will begin to take a look at and "improvise" a response to Cornelius Castoriadis.

February 1987

Notes

1. For a listing of texts to be included in volumes 2 and 3, see the Table of Contents for this volume and Appendix A, respectively. For 10/18 texts omitted from the present translated edition, see Appendix B. Appendix C lists previous English-language versions of 10/18 texts, including those omitted from the present edition. For the "General Plan of Publication" of the 10/18 volumes, along with Castoriadis's reasons for arranging the volumes as he did, see Appendix G.

2. See Appendix F, "English-Language Critical Assessments of and Responses to Castoriadis," for the full bibliographical information on this book.

3. Translated by Arnold Pomerans (New York: McGraw-Hill, 1968; Gabriel Cohn-Bendit is listed as coauthor); the quotations here are taken from Hirsh's book.

4. It was twelve years after the May 1968 rebellion that Castoriadis and Cohn-Bendit first met, right before they were to give their joint presentations to a conference of environmental activists (see 1981a in Appendixes D and E), Castoriadis shaking Cohn-Bendit's hand with the greeting, "Dr. Livingstone, I presume." Castoriadis himself had tried, without success, to regroup the *S. ou B.* comrades during May 1968 (see "The Anticipated Revolution," to be included in volume 3 of this edition, published in *La Brèche*, a collection of assessments of May 1968 written by Castoriadis [under the pseudonym Jean-Marc Coudray], Lefort, and Edgar Morin, the former editor of *Arguments*, another early and influential pioneering journal of the French New Left).

5. Following in the tradition of Lenin and Trotsky, many Marxists and other leftists wrote under and were known by pseudonyms (see Appendix H, "Identification of Pseudonymous Authors"). In Castoriadis's case, he was not a French national until 1970 (and thus liable to immediate deportation by the police without any possible recourse to judicial procedures), he was working a "straight" job, and he was a draft dodger from the Greek Civil War. The tradition, of course, extends back further than Lenin. Samuel Adams had approximately thirty pen names and often wrote (congratulatory) letters under one pseudonym replying to newspaper articles written under another pseudonym.

6. Readers will note that, despite the pioneering work of *Socialisme ou Barbarie* and Castoriadis, who helped introduce feminist questions into debates on the Left in the sixties, the English translations presented here contain such "sexist" phrases as "the worker . . . he." It matters little whether one considers the French language inherently sexist or entirely exempt from sexism: at the time of these writings, Castoriadis used such phrases as "the worker . . . he" when he spoke English (as did almost everyone else) and so I have thought it best to retain "sexist language" for the sake of a faithful translation. As the Solidarity introduction to *Redefining Revolution* says: "Th[is] text was published before the main impact of the Women's Liberation Movement had made itself felt in Western Europe. One of the effects of this movement has been to compel serious revolutionaries carefully to consider their use of words, less [*sic*] they themselves contribute to the sexist assumptions that underlie so much of everyday language. [Such] instance[s] . . . we reproduce for the sake of accuracy in translation, but which hopefully, we would not ourselves now use" (Solidarity Pamphlet 44, page 2, note 5). To this I would add that the project of "carefully considering one's use of words" is no easy task, for it requires not only a number of difficult decisions and a creative use of existing language but also the creation of new words and phrases, and, of course, new social conditions. Certainly one should not historically rewrite existing examples of sexist language, even when translating them, but what should one do when writing today? First, one should recognize that the insertion of "or she" after "he" when referring to a nonspecific subject is not a mere "corrective" but rather a grating, awkward intervention in present-day language, the social and political effects of which work (at least right now) through this very act of awkward insertion (see note 18 in my essay, "A Class and State Analysis of Henry Sidgwick's Utilitarianism," *Philosophy and Social Criticism*, 11 [Summer 1986], p. 295). But does not the insertion of "or she" also serve to hide existing sexism as well as expose it, since, in a "liberal" manner, it voices equality in a still unequal society? And does it not also heighten the emphasis on gender, through its multiplication, instead of effacing the relevance of gender distinctions for a nonspecific subject? Would not the substitution of "co" (for "he or she"), "cos" (for "his or her"), and "com" (for "him or her") be preferable, as is practiced at the Twin Oaks (Skinnerian) Commune in Virginia? Or would that practice merely serve to efface the female gender, just at a time when women are becoming recognized in their own right

through the grating use of "or she"? I do not believe that such questions can be answered a priori, but neither can they be left aside. The goal of rewriting sexist language must not become an Orwellian project of rewriting history, as would have been the case if I had changed Castoriadis's previous usages of "sexist" language. (He now generally inserts "or she" when speaking English, we should note.) This goal cannot be divorced from the feminist movement; if fully and critically developed in concert with it, this effort may even exert a positive, creative influence upon this movement. Occasional insertions of "or she" hardly scratch the surface of possible changes; my discrete use here of the neutral "one should" does not advance things one bit.

7. See Appendix I, "Glossary," for an explanation of this and other terms found in the text of the present translations.

8. See 1961 in Appendix D for "Socialism or Barbarism," a statement by "a conference of revolutionary socialists . . . held in Paris" in May 1961. The statement was drafted by Castoriadis. The conference included representatives from Pouvoir Ouvrier (i.e., S. ou B., France), Unita Proletaria (Italy), Socialism Reaffirmed (later Solidarity, of Great Britain), and Pouvoir Ouvrier Belge (Belgium). At various times, groups in Japan, the United States, and other countries were in contact with S. ou B. or Solidarity. Some of the people involved in the Berkeley Free Speech Movement, including Mario Savio, were at the time subscribers to (London) *Solidarity*, which in turn put out a pamphlet about this student protest that had a "significant influence" on the development of the British student movement, Ken Weller reports. Black & Red of Detroit has reprinted *Solidarity* pamphlets and books while Philadelphia Solidarity has reprinted some of the London group's translations of Castoriadis's writings, including a 1984 reprint of *Workers' Councils and the Economics of A Self-Managed Society*, i.e., *CS II* (see Appendix C).

9. See "Proletarian Leadership" and its postface in this volume as well as "Proletariat and Organization, I" (and the lettered note) in volume 2.

10. See "The Suspension of Publication of *Socialisme ou Barbarie*," to be included in volume 3.

11. As an example of the strange mix of homage and obscurity that surrounds Castoriadis's work in France, the *Magazine Littéraire* (December 1985) speaks of Castoriadis as the founder of *Socialisme ou Barbarie*, "where the anti-Stalinist, antibureaucratic and antitotalitarian discourses from which France fashioned its political philosophy in the course of the decade of the 1970s were sketched out." This arbitrary choice of decade might be explained by the fact that this summary of Castoriadis's life and work also says that *S. ou B.* was founded "at the end of the 1950s." And the bibliography neglects to mention six of the eight 10/18 volumes and his most important work in the past twenty-five years, *The Imaginary Institution of Society*.

12. Bibliographies of Castoriadis's non-10/18 writings in English and French can be found in Appendixes D and E.

13. As an alternative, one could also try to make Castoriadis the "Prophet of Overdeterminacy." In "The Problem of the USSR and the Possibility of a Third Historical Solution," his critique of Trotsky's conception of degeneration as a function of backwardness and isolation is based on the generalized interdependence of economies beyond mere transactions on the "world market." The effects of economic and power concentration are described schematically in "The Concentration of the Forces of Production." "The Yugoslavian Bureaucracy" analyzes this bureaucracy's chances for survival and "independence" in terms of the overdetermination of this specific situation by the presence of superpower conflict. And *SIPP* includes a brilliant section on the growing interdependence and interpenetration of economics, politics, and strategic considerations in its analysis of the world situation. In general, the criticisms made here concerning the first alternative also apply to this second one.

14. A more recent article, "Value, Equality, Justice, Politics: From Marx to Aristotle, from Aristotle to Ourselves" (reprinted in *Crossroads in the Labyrinth*), where he elaborates on what is involved in the instauration of equality, brings Castoriadis's thoughts on the issue of "bourgeois right" up to date.

15. I have discussed the triumph of method over practice in relation to the bureaucratic "impersonality" in "A Class and State Analysis of Henry Sidgwick's Utilitarianism," pp. 259-96 (location cited in note 6). A listing of two dozen "errata" should appear in a forthcoming issue of this review.

16. Translated by Joseph Bien (Evanston, Ill.: Northwestern University Press, 1973), p. 232.

Merleau-Ponty paraphrases part of the first paragraph of "Proletarian Leadership." I quote part of the passage here.

17. The contempt people have at all levels of the hierarchy of these organizations for wishy-washy liberals, "left-wing" intellectuals (whether "engaged" or of the armchair variety), and the hazy-minded members of various "radical" or "Marxist" sects is in most cases entirely justified. How this contempt shared by real activists is actually *used* is what I am trying to bring out.

18. "Subterranean Homesick Blues," words and music by Bob Dylan, © 1965 by Warner Bros. Inc. All rights reserved. Used by permission. I thank Mr. Jeff Rosen of Dwarf Music/Big Sky Music/Ram's Horn Music/Special Rider Music and Mr. Al Kohn at Warner Bros. Music for granting permission and gratis use of these lyrics.

19. We should note, however, that the concern with language and the mode of expression of the texts in *Socialisme ou Barbarie* becomes paramount (an "obsession," he says) in Castoriadis's later writings, such as "For A New Orientation" and "Recommencing the Revolution" (both of which are to be included in volume 3).

20. See "Blues Music as Such," in Albert Murray's *Stomping the Blues* (New York: McGraw-Hill, 1976; issued in 1982 as a Vintage paperback).

21. It is striking how, as Castoriadis points out in "Wildcat Strikes in the American Automobile Industry" (see volume 2) following an article in the Detroit workers' journal, *Correspondence*, the very phrase "local grievances" was coined out of the struggle brought on by the wildcat auto strikes of 1955. We must remember, however, that the spontaneous actions that generated "local grievances" as well as this phrase were, in Castoriadis's and *Correspondence*'s interpretation, an outcome of a mass nationwide struggle against *centralized bureaucracies* (the UAW and the Big Three auto companies) and not in themselves purely local and "decentralized."

22. Presumably the word "revolution," as a "turning around" or even as an "overturning," does not get at the creativity and unprecedented nature of what Castoriadis calls the process of "instauration" (again, see Appendix I).

Preface to the 1979 10/18 Edition

The 10/18 edition reprints all of the texts I published in *Socialisme ou Barbarie* (with the exception of two or three incidental notes), a few others published elsewhere, and numerous unpublished texts, some of which were written before *S. ou B.*; others were the unpublished continuation of *S. ou B.* texts, and still others were written expressly for this series. Among the unpublished texts, a choice was unavoidable; I proceeded parsimoniously.

The texts that already had been published, in *S. ou B.* or elsewhere, are reproduced *without* modification, save for the correction of misprints and of two or three *lapsus calami* by the author. The original notes are designated by arabic numerals; those designated by lowercase letters have been added for the present edition. In the rare cases where I thought a clarification of the original text was called for, the material added to this end is placed in brackets. Most of the references have been updated. I took advantage of the reissuance of this 10/18 volume to correct other misprints that had escaped my attention in the first edition.

Texts drafted over a period of twenty-five years necessarily call, in my opinion, for a host of remarks, observations, criticisms, and revisions. Rather than sprinkle the original text with them, I thought it far preferable for the reader, for me, and for the thing itself to express my current thoughts on the question in postfaces, should the occasion arise. . . .

I would like to emphasize that the publication of *S. ou B.* involved considerable collective labor from beginning to end. All the important texts were discussed in advance by the group; the discussions often were animated, sometimes

---

T/E: This "*Avertissement*" is presented in this volume in abridged form; it first appeared in *SB 1*, pp. 5-8. A similar, but abbreviated, version appeared at the beginning of each successive volume in the 10/18 series. The only additions made in later versions were notes of thanks to authors who collaborated on specific texts.

very long and a few of them ended in scissions. I always learned a lot in these discussions, and all the comrades of *S. ou B.* — those whose names are found in the editorial synopsis of the review and those who do not appear there — have played a part, in one way or another, in making these texts better than they otherwise might have been. I must mention in particular, however, the heroic figure of someone whom I still cannot name and who made clear to me in circumstances where death was present every day and at every street corner — and for him it almost never has ceased to be so — what a revolutionary militant is, and what a politics is whose thought recognizes no taboo. [I am speaking of A. Stinas, who has just published in Greek the first volume of his *Memoirs*. T/E: Another volume has since been published along with a book on the occupation.] I would have liked to mention my comrades who died of want or were assassinated by Stalinists during the occupation or immediately thereafter, a list that would, alas, be too long. Long too would be the list of those whose replies or questions helped me to advance along the path indicated here. My collaboration with Claude Lefort — begun in August 1946, continuing on a daily and sometimes stormy basis for many years, and marked by two political breaks — nourished this rare friendship that in the end permits us to maintain a dialogue across and beyond our differences of opinion. I have learned much from Philippe Guillaume; his texts published in *S. ou B.* do not fully show the originality of his thought. Discussions with Ria Stone [Grace Boggs] played a decisive role at a stage when my thoughts were taking form, and I am indebted to her in part for my having passed beyond the European provincialism that still so strongly characterizes what the former capital of universal culture produces and which continues to take itself for the hub of the world.

My young friend E. N. G., who knew better than I what I have written, has been of valuable assistance to me while preparing this edition. May he be thanked once again.

Acknowledgments

Many people have assisted in making this translation not only possible, but an enjoyable and rewarding experience. First of all, I thank Arthur Hirsh, whose *The French New Left* first introduced me to Castoriadis's work. Next, Henry Louis (Skip) Gates, Jr., who guided me through the labyrinths of the publishing world during the initial stages of this project. My editor, Terry Cochran, responded enthusiastically from the beginning, giving a real life to this hitherto imaginary project and making all that postage for forty publishing proposals worthwhile. I also thank the National Endowment for the Humanities for their tersely worded lesson in self-reliance.

My contacts with various Solidarity members in London and Philadelphia shed light on Castoriadis's work, and showed how one can think, write, organize, and struggle (at the same time!) without feeling guilty about any of it. Besides Maurice Brinton, some of whose excellent translations have been used in this edition, and Benson Perry, let me mention Ken Weller, a working-class British activist and historian who gave new meaning and expression to ideas found in Castoriadis's work. The Solidarity people also helped complete my bibliography of his writings.

For lack of space, I merely mention others who have helped in various ways; they know what their special contributions have been: Nathaniel Berman, Cliff Berry, Grace Boggs, Mary Byers, Elaine Curtis, Grant Curtis, Alex Economu, Louis Eemans and the Centre d'études et de recherches sur les mouvements trotskistes et révolutionnaires internationaux, John Fekete, Bill Ford, Jonathan Friedman, Michelle Gales, Dick Howard, Mary Maxwell, William B. Maxwell III, William McBride, Kathleen McLaughlin, Bruce McVicar, Christopher Miller, Rey Philips, Robert (Woody) Sayre, George Schrader, and Brian Singer.

Through discussions, dinners, and patient answers to too many amateur translation questions, Cornelius Castoriadis, who so generously and trustingly responded to my offer ex nihilo to undertake this translation, has assisted this project in so many ways and on so many levels that I could never recount them. True to the spirit of his work, his assistance has helped me to resolve for myself the problems I have faced. Zoé Castoriadis's myriad forms of assistance have ensured that the critical apparatus is as complete and accurate as possible.

Finally, let me mention the encouragement and support I have received from the start from Clara Gibson Maxwell. This project never would have been begun or completed without her.

Abbreviations

Text Abbreviations for Volumes Written by Cornelius Castoriadis

CL	*Les Carrefours du labyrinthe* (Editions du Seuil, 1978). *Crossroads in the Labyrinth* (MIT Press and Harvester Press Limited, 1984).
CMR 1	*Capitalisme moderne et révolution, 1: L'Impérialisme et la guerre* (10/18, 1979).
CMR 2	*Capitalisme moderne et révolution, 2: Le Mouvement révolutionnaire sous le capitalisme moderne* (10/18, 1979).
CS	*Le Contenu du socialisme* (10/18, 1979).
DH	*Domaines de l'homme* (Le Seuil, 1986).
EMO 1	*L'Expérience du mouvement ouvrier, 1: Comment lutter* (10/18, 1974).
EMO 2	*L'Expérience du mouvement ouvrier, 2: Prolétariat et organisation* (10/18, 1974).
IIS	*L'Institution imaginaire de la société* (Le Seuil, 1975). *The Imaginary Institution of Society* (MIT Press and Polity Press, 1987).
PSW 1	*Political and Social Writings, Volume 1. 1946-1955: From the Critique of Bureaucracy to the Positive Content of Socialism* (University of Minnesota Press).
PSW 2	*Political and Social Writings, Volume 2. 1956-1960: From the Workers' Struggle against Bureaucracy to Revolution in the Age of Modern Capitalism* (University of Minnesota Press).

PSW 3	*Political and Social Writings, Volume 3. 1961-1979: Recommencing the Revolution: From Socialism to the Autonomous Society* (Planned: University of Minnesota Press).
SB 1	*La Société bureaucratique, 1: Les Rapports de production en Russie* (10/18, 1973).
SB 2	*La Société bureaucratique, 2: La Révolution contre la bureaucratie* (10/18, 1973).
SF	*La Société française* (10/18, 1979).

Text Abbreviations for Articles Written by Cornelius Castoriadis

CFP	"La Concentration des forces productives," unpublished (March 1948); *SB 1*, pp. 101-13. "The Concentration of the Forces of Production," *PSW 1*.
CS I-III	"Sur le contenu du socialisme," *S. ou B.*, 17 (July 1955), 22 (July 1957), 23 (January 1958); reprinted in *CS*, pp. 67-102 and 103-221, and *EMO 2*, pp. 9-88. "On the Content of Socialism," *PSW 1* and *PSW 2*.
DC I, II	"Sur la dynamique du capitalisme," *S. ou B.*, 12 and 13 (August 1953 and January 1954).
HMO/HWM*	"La Question de l'histoire du mouvement ouvrier" (1973), *EMO 1*, pp. 11-120. "The Question of the History of the Workers' Movement," *PSW 3* (planned).
IG/GI	"Introduction générale," *SB 1*, pp. 11-61. "General Introduction," *PSW 1*.
MRCM/MCR I-III	"Le Mouvement révolutionnaire sous le capitalisme moderne," *S. ou B.*, 31, 32, and 33 (December 1960, April and December, 1961); *CMR 2*, pp. 47-258. "Modern Capitalism and Revolution," *PSW 2*.
MTR/MRT I-V	"Marxisme et théorie révolutionnaire," *S. ou B.*, 36-40 (April 1964-June 1965); reprinted in *IIS*, pp. 13-230. "Marxism and Revolutionary Theory" is the first part of the translation of *IIS*.
PhCP	"La Phénoménologie de la conscience prolétarienne," unpublished (March 1948); *SB 1*, pp. 115-30.
PO I, II	"Prolétariat et organisation," *S. ou B.*, 27 and 28 (April and July, 1959); reprinted in *EMO 2*, pp. 123-87 and 189-248. "Proletariat and Organization, I," *PSW 2* (part II not included in this series; see Appendix C).

RIB/RBI*	"Le Rôle de l'idéologie bolchevique dans la naissance de la bureaucratie," *S. ou B.*, 35 (January 1964); reprinted in *EMO 2*, pp. 385-416. "The Role of Bolshevik Ideology in the Birth of the Bureaucracy," *PSW 3* (planned).
RPB/PRAB	"La Révolution prolétarienne contre la bureaucratie," *S. ou B.*, 20 (December 1956); reprinted in *SB 2*, pp. 267-337. "The Proletarian Revolution against the Bureaucracy," *PSW 2*.
RPR	"Les Rapports de production en Russie," *S. ou B.*, 2 (May 1949); reprinted in *SB 1*, pp. 205-81. "The Relations of Production in Russia," *PSW 1*.
RR*	"Recommencer la révolution," *S. ou B.*, 35 (January 1964); reprinted in *EMO 2*, pp. 307-65. "Recommencing the Revolution," *PSW 3* (planned). See Appendix C for previous title.
SB	"Socialisme ou Barbarie," *S. ou B.*, 1 (March 1949); reprinted in *SB 1*, pp. 139-83. "Socialism or Barbarism," *PSW 1*.
SIPP	"La Situation de l'impérialisme et perspectives du prolétariat," *S. ou B.*, 14 (April 1954); reprinted in *CMR 1*, pp. 379-440. "The Situation of Imperialism and Proletarian Perspectives," *PSW 1*.

*Planned third volume texts that already exist in translation; see Appendix C.

Text Abbreviations for Frequently Cited Texts

LCW	V. I. Lenin, *Collected Works* (various editions will be cited in notes).
LSW	V. I. Lenin, *Selected Works* (New York: International Publishers, 1943).
LSWONE	V. I. Lenin, *Selected Works. One-Volume Edition* (New York: International Publishers, 1971).
MECW	Karl Marx and Frederick Engels, *Collected Works*. 40 vols. (New York: International Publishers, 1974-86).
MESW	Karl Marx and Frederick Engels, *Selected Works in One Volume* (New York: International Publishers, 1968).

Cornelius Castoriadis
Political and Social Writings
Volume 1

General Introduction

The texts to be read here have been conceived, written, and published during a period of thirty years, years that have not been particularly lacking in cataclysmic events or in profound changes. The Second World War and its aftermath; the expansion of the Russian bureaucratic regime and its empire over half of Europe; the cold war; the bureaucracy's accession to power in China; the reestablishment and unprecedented growth of the capitalist economy; the brutal end of colonial empires founded in the sixteenth century; the crisis of Stalinism, its ideological death, and its real survival; the popular revolts against the bureaucracy in East Germany, Poland, Hungary, and Czechoslovakia; the disappearance of the traditional working-class movement in Western countries and the privatization of individuals in all countries; the accession to power of a totalitarian bureaucracy in certain ex-colonial countries, of a series of psychopathic demagogues in others; the internal collapse of the system of values and rules in modern society; the challenging, in words as well as deeds, of institutions, some of which (schools, prisons) date from the beginnings of historical societies and others of which (the family) were born somewhere in the mists of time; youth's break with the established culture and the attempt of some of them to get out of it, and (less apparent but perhaps most important) the eclipse—who knows, the disappearance for an indefinite period of time—of our inherited bearings and of all bearings for reflection and action, with society dispossessed of its knowledge and this knowledge itself, swelling like a malignant tumor, in a profound crisis as to its meaning and function; the boundless proliferation of a multitude of empty and irresponsible discourses, their industrialized ideological fabrication and the glutting of the market by a plasticized pop philosophy—such are, in an approximately chronological order, a few of the facts that would confront those

Originally published as "Introduction générale," *SB 1*, pp. 11-61.

who, during this period, attempted to talk about society, about history, and about politics.

Given these conditions, the author, an unfashionable product of another era, will be excused perhaps for not being content, as is the present fashion, to write just anything at all today after having published another—and the same—anything at all yesterday. Instead, he shall try to take as much responsibility as he can for his own thoughts, to reflect anew on the path he has taken, to interrogate himself on the relation between these writings and their actual evolution, to try to understand what, beyond some personal or accidental factors, allowed certain ideas to confront victoriously the test of events, rendered others null and void, and lastly made certain among them to which he had clung most tenaciously— but there is no historical novelty in this—and which were taken over and popularized since the time he first formulated them, seem to him sometimes to have become tools in the hands of swindlers used to deceive the innocent.

From the Analysis of Bureaucracy to Workers' Management (1944-48)

As these ideas were beginning to evolve, there came the experience of World War II and the German occupation. There is no point in relating here how an adolescent, discovering Marxism, thought he was being faithful by joining the Young Communists during the Metaxas dictatorship, nor why he might have believed, after the occupation of Greece and the German attack against Russia, that the chauvinistic orientation of the Greek CP and the constitution of the National Liberation Front (EAM) were the result of a local deviation that could be redressed by an ideological struggle within the Party. As arguments were reduced to bludgeons and as he listened to Russian radio broadcasts, his self-deception quickly ended. The reactionary character of the Communist party, of its politics, of its methods, of its internal system of rule as much as the cretinism that permeated it, then as now, no matter what speeches or writings emanated from its leadership, became apparent with a blinding clarity. It was not surprising that, in the conditions of the times and of the place, these discoveries led to Trotskyism and to its most leftist faction, which was working out an intransigent critique of Stalinism as well as of the rightist Trotskyists (about whom it was learned later on—when communications, which had been broken off since 1936, were reestablished—that they represented the true "spirit"—*sit venia verbo*—of the "Fourth International").

Surviving the double persecution of the Gestapo and of the local GPU (the OPLA, which assassinated dozens of Trotskyist militants during and after the occupation)[1] proved to be a problem capable of being solved. Far more difficult were the theoretical and political questions posed by the occupation. Faced with the collapse of the State and of bourgeois political organizations in a society that was disintegrating, was being pulverized (nearly all of the small number of prewar industries had ceased to function, and one could no longer speak in practical terms of a proletariat, but only of a general lumpenization), the population, pushed by appalling living conditions and by the cruel oppression practiced by the German army, went toward the CP, which thereby experienced a period of overwhelming growth, recruited tens of thousands into its front organization (EAM), deployed a pseudopartisan force in the countryside and in the cities (pseudo- because it was completely centralized and bureaucratized) that numbered at the end of the occupation a hundred thousand well-armed men, and established total power over the least accessible regions of the country and, after the departure of the Germans, over the entire country with the sole exception of Constitution Square in Athens.

What made the masses hold to a Stalinist political line, what made them not only deaf to all revolutionary and internationalist talk but ready to cut the throats of those who held such views? For traditional Trotskyism-Leninism, the easily discovered answer lay in an exaggerated repetition of the paradigm of the First World War: War was possible only because of the resurgence of the "nationalist illusions" of the masses, who were to remain prisoners of such illusions until the experience of the war would relieve them of these illusions and lead them toward revolution. This same war only completed the transformation of the Communist party into a reformist-nationalist party, permanently integrated into the bourgeois order, as Trotsky had forecast a long time ago. What was more natural, then, than the CP's hold over the masses, who ascribed all their ills to the "enemy" nation? For the Trotskyists, as for Trotsky until his dying day, the CP only replayed, in the conditions of the era, the role of chauvinist social democracy from 1914-18, and the "national" or "patriotic" fronts it patronized were only new disguises for the "Sacred Union." (I speak here only of the consistent Trotskyist line—even though it was in the minority. The rightest tendencies in the "Fourth International," who were much more opportunistic, tried then, as now, to cling to the Stalinists, and sometimes went so far as to maintain that the "national" struggle against Germany was of a progressive character.)

Up to a certain point, the facts still could be adapted to this schema, provided, as is always the case with Trotskyism, that these facts are sufficiently distorted and that, in adapting them, one avails oneself of an indefinite "tomorrow." For my part, comparing the CP to a reformist party when even just a little was known of its inner workings appeared to me frivolous, and the illusions of the masses seemed to me neither exclusively nor essentially "nationalistic." What had been intellectual malaise was transformed into glaring certitude with the Stalinist insurrection of December 1944. There was no way of forcing this event back into the prevailing schemata, and the unequaled emptiness of the "analyses" the Trotskyists attempted to offer for it during this era and thereafter amply testify to that fact. Indeed, it was obvious that the Greek CP did not act as a reformist party but aimed at seizing power by eliminating the representatives of the bourgeoisie or by tying them up: In the coalitions it was forming, bourgeois politicians were the hostages of the CP and not the other way around. No real power existed in the country besides the submachine guns of the CP's military units. The support of the masses was not motivated simply by hatred of the German occupation; reinforced tenfold after the departure of the Germans, it always contained the confused hope of a social transformation, of an elimination of the old dominant strata, and had nothing to do with a "National Union." The masses behaved in other respects as the passive infantry of the CP; only someone who was delirious could have believed that the masses, militarily commanded, trained, and schooled, with neither an autonomous organ nor the inclination to form one, would have "outflanked" the CP once it was installed in power. Had they, by some remote chance, tried, they would have been mercilessly massacred, the corpses being rigged up with the appropriate epithets.

The December 1944 insurrection was beaten—but it was beaten by the English army. It matters little, in the present context, to know to what extent the Stalinist leadership's tactical and military errors (from its own point of view) or its internal quarrels actually existed or played any real role: Sooner or later, the CP would have been beaten anyhow—but it would have been by the English army. This defeat is thus, if I may say so, sociologically contingent: It resulted neither from the intrinsic character of the CP (which might not have been "willing" or "able" to seize power) nor from the relation of forces in the country (the national bourgeoisie had no force to oppose it), but rather from the country's geographical position and from the international context (the Tehran accords, and then those of Yalta). If Greece had been situated six hundred miles farther to the north—or France six hundred miles farther to the east—the CP would have seized power at the end of the war, and this power would have been guaranteed by Russia. What would it have done with it? It would have installed a regime similar to the Russian regime, eliminated the formerly dominant strata after having absorbed those who allowed themselves to be absorbed, established its dictatorship and installed its men in all posts involving authority and privileges. Certainly at this time all those privileges were just ifs. But the subsequent evolution of the satellite countries, confirming this prognostication as much as a historical prognostication could ever be confirmed, excuses me from having to hark back to this aspect of the argument.

How does one characterize such a regime from a Marxist point of view? Sociologically speaking, it was clear that it should be defined in the same way as the Russian regime. And it is here that the weakness, and ultimately the absurdity, of the Trotskyist conception became evident. For the definition that they gave to the Russian regime was not sociological, it was a simple historical description: Russia was a "degenerated workers' State." And this is not just a question of terminology. For Trotskyism, such a regime was possible only as the product of the degeneration of a proletarian revolution; it had ruled out from its point of view the possibility that property might be "nationalized," that the economy might be "planned," and that the bourgeoisie might be eliminated without a proletarian revolution. Should it characterize the regimes the CP installed in Eastern Europe as "degenerated workers' States"? How could they be, if they never were from the start *workers'* States? And if they were, one must admit that the seizure of power by a totalitarian and militarily organized party was at the same time a proletarian revolution—which was degenerating as it was developing. These theoretical monstrosities—from which Trotskyist "theoreticians" have never retreated[2]—remained, however, of secondary interest. Historical experience, as far as Marx and Lenin were concerned, taught that the development of a revolution is essentially the development of the autonomous organs of the masses—commune, soviets, factory committees or councils—and this had nothing to do with a fetishism for organizational forms: The idea of a dictatorship of the proletariat exercised by a totalitarian party was a mockery, the existence of autonomous organs of the masses and the effective exercise of power by the latter was not a form, it was the revolution itself and the whole revolution.

Likewise, Trotsky's conception revealed itself to be false on the central point on which it had been constituted and which alone could have provided Trotskyism with a foundation for its right to historical existence as a political current: the social and historical nature of Stalinism and of bureaucracy. The Stalinist parties were not reformist, they were not preserving but rather were destroying the bourgeoisie. The birth of the Russian bureaucracy in and through the degeneration of the October Revolution, essential in other respects, was accidental with respect to the latter: Such a bureaucracy also could be born in another fashion and be, not the product, but the origin of a regime that could be characterized neither as working class nor simply capitalist in the traditional sense. If, for a time, some miserable quibblings concerning the presence of the Russian army in Eastern Europe as the "cause" of the CP's accession to power were possible, the installation, since then, of an autochthonous bureaucratic empire over a few odd hundreds of millions of Chinese ought to settle the question for all those who are not trying to blind themselves.

We therefore had to come back to the "Russian question" and set aside the historical and sociological exceptionalism of Trotsky's conception. Contrary to the latter's prognosis, the Russian bureaucracy outlived the war, which had not resolved itself into revolution; it ceased to be "bureaucracy in one country," as similar regimes muscled their way into power all over Eastern Europe. The Russian bureaucracy, therefore, was neither exceptional nor a "transitory formation" in any nonsophistical sense of this term. Nor was it a mere "parasitical stratum" but rather an altogether dominant class, exercising absolute power over the whole of social life, and not only in the narrow sphere of politics. It is not only that, from a Marxist point of view, the idea of a separation (and, in this case, of an absolute opposition) between the alleged "socialist bases of the Russian economy" and the totalitarian terrorism exercised upon and against the proletariat is grotesque; it sufficed to consider seriously the substance of the real relations of production in Russia beyond the juridical form of "nationalized" property in order to discover that these actually are relations of exploitation, that the bureaucracy entirely assumes for itself the powers and the functions of an exploiting class, the management of the production process at all levels, the disposition of the means of production and decision-making authority over the appropriation of surplus production.

A host of consequences of the highest order sprang from these considerations, for the "Russian question" was, and remains, the touchstone of the theoretical and practical attitudes that call for revolution, and this question was also the richest vein, the royal road to the comprehension of the most important problems of contemporary society. The sterility of Trotsky and of Trotskyism is only the reflection of their incapacity to enter onto this route. The historical justification of Trotskyism, which could have laid its foundations as the establishment of a new and independent political current, had been an analysis of the nature of Stalinism and the bureaucracy and of the implications of this new phenomenon. This new stage of the history of the working-class movement as well as of society worldwide required a new effort, a new theoretical development. In place of this, Trotsky never did anything but repeat and codify the classical period of Leninist practice (or rather, what he presented as such), and even this he did after a period of concessions and compromises that ended only in 1927. Completely disarmed before the Stalinist bureaucracy, he was able only to denounce its crimes and criticize its politics according to the standards of 1917. Clouded by the pseudo-"theory" of Stalinist Bonapartism, hampered by his impressionistic view of the decline of capitalism, he refused till the end to see in the Russian regime anything other than a momentary accident, one of his famous "blind alleys" of history; he never furnished anything but superficial descriptions for the bureaucratic regime, and one would seek in vain in *The Revolution Betrayed* for an analysis of the Russian economy: If the productive forces develop, it is thanks to nationalization and planning; if they develop less rapidly and less well than they should have, it is on account of bureaucracy. Here is the substance of what Trotsky and the Trotskyists have to say about the Russian economy. He wore himself out demonstrating that Communist parties were violating Leninist principles and were ruining the revolution—whereas they were aiming at entirely different objectives, and to criticize them from this perspective makes no more sense than to reproach a cannibal, who raises children in order to eat them, for violating the precepts of proper pedagogy. When at the end of his life he agreed to consider a different theoretical possibility concerning the nature of the Russian regime, he tied the theoretical fate of the analyses of Russia immediately and directly to the actual fate of his prognostication concerning the development of the revolution by the war that was just beginning. His pitiful heirs have paid dearly for this theoretical monstrosity; Trotsky had written in black and white (*In Defense of Marxism*) that if the war ended without the victory of world revolution, the analysis of the Russian regime would have to be revised and it would have to be admitted that Stalinist bureaucracy and fascism already had sketched the outline of a new type of exploitative regime, which he identified, moreover, with barbarism. His epigones were obliged for some years after the end of the war to maintain that the war, or the "crisis" issuing therefrom, had not really ended. Probably for them it still has not ended.

Those who, like me, had admired his audacity and his acuity could have been astonished by Trotsky's blindness about Stalinism. But he was not so free. This blindness was a blindness of its own origins: of the bureaucratic tendencies organically incorporated into the Bolshevik party from the start (which he had, moreover, seen and denounced before joining up with the Party and identifying himself with it), and of what, already in Marxism itself, was preparing the way for bureaucracy and making it the blind spot, the invisible and irreparable segment of social reality that made it impossible, beyond a point, to think about this reality within the theoretical framework that Marxism had established (see *RIB/RBI* and *MTR/MRT*).

This new conception of bureaucracy and of the Russian regime allowed us to tear the mystificatory veil from "nationalization" and from "planning" and to rediscover—beyond juridical forms of property ownership as well as beyond the methods adopted by the exploiting class for managing the overall economy (whether these methods be realized through the "market" or through a "plan")—the actual relations of production as the foundation of the division of society into classes. There was in this, obviously, only a return to the genuine spirit of Marx's analyses. If classical private property is eliminated and yet in spite of that the workers continue to be exploited, dispossessed, and separated from the means of production, the division within society becomes the division between directors and executants in the process of production, the dominant stratum assuring its stability and, given the opportunity, the transmission of its privileges to its descendants by additional sociological mechanisms that are hardly mysterious.

This new conception also allowed us to understand the evolution of Western capitalism, where the concentration of capital, the evolution of technique and of the organization of production, the increasing intervention of the State, and, finally, the evolution of the great working-class organizations had led to a similar result: the establishment of a bureaucratic stratum in production and in the other spheres of social life. The theory of the bureaucracy thus was finding its socioeconomic foundations at the same time that it was fitting into a historical conception of modern society. Indeed, it was clear that the process of capital concentration and of its interpenetration with the State, as well as the need to exercise control over all sectors of social life, and in particular over the workers, involved the emergence of new strata managing production, the economy, the State, and culture as well as the proletariat's trade-union and political life; even in the countries of traditional capitalism we were witnessing the increasing autonomization of these strata vis-à-vis private capitalists, and the gradual fusion at the summit of these two social categories. But of course it was not the fate of individuals but the evolution of a system that mattered, and this evolution organically led the traditional capitalism of the private business firm, of the market, of the police state, to the contemporary capitalism of the bureaucratized enterprise, of regimentation, of "planning," and of the omnipresent State. This is why, after having for a brief lapse of time envisaged a "third historical solution" (see "The Problem of the USSR and the Possibility of a Third Historical Solution," this volume), I adopted the term "bureaucratic capitalism." I say "bureaucratic capitalism" and not "State capitalism," the latter being an almost completely meaningless expression that not only improperly characterizes traditional capitalist countries (where the means of production are not State run) but also is unable to put its finger on the emergence of this new exploiting stratum, masks a problem central to a socialist revolution, and creates a disastrous confusion (upon which numerous authors and leftist groups have foundered), for it makes one think that capitalism's economic laws continue to hold after the disappearance of private property, of the market, and of competition, which is absurd (see "The Concentration of the Forces of Production," this volume). How much bureaucratization has become the central process of contemporary society during the following quarter century hardly deserves being mentioned.

More decisive still are the consequences pertaining to the aims of the revolution. If such is the foundation of the division of contemporary society, a socialist revolution cannot stop at barring the bosses and "private" property from the means of production; it also has to get rid of the bureaucracy and the influence the latter exerts over the means and the process of production—in other words, it has to abolish the division between directors and executants. Expressed in a positive way, this is nothing other than *workers' management* of production, namely, the complete exercise of power over production and over the entirety of social activities by autonomous organs of workers' collectives. This also can be called self-management [*autogestion*], provided that we do not forget that this term implies not the refurbishing but rather the destruction of the existing order, and quite particularly the abolition of a State apparatus separated from society and of parties as organs of management and direction; provided also, therefore, that self-management is not confused with the mystifications that for some years now have been circulating under this name or with Marshal Tito's efforts to extract more production from Yugoslavian workers by means of a salary based upon collective output and by taking advantage of their capacity to organize their work themselves. That the experience of being exploited and being oppressed by the bureaucracy, coming on the heels of private capitalism, left the rising masses no other alternative but to demand workers' management of production was a simple logical deduction, formulated as early as 1947 and amply confirmed by the Hungarian Revolution of 1956. That the management of production by the producers, and the collective management of their affairs by those directly involved, in every domain of public life, were impossible and inconceivable except through an unprecedented outpouring of autonomous activity on the masses' part reaffirmed that the socialist revolution is nothing more and nothing less than the explosion of this autonomous activity, instituting new forms of collective life, eliminating as it develops not only the manifestations but also the foundations of the previous order and, in particular, every separate category or organization of "directors" or "managers" (whose existence signifies ipso facto the certainty that there will be a return to the previous order, or rather testifies by itself that this order is still there), creating at each of its stages new bases of support for its further development and anchoring these in social reality.

Finally, there followed some consequences that were just as significant for the revolutionary organization itself as for its relations to the masses. If socialism is the outpouring of the autonomous activity of the masses and if the objectives of this activity and its forms can spring only from the experience the workers themselves have of exploitation and oppression, it cannot be a question either of inculcating them with a "socialist consciousness" produced by a theory or of acting as their substitute in directing the revolution or in constructing socialism. Thus there needed to be a radical transformation of the Bolshevik model, of the types of relations that exist between the masses and the organization as well as of the latter's structure and internal *modus vivendi*.

These conclusions are clearly formulated in "Socialism or Barbarism" (*SB*, in *Socialisme ou Barbarie* [*S. ou B.*], 1 [March 1949]; now in this volume). Nevertheless, I was not able to draw out all of the implications right away, and many ambiguities remained in the first text devoted to this question ("Le Parti révolutionnaire," May 1949), ambiguities already removed in part in a subsequent text ("Proletarian Leadership," July 1952; now in this volume). Beyond the difficulties that are always present when one breaks with a great historical legacy, two factors seem to me to have been determinative of my attitude during this period. The first factor was that I was measuring, in its full breadth, the extent of the problem of centralization in modern society—and, concerning which, I have always thought that it was underestimated by those in the group who opposed me on this question—and that it appeared to me, wrongly, that the Party furnished one element of an answer. As far as I am concerned, this question was resolved, as much as it could be in writing, in "On the Content of Socialism, II" (*CS II*; now in volume 2). The second factor was the antinomy involved in the very idea of revolutionary organization and activity: to be aware, or to understand, that the proletariat has to arrive at a conception of the revolution and of socialism that it can only draw from itself, and yet not to fold one's arms for all that. This ultimately is the formulation of the very problem of praxis, as it is encountered in pedagogy as well as in psychoanalysis, and I was able to discuss it in a manner that satisfied me only fifteen years later (*MTR/MRT III*, October 1964).

The Critique of Marxist Economics (1950-54)

The historical perspective into which we aimed at fitting the first *S. ou B.* texts, and certain interpretations that are found therein, remained prisoners of the traditional methodology. Trotsky had written in his *Transitional Program* (1938) that the premises of the revolution not only no longer were ripening but had begun to rot; he also wrote that the productive forces of humanity had ceased to grow and that the proletariat no longer was advancing, either numerically or culturally. If this were so, it was impossible to understand how the revolution remained the order of the day ten (and now thirty-five) years afterward—just as, conversely, it is impossible to understand how people could think they were being "scientific" revolutionaries and continue to quote Marx as an authority, who wrote "No social order ever perishes before all the social productive forces for which there is room in it have developed" (Preface to *A Contribution to the Critique of Political Economy*). If the proletariat could not make revolution at the apogee of its numerical and cultural strength, how could it do so during its period of decline? As soon as I had begun to study economics seriously (1947-48), I was able to show that in reality capitalist production was continuing to expand. Two factors prevented me nevertheless from drawing all the conclusions from this fact. On the one hand, I retained the historical ultimatism that had characterized Leninism and especially Trotskyism: In the absence of revolution, there will inevitably be fascism; in the absence of a real stabilization of capitalism, there is war on the horizon. On the other hand, under the spell of Marx's economic theory (or what passed for it), I still thought that the exploitation of the proletariat could only continue by growing worse, that a new economic crisis for capitalism was inevitable, that the alleged "tendency of the rate of profit to fall" undermined the foundations of the system. Pushing to its logical limit the theory of capital concentration, and therefore also the theory of the concentration of power (Marx had said that the process of concentration would not stop until a single capitalist or group of capitalists predominated), and finding at the same time that, in contrast to the First, the Second World War had not settled but rather had exacerbated and multiplied the problems that had caused it, and had left alone, face-to-face, two imperialist superpowers—neither of whom would give up the idea of reopening the question of the uncertain partition of the world fixed solely by the advance of their armies in 1945—I concluded from this that a third world war was not only ineluctable (which always has remained, on the whole, true) but also "immediate" in a special sense of this term: Whatever the delays and detours, the historical situation would be determined in a sovereign manner by a process that ends in war. This thesis, formulated in essays explicitly devoted to the international situation (such as *SB* and those texts reprinted in *Capitalisme moderne et révolution* [*CMR 1*]), made its mark on many of the writings of this period. It is superfluous to state today that this thesis is false. Still, we must see that the factors for which it accounted remain at work and continue to be determinative (Cuba, Indochina, the Near East). But what is needed is an analysis of the reasons for the mistake.

Those that seem to me to contain an enduring lesson are of two different orders. The first—indicated in *S. ou B.* texts beginning in the summer of 1953 ("Note sur la situation internationale" from issue no. 12, written in collaboration with Claude Lefort, and then "The Situation of Imperialism and Proletarian Perspectives" [*SIPP*, April 1954]; now in this volume)—was the overestimation of the independence of ruling strata vis-à-vis their own population and the populations of the countries dominated by these two blocs. The American population's hostility to the Korean War, the cracks in the Russian empire that the bureaucracy already should have perceived before Stalin's death and that exploded in broad daylight with the East Berlin revolt of July 1953, no doubt played a decisive role in halting the race toward open war. Behind these facts, there is a profound signification that I was only able to sift out later on, in "Modern Capitalism and Revolution" (*MRCM/MCR*, 1959-60; now in volume 2): A whole world separates postwar societies from prewar ones, insofar as conflict is becoming generalized at all levels of society; insofar as the dominant strata see their power limited, even in the absence of head-on opposition, by a struggle that also is becoming generalized; insofar as their own internal contradictions have changed in character; and insofar as the generalized process of bureaucratization transposes, into the depths of the ruling structure, the irrationalities of the system and imposes upon them constraints that are different from classical constraints but just as powerful.

The second aspect of this lesson involved my adherence to Marx's economic theory and to its—explicit and authentic—conclusions, such as the idea that capitalism can only constantly increase the workers' exploitation, or to its implicit conclusions, as "interpreted" by traditional Marxism, such as the idea of the inevitability of overproduction crises and the impossibility of the system's attaining a state of dynamic equilibrium, however roughly defined. War then appeared—and, as is well known, the entire Marxist tradition explicitly had theorized it in this way—as the system's only outcome, an outcome dictated by its own internal necessities. Now, my daily work as an economist as well as a new and more careful study of *Capital*, occasioned by a series of lectures given in the winter of 1948-49, gradually led me to conclude that the economic basis that Marx had tried to give both to his work and to the revolutionary perspective, and which generations of Marxists considered as an immovable rock, simply did not exist. From the point of view of vulgar Judeo-phenomenal reality, to speak like him, what was happening had no connection with the theory; what Marx had said about economics provided no tool for understanding it now, nor did he help us to reorient ourselves amid contemporary events, and the predictions formulated in his work or deducible therefrom ended up being contradicted—apart from those that had much more of a sociological character than an economic one, such as the universal expansion of capitalism or its process of concentration. More serious still from the theoretical point of view was that the system was more than incomplete; it was incoherent, based on contradictory postulates, and full of fallacious deductions.

And ultimately, the latter aspect was quite closely connected with the former one.

Already during this period the facts forced us to see that there was neither an absolute nor even a relative pauperization of the proletariat, and no growth in the rate of exploitation. Returning to the theory, we found that nothing in *Capital* lets us determine a level of real wages or how this level varies through time. That the unit value of the goods consumed by the working class diminishes with an increase in labor productivity tells us nothing about the total quantity of goods that make up wages (200×1 is no smaller than 100×2); that at the outset this quantity (the working classes' actual standard of living) is determined by "historical and moral factors" tells us nothing about its connection with these factors nor in particular anything about how it evolves; finally, that working-class struggles allow a modification in the distribution of net product between wages and profits, which Marx had seen and written about, is certainly true and even fundamental, since these struggles have succeeded in keeping this distribution roughly constant, thereby providing capitalist production with a constantly enlarged internal market for consumer goods. But precisely for this reason the entire system, inasmuch as it is an economic system, is plunged into a state of total indetermination with respect to its central variable, the rate of exploitation, and, strictly speaking, makes everything that comes afterward a series of gratuitous statements.

Likewise, there was no logical necessity to the empirically debatable thesis of the rise in capital's organic composition (all the existing statistical studies, as

much as they can be depended on, show that there is no clearly defined historical evolution of the capital/net product ratio nor any systematic correlation between this ratio and the level of a country's economic development).

There is, summarily speaking, no reason for the aggregate *value* of constant
capital to increase through time relative to the aggregate *value* of net product,
unless it is postulated that the part of labor productivity producing the means of
production increases less rapidly than average productivity—which would be at
the same time arbitrary and hardly plausible, seeing that for Marx raw materials, etc. enter into the composition of constant capital. In fact, in his definition
of organic composition, Marx related the value of constant capital not to net
product (as should have been done in order to have a less ambiguous concept)
but rather to variable capital (wages alone); this renders his formula more than
suspect since the original statement, the one that gave an apparent plausibility to
the idea of a rise in organic composition, is that "the same number of workers
handle an increasing quantity of machines, raw materials, etc." But the *number*
of workers and the *quantity* of machines are not concepts of *value* but rather
physical concepts. The *number* of workers tells us nothing yet about variable capital—unless wages are introduced; and in this case there will be a rise in organic
composition, everything else being equal, only as a pure reflection of the increase in the rate of exploitation—which leads us back to the previous problem.[3]
Indeed, the great chimera, the sea serpent of Marx's economic theory, the "tendency of the rate of exploitation to fall," appears as the culmination of a series of
fallacious deductions proceeding from incoherent hypotheses that are totally irrelevant no matter what the context.

Indeed, Marxists have lived and still do live on the belief that *Capital* explains
the mechanism of overproduction crises and guarantees that they will recur. It
does nothing of the sort; we can find many passages there that discuss this question and furnish partial and limited interpretations for it, but the sole positive
result is a numerical example (in the second volume) illustrating the case of stable accumulation, though it runs exactly contrary to current prejudices. Moreover, the conditions under which the discussion proceeds are so abstract that the
conclusions, when there are any, have almost no bearing on reality.

The same period witnessed the downfall of the colonial empires. According to
the vulgate in force then as now, this should have led to the collapse of the economies of the home States—and nothing of the sort happened. These questions
had not been treated by Marx—and for good reason; but in the Marxist literature, two incompatible conceptions went at each other head-to-head on this
point. For Rosa Luxemburg, the capitalist economy has an organic need for
noncapitalist surroundings in order to make its surplus value; i.e., this environ-
ment allows the capitalist economy to get rid of all that it produces, and imperialism finds here its necessary cause. Being cut off from its former colonies
could only result in a reduction of colonial capitalism's external outlets for trade
(and in certain cases—China, for example—their total suppression) and therefore should have provoked a crisis in the home countries. For Lenin, on the contrary, capitalist accumulation as a closed circuit is perfectly possible, and the
root of imperialism is to be sought elsewhere (in the tendency of monopolies to-

ward limitless self-aggrandizement of profits and power); but for him too—as well as for Trotsky, when he discussed the consequences of Indian independence for England—the loss of their colonies could not help but plunge the home countries into a deep crisis, since the social and political stability of the system was secured only through the "corruption" of the working-class aristocracy and even of large strata of the proletariat, which is possible only in terms of imperialistic superprofits. (Let us note that run-of-the-mill Marxists today profess in general an incoherent mixture of these two incompatible conceptions.) In both cases the same result was logically and actually predicted, and it did not occur.

Indeed, Marx's theory had in mind a competitive and entirely private capitalism. Certainly, there have been some Marxists recently who were for treating competition and the market as epiphenomena whose presence or absence does not alter in any respect the "essence" of capital and of capitalism. We can find a few rare citations in Marx authorizing this view and others, much more numerous, affirming the contrary. But it is the logic of the theory alone that matters, and in this respect it is clear that the theory of value implies the comparison of goods in a competitive marketplace, for without the latter the term "socially necessary" labor is meaningless; the same goes for the equalization of the rate of profit. What then was the relevance of this theory for an era in which the "competitive" market had practically disappeared, either through the triumph of monopolization and the existence of massive State intervention in the economy or through the complete statification of production? But what we have said shows that it was already irrelevant in the case of the "competitive" economy.

In the midst of this empirical and logical collapse, what remained? The theory was coming apart, separating like an ill-beaten mixture. The grandeur of *Capital*, and of Marx's entire oeuvre, was not in the imagined economic "science" they supposedly contained, but in the audacity and profundity of the sociological and historical vision underlying them; not the "epistemological break," as it is stupidly called today, that would have made of economics and of social theory a "science," but, quite the contrary, the attempted unification of economic analysis, social theory, historical interpretation, a political perspective and philosophical thought. *Capital* was an attempt to realize philosophy and to surpass it as mere philosophy while showing how this attempt could animate an understanding of the fundamental reality of the era—the transformation of the world by capitalism—which would in its turn animate the communist revolution. Now, the element upon which Marx himself had conferred a central place in this unity, his economic analysis, proved untenable. Precisely on account of the nonaccidental, but instead essential, role it played in his overall conception—"the anatomy of civil society is to be sought in political economy," he wrote in the most celebrated of his prefaces—it dragged down with itself in its fall not only the other elements but also their unity. This I saw only gradually— and for yet a few more years I tried to uphold the original whole at the cost of accepting more and more significant modifications—until the day when these modifications, having become far heavier than that which had been preserved from the original, made everything topple over. At that time I was formulating in the "Sur la dynamique du capitalisme" (*DC*, 1953-54) the conclusions summarized earlier here; I also was reaching the conclusion that the type of economic theory at which Marx was aiming was impossible to develop since the system's two central variables—class struggles, the tempo and character of technical progress—were essentially indeterminate; consequently, the rate of exploitation was indeterminate and it was impossible to obtain a measurement of capital that had any real significance. These ideas, already formulated in the first part of *DC*, were developed in the unpublished part of this text.[4] One can see there too that a systematic economic theory of the type universally envisioned till now of necessity has to succumb to the pull of the categories of capitalist economic "rationality"—which is ultimately what happened to Marx himself.

These conclusions were the foundation of the economic part of *MRCM/MCR*, which was worked out beginning in 1959. For them to be raised to their full power, we had to challenge in reflection and ultimately pass beyond the other components of the Marxian unity. But one of the immediate implications, which was drawn at once, played an essential role in the development of my work, and it underlies "On the Content of Socialism" (*CS I-III*).

The way capitalism functions assures permanent economic conflict between proletariat and capital around the issue of how production is to be distributed, but this conflict is, by its very nature and in each specific instance, neither absolute nor insoluble; it is "resolved" at each stage, arises again during the following stage, only to give birth to different economic demands and protests, which are satisfied in their turn sooner or later. From this results the semipermanent nature of the proletariat's protest action, which is of fundamental importance in a host of respects and in particular for its continued combativity, but it provides nothing that prepares the proletariat even remotely for a socialist revolution. Conversely, if the functioning of capitalism made the satisfaction of economic demands impossible, if capitalism produced poverty and increased unemployment for the masses, how could it be said that the masses were prepared, by their very life under capitalism, to construct a new society? The starving unemployed can at most destroy the existing power structure—but neither unemployment nor poverty will have taught them to manage production and society; at best, they could serve as the passive infantry of a Nazi or Stalinist totalitarian party that would use them to take power. Marx had written that with the process of capital accumulation and capital concentration "grows the mass of misery, oppression, slavery, degradation, exploitation; but with this too grows the revolt of the working class, a class always increasing in numbers, and disciplined, united, organized by the very mechanism of capitalist production itself." It is difficult, however, to see how work on the assembly line prepares those chained there for the positive invention of a new society. Marx's philosophical view that capitalism actually has succeeded in completely alienating and reifying the proletariat, philosophically untenable in itself, also had some unacceptable political consequences and had a precise economic translation: The reification of the worker meant that labor power was *only* a commodity, therefore that its exchange value (wages) was ruled *only* by the laws of the marketplace and its use value (extraction of output in the concrete work process) depended *only* upon the will and knowledge of its purchaser. The first point, as was seen, is false, but the second point is false too since there is something more to the lives of workers in the factory and in the course of their work.

The Transcendence of the Capitalist Universe
and the Content of Socialism (1955-58)

If socialism is the collective management of production and of social life by the workers, and if this idea is not a philosopher's dream but a historical project, it ought to be found in what already is its root. And what could that be if not the desire and the capacity of people to give life to this project? Not only does it preclude "socialist consciousness being introduced into the proletariat from outside," as Kautsky and Lenin put it, its seeds must already be present in the proletariat; as the latter is not genetically a new living species, this can only be the result of its experience of work and of life under capitalism. This experience could not be, as it had been abstractly presented in "La Phénoménologie de la conscience prolétarienne" (*PhCP*), merely political; this experience would have to be total for it to put the proletariat in a position to manage the factory and the economy, but also and especially to create new forms of life in every domain. The idea that the revolution necessarily had to put into question the totality of existing culture certainly was not new, but it had in fact remained an abstract phrase. There was talk of putting existing techniques into the service of social-ism—without seeing that these techniques were, from beginning to end, the material incarnation of the capitalist universe; there were demands for more education for more people—or a complete education for everyone—without seeing (or, in the case of the Stalinists, precisely because it was foreseen) that this meant more of capitalism everywhere, this type of education being in its methods, content, form, and up to and including its very existence insofar as it is a separate domain, the product of millennia of exploitation brought to its most perfect expression by capitalism. One reasoned as if there were, in social transactions, or even in any other kinds of transactions whatsoever, a rationality in itself—without seeing that this only reproduces capitalist "rationality," thus remaining prisoner of the universe that one claimed to be combating.

The intention animating *CS I-III* is to give concrete expression in every domain to the break with the inherited ideology. The program, explicitly formulated in the first part (*CS I*, 1955), was to show that the crucial postulates of capitalist "rationality" had remained intact in the work of Marx and had led to some consequences that were at the same time both absurd and reactionary and that the process of challenging capitalist relations and their "rationality" in the domain of work and of power were inseparable from their being put into question in the domains of the family and of sexuality, of education and of culture, or of daily life. The Twentieth Congress of the Russian CP as well as the Polish and Hungarian revolutions momentarily interrupted the drafting of this text; these events lent a particular bent to the choice of themes explicitly treated in *CS II* and *III*.

It cannot be emphasized too strongly what a source of stimulation and inspiration the Hungarian Revolution was for those who, like us, had predicted for years that the proletariat could not but rise against the bureaucracy and that its central objective would be the management of production, as was demanded openly by the Hungarian Workers' Councils. But neither should one underestimate the obligation it created for envisaging, much more concretely than before, the problems the revolution would encounter in the factory as well as in society.

Concerning workers' management of production in the strict sense, the discussion in *CS II* and *III* took its point of departure from a new analysis of capitalist production as it takes place everyday on the shop floor. The worker as passive use value from which capital extracts the maximum technically feasible surplus value, the worker as molecule, the object without resistance of capitalist "rationalization," was the objective contradictorily aimed at by capitalism. As concepts, these were merely some fictitious and incoherent *constructa* inherited unconsciously but in full by Marx, though they were also at the foundation of his analyses. Taking up again some merely philosophical ideas (already expressed in *PhCP* and other texts circulated within the group), incorporating contributions from some American comrades (Paul Romano and Ria Stone, in "The American Worker," *S. ou B.* issues 1 to 5-6),[5] and profiting from discussions with Philippe Guillaume, some comrades from the Renault factories and in particular Daniel Mothé, I was able to show that the real class struggle has its origin in the nature of work in the capitalist factory as a permanent conflict between the individual worker and the informally self-organized workers on the one hand, and the production plan and the plan of organization imposed by the company on the other hand. It thus follows that there exists a working-class countermanagement, which is masked, fragmentary, and changing, and also a radical scission between the official organization and the real organization of production, between the manner in which production is supposed to take place according to bureaucratic plans and their "rationality" (equivalent in fact to a paranoiac's mental construct) and the manner in which it actually takes place, despite and in opposition to this "rationality" that, if it were applied, would lead to the breakdown of production pure and simple. This alleged capitalist rationalization is an absurdity from the very point of view of the miserable objective at which it aims (the maximization of production). And it is absurd not because of the anarchy of the marketplace but because of a fundamental contradiction involved in its organization of production: the simultaneous need to *exclude* the workers from the direction of their own work *and*, having foreseen the breakdown of production in which this exclusion would result if it were ever fully realized (and this can be materially and literally confirmed in the case of the Eastern bloc countries), the need to make them *participate* in it, to continually call upon the workers and their informal groups, considered sometimes as mere cogs in the production apparatus and other times as supermen capable of guarding against any eventuality and even against the unfathomable absurdities of the production plans that management tries to impose on them. This contradiction, under forms that of course vary in each case, is found at every level of organization in society. It is transposed almost exactly as is onto the level of the overall economy when the anarchy of the marketplace is replaced by the anarchy of the bureaucratic "plan," which functions, as in Russia, only insofar as people at all levels, from factory directors to hired hands, act differently than they are supposed to. We also meet this contradiction again in contemporary "politics," which does everything it can to remove people from the direction of their own affairs and complains at the same time of their "apathy," ceaselessly pursuing this chimera of citizens or activists who always can be found simultaneously at the height of enthusiasm and in the depths of passivity. Indeed, it is at the very foundation of capitalist education and culture.

This analysis of production allowed us to see that, on this plane too, Marx had shared the postulates of capitalism till the very end. His denunciation of the monstrous aspects of the capitalist factory remained superficial and moralistic, for in capitalist technique he saw rationality itself, which inevitably prescribed one and only one type of factory organization, itself therefore also rational through and through. Whence comes the idea that the producers will be able to attenuate its most inhuman aspects, those most contrary to their "dignity," but will have to look outside of work (increases in "free" time, etc.) for compensation.

Present-day technique, however, is neither unqualifiedly "rational" nor inevitable, but is rather the material incarnation of the capitalist universe. It can be "rational" as to the coefficients of energy output of its machines, but this fragmentary and conditional "rationality" has no intrinsic interest or significance. It can become meaningful only in relation to the total technological system of the era, which itself is not a neutral means capable of being put in the service of other ends but rather is the concrete materialization of the scission within society, since every machine invented and put in service under capitalism is in the first place one more step toward the autonomization of the production process vis-à-vis the producer, and therefore is one more step toward the expropriation from the latter not of the product of his activity but of this activity itself. And of course this technological system does not determine, but cannot be dissociated from what, from a certain point of view, is only its flip side, namely, the capitalist organization of production, or rather, the capitalist *plan* of this organization—which is constantly being combated by the workers.

The condition for this combat, for its perpetual rebirth, and for its partial success is the fundamental contradiction of this organization insofar as it requires at the same time both the exclusion and the participation of the producers. This contradiction is absolute, in the sense that capitalism simultaneously affirms "yes" and "no." It is not attenuated but is brought to the point of paroxysm by the passage from private capitalism to complete bureaucratic capitalism. It is insurmountable since tautologically its transcendence can be achieved only through the suppression of the scission between direction and execution, and therefore through the suppression of all hierarchy. It is social, i.e., beyond the "subjective" and "objective," in the sense that it is nothing but the manifestation of people's collective activity and in the sense that the conditions of this activity and, to a certain point, its orientation are dictated to it by the system as a whole, which itself is instituted and modified, at each stage, by the results of the preceding stage. And it therefore also is largely independent of "consciousness" or of activity or of specifically "political" factors in the narrow sense (it has been as or more intense in American or English factories than in French ones). It is historical and historically unique. It does not express an eternal refusal of reification by the human essence but rather expresses the specific conditions created by capitalism, the organization of the relations of production that the latter imposes, and the existence of an evolving technology that sets this system in motion while being set in motion by it and that from then on is condemned to be constantly overturned by the internal necessities of the system and in the very first place by the very existence of the struggle within the process of production, against which the system has to and can defend itself only by further developing this technology. This contradiction is indeed the essential element upon which, and upon which alone, the project of collective management of production can be founded, since life inside the capitalist enterprise is what prepares this project to come to fruition.

The clear conclusion from the foregoing was that the goal, the true content of socialism, was neither economic growth nor maximum consumption nor the expansion of free (empty) time as such, but the restoration, rather the instauration for the first time in history, of people's domination over their activities and therefore over their primary activity, work; that socialism was concerned not only with the so-called grand affairs of society but with the transformation of every aspect of life and in particular with the transformation of daily life, "the foremost of important matters" (*CS II*). There is no domain in life in which the oppressive nature of the capitalist organization of society is not expressed, none in which the latter might have developed a "neutral" rationality, none that could have remained untouched.

Existing technology itself will have to be transformed consciously by a socialist revolution; its maintenance ipso facto would be the condition for the rebirth of the directors-executants scission (this is why one need only respond with Pantagruelian laughter to everyone who claims that there can be in this respect the least *social* difference between Russia or China on the one hand, the United States or France on the other). The "self-evident facts" of bourgeois common sense must be denounced and hunted down mercilessly; among them, one of the most catastrophic—it too was accepted by Marx—involves the alleged need for wage inequality during the "transitional period" ("to each according to his work"), based on this other bourgeois "self-evident fact": the possibility of individually "imputing" a product to "its" producer (upon which are based, let it be said in passing, both Marx's theory of value and the theory of exploitation, whose true foundation now turns out to be the artisan's or the peasant's idea that the fruit of "his" work is due back to "him"). There will be no socialist revolution unless from the first day it instaurates absolute equality of wages and incomes of all sorts, for this is the sole means by which the question of resource allocation will be removed once and for all, genuine social protest will be given the means to express itself without distortion, and the *Homo economicus* mentality that is consubstantial with capitalist institutions will be destroyed. (Let us note that the "self-management" types ["*autogestionnaires*"] who, for the past few years, curiously have been mushrooming up at all levels of the social hierarchy, keep silent on this question—which should surprise only the naive.)

The most difficult problem for the revolution, however, is not located at the factory level. No doubt an enterprise's workers could manage it with infinitely more efficiency than the bureaucratic apparatus; dozens of examples (from Russia in 1917-19, from Catalonia, from the Hungarian Revolution, to the Fiat factories recently, and even up to the laughable present-day attempts of certain capitalist firms to give more "autonomy" to groups of workers in their work) prove it. It is situated rather at the level of society as a whole. How do we envisage the collective management of the economy, of the remaining functions of the "State," of social life as a whole?

The Hungarian Revolution was crushed by Russian tanks; if it had not been, it inevitably would have encountered this question. Among the Hungarian revolutionaries who took refuge in Paris, the question was an urgent one, and their confusion was understandable but immense. I tried in *CS II* to respond to this question by showing that not a mechanical transposition of the model of the self-managed factory but the application of the very same profound principles to society as a whole contained the only key to a solution. Universal power for the workers' councils (invoked for a long time by Pannekoek and given new vigor by the Hungarian example), aided by technical devices having no power on their own (the "plan factory," mechanisms for broadcasting pertinent information, reversal of the usual direction of the flow of communication established in class society: ascent of decisions, descent of information), is this solution that eliminates in one stroke the nightmare of a "State" separated from society. This does not mean at all, of course, that properly political problems, those that concern the overall orientation of society and its instrumentation in and through concrete decisions, disappear; but if the workers, the collectivity in general, cannot resolve them, no one can do it in their stead. The absurdity of all inherited political thought consists precisely in trying to resolve people's problems for them, whereas the sole political problem is precisely this: How can people themselves become capable of resolving their own problems? Everything depends, therefore, on this capacity for which it is not only vain but intrinsically contradictory to seek either a substitute (bolshevism) or an "objective guarantee" (almost all of present-day Marxists).

The question of the status of a revolutionary organization is posed once again. It finally became clear, and it was clearly stated, that at no time and in no way would such an organization—which remained and remains indispensable—be able to aspire to any kind of "directorial" or "managerial" role whatsoever without ceasing to be what it was trying to be. This did not mean that it was becoming superfluous. Quite the contrary. But it became necessary to define its function, its activity, and its structure in a radically different manner than had been done in the past. Two years later, when the events of May 1958 (which brought to the *S. ou B.* group a certain influx of sympathizers who wanted to act) posed this question of organization in an acute manner, a scission arose for the second time with Claude Lefort and other comrades who left the group as a result of profound disagreements on this question. The sole coherent position was, and still is, as far as I am concerned, that the function of the revolutionary organization is to facilitate the daily struggles of workers and to help them come to an awareness of the universal problems of society—since society, by the way it is organized, does everything it can to make this impossible—and that this can be accomplished only through war against reactionary and bureaucratic ideological mystifications and above all through the exemplary character of its mode of intervention, which always is oriented in the direction of the workers themselves managing their own struggles, and toward its own existence as a self-managed collectivity ("Proletariat and Organization, I and II").

Modern Capitalism (1959-60)

But once rid of Bolshevik "substitutionism" and objective Marxist guarantees, what could be said of people's capacity to take into their own hands the collective management of their own affairs? In France we were witnessing the instauration of the Fifth Republic, which, if it signified the country's definitive passage to the stage of modern capitalism, was possible only in terms of the population's unprecedented political inactivity in the face of a governmental crisis of the first order. In other Western developed capitalist countries, a profoundly identical situation could be observed. It was not a matter of a temporary "apathy," still less of a cyclical "setback" as in Trotskyist meteorology. Modern capitalist society was fostering an unprecedented privatization of individuals, and not only in the narrowly political sphere. The externalized "socialization" of all human activities, pushed to the point of paroxysm, went hand in hand with an equally unprecedented process of "desocialization"; society was becoming an overpopulated desert. The population's retreat from all institutions clearly appeared at the same time as both the product and the cause of their accelerated bureaucratization, and ultimately as its synonym.

The previously separated strands were now coming together. Bureaucratization, as the predominant process of modern life, had found its model in the specifically capitalist organization of production (which already suffced to differentiate it radically from the Weberian "ideal type" of bureaucracy), but from there it overran the whole of social life. State and parties, business enterprises, certainly, but also medicine and teaching, sports and scientific research more and more were being subjected to it. Bearer of "rationality" and agent of change, everywhere it was begetting the irrational and living only through maintenance of the status quo; its mere existence multiplied to infinity or generated ex nihilo problems for which new bureaucratic authorities had to be created in order for them to be resolved. Where Marx had seen a "scientific organization" and Max Weber had seen the form of "rational" authority, it was becoming necessary to see the precise antithesis of all reason, the mass production of the absurd, and, as I wrote later (*MTR/MRT*, 1964-65), pseudorationality had become the manifestation and the sovereign form of the imaginary in the present era.

What is at the origin of this development? This question has been discussed several times and from several points of view in the preceding pages, but so far the discussion remains inadequate and we will have to return to it at great length; apart from a few unrelated series of events, we know practically nothing at all concerning this fate of the West, now imposed upon the whole planet, which has transformed the logos of Heraclitus and Plato into a ridiculous and fatal logistics. But what allows it to survive, what sustains the functioning and expansion of modern bureaucratic capitalism day after day? The system not only is self-preserving and self-reproductive (like every social system), it is self-catalytic; the higher the degree of bureaucratization already attained is raised, the faster the rate of further bureaucratization. Permeated with "economics," it finds its psychically and ideologically "real" raison d'être in the continuously expanding production of "goods and services" (which obviously are such only in relation to the system of imaginary significations it imposes). If this expansion of production still experiences some fluctuations, if it continues to be bumped along from one accident to another (for, in such a system the recurrence of accidents is necessary), it no longer undergoes profound crises. The management of overall economic activity by the State as well as the latter's own enormous weight allows it to maintain a sufficient level of overall demand. Nor is it limited any longer by the masses' purchasing power, the constant elevation of which now being, it turns out, the condition for its survival. If indeed the class struggle gradually has forced upon capitalism an increase in real wages, the limitation of unemployment, a reduction in the length of working life, of the workyear and of the workday, increased public expenditures, and thus an enlargement of internal avenues of trade, these objectives henceforth are accepted by capitalism itself, which correctly sees them not as mortal menaces but as the very conditions for its operation and its survival. Under such conditions, "consumption for the sake of consumption in private life, organization for the sake of organization in public life" become the system's fundamental characteristics (*MRCM/MCR II*, 1960).

Such at least is what may be called the "bureaucratic capitalist project." It should be pointed out, however, that this project represents, so to speak, only half of the present situation—and this due to an intrinsic necessity: Its complete realization would be its complete collapse. It finds its internal limit in the reproduction, indefinitely repeated within the bureaucratic apparatus itself, of the division between direction and execution, leading to the result that the functions of direction themselves can be carried out, not by observing, but by transgressing the rules upon which they are founded. And, more important, it finds its internal limit also in this same privatization of society as a whole that it is constantly giving rise to, and which is its cancer (as witness the discovery of "participation" by the government's and the bosses' idea men), since modern society can no more be governed through people's contumacy than the business firm can. It finds its limit quite simply in people's struggles—which now take on new forms (this is what prevented Marxists from discovering them before they were staring them straight in the face, as in 1968 for example)—in the *contestation* of individuals and groups who are, at all levels of social life, driven by bureaucratization and its organic products, high-handedness, wastefulness, and absurdity, to put the instituted forms of organization and activity back into question; this can be contestation only if at the same time it is a "search by people for new forms of life that can express their tendency toward autonomy" ("Recommencing the Revolution [*RR*]," 1964; to be included in the proposed third volume of this edition).

Just as workers can defend themselves against the bureaucratic plan for organizing production only by developing an informal counterorganization, so too, for example, do women, the young, or couples tend to put in check the inherited patriarchal organization by instaurating new attitudes and new relations. In particular, it was becoming possible to understand and to show that the questions posed by contemporary youth—students and others—expressed not a "generational conflict" but rather the rupture between a generation and the whole of instituted culture (*MRCM/MCR III*, 1961).

This generalized contestation signified ipso facto—as product and as cause—the progressive dislocation of both the established society's system of rules and individuals' interiorized adherence to these rules. Briefly, and roughly, speaking, there was not a law in place that was obeyed for any other reason than fear of punishment. The crisis of contemporary culture—like that of production—could no longer be seen simply as a "maladjustment," or even as a "conflict" between new forces and old forms. In this respect too, capitalism is an absolute anthropological novelty, where the established culture is collapsing from within without one being able to say, on the macrosociological scale, that a different, new one is already being prepared "in the womb of the old society."

The revolutionary problem thus had become generalized, and no longer just in the abstract, but also in all spheres of social life and in their interconnections. The exclusive preoccupation with economics or "politics" appeared as a matter of fact as the basic manifestation of the reactionary character of traditional Marxist currents. It was becoming clear that "the revolutionary movement must cease to appear as a political movement in the traditional sense of the term. Traditional politics are dead, and for good reasons . . . [It] ought to appear as what it is: a total movement concerned with everything people do and are subject to in society and above all with their real daily life" (*MRCM/MCR III*, 1961).

All this was leading us to break our last ties to traditional Marxism (and provoked the departure from *S. ou B.* of those who claimed to remain faithful to it and who, having accepted the premises step-by-step till then, now were refusing to accept the conclusion). Generalized bureaucratization, the reduced importance of economic problems in advanced countries, the crisis of the established culture, the potential for contestation invading every domain of social life and supported by every stratum of the population (with the exception of the infinitesimal minority inhabiting the summits) were showing that socialism no longer could be defined merely by starting from the transformation of the relations of production, nor could one speak any longer about the proletariat as the privileged bearer of the revolutionary project. Even the concept of the division between directors and executants no longer furnished a criterion for distinguishing between classes since, in the complex of interpenetrated bureaucratic pyramids that forms our social organization, the strata of pure directors and pure executants are seeing their importance constantly diminishing (*RR*, 1964). The very concept of exploitation, taken in its narrowest economic acceptation, was becoming indeterminate; a contemporary Marxist would be obliged to state simultaneously — and generally this is what he does in the interval of a few lines or a few days — that the American worker is exploited by American capital and himself profits from exploitation of the Third World. Must we conclude that the only parties interested in revolution and capable of making one are African bushpeople and the living skeletons sleeping on the sidewalks of Calcutta? (That is the conclusion drawn by another class of confusionists, like Fanon.) And less than ever, even in the long term, could a correlation between the most "exploited" strata and the most combative strata be found: It has not been industrial workers who for the past ten years have been putting forward the most radical demands. Ultimately, it is the very concept of class — even as a sociological-empirical descriptive concept, but in particular with the sociohistorical and philosophical weight Marx conferred upon it — that had ceased to contain any relevance for modern society. This did not mean at all that from now on only movements of "marginal" groups or of minorities were possible and progressive — as certain people more or less have maintained openly since then, thereby transforming into a sort of negative privilege of the proletariat what, in Marxism, was its positive privilege while still remaining in the same world of thought. Quite the contrary: Under its new forms, the revolutionary project was concerned more than ever with nearly everyone. From now on, however, it would be false to assert that in this totality the traditional proletariat retains a sovereign status (as Marx had thought) or even a simply privileged one, and this has been shown in full during May 1968, as well as in events in the United States surrounding the Vietnam War.

The Break with Marxism (1960-64)

Could we, while saving the substance of these analyses and positions, continue to clothe them in the vestments of Marxism and claim that they constituted its continuation and were preserving its true spirit? In a sense, modesty aside, they did so, they are the only ones to have done so. But it had come at the point where continuation required destruction, the survival of the spirit required that the body be put to death. It was not simply the traditional working-class movement that was irrevocably dead — as a program, in its organizational forms and methods of struggle, as a vocabulary, as a system of more or less mythical representations; beyond its distinctive concepts, the very body of Marx's theory, an immense embalmed cadaver profaned by means of this very act of embalming, had become the principal obstacle on the road to a new reflection concerning the problems of revolution. It no longer was a matter of the coherence, of the applicability, or of the correction of this or that economic theory or sociological idea of Marx's; it was the total system of thought that was proving untenable, and, at the center of this totality, was his philosophy of history and, quite simply, his philosophy. What purpose then would it serve to have recourse to Marx? Almost nothing of what had become essential for us had been so for Marx; almost nothing of what had been essential for Marx was so any longer for us — apart from the word "revolution," which today is common parlance, and his passionate search for truth and, whatever he said about it, for justice, which did not begin with him and will not end with us.

Outlined in the "Note sur la philosophie marxiste de l'histoire" which accompanied the first version of *MRCM/MCR* distributed within the group (1959), and clearly formulated in *RR* (1964), this break was explicated in the first part of "Marxism and Revolutionary Theory" (*MTR/MRT*, 1964-65). Profiting from material gathered in the field of ethnology as well as from the evolution of the ex-colonial countries since their emancipation, and especially from an internal critique of concepts, our discussion of the Marxist theory of history made us see in this theory an arbitrary though fecund annexation of the whole of humanity's history to the schemata and categories of the capitalist West; the critique of the Marxist philosophy of history, and of Marxist philosophy itself, brought out behind the "materialist" vocabulary a rationalist philosophy, just an inverted Hegelianism, therefore Hegelianism itself, involving as many mysteries and Procrustean beds as the latter.

Twenty years of effort to develop Marx's concepts and to illuminate them by making them illuminate world history in its most turbulent phases perhaps provides sufficient evidence that this is not some kind of "external" or "superficial" critique. But the critique of Marxism had to face up—and this is why it is so difficult to get people to understand this critique—to a series of difficulties that come not from the particular character of Marx's work—that would be a tautology—but from its absolutely unique character.

The first of these difficulties is that in Marx what we encounter are not "contradictions"—he is teeming with them, as is true with all great thinkers—nor even an opposition between an initial intention and the "system" in its finished form (this is also the case for Hegel), but a central antinomy between what I called the two elements of Marxism. Although the first element, which actually introduced a radical torsion into Western history, was expressed particularly in his youthful writings (rightly considered today as "prescientific" by vulgar rationalists such as Althusser and associates) and reemerged periodically but more and more infrequently in the history of Marxism, it never really was developed; there remain, in essence, only a few striking sentences, some signposts and indications for research much more than complete reflections, and a few exemplary and incomparable sociohistorical descriptions.

The second element, which manifested itself and was elaborated more or less only in the "mature" and "systematic" Marx and which has prevailed among Marxism's theoretical and practical descendants, represents the profoundly persistent hold of Marx's contemporary capitalist world on his thought (and still more so, of course, for his epigones). Marx had wanted to do a critique of political economy; instead he created his own political economics (a false one at that, but had he made a "true" one nothing would have changed; it is important nevertheless to see that it is false *because* its axioms are those of capitalism, the theoretical form it aims at is the form of a positive science and the same holds true for its method. Briefly speaking, this form is abstraction susceptible to quantification). For the living interpretation of a history that always is creating something new there was substituted a so-called theory of history that had classified previous periods of history and had assigned to history the stage to come; history as the history of man producing himself became the product of an omnipotent technological evolution (which one must postulate as autonomous, otherwise everything would become a mere tautology affirming that the elements of social life are in reciprocal interaction), inexplicably progressive and miraculously assuring a communist future for humanity. The transcendence of philosophy had produced solely a "materialist" metaphysics whose only novelty was its monstrous ability for interspecies copulation with a "dialectic" transformed into a law of nature—a copulation capable of producing only sterile offspring, of which Althusserian mules are only the most recent specimens. The question of the relation between the interpretation and the transformation of the world was resolved by dissociating speculative theory of the traditional kind from a bureaucratic politics that itself, it is true, was profoundly innovative in its methods of terror, deceit, and oppression. The enigma of praxis had in the end given birth to a vulgar technical method [*pratique-technique*] for manipulating both militants and the masses.

Certainly, it is always wrong to reduce the thought of a great writer to a few theses; but what can one do when the writer in question is wrapped up in them? Just as certainly it would be stupid to think that the two antinomic elements that we are now sifting out are rigorously and clearly separated in Marx's writings; expressions of the first kind can still be found in much later texts, as a naturalism of the most insipid sort can be found in many passages of *The German Ideology*. But it is history itself that is charged with resolving that difficulty: What very quickly prevailed was not the first element, but rather the second one. If Marxism is true, then according to its own critiques its actual historical truth is found in the actual historical practice it has encouraged—that is to say, ultimately, in the Russian and Chinese bureaucracies. *Weltgeschichte ist Weltgericht.* And if this conclusion is not granted, then the premise must be rejected and Marxism must be accepted as only one system of ideas among others. To appeal against the judgment of actual history in view of the work of Marx the thinker is first of all to treat Marx as a pure thinker, i.e., precisely as what he did not want to be, and to rank him among such other great thinkers as Plato or Aristotle, Spinoza or Hegel, which he certainly merits, but which takes away from him every privilege except merely contingent ones. And, upon closer inspection, is it not truly unbounded arrogance to claim to be saving Marx in spite of himself as well as, ultimately, pure and simple stupidity to try to maintain someone as infallible by asserting that he did not really know what he was saying when he wrote the preface to the *Critique of Political Economy*?

But this is precisely the point—and here we find an even greater difficulty: No one can talk about Marx (no more than one can talk about Freud) as if he were an Aristotle or a Kant; we are not talking about knowing what a solitary thinker sitting in his garret or his ivory tower in 2972 might think again, starting from Marx, but about what, for a century, has made Marx present in contemporary history in a totally different fashion than Lao-tzu, Duns Scotus, or even Kierkegaard. Now, this presence results not from the complexity and the subtlety philosophy tries to reproduce when reconsidering such a work but rather from that which in Marx's work actually is a thesis and is presented as such. Marx is present in contemporary history, not as a great thinker prompting one to think further, but as the founder of a great secular-"rationalist" religion, as the father of a political myth in scientific clothing. (Here indeed is one of the essential reasons for the unbelievable theoretical sterility of the Marxist movement since the death of its founder, and those who today want to "rethink Marx" glance over this without even wondering about it—another strange way of showing its faithfulness to Marx.) In order to rediscover Plato, Aristotle, or Kant, if this is possible, one must break through the conglomeration of interpretations under which the centuries have simultaneously buried them and kept them alive. In order to rediscover Marx, it is Marx himself who must be broken through. Such is the paradoxical historical situation of this man who wanted to be neither Newton nor Mohammed, but is no stranger to the fact that he became both at once; such is the price paid for his unequaled destiny as the Scientific Prophet.

There are no limits—this is true and this is one of the most astonishing things in history—to the transformation, to the transsubstantiation that subsequent epochs can inflict upon a great work. Uncultured scientists (this is not necessarily a pleonasm) today go on repeating that the dogmatism of Aristotle had to be shattered in order for modern science to develop. Yet, for those who know how to read, of all the great philosophers Aristotle is one of the least "dogmatic"; his writings teem with aporias abandoned in midstream, with interrogations left open, and with "but concerning this we must take up this subject again . . ." Over the centuries the Middle Ages succeeded in making this author the source of truth and every truth: *ipse dixit*. The Middle Ages did it, not Aristotle. The contemporary age perhaps would have succeeded in any case in making Marx's work this Bible that no one really reads and that can be considered all the more easily as the guarantee of revolutionary truth. But the fact that cannot be conjured away is that this work lends itself too easily to such an interpretation.

Why does it lend itself so? Because in it is incarnated the last great avatar of the West's rationalist myth, of its religion of progress, of its historically unique combination of revolution and conservation. On the practical plane as well as the theoretical plane, Marxism prolongs and continues the lineage of the revolutions of the Western world since the seventeenth century by leading it explicitly to its apparent limit; but under its perfected, systematic, and realized form, it preserves what is essential to the rationalist-bourgeois universe at the deepest level. Whence comes its essential "progressivism," the absolute confidence in a historical reason that would have everything arranged in secret for our future happiness and in its own capacity to decipher its workings; whence comes the pseudo-"scientific" form of this decoding process; whence comes the complete dominance of concepts like work or production, the accent being put exclusively upon the development of the forces of production. Analogous in this respect to all religions, it necessarily contains the simple and strong assurances it needs for the faithful and humble, and subtle ambiguities for the Doctors' endless disputes and for their mutual excommunications.

To the vulgar scientism provided for the consumption of the average militant there is counterposed on a sophisticated level, and according to taste, the Hegelian filiation, the enigmas of surplus-value realization or of the falling rate of profit, the dazzling acuity of some of the historical analyses, the grand theory itself; but this theory remains speculation, precisely in the sense that Marx himself and above all Lukács (the Lukács of 1923) gave to this term: a theory that is contemplation, sight. Practice follows merely as an application. There is a truth to be possessed, and theory alone possesses it—here is the ultimate postulate that Marx, whatever he might have said at certain moments, shares with the culture of his age and, beyond it, with the whole history of Greco-Western thought. Being is to be seen, just as it is—and when it has been seen, the essential thing, if not everything, has been said. For an instant, Marx had the brilliant intuition that he must get off this path stretching from Parmenides to Heidegger, along which the sights seen and speculated upon quite obviously have always been changing while the speculative relation between being and its *theoros* has not. But he quickly came back to this path. Thus for one more time was it covered over [*occulté*] that being is essentially a having-to-be [à-être], that vision deludes itself about itself when it takes itself for a vision, since it is essentially a making/doing [*faire*], that every *eidos* is an *eidos* of a *pragma*, and that the *pragma* is never maintained in having-to-being except by the *prakton*.

The Instituting Society and the Social Imaginary (1964-65)

Marxism had not achieved the transcendence of the antinomy between theory and practice. The theory, having turned speculative again, had become dissociated into a metaphysics that will not say its own name and a so-called positive science founded upon the former's prejudices and mimicking the sociologically dominant model of science. To these two was annexed a practice conceived of as the application of truths derived from the theory, i.e., conceived of ultimately as technique.

We therefore had to take up again the question of how knowledge and action are related; we had to rid ourselves of a several-thousand-year-old heritage that sees in theory the sovereign authority and sees theory itself as the possession of a system of truths given once and for all; we had to understand that theory is nothing less, but also nothing more, than a project, a making/doing, the ever-uncertain attempt to arrive at an elucidation of the world (MTR/MRT III, IV, and V). We had to establish the radical difference separating political praxis from all forms of practice and all forms of technique, and we had to understand this making/doing, which aims at others as autonomous beings and considers them agents for the development of their own autonomy. We had to understand that this praxis, which can exist only as conscious and clearheaded activity, is something completely different from the application of a previously existing knowledge; the knowledge upon which it depends for its support is necessarily fragmentary and provisional, not only because an exhaustive theory cannot exist, but also because praxis itself constantly gives rise to new knowledge, because only making/doing makes the world speak. Thus do we find, not resolved, but relativized, the antinomy that I once had formulated (*S. ou B.*, no. 10 [July 1952], pp. 10-17)[6] between the activity of revolutionaries, which is based upon the attempt to anticipate developments rationally, and the revolution itself as the explosion of the masses' creative activity, which is synonymous with an overthrow of historically inherited forms of rationality.

Also and above all we had to resume our reflections upon history and society. Once rid of the traditional schemata it was not difficult to see that they represented all the illegitimate transpositions into history and into society of the schemata borrowed from our commonplace experience of the world, the world of familiar objects or of individual life. Thus history is a "life," whether it be a developing life and an *Erziehungsroman*, or aging and degradation, or a combination of the two in a "cycle" or a "succession of cycles." Thus society would be a "contract" or a "war," a "prison" or a "machine." But it is only in history that a life or a succession of lives is possible; it is only in and through society that contracts, wars, prisons, and machines exist. What then can we avail ourselves of in order to think about history and society? Nothing—nothing except a recognition of the absolute specificity, of the unique mode of being of what I called the *social-historical*, which is neither an indefinite addition of individuals or of intersubjective networks, nor their simple product, but which is rather "on the one hand, the given structures, the 'materialized' institutions and their works, whether these be material or not; and, on the other hand, *that which* structures, institutes, materializes . . . the union *and* the tension of the instituting society and of the instituted society, of history made and of history-in-the-making" (*MTR/MRT IV*, May 1965).

That which institutes in each instance, that which is at work in history-in-the-making, can only be thought of as the *radical imaginary*, for in each specific instance it is simultaneously the emergence of something new and the capacity to exist in and through the positing of "images." Far from incarnating some kind of "rational" Hegelian-Marxist process of development, history is, within its ample limits, unmotivated creation.

The organization of every society, far from representing a functional machine (whatever might be the definition, at any rate impossible, of the end to which this functionality would be subjected) or a logical ("structural") combinatory, far exceeds what functionalism or symbolic logic (which indeed always is in its essence indeterminate) can enjoin. Every society exhibits in all its manifestations an unending profusion of elements that have nothing to do with either the real or the rational or with the symbolic, and which is dependent upon what I called the imagined or the secondary imaginary. But what is "rational" and even "real" for society can be grasped, defined, and organized only through the primary and unmotivated positing of areal and arational significations; this positing is its very institution, in the originary sense of the term, the articulation it performs upon itself and upon the world. These imaginary social significations are dependent upon the radical imaginary as it manifests itself in the action of the instituting society (insofar as the latter is to be contrasted with the instituted society). Let us emphasize in passing that the term "imaginary" as it is used here has nothing to do with the meanings currently attributed to it, such as the "fictive" or even the "specular." Therein originate the schemata and the figures that are the ultimate conditions for the representable and the thinkable, hence also that which overturns them during a period of historical change. Whence also proceeds what we call the rational without further qualification (which encounters, in that which exists, an enigmatic correspondence). The imaginary is incarnated in imaginary social significations that are indispensable for all individuals—which they do not think about, insofar as it is only by means of these significations that they can think at all—and which allow them to be transformed from wailing newborns of the species *Homo sapiens* into Spartans, Dogons, or New Yorkers. These significations are instituted because they are established, sanctioned, materialized in and through all social objects (and, to begin with, in and through language). These significations, from the moment they are instituted, lead an independent life; they are creations of the instituting society to which this society is subjected as soon as it has instituted itself. From then on it became clear that alienation, in its social-historical sense, was nothing but the process by which imaginary significations become autonomous in and through the process of instituting, or the independence of the instituted in relation to social instituting, which is just another way of saying the same thing.

What becomes then of the content of the revolutionary project? Obviously, it can be neither the absurdity of a society without institutions nor one of good institutions given once and for all, since every set of institutions, once established, necessarily tends to become autonomous and to enslave society anew to its underlying imaginary significations. The content of the revolutionary project can only be the aim of a society that has become capable of a perpetual renewal of its institutions. Postrevolutionary society will not be simply a self-managed society; it will be a society that self-institutes itself explicitly, not once and for all, but continuously.

This is the new meaning that must be given to the much sullied term "politics." Politics is not a struggle for power within given institutions, nor is it simply a struggle for the transformation of institutions called "political," or of certain institutions or even of all institutions. Henceforth politics is the struggle for the transformation of the *relation* of society to its institutions, for the instauration of a state of affairs in which man as a social being is able and willing to regard the institutions that rule his life as his own collective creations, and hence is able and willing to transform them each time he has the need or the desire. It will be said, "Without an established and fixed set of institutions the individual cannot be humanized and society cannot exist." Certainly so. The question to be answered is: "Until what point should the individual, once raised, remain of necessity the slave of this upbringing?" The question to be answered is whether the fixity of institutions in the contemporary world is a condition for society's continued functioning rather than one of the major causes for its chaotic state. We know for a fact that some people have been able to avoid being slaves of their upbringing, even in societies where everything conspired to make them so. We know for a fact that societies have existed that do not place an a priori limit upon their own law-making activity. Certainly, for these people and especially for these kinds of societies there always have been innumerable blind spots, and what we are aiming at goes infinitely further than whatever may have existed till now. But the contemporary situation—where there are no longer any institutions that cannot be put into question explicitly and where the social imaginary no longer can be incarnated except in a pseudorationalism dedicated essentially to a constantly accelerated erosion and self-destruction—also goes infinitely further.

Today we know that there is no genuine knowledge except for knowledge that raises the question of its own validity—which does not mean that everything is dissolved into an indeterminate process of interrogation; a question can have a meaning only by presupposing something not in question, but this questioning can return to the unquestioned in order to question it in its turn, and thinking is this very movement. We are aiming at a state in which the question of the validity of law will remain permanently open. Not so that everyone might be able to do anything whatsoever, but so that the collectivity might always be able to transform its rules, knowing that these rules proceed neither from the will of God nor from the nature of things nor from the Reason of History, but rather from itself, and knowing that if its field of vision always is necessarily limited, it is not by necessity chained to a position and that it can turn around and look at what till then was behind its back.

The Present Question

This was the point I had reached when, after long and difficult internal debates, I decided during the winter of 1965-66 to propose to the comrades with whom I was working (and who ultimately, and not without great reservations, accepted) that the publication of S. ou B. and the operation of the group be suspended *sine die*. The external or circumstantial reasons that led to this decision were minor; among them I must mention the attitude of the readers and sympathizers of the review, who remained passive consumers of ideas and who attended meetings but shied away from all activity. Even this was not decisive, however, for I was convinced that these ideas were making their progress under the surface, and what happened later on has proved this. The decisive motives were of a different order. The preceding pages would remain essentially incomplete if these motives were not rendered explicit here.

The first motive was homologous to the theoretical exigencies created by the development of these ideas. What has been said here helps one to understand that a theoretical reconstruction going infinitely further than I thought would be required when I began writing "Marxism and Revolutionary Theory" had become necessary; and that, beyond Marxism, all of the frames of reference and categories of inherited thought were open to question along with the conception of what theory is and what it tries to be. This reconstruction, assuming that I was capable of broaching it, required an effort of such a breadth and of such a subject matter as could not easily be made compatible with the publication of this review, or even with its character.[7]

The second motive, about which I can and should speak at greater length, concerned the relation between the course of social and historical reality and the content of the aims of the revolution. The development of the ideas and the evolution of the situation had led to an immense enlargement of this aim. Even the term "revolution" no longer was appropriate to describe this thing. It was not a matter simply of a social revolution, of the expropriation of the expropriators, of people's autonomous management of their work and of all their activities. It was a matter of the permanent self-institution of society, of a radical uprooting of the several-thousand-year-old forms of social life, challenging man's relation to his tools as well as to his children, his relation to the collectivity as well as to ideas, and ultimately all the dimensions of his possessions [avoir], of his knowledge [savoir], of his powers [pouvoir]. Such a project, which, by definition, tautologically, can be carried forth only by people's autonomous and clearheaded activity and which is nothing but this activity, implies a radical change in individuals, in their attitudes, in their motivations, in the way they are disposed toward others, toward objects, toward existence in general. This is not the age-old problem of changing individuals as a prerequisite to social change or vice versa, which is meaningless even in its own terms. We never envisaged revolutionary transformation except as an indissociable transformation of both the social and the individual where, under changed circumstances, changed people blaze a new trail, thus making their own development toward the next stage easier rather than more difficult. And it is plain to see that our central concern always has been to understand how and to what extent life in present-day society prepares people for this transformation. Now, the deeper the content of this transformation grew, the wider the gap separating it from people's real life seemed to grow, and the more momentously did the following question crop up: To what extent does the contemporary social-historical situation give birth in people to the desire and the capacity to create a free and just society?

I always knew that no merely theoretical answer exists for this question; still more, that it would be ridiculous to relate this discussion to circumstantial phenomena. But also I never could be content with the proverbial saying, "Do what you ought to do, come what may." For, the question here is precisely that of the doable, which in this domain certainly is not theoretically deducible, but which, according to the very things we are saying, should be susceptible to elucidation [élucidible]. One may judge the extent to which I was able to make headway with this elucidation by reading the hitherto unpublished and new texts that will appear in CS, EMO 1 and 2, and IIS.[8] Here I simply want to jot down a few points to bring this question up to date.

The "combination of circumstances," as it turned out, was particularly ponderous in 1965-66. But in this set of circumstances, what we saw going on was just the opposite of circumstantial: privatization, desocialization, the expansion of the bureaucratic universe, the increasing ascendancy of its form of organization, of its ideology and of its myths as well as the concomitant historical and anthropological changes. What has happened since has confirmed again that this is only part of contemporary reality, but it has not altered fundamentally the terms of the problem. If May '68 showed vividly the accuracy of our analyses concerning the character and meaning of the youth revolt, the spread of social protest, and the generalization of the revolutionary problem, it has also made us see the immense difficulties involved in a nonbureaucratized collective organization, in taking responsibility for the overall problem of society, and above all it showed the profound political inertia of the industrial proletariat, the hold its way of life exerts upon it and the mentality that predominates. The unprecedented ideological confusion that followed these events—where we saw some people appealing to Mao in the name of ideas that would get them shot on the spot if they were in China, while others, awakened to political life by May's essentially antibureaucratic movement, went toward the Trotskyist microbureaucracies—and that, to this day, has only grown worse, is no longer just a circumstantial phenomenon.

Whatever may seem to be the case, there is a narrow and direct connection between these two orders of considerations: the need to have as broad a theoretical reconstruction as possible and an investigation into the capacity and the desire of people today to change their history. The break with the dialectical mythology of history, the expulsion of the theological phantasm from its new refuge (which today is "rationality" and "science") is fraught with incalculable consequences at every level. Indissociably teleological and theological, the Hegelian-Marxist view is that of a history that, perhaps through accidents, delays, and detours, in the end is accumulation and centralization, clarification and synthesis, re-collection. This could be so over certain distances and for some period of time. But we also know from blinding evidence that history is just as much syncretism and confusion, decay and neglect, dispersion. These consequences, about which it may be asked to what extent even those who might understand them would be capable of bearing their burden, are dramatically illustrated in the contemporary historical situation. There is not, as Marxism implied, borrowing a three-thousand-year-old belief, an irresistible advance toward truth in history, neither under its liberal-naive-scientistic form nor under some form of dialectical accumulation. Confusion, illusions, and mystifications are constantly being reborn from their own ashes. The gap between what truly exists, the actuality and potentiality of society, and the representations people currently make of these is always ready to widen further; never, perhaps, has this gap been as great as it is today, and this is not in spite of, but precisely as a function of the overwhelming mass of so-called knowledge, of information, and of discourses that fill the air.

The aim, the will, the desire for truth, as we have known it for twenty-five centuries, is a historical plant that is hardy and frail at the same time. We question whether it will survive the period we are passing through. (We know that it did not survive the rise of Christian barbarism, and a millennium had to pass before it reemerged.) I am not talking about the truth of philosophy, but rather about this strange fissure that *has been instituting itself* in society since Grecian times and enables society to put its own imaginary into question. This truth, the only one that in a sense matters for us, has and only can have a social-historical existence. This means that the conditions that make it possible for it to function have to be incorporated in a certain fashion into our social organization as well as into the organization of individuals' psyches, and these conditions are situated at a much more profound level than the mere absence of censure or repression (these conditions sometimes could be brought together under tyrannical regimes, which ultimately encountered in them the reason for their demise, and cannot be brought together under apparently liberal regimes). Today, in a continually accelerating race, everything—the very dynamic of institutions as well as the overall functioning of society—seems to conspire to destroy these conditions: the power of propaganda and illusion-making machines, neoilliteracy spreading as quickly as and at the same pace as the broadcasting of "knowledge," the delirious division of scientific labor, the unparalleled erosion of language, the de facto disappearance of writing (which is a consequence of its unlimited proliferation), and, above all, the established society's unbelievable capacity to reabsorb, divert, and recoup everything that challenges it (which was noted, but certainly underestimated in *S. ou B.* texts and which is a historically new phenomenon) are only a few of the social aspects of this process. Taking all this into account we may ask whether the type of human being for whom these words have weighed as heavily as the ideas to which they refer and for whom the latter were something other than and more than the current season's set of consumer objects, who has remained responsible for the coherency of its statements and as the sole guarantor, in its own eyes, of their veracity, we may ask whether this psychical type of human being is still being produced today. Glancing at the collages that are the principal product of contemporary pop ideology and hearing some of their stars proclaim that responsibility is just a cop's word, we are tempted to respond in the negative. It will be said that this accords them too high a place of honor. But where then would these nothingnesses extract their simulacrum of existence if they are not empty reflections of an emptiness that infinitely surpasses them?

This connection is a narrow and direct one also because henceforth the truth in question is of a different order and of a new character. We cannot, we should not seek—and this again is flipped upside down, diverted, turned into an instrument of mystification and an excuse for irresponsibility in the hands of today's imposters—a "scientific" theory or even a total theory in the area of society, and still less in any other domain. We cannot for a single instant let ourselves believe that the articles of a political program contain the secret for the future liberty of humanity. We do not have any Good News to proselytize concerning the Promised Land glimmering on the horizon, any Book to recommend whose reading would exempt one from having to seek the truth for oneself. Everything we have to say would be inaudible if it is not understood from the outset as a call for a critique that is not a form of skepticism, for an opening that does not dissolve into eclecticism, for a lucidity that does not halt activity, for an activity that does not become inverted into a mere activism, for a recognition of others that remains capable of vigilance. The truth with which we are henceforth concerned is neither a possession nor the return of the Spirit to itself. It is the movement of people through a free space within which there are a few cardinal points. But this appeal, can it still be heard? Is it really this truth that the world today desires and is this the one it can attain?

No one person, whoever it may be, or theoretical thought as such has the power to answer this question in advance. But it is not vain to pose it even if those who try to and are able to understand it are few in number. If they can do so without arrogance, they are the salt of the earth. Neither does any one person, whoever it may be, have the power to found (in the traditional sense of this term) the project of historical and social transformation, which ultimately is consubstantial with such an aim of such a truth, since the two appear to us today as the new exigency for a new self-positing of social-historical man. It is not a matter of establishing a foundation, and still less of indoctrination, but rather of an elucidation that will help this new exigency to propagate itself and take shape.

October-November 1972

Notes

1. T/E: The GPU was the Soviet secret police of the era; the OPLA was the Greek partisans' "Organization for the Protection of the Popular Struggle."

2. In fact, they maintained for a long time and until quite recently that the satellite countries were still "capitalist."

3. We know that some of these points were discussed laboriously and at great length in *Capital*. This does not change the overall theoretical situation, which is similar to Ptolemaic theory saying that the universe's fundamental tendency to turn around the earth is thwarted and sometimes prevented from manifesting itself in the world of appearances due to the action of some secondary factor.

4. T/E: The author notes parenthetically here that *DC* would be "published in Volume II of this edition." This volume, however, never appeared.

5. T/E: *The American Worker* was originally published in English in 1947. *S. ou B.* presented a French translation of the two articles it contains in issues 1-8 of the review. See the Bibliography for information.

6. T/E: Castoriadis is referring to "Proletarian Leadership" (included in this volume).

7. The interested reader can find a few fragmentary indications of the direction of this work in "Epilégomènes à une théorie de l'âme que l'on a pu présenter comme science" in *L'Inconscient*, 8 (October 1968) and "Le monde morcelé" in *Textures*, 4-5 (Autumn 1972). [T/E: Reprinted in *Les Carrefours du labyrinthe* and translated in *Crossroads in the Labyrinth*, pp. 3-45 and 145-226, respectively.]

8. T/E: Among the "hitherto unpublished and new texts that will appear in *CS, EMO 1* and *2*" are seven of the final nine texts to be included in volume 3 of this edition ("The Diversionists" and "The Evolution of the French Communist Party" being the two exceptions). The new parts of *IIS* are found in Part II of that volume.

1

On the Regime and against the Defense of the USSR

Only a short time ago revolutionary politics consisted essentially of the struggle against the overt instruments of bourgeois domination (State and bourgeois parties). For a long time, however, it has been complicated by the appearance of a new and no less fundamental task: the struggle against the working-class's own parties. The working class had created these parties for its liberation, but, one way or another, they have been betrayed by them. This process of permanent deterioration from the top has taken on such importance that it is impossible to elaborate a coherent and effective revolutionary politics today without having a clear conception of its nature and its dynamic.

The key issue here can be expressed as follows. Social democracy, created in a period in which the proletariat and the bourgeoisie were the only forces of polarization, the only sources of autonomous power on the political scene, could betray the former only by passing into the latter's camp, only by following a more and more overtly bourgeois politics. Inasmuch as it has monstrously betrayed the proletarian revolution, Stalinism, in contrast, follows an equally independent political line and autonomous strategy opposed to that of the bourgeoisie no less than to that of the proletariat.

Where can we find the cause of this phenomenon and how can we eliminate the obstacles it creates for the revolution? At the present time everything depends upon the correct solution to this problem. But this solution is possible only if we start from a realistic analysis, stripped of all doctrinaire prejudice, of the society in which Stalinism has been fully realized and from which it draws most of its political virulence—of Soviet society.

Originally published as "Sur le régime et contre la défense de l'URSS," *Bulletin Intérieur du PCI*, 31 (August 1946). Reprinted in *SB 1*, pp. 63-72.

Soviet Society

The Economy

If it is incontestable that Soviet society can be understood only through an analysis of its economic foundations, it remains no less true that in order to study these foundations it is indispensable that we rid ourselves of all juridical formalism. Up till now, indeed, it was thought that everything had been said about this economy when one had mentioned nationalization and planning, its dominant traits; then, without asking oneself what real signification these traits have taken on in the dialectical whole of Soviet social life, one looked at the parties associated with the socialist program and wrote triumphantly, "Nevertheless, the socialist bases of Soviet society remain." A similar semblance of reasoning, which forgets that social and economic realities very often are to be found under the juridical formula that covers them over, would have led us to recognize in bourgeois democracy, whose deceptiveness was so often denounced by Lenin, the perfect realization of civil equality; likewise, it would have led us to ignore the exploitation that takes place in capitalist society, since bourgeois law knows nothing of the words "capital," "surplus value," etc. It would have taken us back from Marx's materialist economic analysis to classical and eighteenth-century juridicism.

Hence, in studying the Soviet economy or any other economy, we need to know how production and distribution are carried out, through and beyond juridical camouflage. In other words, who manages production and, consequently, has possession of the apparatus of production? And who profits from it?

The fundamental social groups through whom the economic process takes place are (a) the proletariat, made up of all the laborers charged with mere tasks of execution; (b) the labor aristocracy, which includes all skilled workers; and (c) the bureaucracy, which is made up of all the people who do not participate in the tasks of execution and who manage the work of others. As always, the boundaries between these three categories obviously are not rigid.

This distinction is essentially based upon a technical criterion. This technical basis, however, necessarily has a number of economic, social, and political consequences. For the solution to the two main problems of every economic organization—the problem of the management of production and that of its distribution—is based in the USSR upon this distinction.

1. The bureaucracy alone is entrusted with the responsibility for managing production. Neither the labor aristocracy nor the proletariat takes any part in this management process. Even within the bureaucracy this process takes place in a dictatorial manner, which grants to the average bureaucrat only extremely limited margins of initiative in implementing that part of the plan that is in his sector of responsibility. This is true as to the form of management. We will examine here those aspects of management that pertain to its substance, i.e., to the directions the bureaucratic summit imposes upon the economic process and to the conscious, unconscious, or situational motivations that dictate them.

2. The conditions that make the law of value valid (principally property and

private appropriation, the separate profitability of each enterprise, the free market, etc.) are lacking in the Soviet economy. On the other hand, planning combined with state control and embracing the economy as a whole eliminates the automatic functioning of the economy and replaces it, within certain very general limits, with conscious human management of the economy. This is why it can be said that in the Soviet economy nothing remains of the law of value but this very general formula: The value of all products taken together is equal to the sum of abstract work socially necessary for their production. Apart from that, it is bureaucratic arbitrariness that regulates distribution, i.e., that determines wages. This arbitrariness knows only two objective economic limits: For simple labor, wages cannot be lower than the bare minimum for existence (a limit that indeed is extremely elastic, as the experience of the first two five-year plans has demonstrated); for skilled labor, salaries are determined according to the relative scarcity of this kind of labor, taking into account consumer needs or those the plan considers as such. Other than that, bureaucratic arbitrariness rules everything—though bound, of course, by the psychological laws of optimal emotional satisfaction and by general political considerations. Within the bureaucracy, distribution takes place in accordance with relations of force similar to the way in which the distribution of total surplus value takes place among imperialist groups and trusts.

The dynamics of this economy are characterized by the absence of organic crises, an effect of quasi-complete planning. Consequently, its equilibrium can be upset only when affected by external factors. It seems then that this equilibrium ought to confer upon it an internal stability never before known in history, should it one day come to dominate the planet.

When we try to define this economic formation it becomes obvious that it bears no resemblance to the capitalist economy, for despite the persistence of exploitation and one social stratum's monopoly over the management of production, the economic laws in force are fundamentally different. On the other hand, of the four fundamental and indivisible characteristics of a socialist economy (namely, abolition of private property; planning; abolition of exploitation; and management of production by the producers), it exhibits only the first two (and these with many reservations), which are the least important ones. Instead of coming closer and closer to the realization of these fundamental goals, the Soviet economy has abandoned them completely—without, for all that, moving back toward the capitalist mode of production. Neither capitalist nor socialist, nor even moving toward either one of these two forms, the Soviet economy presents us with a new historical type. Its name is of little importance once its substance is known.

Politics

As for the political regime, its totalitarian character has been described so many times that it is superfluous to dwell on it here. We need only mention that, along with its police-state dictatorship, this regime entails an ideological hold upon the masses, a "statification of ideas," to such a degree that we may speak of the "im-

pairment of the consciousness of the masses" in Soviet society at the present
time.

"Degenerated Workers' State"

Clearly, the labeling of a state of fact is a mere convention; any terms are appropriate provided their content is understood and they do not engender dangerous
misunderstandings through their political effects. It is from this perspective that
the term "degenerated workers' State," employed in connection with the USSR,
should be considered and condemned. The structure of this expression implies
that the fundamental fact of present-day Soviet reality is to be found in its character as a workers' State and that, in order to explain certain nuances, one
should have recourse to the notion of degeneration. There is nothing of the sort.
It went beyond the point of degeneration a long time ago, for this degeneration
has reached complete maturity; it has evolved to the point that, creating new
forms for new contents, we now can comprehend the phenomenon in its
present-day functioning "independently," so to speak, of its provenance.

Statification and planning today play a fundamental role in the Soviet economy. But to say that with their current content they are enough to give to the
Soviet State even a bit of "working-class" character is to attach to law a signification independent of the real economic process. It is to replace Marxist economic analysis with abstract juridicism. It is to once again separate the economic
from the political in a fashion that is schematic and unacceptable for the study of
the present epoch.

If statification [*étatisation*] in the USSR is sufficient to confer upon this State
the name "workers' State in degeneration" (taken in an active sense), why
wouldn't nationalizations [*étatisations*] in a bourgeois country suffice to confer
upon it the name "workers' State in gestation"? The question is not whether
there is State control [*étatisation*], but by whom and for whose profit this State
control is instaurated or maintained. If in classical capitalist society economic
strength remains distinct from political power and takes control over the latter
insofar as political power still is external to economic strength, the historical
process has little by little reversed this schema: Already in the imperialist epoch,
the real as well as personal distinction between political power and economic
power appeared to be crumbling; in Soviet society, it is impossible even to conceive of it.

A certain technical and economic state determines a political structure, which
from then on governs the economy while the importance of the automatic
functioning of economic laws diminishes more and more. This is why we can
provide a sociological definition for the USSR by answering the following question: Who holds political power and for whose profit is it exercised? The answer
to this question can only be the following: Political power (and consequently,
economic strength as well) is held by a social stratum whose interests are absolutely contradictory in substance to those of the Soviet proletariat; it exercises
this power instead in its own counterrevolutionary interests. This stratum has
nothing in common with the working class or with the capitalist class. Like the

State that it directs and to which it gives expression, it constitutes a new historical formation.

Revolutionary Politics in the USSR

Political Revolution or Social Revolution

The strategy and tactics of the Fourth International and its Russian section toward this state of affairs ought to be distinctly and completely revolutionary. The question of whether the revolution to be achieved in the USSR can be defined scholastically as a "political" or "social" revolution is of little interest as long as we are aware of the tasks to be carried out there. It must be understood, moreover, that the practical basis of this distinction is to be found not in whether a transformation of property relations is to be carried into effect but in this: Can we preserve the State apparatus with a few mere changes in the ruling personnel and in positions of trust (political revolution), or should this apparatus be smashed and rebuilt anew under new forms (social revolution)? Now, it is obvious that it is this second case that will arise in the USSR when the working class becomes capable of overthrowing Stalin, for the real structure of the Soviet State retains essentially nothing that might differentiate it in general from any other historical apparatus for the domination of one class over another. When the revolution happens in the USSR, not only will we have to replace the party in power with ours, not only will we have to revive the instruments of working-class power — the soviets — or rather make them reappear (for "soviets" today exist in name only), but we will also have to create new instruments for the working class to exercise supervision and control. One of the factors favoring the development of bureaucracy is that during the period from 1917 to 1923 the Bolshevik leadership was not able to express in practical terms all of the distrust with which this bureaucracy should have imbued it. What Trotsky called the second aspect of the permanent revolution, and which concerns the socialist revolution itself, the continual shedding of its own skin, also should be applied to the regulation of political and State relations after the victory of the revolution.

The Defense of the USSR and Revolution

The major features of revolutionary strategy and tactics also remain valid, therefore, for the antibureaucratic revolution, subject, of course, to adequate adjustments. This is what today urgently dictates the abandonment of the "Defense of the USSR" line. Even for those who assume the existence of socialist bases in the Soviet economy, it is clear that the ultimate salvation of these vestiges depends upon the victory of revolution on a world scale and that the number one obstacle to this victory is to be found in the Stalinist bureaucracy. The struggle against this bureaucracy therefore constitutes the fundamental task for the Soviet proletariat. Can this wartime struggle be made compatible with the "Defense of the USSR"? Obviously not. To foster this struggle means, for example, to encourage strikes and demonstrations, to undermine the apparatus of repression and to jam up the general functioning of the State apparatus, to provoke insurrection in the army, to withdraw mutinous regiments from the front and to get them to march on the capital, etc. War, like revolution, is of a piece. One cannot conduct one without abandoning the other. The "struggle on two fronts" is an armchair strategy and it has never existed in practice, for inevitably the moment arises when one of the two struggles has to take precedence.

Very often we are asked, "Aren't you really wishing for an imperialist victory over Stalinism, aren't you really indifferent even to the outcome of this struggle, which would result in the suppression of the 'socialist bases' of the Soviet economy?" This question may be answered very easily by asking how the existence of these bases today favors the development of world revolution. We also could point out that these objections show a backward way of thinking that believes in the solitary significance of local and isolated victories or nondefeats over the past twenty or thirty years independent of the international course of events. But the main point lies elsewhere. It lies in the complete ignorance of the ABCs of Marxism as exhibited by people who believe that in the present epoch a wartime revolution is possible within a country without this implying a high world-revolutionary temperature and without the victory of this revolution engendering for other countries a crisis capable at least of preventing a counterrevolutionary intervention. It is, in fact, this consideration that has dictated or that ought to have dictated our defeatist policy within the countries at war against the Axis. It is also this confidence in our ideas and in the international solidarity of the proletariat that ought to guide our policy in the USSR.

Of course, it is not a matter of replacing, at this time and on the international scale, defensist propaganda with defeatist propaganda. The slogan "Revolution Irrespective of All Risk of Defeat" has a signification principally for the Russian section. It would be inopportune and dangerous for the International in general to emphasize this slogan in an especial fashion and to make it a central point in our propaganda. Without ever losing sight of the movement's international solidarity, the proletariat of each country ought to struggle against its own oppressors. What matters for the International today is to have a clear conception of the nature of Stalinism and to rid itself of the lamentable confusion created by the monstrous coexistence of the "Revolution against the Bureaucracy" and the "Defense of the USSR" slogans.

Note on the Lucien, Guerin, Darbout Thesis

This thesis, with whose practical conclusions we are in accord (abandonment of "defensism," revolutionary defeatism in the USSR), exhibits, aside from lacunae (lack of justification for defeatism, lack of a test to establish the organic tie between the phenomenon of Russian degeneration and capitalist society), certain errors that in our opinion are important enough to merit a few words.

After having justifiably criticized the kind of juridicism that sticks to legal formulas instead of looking at economic reality, and after having said in substance that the collectivization of the Soviet economy does not mean anything because the proletariat is dispossessed politically, Comrades L., G., and D. write apropos of Eastern European nationalizations that "they differ in no way from those that can be observed in Western Europe." Now, in this case it is precisely the political dispossession of the bourgeoisie that makes these nationalizations significant: The CP's monopolization of political power, already carried out or in the process of taking place in these countries, makes the Stalinist bureaucracy master of the nationalized means of production in the same general way that the Russian bureaucracy is, though under different modalities. This shows once again that in these countries Stalinism pursues, with a short-term or intermediate-term perspective, the same policy as it conducts on a world scale with a long-term perspective, namely, a policy of *assimilation*.

This leads us to another fundamental error made by Comrades L., G., and D. They identify the antithesis of Stalinism-imperialism with just any antithesis of imperialism. This implies that they are indifferent to the nature of the domestic regimes in the countries occupied by the Red Army and to the fundamental differences (according to their own confession) between these regimes and those of the countries occupied by imperialism. This leaves us completely in the dark when what what we need to know is why Stalinism, in its struggle against the imperialists, relies upon the working-class movement of other countries. Our comrades understand perfectly well that the Soviet regime is not socialist and that it is not compelled thereby to be capitalist. Why are they unable to understand that its foreign policy, while not being revolutionary, can very well be *non*capitalist, i.e., *anticapitalist*? This is why the term "bureaucratic expansionism" is much preferable to "imperialism," whatever the nuances.

2
The Problem of the USSR
and the Possibility of a
Third Historical Solution

Some Elementary Notions Concerning Revolutionary Theory

1. The most striking manifestation of the crisis of the Fourth International is to be found in its theoretical stagnation. Since the death of Trotsky, not only have we searched in vain for a trace of one new idea in all the Fourth's publications, but also the level of theoretical and political discussions has suffered a tremendous decline. An atmosphere of suspicion surrounds every attempt at renewal.

2. The historical cause of this sterility is to be found in the impossibility of making any theoretical advance during a period of momentous defeats for the revolutionary movement, as is the case with the period through which we just have passed. The influence of this objective factor has been reinforced by the ecclesiastical and scholastic attitude vis-à-vis revolutionary theory that characterizes the ruling apparatus of the International.

3. Revolutionary theory is not a dogma revealed once and for all but rather an integral part of revolutionary action constantly evolving in the same manner as the latter. Proletarian revolutions are not uniform applications of invariant principles and of "tradition," but rather they "criticize themselves constantly, come back to the apparently accomplished in order to begin it afresh, deride with unmerciful thoroughness the inadequacies, weaknesses and paltrinesses of their first attempts" (K. Marx, *The Eighteenth Brumaire*).[1] Likewise, revolutionary theory is continually obliged to put itself into question, to reassert itself in light of every new scientific discovery and through the assimilation of new his-

Originally published as "Le Problème de l'URSS et la possibilité d'une troisième solution historique," in *L'URSS au lendemain de la guerre et la politique des Partis communistes* (preparatory discussion material for the Second Congress of the Fourth International), vol. 3 (February 1947). Reprinted in *SB 1*, pp. 73-89.

torical experiences. To each stage of the revolutionary movement there corresponds a more or less profound theoretical upheaval.

4. The same conclusion follows from the theory of permanent revolution, according to which "all social relations are transformed for an indefinite period of time in the course of continual internal struggle." "Revolutions in economy, in technique, in science . . . develop in complex reciprocal action and do not allow society to achieve equilibrium."[a] To the permanent revolution in transitional society there corresponds the permanent revolution in revolutionary theory.

5. Moreover, revolutionary theory remains a mere ideology until communism is achieved. Consequently, some parts of this theory are revealed sooner or later to be more or less *ideological*, i.e., false. Other parts, adequate at first, become increasingly abstract until a new examination brings them back in touch with reality.

6. This new examination is indispensable today when it comes to the problems of the USSR, of the degeneration of a proletarian revolution, and of the inevitability of socialism. From the theoretical point of view, let us note that, except in passing, neither Marx nor Lenin had envisaged the case of a revolution degenerating. Trotsky, while he examined this case, refused till the end to relate this problem to that of barbarism, though he deemed it necessary to bring the latter phenomenon to the proletariat's attention. From the political point of view, we urgently need to take a stand against the International's present line, which, with its "Unconditional Defense of the USSR" and the theory of the "socialist bases of the Soviet economy," does everything it can to polarize the masses toward the Russian side and constitutes in fact a "leftist" cover for Stalinism.

7. For us, to reexamine the problem of the inevitability of socialism and to speak of a "third solution" does not mean to challenge the revolutionary stance, as is the case with ignorant confusionists of the D. MacDonald sort, or to bow to the inevitable, along with the conformism of Leblanc, but to render the revolutionary perspective more complete and to seek the means to struggle against the new dangers that menace it.

Inevitability of Socialism and the
Possibility of a Third Historical Solution

8. As with Marx's and Lenin's similar formulations, the dilemma posed by Trotsky, "Socialism or Barbarism?", explicitly recognizes that socialism is neither fated nor inevitable, that it is simply possible.

9. This fact entails two conclusions relative to the nature of the historical process.

First, the historical process is neither fated nor necessarily determined in advance. Even if the evolution of nature and of History were set in advance like clockwork, our knowledge of this evolution and consequently every prevision could only be relative. But reality is not a clockwork mechanism: Causal laws, which seem to us to rule reality, constitute merely a first approximation, and scientific investigations have demonstrated that at a deeper level reality is regulated only by statistical laws of probability. History is determined in a definitive manner only by the determinate action of man. Just as the philosophical problem of free will on the individual level is merely a pseudoproblem, for it is only through his action alone that man can show at any time to what extent he is free, i.e., determined by an authentic [*vraie*] consciousness, so also on the historical level does the conscious action of humanity and of the revolutionary class determine, within the limits of possibility, the direction of History.

Second, the historical process does not follow a straight and narrow line of ascent. As Trotsky said, "History often passes by blind alleys like Stalin."[2] More generally, History, along with its periods of progress, also experiences its periods of breakdown and collapse, periods of barbarism, as occurred, for example, during the period following the fall of the Roman Empire (from the fourth to the tenth century). It is not through a priori reasoning that the extent and depth of such periods can be determined but rather through the study of facts and above all through revolutionary action itself. The only things that can be determined in advance are possibilities: today, the possibility of socialism as opposed to the possibility of a period of definite historical collapse such as barbarism.

The Classical Schema for the End of Capitalism from Marx to Trotsky

10. That capitalism, like every social system, is constantly wearing itself down and is approaching its own violent collapse is a truth that hardly needs to be demonstrated. Marx's essential contribution was to elucidate and to put forward these two additional ideas, namely (a) that the proletariat constitutes the fundamental lever for the overthrow of capitalism and (b) that the result of the conquest of power by the proletariat will be the instauration of socialism. It is indispensable to follow the fortunes of these two fundamental Marxist propositions in the three periods through which they have passed to date: the period of classical Marxism, that of Leninism, and the one through which we have been passing, ever since the conclusion of the process of degeneration of the Third International.

11. In classical Marxism, the idea that the overthrow of capitalism will be the work of the proletariat is founded upon the conception that in the last analysis there are in capitalist society only two sources of historical power: the bourgeoisie and the proletariat. Many social strata can enter into conflict with capitalism, but only the proletariat is willing and able to lead this conflict up to the point of social revolution. This fact is based not upon a proletarian messianism but upon an analysis of the working class's economic, political, and social condition, which we cannot dwell upon here.

We therefore can sketch Marx's schema for the end of capitalism in the following manner: deeper and deeper crises of capitalist society, middle-class disintegration, heightened proletarian consciousness. It is the most advanced societies that will bring the rest of the world into this evolutionary schema. For

Marx, the socialist revolution is a product of the overdevelopment of capitalist society.

12. In the Leninist period, however, new factors arise. On the one hand, this overdevelopment of capitalism entails a diminution of revolutionary potential in the most advanced nations (corruption of the labor aristocracy and of the trade-union and political bureaucracy, imperialistic pay bonuses granted to a part of the proletariat in the imperialist countries). Consequently, the "backward" countries take on a particular importance for the revolutionary struggle. But if the center of gravity is displaced toward the backward countries, if the weakest link is to be found most often in the countries where capitalist development is the weakest, a significant part of the classical schema is overturned, and it may be asked how the weak proletariat of a backward country can achieve victory. And how could this victory, on such a technically, economically, and culturally low level, inaugurate the realization of socialism?

The theory of permanent revolution provides the answer. As a matter of fact, even in a backward country, only the proletariat would be able to resolve for good the country's social problems, even those of national liberation and democratic transformation. On the other hand, if the revolution begins in a backward country it will culminate in victory by extending itself into the rest of the world, by bringing in its wake the advanced countries that alone can resolve the problem for good. In this way the two classical propositions are rescued.

13. This rescue, however, is only apparent. As a matter of fact, the permanence of the revolution is not a law that obtains at all times and in a positive direction. It is a condition, a simple hypothesis. The theory of permanent revolution neither affirms nor could it affirm that "in *every* revolution occurring in a backward country, the proletariat *will take* power and *will set up* its dictatorship; every revolution begun on the national level *will extend itself* onto the international level and *will bring in its wake* the advanced countries." It says simply that "only if the proletariat takes over the direction of the revolution *will* the revolution *be able* to reach a culmination; only if the revolution extends itself onto the international level *will* it *be able* to bring the worldwide victory of socialism in its wake." Far from settling this question, the revolution, once begun, can only pose it. But what if the proletariat does not assume the direction of the revolution (China)? What if the revolution is not extended to the rest of the world (Russia)? For Trotsky, the answer is simple: In this case, there will be a victory for the counterrevolution that itself also is permanent; the revolution will be crushed for a definite period of time, and the counterrevolution will triumph worldwide, bringing things back, so to speak, to their point of departure.

At this point two factors intervened that Trotsky obstinately ignored. The first was that this process could not go on indefinitely. Defeats of the proletariat have profound results that put a mortgage on the future, and their accumulation signifies more than simple arithmetic addition. The second was that, in the case of an isolated revolutionary victory, the crushing of the movement in the rest of the world did not entail the immediate restoration of capitalism in this country. A period of time elapses during which this revolution degenerates almost by fate. Trotsky established the fact of this degeneration, but, following the schema of permanent revolution, he stubbornly repeated that this degeneration was an episodic and passing phenomenon, a contradiction that ultimately would be resolved either by the restoration of capitalism or by the worldwide victory of socialism. We are obliged today to state that degeneration itself also is permanent. In the country where it became installed, it develops into a new and consummate form of class society and from there it influences the rest of the working-class movement, enslaves this movement, employs it in order to maintain itself against capitalism and tries to encroach upon the rest of the world. Before examining the fate of the two classical propositions in the present era, it is incumbent upon us, therefore, to analyze more thoroughly the problem of degeneration.

The Degeneration of the Proletarian Revolution In General

14. Was the degeneration of the dictatorship of the proletariat in Russia, and will it remain in history, a specifically "Russian" phenomenon or a phenomenon peculiar to backward or isolated countries? Or is it the general fortune of every revolution?

To avoid meeting up again with the theory of "socialism in one country" on the opposite side, we should recognize that we are dealing here not with Russia's miraculous and peculiar properties but with more deep-seated factors in the evolution of history that begat Stalinism. Just as the Russian Revolution expressed not only the state of Russian society but principally the contradictions of world capitalism, likewise its degeneration is not an accidental outcome but instead reveals highly significant tendencies in our overall historical situation. Indeed, Trotsky no less than Stalin marveled at the Russian phenomenon. Despite all his analyses, it remained for him isolated, episodic, monstrous, having no organic relation to the state of the world economy or to the essential characteristics of the proletarian movement. Having from the first put his finger on the two fundamental factors of Russian degeneration—the ebbing of the world revolution and the backward state of the Russian economy—he refused till the end of his life to examine the extent to which these two factors were general and capable of appearing in every revolution.

It is clear, however, that the isolation of a victorious revolution is not "fortuitous" in the historical sense of the word and that it can happen again in the future. The all-round development of capitalism never will signify that the world will become completely standardized and especially not with respect to the political consciousness of the proletariat. The revolution's process of maturation takes place at different paces in different countries. All our efforts are aimed toward synchronizing the international revolution, but their success is never guaranteed in advance. In contrast to the bourgeois revolution, whose permanence on an international level is founded above all on the automatic functioning of industrial expansion, no automatic economic mechanism guarantees the rapid expansion of the proletarian revolution.

But why is an isolated revolution fatally doomed to degenerate—when it is

not defeated immediately? First of all, for political reasons. The victorious proletariat, as it becomes aware of how the revolution is being crushed in other
countries and of its own isolation, becomes demoralized and abandons the State
to the bureaucracy. But where does this bureaucracy come from? From the
"backward state of the country," from the economic scarcity that makes one
need a "guardian of inequality," a role "the masses cannot and do not want to
play."[3] But what if the country is not backward? *Every* country is "economically
backward," or rather economically inadequate to the task when it is isolated
from the world economy.

But what if the revolution is vanquished on the world level? Here too there is
no economic *or* other type of automatic mechanism that necessarily excludes the
possibility of degeneration. Only the phase of higher communism constitutes
such a guarantee. Until then, the economy will furnish necessary but by no
means sufficient bases for the building of socialism. The rest depends upon the
proletariat's political maturity and vigilance. Indeed, up until the phase of
higher communism, society continues to pass through a period of economic
scarcity. Socialism itself is a regime ruled by goods shortages, and it continues to
be a regime of inequality. For a period of time, consequently, the "war of all
against all" over the hoarding of products that exist in limited quantities will
continue, and people centered around the political and economic ruling circles
will inevitably try to lay hold of this power for themselves in order to guarantee
privileges for themselves. Once these people are installed in power, the inevitable cycle of degeneration begins.

Revolutionary Marxism has nothing to do with fatalism. Present-day technique renders socialism possible, but not at all inevitable. The achievement of
socialism depends upon the proletariat's conscious revolutionary action, even
and especially after the seizure of power. Things then become much more difficult. Fluctuations in proletarian consciousness and internal differentiations
within this class are not automatically abolished by the seizure of power. Degeneration can always be grafted onto these difficulties.

Marx was mistaken about many things, but he brilliantly foresaw the general
direction of historical development: abolition of capitalism's social forms and
worldwide economic and political concentration. This outcome is determined
today almost fatally by the development of technique. Whether this process of
concentration will operate upon a bureaucratic basis or upon a proletarian basis,
however, cannot be settled by a process of reasoning. It will be settled by the action of the proletariat. To the revolutionary consciousness of the proletariat, to
its power of mass action, there corresponds the socialist solution. To a prolonged
drop in its level of consciousness, to the problems involved in its becoming concentrated, to its breakdown as brought about by the agony of imperialism and
the degeneration of the State and of the "working-class" parties, there corresponds the bureaucratic solution. Both solutions are contained organically in the
ambiguity of the social situation of capitalism in its death throes, which signifies
on the one hand a liberation of progressive forces and, on the other hand, a profound breakdown of society.

Two New Factors in the Present Period

15. We can mention here only very briefly the appearance of two new factors that make the prospects for bureaucratization grow even more likely.

The first factor involves the spread of this degeneration from the USSR toward the capitalist countries through Stalinist parties. The political and trade-union bureaucracy of these parties, unlike that of social democracy, does not join up organically with capitalism but rather prepares to bring its respective countries into the Soviet zone. And if this is impossible at the present time, it prepares to take the most advantageous positions in the capitalist State with an eye toward the next conflict between the USSR and the United States. Because of the military-like form of organization of these parties, the masses who follow this leadership are much more difficult to lead toward genuine revolutionary action.

The second factor involves Europe's devastation by the war. In a number of countries the war set off an unprecedented social crisis. The bankruptcy of the revolutionary movement during this period and the character of the particular conjunctural situation made the exploited masses of these countries easy prey for Stalinist demagogy. The result was that the Stalinist parties almost came to power in all these countries, and now, in accordance with their own tactics and with a tempo derived from these tactics, they subject them to a process of structural assimilation with Russia, i.e., to a process of bureaucratization. Like the Soviet bureaucracy itself, the new class that is in the process here of coming into being did not have to be contained in advance in the economic structure of capitalist society, for its appearance corresponds not to a phase of progress but rather to a phase of historical collapse and social breakdown.

16. To sum up: A third historical solution, beyond the dilemma of capitalism or socialism, is possible. It corresponds to the proletariat's potential revolutionary bankruptcy. And its historical meaning would be that of a fall into an unprecedented modern barbarism, entailing an unbridled, rationalized exploitation of the masses, their complete political dispossession, and the collapse of culture.

The socialist solution remains today the only progressive solution. To choose between bureaucratic barbarism and ultra-imperialist barbarism has no meaning for us, neither before the question is settled (for until then we are struggling for the socialist revolution) nor afterward (since we will then try anew to organize the struggle of the exploited against the new regime on the basis of a revolutionary program).

The Bureaucratic Society

Juridical Forms and Economic Realities

17. Every discussion of the Russian question has been obscured by the confusion (unpardonable for Marxists) between the real relations of production in Russia and the juridical formulas employed by the bureaucracy to camouflage

these relations. Maintaining this confusion within the proletariat by means of the theory of the "socialist bases of the Soviet economy," the Fourth International is indulging in the same kind of mendacious and hypocritical apologetics that bourgeois professors employ when they talk about the sovereignty of the people and civil equality, as guaranteed by the Constitution.

18. The relations of production that determine the structure of a society are the social relations of exchange, the real, daily relations of man with man and of class with class. Real property relations, or the relations of possession, people's relations with the material objects that enter into their economic activity are purely and simply a function and result of the relations of production. As for the juridical expression of these relations (i.e., the formal system of property ownership in a juridical sense), its role is not to disrupt the economy's functioning but rather to mask in the best fashion possible its class content. Originally, the sole function of law was to reflect economic relations. The more culture develops and the more the masses enter into daily political life, the more the principal function of law becomes not to reflect but to camouflage economic realities as effectively possible. (See Engels's Letter to Schmidt, October 27, 1890.)[4]

The Bureaucratic Economy

19. The economic process in Russia takes place basically between two social categories: the proletariat, made up of all unskilled workers and having at its disposal only its labor power, and the bureaucracy, which includes the people who do not participate in material production and who alone assume the management and control of the work of others. Between these two categories is inserted a more or less privileged laboring and intellectual aristocracy. What defines the two fundamental categories *qua* classes is their absolutely different role in relation to production.

20. The class character of the productive process in Russia is guaranteed by:
   a) The bureaucracy's actual possession of the productive apparatus, which the bureaucracy has totally at its disposal, and by the proletariat's total dispossession therefrom;
   b) The monopoly the bureaucracy exercises over the management of production; and
   c) The objectives the bureaucracy imposes upon production and which are designed to serve bureaucratic interests. Production plans are only the numerical expression of bureaucratic interests.

21. Neither production plans nor the "nationalization" of the means of production by themselves have anything to do with the collectivization of the economy. To collectivize the economy means to give the actual possession, the management, and the enjoyment of the fruits of the economy (each being inseparable from the others) to the collectivity of workers. On the other hand, this is possible only if the latter really exercises political power. None of these conditions are fulfilled in Russia.

22. The same class character in Russia determines the distribution of social revenues among the various social categories. Whereas for the proletarian the

only sources of income are the proceeds from the sale of his labor power (wages), the bureaucrat enjoys a surplus income unrelated to his productive contribution and proportional to his place in the bureaucratic pyramid.

This surplus income comes from the exploitation of the proletariat. In capitalist society, exploitation has objective limits, which are expressed by laws regulating the rate of surplus value and by the objective value of labor power. In Russia, the sole limit on exploitation is the corporeal resistance of the worker, for the rate of surplus value (the percentage of exploitation) is "freely" determined by the bureaucracy, and the law of value loses its meaning as the conditions for its application do not exist there.

23. Indeed, the law of value implies individual property, competition, and an absolutely free market. All these conditions are absent in Russia. This is why, within given physical and technical boundaries, the interests of the bureaucracy replace the automatic functioning of economic laws as the factor determining the orientation of the economy.

24. Whereas the class character of this economy is manifest, the system of actual property ownership that forms its basis can be compared to no other historically extant system of rule. Bureaucratic property is neither individual nor collective. It is a form of private property since it exists only for the bureaucracy, and the rest of society is completely dispossessed therefrom. But it is a private form of property exploited in common by a class and a collective form of property within this class, whereas in other respects internal differentiations still exist. In this sense, it can be defined in summary terms as a form of collective private property.

The Bureaucratic State

25. The bureaucracy's class position rests upon and is guaranteed by its exclusive possession of the State apparatus. In the bureaucratic State we witness the point of culmination of the phenomenon that already is characteristic of imperialism: the merger, even on the personnel level, of economic strength and State power.

26. In light of the nature of bureaucratic society, the classic definition of the State has to be supplemented. The State today is the monopoly over material violence plus the monopoly over ideas.

The Collapse of Culture

27. So-called Russian culture today is an appalling example of ignorance, self-complacency, oversimplification, brutishness, and "Asiatic" dogmatism. As such, it can be compared to no other epoch of human civilization, and it constitutes in fact the negation of culture. The revival, in the bureaucracy's "ideological" fabrications, of well-known reactionary themes (Fatherland, Family, Religion, etc.) does not signify a trend toward the return of capitalism but derives simply from the stabilization of a class that, in order to justify its domination, gives itself an "ideology" by grabbing it up wherever it can.

The Social and Historical Character of the Bureaucracy

28. The class character of bureaucracy follows from the specific role it plays in the economy. In production, the bureaucrat carries out a role that is the absolute negation of the proletarian's. *Qua* member of the dominant class, he possesses the productive apparatus from which the proletarian is alienated. If given the opportunity, the bureaucracy will fulfill, in addition, a historical role: the realization of humanity's fall into barbarism. That this historical role is negative does not change the bureaucracy's class character one bit: History also experiences periods of collapse, and during these periods society's class divisions continue to exist; the role of the ruling class during such a period can only be regressive. Economic "progress" in Russia is progress only for the privileged class, and even as such, in the long run it is incompatible with bureaucratic control over society. Finally, the bureaucracy's class character is not affected by the fact that this bureaucracy is not an organic product of capitalist society; Marx had already considered instances where the class struggle ends "in the common ruin (and defeat) of the contending classes"[5] (and, consequently, with the appearance of a new ruling class).

29. In order to safeguard its position of predominance, there is no need at all for the bureaucracy to have recourse to the restoration of private capitalism. On the contrary, both from an economic viewpoint (complete elimination of economic crises) and from a political viewpoint (socialist camouflage for its totalitarian dictatorship), it is infinitely preferable for it to maintain the present system. The inheritance of privileges is fully guaranteed, not by juridical rules, but by social laws governing the bureaucratic world. Just as the bourgeois understood that they in no way need to secure their possession of the State through juridical means—as feudal lords and absolute monarchs had done—in order to have effective control over it, so too do the bureaucrats know (and in this they are more Marxist than today's "Trotskyists") that they in no way need to secure their ownership of the means of production through juridical means in order to actually possess them. Capitalism in Russia could not be restored from within. It could only be restored as the result of armed foreign intervention.

30. The theory of the "degenerated workers' State" ought to be resolutely rejected. This theory is scientifically incorrect, for it designates only the evolutionary process from which the present regime is descended while saying nothing but falsehoods about the regime's present character. The workers' State is characterized in essence not by its economic bases but rather by the actual political power of the working class (the Commune of 1871, the Russian Revolution up to 1921-23); as soon as the real exercise of this power is undermined, the State becomes a degenerated workers' State (Russia from 1921-23 to 1927). At the moment when there no longer remains even a bit of power in the hands of the working class, the circle is closed and the "degenerated workers' State" is transformed into a State that no longer has a working-class character [*Etat non ouvrier*]. Moreover, this theory is politically disastrous, for it reinforces all the illusions and confusion that reign among the masses concerning Soviet society.

31. Equally false is the conception of the Russian regime as a regime of

"State capitalism." This theory serves to conceal the inability of the theory's supporters to study a new phenomenon without having recourse to well-known formulas, and usually rests upon deplorable confusions (as with Georges Munis, who identifies any form of exploitation with capitalism). In fact, adherents to this theory are obliged to acknowledge that, aside from the traits common to every exploitative society, Russian society exhibits none of capitalism's characteristics (complete elimination of crises, lack of any objective determination of the rate of surplus value, lack of any law of wages, absence of any law of value, distribution of profit to the bureaucrats in accordance with their positions and not according to property titles). The quarrel would revert accordingly to a mere dispute over terminology if the falsity and the superficial character of the theory of "State capitalism" were not established by highly significant facts. Some of these facts are (a) the instauration and stabilization of this regime (which normally ought to have been the product of an overdevelopment of capitalism) not in the advanced countries (the United States, Germany, England) but in a backward country; (b) the absence of almost any connection between today's bureaucrats and former capitalists; (c) the way in which the bureaucracy came to power; and (d) the Russian policy in the glacis,[6] a policy of assimilation that in its first phase totally dispossessed the capitalists (which would be absurd if the regime to be set up were State capitalism). Moreover, the "logic" of their ideas pushes the adherents of this theory toward theoretically and politically stupid conclusions, like their correlation [*assimilation*] of Stalinist parties with the fascist parties.

Stalinist World Policy

32. Supported by the masses' illusions, the bureaucratic State and the Stalinist bureaucratic stratum in capitalist countries form the social basis for the prospect of a possible fall into barbarism. The historical interests of this base are irreducibly opposed to those of the proletariat, and for twenty years the bureaucracy has consciously forced a series of defeats upon the revolutionary movement. The bureaucracy's interests, however, cannot be reconciled with those of imperialism either; the monopoly over foreign trade in the Russian zone and the political influence of Stalinism in capitalist countries are intolerable for the United States as are American economic penetration into its zone and the installation of rightist dictatorships in European countries intolerable for the bureaucracy. The common fear of revolution and of German and Japanese imperialism made compromises during the war and till now possible. If they succeed once again in crushing the revolution, imperialism and the bureaucracy will find themselves face-to-face on an inevitable collision course.

33. If the ultimate aim consciously pursued by the bureaucracy is world domination, its immediate aim is to prepare for war and to secure for itself the most favorable positions for this war. This strategy, as well as its class nature, imposes a particular tactic upon the bureaucracy.

In the countries of the glacis, this tactic is expressed through the pursuit of structural assimilation according to the methods and rhythms necessitated by its fear of the masses and by its compromises with imperialism. In other European countries, the Stalinist parties pursue the bureaucratic conquest of the State and the reinforcement of their influence over the masses.

Stalinism's Historical Chances

34. If today, in the face of imperialism on the one hand and the proletarian revolution on the other hand, Stalinism's chances appear minimal, this nevertheless changes neither the social character of Russia nor the historical significance of the phenomenon of bureaucracy. The degeneration of the revolution will always remain a possibility during every transitional period in history, right up till the time communism is achieved. In the struggle against this possibility of degeneration, theoretical analyses certainly are indispensable, but the definitive solution will be given only by the revolutionary combat of the proletariat.

The Fourth International indeed ought to become aware of the fact that it is struggling on the one hand against capitalism in its death throes and on the other hand against nascent barbarism.

Notes

1. T/E: "The Eighteenth Brumaire of Louis Bonaparte," in *MESW*, p. 100. Castoriadis's quotation omits the phrase "interrupt themselves continually in their own course" after "constantly."

2. T/E: Castoriadis has quoted Trotsky from memory.

3. T/E: Castoriadis has quoted Trotsky from memory.

4. T/E: Engels to C. Schmidt in Berlin, London, October 27, 1890, in *MESW*, pp. 694-99.

5. T/E: "Manifesto of the Communist Party," in *MESW*, p. 35. The parenthetical phrase "and defeat" is Castoriadis's addition.

6. T/E: "Glacis" is a term borrowed from military terminology by Trotskyists and others to describe Russia's postwar "buffer zone": Eastern Europe.

a) L. Trotsky, "The Permanent Revolution," in *The Permanent Revolution & Results and Prospects* (New York: Pathfinder Press, 1970), p. 132. [T/E: Castoriadis's quotation skips the phrase "the family, morals and everyday life."]

3
Stalinism in France

A few preliminary remarks are indispensable.

There was a time—not so long ago—when the question of Stalinism was not raised in the Party on a practical level, in any case not in a way that differs from how it is employed by reformism. Stalinism was a "traitorous" party. It was understood to be a little more traitorous and at the same time a little more left-wing than social democracy, just by a point. In these happy times, just over a year ago, Comrade Bleibtreu, then secretary-general of the Parti communiste internationaliste (PCI), declared to the Central Committee that we did not have to become obsessed with distinguishing ourselves from Stalinism. After that, people immediately went back to charting the ups and downs of the mass movement. This happened in the spring of 1946.

At the Third Congress of the PCI, it was practically the same thing. In their speeches, the comrades of the Frank[1] tendency did not deign to bother themselves with Stalinism. Since then, something has changed. Under pressure from a left wing of the Party, which was weak at first but grew constantly stronger as it used this issue in its struggle against the right wing, these same comrades finally "discovered" Stalinism. Nevertheless, their attitude deep down remains the same. Later on we will discuss the demagogy of the current minority wing that, while howling all along about the need for a "relentless" struggle against Stalinism, not only does not propose any slogan, any concrete means for con-

Originally published as "La Crise du capitalisme mondial et l'intervention du parti dans les luttes." Draft of a report for the Fourth Congress of the Parti communiste internationaliste (French section of the Fourth International), published in the *Bulletin Intérieur* of the PCI in October 1947. Written by myself, the report was signed by Chaulieu (C. Castoriadis), Marchesin, Mercier, Montal (Claude Lefort) and Robert. Reprinted in *CMR I*, pp. 15-118. [T/E: The present translation excerpts only the third section of the second chapter, which was entitled "The Crisis of French Capitalism" (pp. 61-79).]

ducting this struggle, but, with its basic outlook—"Defense of the USSR," "For a PC-PS-CGT Government," and CGT fetishism—does everything it can to reinforce the Stalinists' influence within the proletariat. What interests us here is the manner in which these comrades "analyze" Stalinism, how, with their "theoretical appraisal," they prepare the Party for war in its struggle against Stalinism.

This "theory" of Stalinism can be summed up in a few words: The CP is "a reformist party of a new kind" in the service "not only of the bourgeoisie but especially of the Kremlin." That is it. That is the key to understanding all the political phenomena of our age. There is not much to it.

These "theoreticians" state that the CP is "a reformist party of a new kind," and yet they don't even ask themselves the following question: But why then would there be two reformist parties? Why two reformist parties at the time when, according to Lenin's theory—for whom reformism already was an anachronism in 1919, a historical relic—there should no longer be even one? If, in a pinch, we might explain the lengthy continued existence of reformist parties by consciousness's lagging behind reality, the birth and development of new "reformist" parties that are enjoying a very stable existence in capitalism's present period of crisis must be due to some sort of historical sleight of hand. Consciousness no longer just lags behind reality, it becomes independent of it; without any difficulty, it can even go backward. Perhaps tomorrow it will give birth to parties advocating feudalism.

For Lenin, reformism was not born from the masses' illusions, as the minority wing's unconscious idealism would have it. On the contrary, the masses' reformist illusions are born upon the basis of the reality of certain social reforms that an ascendant capitalism is able to grant. The reality of these reforms, on the one hand, and a specific "social base," on the other—labor aristocracy and trade-union and political bureaucracy—are, according to Lenin's materialist theory of reformism, the roots of social democracy. For the Frank tendency, in contrast, a "new reformism" can be born independently of all objective reality: It suffices that people have "illusions" for large parties to be born and to grow. People's stupidity becomes the motive force of history. Or else, then, these "reformist illusions" have a real basis, and then the minority wing would be obliged to admit that capitalism right now is conceding "reforms" to the working class and, what is worse, that it is possible to concede them. Thus we, and the minority wing before anyone else, would have to revise our whole conception of this era as a period of crisis for capitalism and of decomposition for bourgeois society.

There is more. If the CP is a reformist party, what we have said about the social base of Stalinism—labor aristocracy and trade-union and political bureaucracy—is automatically true. As a matter of fact, for Lenin these strata have always been the social base of social-democratic reformism. CP = reformist party necessarily entails: The social base of the CP = labor aristocracy, etc. Why in that case have they howled so loudly against the theory of social bases and "its dim-witted author"?

But here is the real clinker. The Stalinists "express at the same time the interests of their national bourgeoisie and especially (!) those of the Kremlin."

Those in the minority do not even ask whether the interests of the bourgeoisie and the Kremlin are compatible, apart, of course, from the times when it is a matter of crushing the proletariat. Can one serve both at once? It is obvious that the Stalinists' efforts objectively benefit the bourgeoisie, especially at times when the proletarian revolution becomes a threat, but it is not the advocates of "Power to the CP" who will teach us this. And this is not in the least bit sufficient to describe the core of Stalinist politics, which pursues its own goals independently of all bourgeois politics, as can be seen every time, the proletarian threat having been set aside, Stalinism and the bourgeoisie confront each other in a fight to the death. Let the minority wing explain to us, for example, how and why the Greek or Chinese Stalinists, in order to serve the interests of their "bourgeoisie," have found no better means than to conduct a civil war against this very same bourgeoisie.

How Ought the Problem to Be Posed?

In order to respond to the question about Stalinism's character and role, we first must resolve the following problems:
1. Is it true or not true that the CPs of every country evince the same policy worldwide, despite possible differences in tactics?
2. Is it true or not true that this worldwide Stalinist policy is determined by the need to preserve the USSR's bureaucratic regime, to consolidate itself in the glacis, and occasionally to expand itself into other countries?
3. If the response to these two questions is yes, what factors allow the CPs to have such an influence within a very significant number of capitalist countries?

For us the answer is clear. There is no doubt about the uniformity and coherence of Stalinist policy around the world. The apparent "contradictions" in the policy of various national CPs are contradictions only in the naive view of certain Trotskyists. Tito and Dimitrov lay claim to northern Greece, and Zachariadis claims indignantly that he will defend the integrity of Greek territory against anyone. This does not prevent any of them from sitting together in the Stalinist "Balkan Directorate" and jointly organizing the partisan civil war in Greece. If the Trotskyist leadership does not understand anything at the present time about Stalinist policy it is because they continue to see the CPs as workers' parties that "make mistakes" or that "betray," instead of understanding that the policy of the CPs has its own logic and a set of tactics that follow therefrom as determined by the specific goals of this policy, the means it is obliged to employ, and the nature of the social bases upon which it depends in various countries.

The orientation of this policy is no less clear. It can be characterized in general terms as "defense of the USSR and its bureaucratic system," as long as "defense" is not taken in a static sense, understanding that in the atomic age "to defend" means to conquer the world. But here too we should not be misunderstood: This defense of the USSR takes many forms, depending upon the country in which the CP in question is acting and upon the historical situation;

according to circumstances, it can mean the crushing of a proletarian revolution—in Spain—or the extermination of the bourgeoisie—in the glacis.

We started out with the uniformity of Stalinist policy and the definition of its means and goals in order to facilitate understanding. Indeed, we are dealing with phenomena that are tangible for anyone who has not been completely bewildered by the International's "official" mythology. For the Marxist, however, the principal and genuine question is the following: What then are the material and social bases of this policy? On this question the minority wing obstinately remains silent; the PCF, for example, is for it "a band of Stakhanovites in the pay of the Kremlin"—"the pure revolutionary illusions of the masses." The vulgar idealism of this explanation is quite obvious. The venality of individuals and the illusions of the masses can play a role only if they are put in the service of historical and social factors. In Marxism, a political party always expresses the material and social interests of a particular social stratum. What is this stratum in France whose material interests are expressed by the PCF? That is the real question. For the minority wing this stratum is . . . the Kremlin's clique. By what kind of conjuring away of all historical and sociological laws can a "clique" from a foreign country win the allegiance of the majority of a proletariat it is constantly deceiving and betraying? Only the detective-novel imagination of the minority wing's leaders could explain this to us. Sad to say, the minority wing offers us nothing more about Stalinism than the *Paroles Françaises*[2] theory of "Moscow's fifth column."

As for us, the obvious connection between the policy of the PCF and the policy of Moscow only makes it more pressing to identify the social strata in France whose interests tally with those of the Soviet bureaucracy to such an extent that they can be expressed in the same policy. That is what we have always meant by the "social base of Stalinism in France."

The Social Base of the PCF

In Marxist terminology, the "social base" of a party means the social stratum whose material interests are really expressed by this party and that follows this party, not because it is mystified or deceived by it, but because it is connected with it in an organic way. It is obvious that this means neither that all the individuals of this stratum follow the party in question nor that all those who follow it belong to this stratum. But the party expresses in the final analysis the interests of this stratum, and it derives its basic strength from it, not in the numerical sense but in the social sense. It is in this sense that we have defined the labor aristocracy and the political and trade-union bureaucracy as the social base of the PCF.

At this point a historical explanation is necessary.

In the period of capitalism's ascendancy, these strata were what Lenin had defined as the social base of reformism. The whole historical combination of circumstances as well as their social position, which drew them closer to the petty bourgeoisie than to the proletariat, turned the politics of the party that had expressed the political voice of these strata into a bourgeois politics within the working class. In the period of capitalism's decline, the problem arises on a completely different basis. A "labor aristocracy" does not cease to exist, despite the overall crisis of the system. Obviously, it does not enjoy the same standard of living as before. But it continues to enjoy privileges compared to the great mass of workers, and even more so today than yesterday. These two factors determine its political aspirations. On the one hand, the overall crisis of the capitalist system, tangibly experienced every day, and the fall in its standard of living, have destroyed the reformist mentality within this stratum. Continued "progress" within the capitalist system appears completely utopian. The parasitic role of the bosses has become plain for everyone to see; the Russian example has shown that "technicians," bureaucrats, and "capable people" can run the economy and the State without the bosses. On the other hand, their specific interests, their differentiation from the proletariat, the fact that the proletarian revolution is overdue (proof to them that the proletariat is incapable of imposing its own historical solution), their aspiration to remain a privileged stratum, takes them off the road to revolution. Quite naturally, then, they rally to the PCF, which claims to be the enemy of the bourgeoisie and of "capitalist chaos," as well as the promoter of an economically rationalized society; which has a place for genuinely privileged strata; which makes sure the proletariat keeps working by keeping it on a tight leash; and which promises to kick out the bourgeois parasites.

As for the trade-union and political bureaucracy, it is a stratum whose size and effectiveness cannot be underestimated. The people who at the present time hold positions in the trade unions or in politics thanks to their adherence and allegiance to the PCF number in France at minimum several tens of thousands. Their allegiance guarantees their material existence, and they know that in case there is a total victory for the PCF they would be the undisputed masters of society. Their rabid opposition to any autonomous proletarian movement that might upset their schemings and maneuverings is only stronger and more resolute for these reasons.

From a political point of view, this analysis is of great import. It is the only one capable of explaining the relative stability the PCF enjoys. Welded to Stalinism through their interests, these strata provide the PCF with a material foundation within the proletariat. They weigh down on the rest of the class as they occupy posts of responsibility. They are the relatively firm base that gives the PCF room to maneuver and provides a continuity to its politics. Taken as a whole, these factors have allowed us to see in advance that outflanking it would be infinitely more difficult and more complicated than the minority wing previously has said it would be, precisely because Stalinism is not a thin stratum superficially overlaying a proletariat that remains altogether alien to it. Rather it is a body resting on top of a specific and well-defined social base that penetrates into the proletariat and, with its many tentacles, is in a good position to keep a tight grip on it. For the minority wing, in contrast, the "difficulty" of outflanking Stalinism that they have belatedly discovered is just a glaring afterthought clashing with their entire view of Stalinism.

The Social Composition of the PCF; the Proletariat's Illusions

As opposed to what is happening in the countries of the glacis or in Greece, where the percentage of workers in the CP is quite small, in France the social composition of the CP is principally working class. The PCF is born of the proletariat; it has strength against the bourgeoisie only through the working class. A massive defeat of the latter would mean a considerable loss for it too.

If that is the case, it is of the highest importance to have a clear image of the nature of the illusions of the working-class members of the PCF and to analyze the ways in which they adhere to Stalinist policy. First, we must rule out the theory of the Party's right wing concerning the "reformist illusions" of Stalinist workers. Only Trotskyist leaders have reformist illusions about the PCF. Let us note, on the other hand, the logical consequence of the minority wing's incoherent view of Stalinism: If the CP is a "reformist party," the workers who follow it ought to do so on the basis of reformist illusions. We have never seen workers who follow a "reformist" party on the basis of "revolutionary illusions." But this upsets the minority wing's efforts at "permanent radicalization." On the contrary, a further contradiction does not even scare them off: They rashly proclaim that the workers are following the CP on the basis of a "pure," yet "superficially duped," "revolutionary consciousness," while the CP nevertheless remains a "reformist" party.

It is undoubtedly true that a certain—extremely limited—number of workers follow the CP on the basis of reformism and that some others, either very young or faithful to their party's revolutionary past, though superficially duped, are, so to speak, "Stalinists by mistake." But the overwhelming majority of pro-Stalinist workers are tinged *in part* with Stalinist ideology. They are convinced that the CP wants to overthrow the bourgeoisie and instaurate a new society wherein exploitation would be "limited," but they also are persuaded that the Party is a supreme authority that transcends them, that alone is conscious and responsible.

Their confidence is undermined by the spontaneous power of the masses. For the most part, it is not they who launch struggles. They make up the mass of those who will follow along; in the best of cases, they are those who in a period of revolutionary growth will even end up breaking with Stalinism. On the other hand, during each period of retreat, they will line up behind Stalinism; in the best of cases, it will be difficult to get them in line.

To think that Stalinism could weigh down on the workers as it has over the years without affecting them is a delirious fabrication. Because problems of consciousness are in the last analysis secondary, and because the proletariat in a period of struggle evolves rapidly, determined in its course by its interests, the vanguard can lead the most apathetic strata as well as those infiltrated by Stalinism. For this reason we do not see in this a decisive element. But this analysis of the illusions of the workers who follow the CP ought to help us once again to understand the proper timing for outflanking the CP and the difficulties involved in doing so. And in particular it ought to help us carry on effectively our propaganda efforts by attacking the mystifications of Stalinism at their source, i.e., on the question of the USSR.

The "Middle Strata" and the Social Composition of Stalinism

No one in the Party denies that, since the "Liberation," Stalinism has made great inroads into the middle classes, and yet, strangely, the importance of this phenomenon has been underestimated.

We reject the conception of the Party's right wing, according to which the middle classes are going over to Stalinism today as they went over to radicalism before, as well as that of the Frank minority wing, which sees in this movement a kind of "radicalization." Reality is not somewhere in between these two incorrect assertions, it is totally different. We cannot determine why large sections of the middle strata are joining the PCF by taking into account only the outward appearance of its program. The bourgeoisie's hostility to the CP and to its international ties leaves no doubt about its allegedly "radical" character. On the other hand, the CP constantly proclaims itself to be the fervent partisan of purging and exterminating the people's enemies and oppressors, of the struggle against the trusts, and of great structural reforms. And yet, it would be just as wrong to ignore the clearly counterrevolutionary policy of the CP and to see in it, as the Frank minority wing does, a "progressive pole of attraction" for the middle classes. It is no accident that these classes joined the CP when it began developing a policy openly opposed to the interests of the proletariat, when it began preaching the necessity of avoiding revolution and disapproving of the idea of the dictatorship of the proletariat.

We must understand what the situation of the "middle classes" is today and what their aspirations are. The crisis of the system has hit the petty bourgeois terribly hard. Trotsky already has explained that while the French petty bourgeoisie usually has been both strongly in favor of maintaining order and hostile to extreme solutions, nevertheless at certain times—when driven by despair and overcome by crisis—it inevitably has been led to search feverishly for salvation behind a leader, whether it be the proletariat or fascism. More than ever, the current crisis of the system has removed a significant number of the middle strata from the traditional "democratic" parties. At the time of the "Liberation," fascism could not show its face. An autonomous revolutionary proletarian politics was not appearing on the scene either. Given the bankruptcy of the traditional parties, only the CP—with its totalitarian structure, its powerful propaganda, its clever demagogy, and the particular care with which it applied itself to the conquest of the middle classes—was seen as having a clear-cut set of features. It is not surprising that the CP appeared to a significant number of petty bourgeois to be a savior, a savior with respect to big business as well as to the proletariat.

The myth of the "New Democracy" essentially is addressed to these strata. Several themes hark back constantly to the middle classes' habits of speech.

1. The struggle against the trusts: All evils issue from this handful of vam-

pires who feast upon society, unleash economic crises, carry on behind the scenes a fascist policy, and want war so they can put everything at the disposal of the Great American Trust. The CP will destroy the trusts and will put the great wellsprings of the economy back into the hands of the people.

2. Only by relying on the proletariat, "the great progressive force in history," will we be able to wipe out the vampires. But the proletariat itself has its duties: to work under the CP's discipline and enlightened direction. Only traitors strike in a "Popular Democracy." Unions, which are the best servants of the State, keep order.

3. The new society will be rationalized on the economic level, there will be a plan, crises will be banished, and social stability will be assured.

4. The middle classes — especially intellectuals and technicians — are implicitly invited to become the cadres of the new society, for the proletariat will have need of cadres.

The relationship between this mythology and that of fascism is manifest. Fascism howls about the struggle against the trusts. It promises jobs, it promises social discipline, it even pretends to rely on the "real workers," it promises emancipation to the middle classes in particular. Like Stalinism, it says to them, in short: "You who have no independence, who have been crushed by the feudal lords of the economy, you will finally run the State." But in reality the mystification of Stalinism is much more thorough.

Fascism engages in pure demagogy. It preaches the struggle against the trusts, but it is their instrument. It promises the triumph of the middle classes, but it crushes them after taking power; only a thin layer can be accommodated in the fascist politico-military bureaucracy. Stalinism, in contrast, actually fights against the trusts, certainly according to its own methods, but it is a fact that where it has power, it dispossesses and usually wipes out the big capitalists: The experience of the "glacis" is there as conclusive evidence for all but the blind. On the other hand, in order to fulfill the requirements of its economic policy (which depends upon continuous State growth), and by carrying out its social policy (which requires a large base of support against both the bourgeoisie and against the proletariat), it actually prepares for the triumph of new strata that are to form its political and economic bureaucracy. Incidentally, the character of these ties between certain strata of the petty bourgeoisie and Stalinism also explains the slowness with which fascism has been able to rebuild itself in France.

Conclusions

If the Party's right wing really is becoming adjusted to Stalinism and is seeking only to "move it to the left," the Frank minority wing itself has a subtler, but equally dangerous, method of adaptation: the slogans "Defense of the USSR" and "For a PC-PS-CGT Government," the simplistic move toward "replacing the leaders of the CGT," the idea that the CP might be transformed "under pressure from the masses" (Privas's article in *BI* no. 37),[3] the idea of an automatic outflanking of Stalinism—this whole set of catastrophic errors, capable on their own of stifling a future revolutionary situation, has a common theoretical source: They all confuse the CP with reformism. The experience in the "glacis," where Stalinism is wiping out the capitalist class more and more, both economically and politically, and is pushing society down the road toward assimilation with the USSR, does not even exist for these comrades. Unable to understand that the Stalinist strategy (conquest of State power) occurs in various countries in various ways and through various tactics, they pose such puerile questions as: "If things are as you say, why then doesn't the CP take power in France?", without seeing that, beyond the risks of being outflanked that this would entail for them, and against which they had been protected in the countries of the glacis by the presence of the Red Army, such an endeavor for the Stalinists of 1944 as well as of today would immediately unleash war between the Soviet Union and the United States, a war they wish to delay as long as possible. These comrades are so blind that they have swallowed whole the pronouncements for petty bourgeois consumption of Thorez[4] and company concerning the "peaceful conquest" of power, declarations whose true value fools neither the bourgeoisie nor the partisans of the CP.

Their inability to understand anything at all about the phenomenon of Stalinism can be measured by the vulgarity of the concoctions to which they are obliged to have recourse in order to "refute" our account of Stalinism. Thus, when the authors of the minority wing's thesis write (p. 20): "If the CP is a new class in the process of formation, all the organizations that depend on it or that it controls represent organic components of this class and of its future domination. Thus the unions may be compared to the imperialist army, i.e., to a body constituted by the class enemy that ought to be smashed," the fervor they exhibit while drawing the "logical consequences" from our position, and which is completely lacking when it comes to drawing conclusions from their own positions, can be turned completely against them. We have never said that the CP is a "new class in the process of formation." Do these comrades have to be taught that a party is never a class, that it is only its political expression, and that even in the USSR it is not the CP that is the dominant class but the infinitely more immense bureaucracy, the CP being only its instrument? We have explained only that the CP—like every political party—has to express the material interests of a social stratum, and we have tried to define this stratum. For them, the CP expresses only the treachery of Thorez and the stupidity of the masses that follow him. It is easy to see where genuine Marxist analysis is to be found. As concerns the "consequences" for the trade unions, they call to mind with their logic the famous 1936 "deductions" of Vyshinsky:[5] "You are against the regime, therefore you are advocates of sabotage." The minority wing says to us: "If the CP is a new class (?), the unions are its organic components; therefore they should be smashed." The monumental absurdity of this kind of "reasoning" is manifest. The unions are for us above all the rallying point of the working class. Our attitude is not changed by the fact that the Stalinist bureaucracy dominates them, just as it was not changed before when the (reformist) agents of capital dominated them. And another thing: In order to win them over we are proposing a tactic (Committees of Struggle) that differs from the opportunistic and in-effective tactics of Lambert. When, on the other hand, the minority wing ac-cuses us of defining a class "by how much of the national income it consumes," all they have done is reinvent the wheel. We were the first to explain that it is precisely because the strata that form the social basis of Stalinism in capitalist countries have no independent position with respect to the means of production that they cannot be characterized as a "class" but rather only as a social "stra-tum." Only if they come to power and have complete domination over the ap-paratus of production—as has happened in Russia and is occurring in the "glacis"—will they become a class in the full sense of this term.

A final question is posed: If all this is true, is the CP still a "working-class party"? We answer: If by working-class party you mean a party made up mostly by workers who consider it as such, then the CP undeniably is a working-class party. But posed in this way the question is merely scholastic. Apropos of social democracy, Lenin already had explained that this "working-class party" was in fact capital's agent within the working-class movement. It is by starting out with this kind of analysis that we can resolve the political problems raised by Stalin-ism. Precisely because we are taking the working-class composition of the PCF into account, we believe that the policy of a United Front with the PCF cannot be ruled out a priori, independent of the fact that today it generally is imprac-ticable for other reasons. On the other hand, the slogan "For a PC-PS-CGT Government" is the most glaring proof of the opportunism to which the inten-tion of determining one's politics solely on the basis of the "working-class na-ture" of the CP is led.

The Problem of Outflanking Stalinism

This conception allows us to understand the process of outflanking Stalinism and its timing. The difficulty and the complexity involved are for us not a con-cession to reality as they are for the Frank minority wing but the clear result of an analysis of the social basis of Stalinism, which confers upon it a relative de-gree of stability, as well as of the nature of the illusions of the masses who follow Stalinism. On the other hand, it is precisely the CP's heterogeneous character, the fact that its support comes not from a class with an autonomous position within the production process, but rather from strata whose ideological crystal-lization is due only to the fact that the proletarian revolution is overdue, that makes the outflanking of Stalinism remain an ever-present possibility—but on the condition that the Party carries out a revolutionary, nonopportunistic poli-tics. What we need are not useless verbal attacks that only serve to hide a de facto capitulation to Stalinism: first off, we need to explain patiently the com-plete workings and the material roots of Stalinism's betrayal. On the other hand, above all we need to propel this tactic of outflanking into action through appro-priate slogans; we will come back to this in our third chapter.[6] For the moment let us state that if the minority wing has finally discovered the necessity of strug-gling against Stalinism, it has done nothing to change its tagalong political style.

Notes

1. T/E: Pierre Frank (b. 1905) was a prominent French Trotskyist theoretician.

2. T/E: *Paroles Françaises* was an ultra-right French magazine of the era.

3. T/E: Castoriadis is evidently referring to an article written by "Privas" published in the Parti communiste internationaliste's *Bullétin Intérieur*, 37 (December 1946), pp. 9-19. (This "article by Privas"—also signed by "Dumas," another pseudonym for "Privas"—is entitled "Résolution sur la necessité du mot d'ordre 'Gouvernement PS-PC-CGT.' ") The phrase he quotes, "under pressure from the masses [*sous la poussée des masses*]," however, does not appear there. Nevertheless, a very similar phrase, "*sous la pression des masses*" (which would also be translated as "under pressure from the masses"), does appear in the draft report of the Frank tendency for the same Fourth Congress of the PCI (p. 24 of the Frank report). It was signed, but not written, by Privas. The authors of this report did not say that the French Communist party was "transformed" by mass pressure (as Castoriadis had said was the Frank tendency's thesis); rather they claimed it had been "turned around" or it had "changed sides" (the French word is *virer*, whence the English "veer") because of pressure from the masses. "Privas" informed me in a 1987 personal interview that he does not think the Frank tendency believed the nature of the Communist Party could have been *transformed*—though it might have changed its policies under mass pressure. He says that the key to the Frank tendency's position was to be found in its (mistaken) belief that the CP would act out the same role as the one Kerensky's Social Democrats played in Russia in 1917: Neither the Frank tendency nor Lenin held any illusions about the "progressive" character of these respective political parties, "Privas" explains. Castoriadis maintains that the Frank tendency's advocacy of a government with CP participation as a "transitional" formation on the way to socialism meant that the Frank tendency mistakenly believed France's Stalinist CP itself could play a progressive role.

4. T/E: Maurice Thorez (1900-64) was secretary-general of the French Communist party from 1930 to 1964.

5. T/E: Andrey Vyshinsky (1883-1954) was the public prosecutor at the Moscow trials.

6. T/E: The third chapter, entitled "Vers la dualité du pouvoir (l'intervention du parti dans les luttes)" (Toward dual power [the Party's intervention in struggles]), is not included in the present edition.

4

The Concentration of
the Forces of Production

1. In present-day society the need to concentrate the forces of production is expressed in two profoundly contradictory ways. One of the ways in which this need is expressed is found in the proletariat's movement toward socialist revolution. The other way it expresses itself is through the continual merger of capital and the State on a national and international scale.

This merger exhibits itself in two radically antagonistic modes. Either, in taking as its point of departure the most highly developed sectors of monopoly capitalism, concentration grows organically within present-day capitalism, pivoting around the most concentrated and the most powerful stratum of finance capital. In this case, the state bureaucracy and labor bureaucracy of finance capital's home country as well as those of the rest of the capitalist world are integrated into this stratum (this is what is happening with the United States). Or else, concentration essentially takes place around the labor bureaucracy itself, which, in a struggle to the death, dispossesses the most powerful capitalist strata. In this latter case, petty bourgeois elements and other intermediary strata are integrated into this bureaucracy *qua* individuals (this is what happens with the USSR).

2. Despite their violently antagonistic character and the differences in their respective content, these two modes of merger express the same historical essence: the brutal increase of barbarism in the decaying capitalist world. Barbarism is not a historical stage suddenly appearing *after* the capitalist system has reached its point of impasse. It already makes its appearance in decaying capitalism too. Here it is only the product of a continuous alteration [*transcroissance*] of the rotting capitalist system, which more and more is becoming something

Originally entitled "La Concentration des forces productives"; unpublished (March 1948). First published in *SB 1*, pp. 101-13.

different than it was before. The essential identity of these two modes is nothing other than one identical social and historical need that can be described as follows: absolute concentration of the forces of production on the national and international scale, "planning" of the production that has thus been concentrated, world domination, fusion of the economy with the State, statification of ideology, and the complete reduction of the proletariat to the status of a cog in the productive apparatus. This historical and social need itself is dictated by the state of technique and of the forces of production, but also by the entire social and historical situation.

3. The key to understanding the world situation today rests, however, on the knowledge of the identity of these two phenomena as well as on the knowledge of their profound antithesis. We must distinguish three moments in this antithesis.

a) *The historical origin of this antithesis and its social basis.* In the process of concentration as it is taking place today, both nationally and internationally, around U.S. finance capital, the active role is played by (and the principal interests boil down to) the most concentrated and most powerful stratum of monopoly capital. Into this stratum are integrated the State bureaucracy and the labor bureaucracy of its own country as well as the corresponding strata of the population (capitalists and bureaucrats) of the other capitalist countries. Historically speaking, this stratum is the natural and organic product of the entire evolution of capitalism. No kind of gap exists between its complete predominance over the economy and society, down to its tiniest cogs, and what the situation was under "classical" capitalism. Moreover, its position of complete predominance presupposes the extermination of every constituent element that does not accept being a pure and simple agent of its domination. Whence its struggle to the death not only against the proletarian revolution but also against that part of the labor bureaucracy that demands for itself and itself alone all economic and political power.

In contrast, in the process of concentration taking place around the Soviet bureaucracy, the active role is played by (and the principal interests are represented by) this bureaucracy—a trade-union and political, State and military, economic and technical bureaucracy—which groups around itself key sections of the workers' trade-union and political bureaucracy of other countries, as well as petty bourgeois elements and members of the intermediate strata of society. Historically speaking, the accession to power of this stratum is the product of the degeneration of a proletarian revolution and of the entire process that has followed therefrom, both as concerns this country as well as most capitalist countries, as far as their labor movements are concerned. Its complete domination, both nationally and internationally, presupposes the complete extermination of capitalist strata. Whence its struggle to the death not only against the proletarian revolution but also against these capitalist strata. Whence also its need to make use of the proletariat in a relatively active way, distinguishing between the working class and other strata of the population in its bid to take power. Whence, finally, its specific ideological armature, which, while being just as reactionary as that of decaying capitalism, is nonetheless radically different from it.

If these two factors are rightly the products of the overall situation of decaying capitalism and if the general conditions of their existence and of their strength are the objective conditions of the present age as well as the reason for the "delay" or difficulties experienced by the proletarian revolution, it remains no less true that, starting from this overall situation, each expresses a different element in this dialectical whole. For the former, capitalism itself is its starting basis, and what it represents is rising barbarism within the capitalist world. The latter is born within the proletariat as its own internal negation, and within this negation there persists the opposition to capitalism that also determines the proletariat. What it expresses is the possibility of barbarism contained in the no longer material but now essentially ideological alienation of the proletariat.

b) *Its present stage of evolution.* At present these two factors find themselves at essentially different stages in their respective historical cycles. In the system created by the labor bureaucracy on the basis of the degeneration of the workers' State in Russia and on the basis of the political exploitation of the labor movement in other countries, the movement toward total concentration has been almost completely realized: On the whole, the fusion of the economy with the State already has been accomplished; the same goes for "planning," inter-State concentration, statification of ideology, and the reduction of the proletariat to the status of raw material for the economy.

By way of contrast, in the evolution of American imperialism we still are able to observe only the first embryonic stages of these phenomena. The merger of capital and the State is still in its beginnings, and in most instances it has taken place only in the area of personnel rather than objectively; progress occurs only through a series of mediations. It continues to appear in the form of finance capital's absolute stranglehold over State power and of the fusion on the personnel level of the leading circles of society. The unity of capital and the State still has not become an immediate one, as in Russia, but remains an internally differentiated unity that still has need of mediation in order to assert itself. "Planning" is carried out only within each monopoly group; the beginnings of intersector coordination, which was forced on American imperialism by the Second World War, have suffered a setback with the end of the war. Consequently, the ruling stratum retains its internal antagonisms and overcomes them only when faced with opposition by an external enemy (the proletariat or the Russian bureaucracy); such antagonisms have been suppressed in the abstract universality of the bureaucracy *qua* ruling class in Russia. The same thing holds on the international level. Finally, on the social level, efforts to achieve the statification of ideology and the reduction of the proletariat to material existing merely for purposes of exploitation still have a long road ahead of them.

Nevertheless, it would be completely wrong to limit ourselves to these statements, and not to see the dynamic at work in the evolution of the process of concentration. Faced with the vulgar empiricism of the majority of the Fourth International and its complete lack of historical perspective, and faced too with the abstract generalizations of adherents to the idea of "State capitalism" (in such generalizations, all cows are black), we must reaffirm the need for, and provide illustrations of, a dialectic of the concrete capable of grasping the boundless differentiation of external reality as well as of rendering explicit the profound symmetry of American imperialism and Russian bureaucratism, the identity of the social and historical necessities underlying them, and the dynamic that, through a series of deepening contradictions, ultimately leads them to the point of complete unification.

The initial result of this dynamic, quite clearly, is a rapid development of the traits of concentration within American imperialism. The simultaneously political and economic control over other countries exercised by U.S. finance capital; the increasing role of the American State in the establishment of this control; the direct stranglehold over German, Japanese, and Italian capital; the acceleration of vertical and horizontal concentration imposed by the need to control and regulate more and more completely its sources of raw materials and its domestic as well as foreign markets; the expansion of its military apparatus, the likelihood of "total" war, and a war economy; the need for increased exploitation of the working class imposed by the falling rate of profit—all these factors drive the American economy beyond capitalism "run by the monopolies" (just as these monopolies went beyond the stage of competitive capitalism) in order to arrive at the stage of a *universal monopoly* that is identical with the State. A new crisis of overproduction—more acute even than the present crisis—but, above all, *war*, will signal an extraordinary acceleration of this process.

But if the only possible meaning of the culmination of this two-sided process of concentration is that the two systems have become identical, the process of identification that results from it presupposes the complete destruction of one side by the other and the total absorption of the losing side by the winner. Any idea of a peaceful interpenetration or merger of the two systems ought to be resolutely dealt with as the mystification that, in our age, is the complement of the one Kautsky nourished in his time. The most thoroughgoing form this opposition between these two systems can take will be manifested in *war*. And if the proletariat does not intervene to abolish this opposition and suppress its bases, this opposition will be resolved through the destruction of one of the two factors of world concentration for the benefit of the other. The winner will totally absorb all substantial parts of the vanquished, amputating anything that might pose a danger to it. In the absence of revolution, war will end with world domination for the benefit of the victor, a total stranglehold over the world's capital and over the proletariat, and the regrouping around the victor of most of the economic and State ruling strata, after having crushed the summits that, in both of these systems, crystallize the will to power, the for-itself and the awareness of autonomy of these strata. Clearly, Russia's victory over America would signify its complete stranglehold over America's and the world's apparatus of production. It would take the form of a total "nationalization" of big American capital and the physical extermination of the capitalists and their principal political, trade-union, and military agents. This would be accompanied by the integration into the new system of almost all technicians and a large part of the State, economic, and labor bureaucracy. Conversely, it is equally obvious that an American victory over Russia would signify the extermination of the summits of the latter's bureaucratic apparatus, American capital's direct stranglehold over

Russia's apparatus of production and its proletariat, preserving the form of "nationalized" property as the most convenient and concentrated form for continued exploitation. And this victory would be accompanied by the integration into the American system of the overwhelming majority of the administrative, economic, and labor bureaucracy as well as its technicians.

c) *The laws of the two systems and their mutual interconnection. The world "market."* The fact that these two systems are at different stages in their respective evolutions forms the basis for the differences in the economic laws governing these two systems. Whereas the American imperialist economy still finds itself under the hold of the laws governing the capitalist system during its monopoly stage (though these laws might experience a few distortions and a few modifications under the pressure of the growing merger of capital and the State), the Russian bureaucratic economy already has freed itself from the hold of such laws and now constitutes a new whole that negates capitalism (though there might be a few distortions in the manifestations of this new totality and a few modifications under the pressure of its "capitalist surroundings"). To prove this assertion, we need only take as an example the law that forms the basis of the classical capitalist economy: the law of value.

The law of value is the foundation for the concrete operation of the capitalist economy as such. As the central expression of the laws of exchange within the framework of this system, it already expresses through its variations within the capitalist system the evolution of that system. But since the general presupposition for its validity is the existence of a free market and competition, one cannot exit completely from these conditions without thereby going beyond the law of value in its concrete form.

Insofar as it presupposes the "absolute" isolation of different enterprises, i.e., that they communicate solely through the intermediary of the market, the law of value finds its simplest and most immediate expression in the simple production of commodities wherein the value of the product is measured solely by labor time, labor appearing here under three forms: as dead labor (constant capital, C), paid, living labor (variable capital, V) and nonremunerated, living labor (surplus value, S). The value formula thus is $C + V + S$. Already in classical capitalist production this formula finds itself surpassed insofar as value is constituted, through the formation of an average rate of profit, in a mode that is more profoundly—although still indirectly—social. What in classical capitalist society is called the cost of production (which increasingly covers over value as such and which contains a more profound abstraction than immediate value) replaces concrete surplus value with a fraction of universal surplus value (i.e., with average profit, P), and thus give us the formula $C + V + P$. In monopoly production, which is the organic outcome of competitive capitalism, this abstraction reaches a new stage, insofar as it adds monopoly profit as such to average profit. The fraction of surplus value contained in a monopoly's synthetic profit has suppressed its concrete mediation by competition, which was its presupposition in the antecedent phase, as well as its concrete relation no longer merely to the *structure* (organic composition) of capital from which it precedes (this relation to its structure already having been suppressed by the average rate of profit) but also to the most abstract expression of this mass of capital, i.e., the *magnitude* of the latter.

Finally, in State-run production in its most thoroughgoing form (the Russian economy), the law of value, as far as this economy in itself is concerned, loses all concrete content and becomes the abstract and completely empty generality that "the value of social production as a whole is equal to the total amount of labor contained in this whole," which is a simple tautology. Profit becomes abstract universal profit, which has suppressed its relations both with the structure and the magnitude of a concrete mass of capital as well as with the very possession of such a mass of capital. Profit is only total profit based on the universal possession of the productive apparatus by this abstract universal that is the State. Insofar as this State is only an abstraction; insofar as profit, by way of compensation, demands to be given concrete form through accumulation and through unproductive consumption (consumption being, in a word, the only real way in which it can be made *concrete*); insofar, consequently, as the State can make profit concrete only under the abstract form of abstract accumulation (abstract meaning here: not determined in its specific form, since concrete accumulation is, in a word, accumulation for the purpose of *consumption*), and given that consumption is always concrete consumption (i.e., consumption of something by someone), we then can say that the concretization of profit can only consist of its consumption by the concrete contents of the State, i.e., by the bureaucracy. But in this process of concretization, its relation with a determinate mass of capital is suppressed *qua* mediation. The mediation necessary to the process of concretization can take place, therefore, only on a different basis than its relationship with a determinate mass of capital. It thus takes place on the basis of relations that no longer are economic but rather extraeconomic. And hereafter these relations will determine the allocation of total profit between the different strata of the bureaucracy and among the bureaucracy as individuals.

On the other hand, all concrete expressions of the law of value likewise have disappeared. When it comes to the exchange of goods, the separate profitability of business firms, investment (i.e., the concrete form of accumulation), and the "purchase" of labor power (which no longer takes place upon the basis of the value of this labor power, since the very notion of "the value of labor power" disappears insofar as the market for labor power and a standard of living having any objective content have disappeared) no longer are determined by the law of value but rather by the universal interest of the bureaucracy.

It remains for us now to integrate this new totality into the whole that continues to dominate it, that is to say, the world economy and society. First of all, however, we must deal resolutely with the wholly external and superficial argument advanced both by Trotskyists as well as by those who believe in "State capitalism." This argument consists merely in stating that the Russian State-run economy is directly dependent upon the "world market." This notion of a "world market" becomes a convenient instrument for building upon abstract constructions, the possibility for which is based upon having forgotten about recent transformations in the structure of this market and having ignored the specific mode in which Russian production participates in it. In this way they conjure away the fact that the more and more advanced state of decomposition of the world market goes along precisely with the greater and greater international interdependence of various economies. The result of this growing international interdependence has been that the competitive aspects of the market (in the strict sense of the term "competitive") are being abolished for the same reason that competition between monopolies and monopolistic nations is increasingly losing its connection with value. They forget that the advent and expansion of the Russian economy have as a matter of fact powerfully contributed to this process of decomposition. Finally, they forget quite simply Russia's monopoly over foreign trade and what it implies—obviously not as concerns its supposed isolation and total immunization from the rest of the world, as Stalin and Bukharin would have had it, but rather as concerns the transformation of the mode of participation of a "national" economy on the universal market.

Value as the general form of unity in difference contains mediation. Not any kind of mediation whatsoever, but determinate mediation, which is comparison. And not any kind of comparison whatsoever, but the kind of comparison that is competition. Another form of mediation (for example, the direct comparison of labor productivity that is expressed in war between two primitive tribes) does not suffice to constitute value. Value proceeds from labor productivity but is not identical with the latter inasmuch as it is its expression as mediated by competition. But this competition can constitute mediation only insofar as it connects the universal of abstract social labor to the singular of a determinate commodity in passing through the particular of the movement of masses of capital in the various branches of production. In contrast, what remains of competition in Russia's productive relations with the world market is only the abstract universality of general competition, which suppresses the mediation both of the particular mass of capital and of the singular commodity, inasmuch as value has no more than an abstract meaning in Russian production and inasmuch as this abstraction of value is protected by this other abstraction, the monopoly over foreign trade. As the sale price of every Russian commodity on the world market is determined—or can be determined, which is precisely the same thing—not on the basis of the concrete fraction of abstract labor contained in this commodity but rather on the basis of the universal interest of the bureaucracy (dumping, when it comes to sales; "use value"—basically its "use value" for production—when it comes to purchases), competition is no longer anything but total competition that has immediately suppressed all concrete comparisons. This empties competition of all concrete content as far as value is concerned.

The relationship between these two systems will be expressed under the most direct and immediate form of comparison between different rates of labor productivity, i.e., in the form of war. If the ineluctability of this war irrefutably proves the reciprocal determination of the two systems encompassed within a vaster totality that is the world economy, it proves too that the ultimate form of economic confrontation—just as it also is its most primitive form—goes well beyond the economic plane and becomes total confrontation. But this war totality that in its primitive form is an immediate totality now becomes an infinitely differentiated totality in which the economy, politics, military considerations, and ideology coexist synthetically.

4. If the proletariat does not succeed in suppressing this contradiction and its basis before, during, or immediately after this war through a victorious international revolution, ultra-imperialism will be realized. What constituted the essence of the opportunistic mystification in the Kautskyist conception of ultra-imperialism was its pacifist aspect, the idea that imperialist States would be able to agree peacefully on how to carve up the world. Reality has definitively refuted this mystification, showing that only total violence could serve as the motive force for an apparent "unification" of the imperialist world. Today we must vigorously affirm that this prospect is possible, not only when faced with the vulgar confusionism of the majority of the Fourth International—for whom ultra-imperialism ought already to be achieved, since we undeniably have, in their opinion, *a single* imperialist State (the United States) dominating the capitalist world, and which is faced with a nonimperialist State, a degenerated workers' State that ought to be defended—but also and especially against the "retrogressionist" opportunism that more and more is penetrating into the majority of the Fourth itself. The movement toward national and international concentration (just like the progressive fusion of the economy with the State and the forms of political power that are becoming increasingly totalitarian) not only does not signify a "retrogression" from any standpoint—except that of petty bourgeois sentimentalism—but expresses instead the inexorable tendency of present-day history (a tendency that will go on accelerating and deepening) to adapt itself to the evolution of the forces of production. And this adaptation will develop in a reactionary mode as long as the revolutionary mode does not win out. In this sense, to again put forward "national and democratic demands" or to talk of a "necessary democratic interlude," etc., signifies only that one wants to turn back the wheel of history, to throw oneself in front of a train going at full speed with the illusion that one will be able to stop it. Just as Trotsky said in 1938 that we take no responsibility for the defense of bourgeois democracy—for, he added, it is *indefensible* (and *objectively undefendable*)—so we can have nothing in common with any defense of "national independence," for many reasons, but essentially because such "independence" is today completely utopian. In case ultra-imperialism is achieved, within revolutionary ranks "retrogressionist" ideology will be the principal form in which petty bourgeois and national bourgeois strata will be able to put political and ideological pressure on the proletariat. Not only is it incumbent upon us to arm the proletariat from here on out against this disastrous and fatal illusion, but this response alone allows us to grasp the depth of the opportunism of the present majority of the Fourth International on a series of questions of immediate import (the "national question" in Europe during the occupation, the "national question" in Greece today, the colonial question).

On the other hand, the possibility of ultra-imperialism does not mean in the least that "the socialist program would be reduced to a utopia," as Trotsky hastily affirmed in 1939. The socialist revolution is not the exclusive business of one generation or even of one century. It goes without saying that the extreme transformation that will take place after the Third World War (assuming the proletarian revolution does not intervene in time) will necessitate a profound readaptation, an almost complete revolution in revolutionary methodology and thought. The prospect for the proletarian revolution will be definitively postponed only when statist ultra-imperialism brings the forces of production first to a state of stagnation and then to one of regression, thus sapping the objective bases not only of action but also of the very existence of the proletariat as such. In contrast, the current phase of history as well as the phase that will follow immediately upon the Third World War are phases during which the productive forces will continue to develop. During the period between 1939 and 1948 we witnessed a new development of the forces of production on a world scale—certainly a limited, contradictory development going hand in hand with the destruction of existing productive forces, but on the whole a real development nonetheless. Likewise, the phase that will follow upon the Third World War will still be a phase of development, resulting from the complete internationalization of the forces of production. What will determine the gradual slowdown, then stagnation, and finally the regression of the forces of production will be the absence of any motive force for accumulation, the reduction of the ruling strata to a totally parasitic role and the intellectual regression that will come about with the establishment of totalitarian regimes. This will be the complete realization of barbarism. Then—and only then—will there be an indefinite postponement of the proletarian revolution.

5
Socialism or Barbarism

A century after the *Communist Manifesto* was written and thirty years after the Russian Revolution, the revolutionary movement, which has witnessed great victories and suffered profound defeats, seems somehow to have disappeared. Like a river approaching the sea, it has broken up into rivulets, run into swamps and marshes, and finally dried up on the sands.

Never has there been more talk of "Marxism," of "socialism," of the working class, and of a new historical era. And never has real Marxism been so distorted, socialism so abused, and the working class so often sold out and betrayed by those claiming to represent it.

The bourgeoisie, in various superficially different but basically identical forms, has "recognized" Marxism and has attempted to emasculate it by appropriating it, by "accepting" part of it, by reducing it to the rank of one of a number of possible doctrines. The transformation of "great revolutionaries into harmless icons," of which Lenin spoke forty years ago, is taking place at increasing tempo. Lenin himself has not escaped the common fate.

"Socialism," we are told, has been achieved in countries numbering four hundred million inhabitants, yet that type of "socialism" appears inseparable from concentration camps, from the most intense social exploitation, from the most atrocious dictatorship, and from the most widespread brutish stupidity. Throughout the rest of the world the working class has been faced for almost twenty years now with a heavy and constant deterioration of its basic living standards. Its liberties and elementary rights, achieved only through years of strug-

---

Originally published as "Socialisme ou Barbarie," *S. ou B.*, 1 (March 1949). Reprinted in *SB 1*, pp. 139-83. [T/E: Originally translated as "Socialism Reaffirmed" by Bob Pennington and printed as a *Solidarity Pamphlet*, 1961; revised by T/E.]

gle against the capitalist State, have been abolished or gravely threatened [see the Postface].

On top of all this, millions of people are now realizing that we have no sooner emerged from the Second World War than we face a third one, which, it is generally held, will be the most terrible ever seen.

In most countries the working class is organized in gigantic trade unions and political parties, numbering tens of millions of members. But these unions and parties are every day more openly and more cynically playing the role of direct agents of the ruling class and of the capitalist State, or of the bureaucratic capitalism that reigns in Russia.

Only a few minute organizations seem to have survived the general shipwreck, organizations such as the "Fourth International," the Anarchist Federations, and a few self-described "ultraleftist" groups (Bordigists, Spartacists, Council Communists). These organizations are very weak, not only because of their numbers (numerical strength by itself is never a criterion), but above all because of their political and ideological bankruptcy. Relics of the past rather than harbingers of the future, they have proved themselves utterly incapable of understanding the fundamental social transformations of the twentieth century and even less capable of developing a positive orientation toward them.

Today the "Fourth International" uses a spurious faithfulness to the letter of Marxism as a substitute for an answer to the important questions of the day. Some vanguard workers are to be found, it is true, in the ranks of the Trotskyist movement. But there they are constantly twisted and demoralized, exhausted by an activism devoid of all serious political content, and, finally, discarded. With the small amount of strength it can muster, the Fourth International plays its comical little role in this great tragedy of the working class's mystification when it puts forward its class-collaborationist slogans, like "Defense of the Soviet Union," for a Stalino-reformist government or in more general terms, when it masks the reality of today behind the empty formulas of yesterday.

In some countries, the Anarchist Federations still enjoy the support of a number of workers with a healthy class instinct—but those workers are very backward politically, and the anarchists keep them that way. The anarchists' constant refusal to venture beyond the sterile slogan "No Politics," or to take theory seriously, contributes to the confusion. This makes anarchism one more blind alley for workers to get lost in.

Meanwhile, various "ultraleftist" groups cultivate their pet sectarian deviations, some of them (like the Bordigists) even going so far as to blame the proletariat for their own stagnation and impotence, others (like the Council Communists) living happily in the past and seeking therein their recipes for the "socialist" kitchens of the future.

Despite their noisy pretensions, all of them, the "Fourth International," anarchists, and "ultraleftists," are but historical memories, minute scabs on the wounds of the working class, destined to be shed as the new skin readies itself in the depths of its tissues.

A century ago, the proletarian revolutionary movement was constituted for the first time when it received its first charter, the *Communist Manifesto*, from the brilliant pen of Marx and Engels. Nothing shows better the strength and depth of this movement, nothing can give us more confidence as to its future than the fundamental and all-embracing character of the ideas on which it was founded.

The imprescriptible merit of the *Communist Manifesto* and of Marxism as a whole was that it alone provided a granite foundation upon which a solid, unassailable edifice could be built. The *Manifesto* had the ever-lasting merit of helping us understand with blinding clarity that the whole history of humanity—until then presented as a succession of chance events, as the result of the action of "great men," or even as the product of the evolution of ideas—was the history of *class struggle*. It showed that this struggle between exploiters and exploited has gone on in each epoch, within the framework set by given levels of technical development and given economic relations created by society itself.

The *Manifesto* showed that the present period is that of the struggle of the proletariat against the bourgeoisie, of the productive, exploited, and oppressed class against the idle, exploiting, and oppressing class; that the bourgeoisie develops the productive forces and the wealth of society ever further, unifies the economy, the conditions of life, and the civilization of all peoples while at the same time it increases both the misery and the oppression of its slaves.

The *Manifesto* proclaimed that the bourgeoisie is developing not only the forces of production and social wealth but also an ever more numerous, more cohesive, and more concentrated class of proletarians. The bourgeoisie educates this class and even drives it toward revolution. The bourgeois era allowed one, for the first time in history, to raise the question of the total abolition of exploitation and of the building of a new type of society, and to raise it not on the basis of the subjective wishes of social reformers but on the basis of the real possibilities created by society itself. Finally, the *Manifesto* showed that the proletariat can be the essential motive force for the social revolution. Driven forward by the conditions of its life and disciplined over a long period of time under the capitalist system of production and exploitation, the proletariat would overthrow the ruling system and reconstruct society on a communist basis.

From the very outset, Marxism outlined a framework and orientation for all revolutionary thought and action in modern society. It even succeeded in foreseeing and predicting many of the delays and difficulties the proletariat would encounter on the road to its emancipation. But the evolution of capitalism and the development of the working-class movement itself have given rise to new difficulties, unforeseen and unforeseeable factors, and previously unsuspected tasks. Weighed down by these new difficulties, the organized revolutionary movement folded. At the present time, it has disappeared.

The first job confronting those who wish to rebuild this movement is to become aware of the tasks confronting the movement today and to respond to these problems.

Roughly speaking, we can say that the profound difference between the situation today and that of 1848 is the appearance of the bureaucracy as a new social stratum tending to replace the bourgeoisie in the epoch of declining capitalism.

Within the framework of a world system based on exploitation, new economic forms and new types of exploitation have appeared. While maintaining the most fundamental features of capitalism these new forms differ significantly from traditional capitalism in that they have superseded and broken radically with such traditional capitalist forms as the private ownership of the means of production. These new economic forms even superficially resemble some of the objectives the workers' movement had set itself, objectives such as the statification or nationalization of the means of production and exchange, economic planning and the coordination of production on an international scale.

At the same time, and intimately connected with these new forms of exploitation, appeared the bureaucracy. This is a social formation that previously existed in embryonic form, but which now, for the first time in history has crystallized and established itself as the ruling class in a whole series of countries.

The bureaucracy was the social expression of these new economic forms. As traditional forms of property and the bourgeoisie of the classical period are pushed aside by State property and by the bureaucracy, the main conflict within society gradually ceases to be the old one between the owners of wealth and those without property and is replaced by the conflict between directors and executants in the process of production. In fact, the bureaucracy justifies its own existence (and can be explained in objective terms) only insofar as it plays a role deemed essential to the "management" of the productive activities of society — and, thereby, of all other forms of activity.

The importance of this replacement of the traditional bourgeoisie by a new bureaucracy in a whole series of countries resides in the fact that, in the majority of instances, the roots of this bureaucracy lie within the working class itself. The core around which the new ruling strata of technicians, administrators, and military personnel crystallized was none other than the leadership strata from the trade unions and "working-class parties" who have achieved various degrees of power after the first and second imperialist wars. This bureaucracy, moreover, seems capable of achieving some of the original objectives of the workers' movement, such as "nationalization" and "planning." And these achievements seem to provide the bureaucracy with the best basis for its continued domination.

The clearest result of a whole century of economic development and of the development of the workers' movement itself appears to be as follows. On the one hand, the traditional organizations (such as trade unions and political parties) that the working class continually created for its emancipation regularly transformed themselves into the means for mystifying the working class. Oozing out of every pore came the elements of a new social stratum. Climbing onto the backs of the workers, this social stratum sought to achieve its own emancipation, either by integrating itself into the capitalist system or by preparing and finally achieving its own accession to power. On the other hand, a whole series of measures and programmatic demands, once considered progressive and even revolutionary (such as agrarian reform, nationalization of industry, planning for production, monopolization over foreign trade, international economic coordination), have been fulfilled, usually by the actions of the workers' bureaucracy, sometimes by capitalism itself in the course of its development. This has taken place without there resulting for the toiling masses anything other than a more intense, better coordinated, and, in a word, rationalized exploitation. The objective outcome of this evolution has been a more efficient and more systematic organization for exploiting and enslaving the proletariat.

These developments have given rise to an unprecedented ideological confusion concerning the problems of how the proletariat should organize for struggle and of how working-class power should be structured and even of what the program for the socialist revolution should be.

Today it is this confusion concerning the most fundamental objectives of the class struggle that constitutes the main obstacle to rebuilding the revolutionary movement. To dispel it, we must analyze the main features of capitalist development and of the evolution of the working class during the last hundred years.

Bourgeoisie and Bureaucracy

From the beginning of the nineteenth century until about 1880, capitalism (i.e., the system of production based on the extreme development of mechanization and on the exploitation of the proletariat for the purpose of making a profit) was essentially a national capitalism, and it relied on a national bourgeoisie. It developed within the framework of free competition. During this entire period, competition between individual capitalists was the main driving force behind the development of the productive forces and of society in general.

Production was blindly and automatically regulated by the market. The balance between production and consumption (achieved by the "free play" of the market) was necessarily temporary. Each period of equilibrium was preceded and followed by periods of profound imbalance, i.e., by economic crises. This whole historical period was dominated by the anarchy of capitalist production, which periodically and regularly resulted in crises. During each of these crises, part of society's wealth was destroyed, masses of laborers were forced out of work, and the weaker capitalists were driven to the wall and bankrupted.

Driven on by technical development (which necessitates increasingly large investments), capital became more and more concentrated. As a result of crises and competition, many small and even medium-sized capitalists were eliminated. Increasingly large amounts of capital (and increasingly large armies of workers) were managed by a decreasing number of employers and capitalist companies. This process of concentration of the productive forces—of capital and of labor—reached a first plateau when all the important sectors of production came to be dominated completely by a capitalist monopoly and when industrial capital and bank capital began to merge as finance capital.

As the competitive capitalism of the nineteenth century gave way to monopoly capitalism, it left in its wake a world transformed. Industrial production, previously of no great significance, became the main activity of human beings and the main source of the wealth of civilized society. Hundreds of large towns developed. Hundreds of thousands of industrial workers were forced to live in them. They worked in factories of ever-increasing size. The similarity of their conditions of life and work rapidly gave rise to an awareness of their essential unity as a class.

Over a period of a few decades production and international trade increased tenfold. Having conquered and organized the great "civilized" nations (England, France, the United States, and Germany), capitalism then set out to conquer the world. This conquest was not to be achieved, however, by competitive capitalism. Its own internal tendencies had converted it, at the turn of the century, into monopoly capitalism. This transformation was to have a series of consequences of tremendous importance. On the strictly economic level, first of all, the concentration of capital and the development of increasingly large concerns led to rationalization and an "improved" organization of production. It also led to a speed-up of the labor process, greater exploitation of the working class, and a considerable reduction in manufacturing costs. On the social level, the concentration of capital, by gradually eliminating the owner-manager (the pioneer during the heroic period of capitalist development) and by centralizing numerous large concerns in the hands of a small number of owners, brought about a gradual separation of the functions of ownership and management of the productive process and increased the social significance of the stratum of managers, administrators, and technicians. At the same time, capital was losing its exclusive ties to its own national bourgeoisie. By means of trusts and cartels, its influence began to spread into other countries. Capital was becoming international. Finally, the development of monopolies, while suppressing competition within particular monopolized sectors of the economy, accentuated at the same time the struggle between the various national and international monopolies and monopolistic groupings. The forms of struggle between various groups of capitalists were altered. "Peaceful" competition (based on an expansion of production and on a reduction in selling prices) was replaced more and more by "extraeconomic" methods of struggle, such as the erection of customs barriers, dumping, the development of sheltered markets in the colonies, political and military pressures, and finally war itself, which broke out in 1914 as a "last resort" attempt at solving the economic problems confronting society.

The struggle for colonies became the main expression of the antagonisms between various monopolies and imperialist nations. From the time of the discoveries of the fifteenth century until the second half of the nineteenth century, "backward" countries overseas (whether or not they bore the status of "colonies") were essentially areas in which the "advanced" capitalist countries could indulge in the direct and brutal appropriation of wealth and in which they could sell their products. Capitalism's invasion of these countries during the first half of the nineteenth century appears essentially as an invasion by cheap commodities.

The transformation of competitive capitalism into monopoly capitalism altered the character of the economic links between capitalist countries and their colonies. Monopolies require a well-ordered market with stable sources of raw materials and stable outlets. The colonies therefore became integrated into this general tendency toward market "rationalization," which monopolies try to achieve for their outlets and for the sources of their raw materials. The colonies became above all a field for the investment of overabundant capital from the home countries, which is now exported on an increasing scale from these metropolitan countries to their colonies and to backward countries in general. In these areas the high rate of profit, tied to the very cheap labor costs that prevail there, allows capital to exploit labor to a much greater extent.

Already before 1914, the whole world had been divided among six or seven big imperialist nations. The tendency of the monopolies to extend their power and to increase their profits can henceforth express itself only by putting into question the current division of the world and eventually by struggling for new, more advantageous divisions. This is the real signification of World War I.

The result of the war was the spoliation of the vanquished by the victors and their confinement within their national boundaries. But the euphoria of the victorious imperialist powers proved short-lived. The continuous export of capital into backward areas and the abrupt cessation of European exports as a result of the war had brought about the industrialization of many overseas countries.

For the first time, the United States appeared on the world market as an exporter of industrial goods. Moreover, as a result of the 1917 revolution, Russia was lost to the capitalist market. The expansion of production in the capitalist countries was running up against an increasingly reduced market. Since 1913, the production of manufactured goods had increased constantly, whereas the imports and exports of these same goods had remained at a fairly static level, when they did not actually fall off. A new crisis of overproduction was becoming inevitable.

The crisis broke out in 1929 with unparalleled violence. The year 1929 saw the last of the classical cyclical crises of capitalism as well as the entrance of capitalism into a phase of chronic crisis, from which it has never lastingly recovered its balance, even to a limited and temporary extent.

The crisis of 1929 accelerated certain economic developments within imperialism itself. Previous capitalist crises had accelerated the concentration of capital by eliminating the less resilient capitalists. The process had progressed to the point of complete monopolization of every important sector of the economy. Competition had been eliminated within these sectors. After 1929 we see the same process developing, this time on an international scale. The most developed European imperialist countries (and those most richly endowed with colonies) are now revealed as utterly incapable of competing on the world market. A new era, that of the international concentration of the productive forces on a world scale, began.

Until then the world had been divided into a number of rival countries or groups of countries, each of which had lived in alternating states of economic, political, and military equilibrium and disequilibrium. Now the tendency was toward total world domination by a single imperialist country, whichever was the strongest in the economic and military fields.

Although their first effects were on international relations, these developments were to have a profound influence on the capitalist economy of every country. The European countries, incapable of struggling any longer on the world market, inevitably reacted to the crisis by retreating into their shells and by gearing production in the direction of economic autarky. This autarkic policy was merely the expression of the high degree of monopolization already achieved in these countries and of the control of the national economies the monopolies had already secured. This policy, however, was to have an important effect. A new phase in the process of capital concentration was developing: the concentration of capital around the State.

A slow and gradual fusion between capital and the State had in fact been evident since the very beginning of the industrial era. It had developed rapidly during the monopoly phase. It was now to take a great leap forward. As these "national" imperialist economies geared themselves toward autarky, the capitalist State assumed a new function. In addition to its classical function of political coercion, it now increasingly became the central organ for the coordination and management of the economy as a whole.

Imports and exports, production and consumption had to be regulated by a central agency expressing the interests of the monopolistic strata. Thus the whole of economic development between 1930 and 1939 is characterized by the increasingly important economic role played by the State *qua* supreme organ of coordination and management of the national capitalist economy, and by the beginnings of an organic fusion between monopoly capitalism and the State. It is not by accident that in Europe the most extreme expressions of this tendency were encountered in countries such as Nazi Germany and fascist Italy, nations that, as a result of a lack of colonies, were in the most unfavorable position in comparison to the other imperialist countries. Nevertheless, Roosevelt's policies in the United States expressed the same tendency within the context of a much sounder capitalist system.

This period of "falling back" on one's national economy was, however, to prove very short lived. This stage in no way implied any changes in the tendency of national capitalist production to be increasingly dependent on the production of other capitalist countries. On the contrary, it is merely an initial reaction of monopolies and capitalist States to precisely such a tendency toward interdependence, a tendency that of necessity has catastrophic results for the weakest capitalist countries. The reaction against this tendency and the suggested remedy of economic autarky were both to prove completely utopian.

World War II furnished the proof. This war was directly provoked by the stifling of German, Italian, and Japanese production within their own restricted markets. World War II also was the first direct expression of the tendency toward total concentration of production on an international scale, toward the regrouping of world capital around a single dominant pole.

German capital tried to play this unifying role by subordinating and attempting to draw in around itself all European capital. It no longer was a question, as in World War I, of a new "partitioning" of the world. The objectives of the war, on both sides, were far vaster: The victorious power would annex not only backward countries, overseas markets, etc., but also the capital of the other imperialist countries, in an attempt to organize the world economy and human life itself in relation to the interests of a single, all-dominating imperialist power. The defeat of the Axis powers left the field wide open for the "Allies" to dominate the world.

World War I had provided a very temporary solution to the problems that had provoked it. The end of World War II was to pose again, but in an immeasurably deeper and more intense, urgent, and imperative manner, the very problems that had provoked it. The total failure of all "secondary" imperialist powers and of all autarkic structures was now clear for everyone to see. The European imperialist powers proved themselves utterly incapable either of competing with American production on the world market or of living off their own resources. Yankee imperialism did not even have to try to subjugate them: They subjugated themselves. They recognized that henceforth they could live only by sponging off Uncle Sam and by remaining under his tutelage. But above all, World War II laid bare the last great antagonism between exploiting States, the antagonism that now tears clear through the world system of exploitation: the struggle between Russia and America for world domination.

This antagonism now dominates our epoch. It presents profoundly new features. Not only is it the ultimate form of rivalry between contending States in modern society, but it is also an antagonism between two systems of different structure, each representing a different stage in the concentration of the forces of production.

Concentration has now gone well beyond the classical monopoly stage and has taken on a new role. In each country, the State has become the backbone of economic life. Either all production, and hence the whole of social life, is in its hands (as in Russia and its satellites) or (as in the rest of the world) the leading capitalist groupings are necessarily compelled to utilize the State as the most efficient tool for their control and management of the national economy.

In the field of international affairs, not only have the countries that always have been subordinated to the "Great Powers" revealed their inability to maintain their economic, military, and political independence, but so have the "Great Powers" themselves. One and all have fallen under the open or disguised domination of the only two States whose power guarantees them autonomy. Russia and the United States have become the Superstates of the contemporary era, the devouring Molochs before whom all must bow or disappear. In this way, both Europe and the rest of the planet find themselves split into two zones: one dominated by Russia, the other by America.

But the profound symmetry that exists between the two zones should not allow one to forget the essential differences separating them. The United States has reached the present stage of concentration of its economy and its present position of transcontinental domination as a result of the organic development of its own capitalistic system. As a result of monopolization, the American economy has reached its present stage, a stage where a dozen supergroupings of formidable power, united among themselves, own everything essential to production. They control the entire production process, from the smallest cogwheel right up to the central organ of coercion and coordination, the American federal State. Big business, however, has not yet become completely identical with the State. In the formal sense, ownership and administration of the economy on the one hand, and ownership and administration of the State on the other, remain separate and distinct functions. Only the identity of the managing personnel of each ensures coordination. Economic planning, however, remains confined within each sector of production. It was only during World War II that the economy as a whole was totally coordinated. Since then, there has been a partial dismantling of this total coordination.

In the Russian sphere and above all in Russia itself, on the other hand, the concentration of the productive forces is now complete. The whole of the economy is State-owned and is administered by the State. The beneficiary of this exploitation of the proletariat is an enormous and monstrous bureaucracy (consisting of the bureaucrats in the political and economic apparatus, of technicians and intellectuals, of leaders of the "Communist" party and of the trade unions, and of the top military and police personnel). Economic "planning" proceeds in the interests of the bureaucracy and affects all areas of production.

On the international level, there are also certain differences between the two systems. The Russian satellite States have been completely assimilated, both with respect to their economic and their social regimes. Their production is geared directly to the economic and military requirements of the Russian bureaucracy. In the zone of American influence, on the other hand, the process of economic and political subjugation has several further stages to go through. Compared to the "Molotov Plan," the "Marshall Plan" was just a beginning. Only the Third World War will bring this process to completion.

Finally, from the proletariat's point of view, if both systems show the same fundamental tendency of modern capitalism toward an increasingly complete exploitation of labor power, this trend has advanced to different degrees in the two systems. In the Russian sphere there are no obstacles of a juridical or economic kind that might thwart the desire of the bureaucracy to exploit the proletariat to the limit, to increase production as much as possible in order to satisfy its parasitic consumption patterns, and to build up its military potential. Under such conditions, the proletariat is completely reduced to mere raw material in the production process. Its conditions of life, the pace of production, and the length of the working day are all imposed upon it by the bureaucracy, without any possibility of discussion. This process has not achieved a similar state of development in the American sphere, except in colonial and backward countries. Europe and the United States are only beginning to advance in this direction.

Profound as these differences may be, we must not forget that the very conditions under which the two systems are forced to develop inevitably lead them in the exact same direction. The primary effect of this dynamic of social change is to accentuate the process of concentration within American imperialism. American capital now dominates many countries both politically and economically. The American State is playing an increasingly important role in this domination. After World War II, American monopolies grabbed up for themselves a considerable proportion of German and Japanese capital and have shown little or no inclination to abandon such spoils. Within the American economy, concentration has proceeded both horizontally and vertically. This development has been dictated by the needs to control and regulate more completely both the sources of its raw materials and its markets, and this both within the United States and overseas. The American military apparatus has been immeasurably expanded. The threat of World War III has gradually converted the "peacetime" economy into a "permanent war economy." The falling rate of profit and the need for ever-greater investments had made it necessary to exploit the working class to the full. These factors tend to drive American capitalism toward world domination, a domination that identifies itself more and more openly with the American State. All this leads the American State itself toward increasingly totalitarian forms of political rule. A new crisis of overproduction or war itself would accentuate these tendencies immeasurably.

The process of total concentration of the productive forces can come to fruition only through the unification of capital and the ruling class on a world scale, i.e., through the merger of the two systems that today oppose one another. War alone could bring this about. American imperialism and the Russian bureaucracy can attempt to solve their contradictions only through an external expansion of their spheres of influence. Short of revolution, war is inevitable. The world economy cannot remain divided into two hermetically sealed sectors.

The inexorable tendency of the dominant strata of both systems to increase their wealth and power obliges them to seek ever-wider fields to plunder. The wish to increase their privileges—or even merely to preserve them—obliges both ruling strata to continue developing their productive forces. But each ruling stratum is confronted with an adversary with similar appetites. Expansion therefore becomes increasingly difficult. In a world divided into two zones the limits of possible expansion are strictly defined for each contender.

The concentration of capital and technical developments necessitate ever-larger investments. These requirements can only be met through increased exploitation of the proletariat. But this very exploitation soon comes up against an insurmountable obstacle, namely, the fall in the productivity of labor when labor is overexploited. From this stage on there is only one solution possible for the exploiters, whether bourgeois or bureaucrats: external expansion through the annexation of the capital, the raw materials, and even the proletariat of their opponent.

This is merely the supreme expression of the fundamental tendency of concentrated capital, the tendency to expand not merely in relation to its own absolute size but in accordance with its dominant position in the worldwide relation of forces. Today this means the appropriation not merely of a larger share of the profits but of *all* the profits. One can appropriate all the profits for oneself, however, only if one appropriates all the conditions and sources of profit, in other words, if one secures domination over the entire world economy.

The struggle for world domination now becomes the ultimate and supreme form of competition between the highly concentrated and centralized productive machines of the contemporary era. When the stage of total concentration of the productive forces has been reached, competition inevitably and directly is transformed into military struggle. Total war replaces economic competition as the expression of the conflicting interests of the two ruling strata and of the more fundamental tendency toward a worldwide concentration of the productive forces, which is necessitated by the very development of the economy.

Conversely, as soon as the insoluble antagonism between the Russian bureaucracy and American imperialism makes war an inevitable prospect, war itself becomes the nodal point of all human activity. The eventuality of war determines from now on every manifestation of social life. It has repercussions in the fields of economics, politics, technique, and religion. This domination of all social activities by the threat of war aggravates the contradictions that already exist between the two regimes to a point hitherto unknown. The mere threat of war reinforces and deepens the processes that drive toward war.

If the proletariat does not intervene to smash this antagonism and its bases, not only is war inevitable, but so is the identification of the two systems, which would result in a worldwide system of exploitation of the laboring masses. Short of revolution, the war will be "resolved" by the destruction of one of the two opponents, by world domination for the winner, by the total appropriation of both the capital and the proletariat of the vanquished, and by the regrouping around the victor of most of the exploiting strata in the vanquished countries (after eliminating their top personnel).

A victory for Russia over America would mean the total takeover by Russia of America's (in fact of the world's) productive apparatus. This would take the form of a complete "nationalization" of American big business. Yankee capitalists and their principal political, trade-union, and military agents would be eliminated. At the same time, the bulk of the technicians and a large part of the economic and labor bureaucracies of the American State would be integrated into the new system.

Conversely, an American victory over Russia would imply the elimination of the top personnel of the Russian bureaucratic apparatus, the direct takeover of Russia's productive machine and of the Russian proletariat by American capital, which would preserve "nationalized" property as being the most concentrated and hence the easiest to administer for purposes of continued exploitation. This would be accompanied by the integration into the American system of the great majority of Russian planners and technicians and of trade-union and administrative bureaucrats. The complete assimilation of Russian capital and of the Russian proletariat by Yankee imperialism would be possible, however, only at the expense of considerable internal adaptations of the U.S. economic structure, changes that would in turn propel its economy in the direction of total statification.

Whoever wins, war will be a turning point in the evolution of the modern world. It will accelerate the drift of this society toward barbarism unless the exploited and war-ravaged masses of the whole world intervene, unless the proletarian revolution overflows onto the historical stage in order to exterminate the exploiters and their agents and to rebuild the social life of humanity. Contemporary society has developed the productive forces to a hitherto unknown degree but is capable of utilizing them only as instruments of exploitation, oppression, destruction, and misery. Socialism will utilize these productive forces to free man and to allow him to control his own destiny. The fate of civilization and of humanity is linked directly to the revolution.

Bureaucracy and Proletariat

From its earliest days, capitalism tended to convert the proletariat into mere raw material in the production process. It tended to reduce the worker to the rank of a mere cog in the productive machine. In the capitalist economy the worker is an object, mere merchandise, and the capitalist treats him as such. The capitalist seeks to purchase labor power as he would any other commodity, at the cheapest possible rate. The worker is not a human being, entitled to live his own life. He is only labor power, a possible source of profit. The capitalist consequently tries to reduce wages to a minimum, thus making the worker's living conditions the worst possible, and to extract from the worker, as from any other merchandise, the maximum amount of usefulness. To this end he imposes on the worker the longest possible working day and the fastest pace of production possible.

But the capitalist system cannot give free and unlimited vent to this fundamental tendency toward total exploitation. First of all, this trend rapidly comes into conflict with one of the objectives of production itself. The fulfillment of one capitalist objective (the unlimited exploitation of labor power) clashes with another of equal importance (the increase in the productivity of labor).

From the strictly economic point of view, the worker is more than a machine. He produces for the capitalist more than he costs. Moreover, in the course of his work he exhibits creativity, an ability to produce goods in ever-increasing quantities and of ever-better quality. This is a capacity scarcely shown at all by the productive strata of previous historical epochs. When the capitalist treats the worker as a dumb beast he soon learns (to his cost) that a dumb beast cannot be substituted for the worker. The productivity of overexploited labor falls rapidly. This is the fundamental contradiction in the modern system of exploitation. This is the historical reason for its failure, its inability to stabilize itself.

But in addition—and this is even more important—the capitalist system soon comes up against the proletariat as a class conscious of its own interests. The worker rapidly acquires an awareness that under capitalism it is his lot to produce ever more and cost ever less. To the extent the worker comes to realize that the purpose of his life is not simply to be a source of profit for his employer, to be a mere victim of exploitation, he becomes conscious of exploitation itself and begins to react against it.

The capitalist system produces and reproduces exploitation on an ever-increasing scale. As it does so, the workers' struggle tends to become a struggle for the complete abolition of exploitation. It becomes a struggle against the very *conditions* of exploitation, which are to be found in the total and exclusive appropriation of the means of production, of State power, and of culture itself by the exploiting class.

This struggle for the abolition of exploitation is not peculiar to the working class. It has existed among all previous exploited classes. Two aspects of this struggle, however, are peculiar to the working-class struggle against exploitation. First, this struggle takes place under conditions that permit it to achieve the ends it has set for itself. Today the extreme development of social wealth and of the productive forces, a result of industrial civilization, makes it entirely possible to build a society from which economic antagonisms would be absent. Second, the modern working class finds itself placed in conditions that allow it to undertake this struggle and to wage it to a successful conclusion. In the proletariat there appears for the first time in history an exploited class disposing of immense social power and capable of developing an awareness of its historical situation and interests.

Living and producing collectively, the working class rapidly passes from individual reactions to collective reaction and action against capitalist exploitation. The development of industry and the centralization of the productive apparatus of society into factories, towns, and industrial areas of increasing size have concentrated the proletariat. Living and producing together, the workers rapidly come to realize the unity of their class, and also the unity of the exploiting class that faces them. They know they are the only real producers of wealth. They soon come to realize the parasitic role of the bosses. At this stage it becomes possible for them to see as their goal not merely the limitation of exploitation but its total abolition and the reconstruction of society on a communist basis. This would be a society managed by the producers themselves in which all wealth would come from productive labor.

From the earliest days of its history, the working class has made grandiose attempts at abolishing exploitation and at constituting such a proletarian society. In the nineteenth century, the most advanced attempt of this kind was the Paris Commune. These early attempts, however, ended in failure. The conditions of the time were not yet ripe. The economic basis of society was as yet insufficiently developed, the working class itself was still numerically weak and had only a vague awareness of the means it should employ to arrive at its goals.

After the failure of these early endeavors, the working class began to organize itself to achieve its objectives. It created economic organizations (trade unions) and political organizations (the parties of the Second International). At their beginning at least, both were oriented toward the same objective, the abolition of class domination and the building of a proletarian society.

In the period of their historical ascendancy—until about 1914—these trade unions and political parties accomplished an immensely important task. They provided the framework within which millions of workers—having acquired class consciousness and an awareness of their historical interests—prepared for the struggles that lay ahead. These struggles brought about a considerable improvement in the living and working conditions of the working class. They led to the political and social education of wide strata of workers. Many workers began to understand the decisive strength represented by the proletariat in any modern society.

At the same time, however, the trade unions and the parties of the Second International, carried away by the successful reforms that had been extracted from the bosses as a result of working-class struggle in this period of early imperialist expansion, were becoming more and more imbued with reformist ideology. The leaders sought to make the class believe that it was possible to suppress exploitation and to transform society without violent revolution and without any great expenditures of effort, by means of an infinite succession of reforms. In so doing, they were hiding the fact that capitalism was approaching its period of organic crisis, a period that would prevent it from making any further major concessions and that would even oblige it to go back on concessions already granted. The idea of proletarian revolution as the indispensable means of ending capitalist exploitation appeared as a gratuitous utopia or as the vision of sanguinary mystics.

This degeneration of the Second International obviously was not an accidental phenomenon. Taking advantage of the overexploitation of the colonies, imperialism had been able to grant certain reforms, which appeared to give some substance to the reformist mystification. Imperialism had corrupted an entire labor aristocracy, which itself had become increasingly bourgeois in its outlook. For the first time, a labor bureaucracy appeared that sought to separate itself from the exploited class and attempted to satisfy aspirations of its own.

The recruitment of the working class into enormous organizations numbering millions of dues-paying members, keeping large and powerful apparatuses going, creating newspapers, having deputies and offices to run them, led to the development of a broad stratum of political and trade-union bureaucrats. This stratum emerged from the labor aristocracy and from the petty bourgeois intelligentsia. It began to seek the satisfaction of its own interests. It saw those interests not in the struggle for the proletarian revolution but in the assumption (by the labor bureaucracy) of the role of shepherds to the working-class flock, grazing on the prairies of capitalist "democracy." These political and trade-union leaders became intermediaries between the embattled workers and the bosses. They began to feed at the capitalist trough.

Thus it came about that the very apparatus the working class had created for its own emancipation, the trade unions and political parties to which it had delegated its historical tasks and to whom it had entrusted the responsibility of defending its interests, gradually became one of the bosses' tools within the labor movement, a means of mystifying the working class and of keeping it docile and half-asleep.

There was a rude awakening. When capitalism, driven by its own internal logic, plunged headlong into the universal carnage of 1914, the workers discovered that their "leaders" were all deputies of the bourgeoisie or ministers in governments of National Unity. All that these "leaders" could call upon the working class to do was to allow themselves to be butchered for the defense and glory of the capitalist "fatherland."

The workers' reaction was slow, but all the more radical for that. In 1917, six months after having overthrown the czarist regime, the Russian workers and peasants swept aside the social-patriotic government of Kerensky and began to instaurate, under the aegis of the Bolshevik party, a soviet democracy, the first Republic of the Exploited in human history. In 1918, the workers, soldiers, and sailors of Germany were overthrowing the kaiser and creating soviets throughout the country. A few months later the Hungarian Soviet Republic was born. In Finland, the proletariat launched a mass struggle against the landowners and capitalists. In 1920, the Italian proletariat was occupying the factories. In Moscow, Vienna, Munich, Berlin, Budapest, and Milan, the proletarian battalions were entering the fight, determined to win. The European revolution seemed on the verge of success.

In other countries feelings ran high. The militant solidarity of the French and British workers proved the main factor in preventing Clemenceau and Churchill from crushing the Russian Soviet Republic by force of arms. The vanguard of the class was breaking off from the reformist parties on a massive scale. In 1919, the Third (Communist) International was founded in Moscow. It called for the creation of new revolutionary parties, which would break completely with the opportunism and the reformism of social democracy and which would see as their task the leadership of the working class to the revolutionary conquest of power.

But the hour of mankind's liberation had not yet struck. The capitalist system and its State proved strong enough to withstand the assault of the masses. The parties of the Second International in particular successfully played their role of protectors of the bourgeois order. The influence of reformism on the working class, the weight of intermediate social strata, the shock-absorbing role of the labor aristocracy all proved more important than had been anticipated. Defeated in Europe, the revolution was able to hold on only in Russia, an immense but extremely backward country, where the proletariat constituted only a small minority of the population.

The revolutionaries of that period, although they gave it a certain practical importance, did not consider this defeat of the European revolution between 1918 and 1923 as having any deep, *historical* significance. They remained convinced that this defeat stemmed essentially from a lack of adequate "revolutionary leadership" in the European countries. They felt confident that this deficiency could be made up for through the construction of the revolutionary parties of the Third International. These parties, supported by the revolutionary power that had succeeded in maintaining itself in Russia, would win the next round.

Events developed quite differently, however. In the land of the "victorious" revolution, Bolshevik rule underwent a rapid degeneration. We can characterize this degeneration in summary terms by saying that it brought to enduring political and economic power an all-powerful bureaucracy, formed from the cadres of the Bolshevik party, from the managers of the State and of the economy, from technicians, intellectuals, and army officers. As it gradually consolidated its power, this bureaucracy transformed the embryonic socialist organs engendered by the revolution of October 1917 into instruments of a new system of oppression and exploitation, the most highly perfected one ever known.

Thus there evolved a system that cynically calls itself "socialist," yet where side by side with the appalling poverty of the working masses can be seen the life of luxury led by about 10 or 15 percent of the population who make up the exploiting bureaucracy. This is a system where millions of people are held in concentration and forced labor camps, where the State police (of which the Gestapo was but an imitation) exercises total terror, where "elections" and other "democratic" procedures would be deemed sinister farces were they not the tragic expressions of the terrorization, the brutalization, and the degradation of man under the most overwhelming dictatorship alive today.

Simultaneously we have seen the "Communist" parties in the rest of the world become, through a series of apparent zigzags in their policies, the docile instruments of the Russian bureaucracy's foreign policy. These parties and even workers who follow them attempt by all means possible to help this bureaucracy in its struggles against its imperialist opponents. Should the occasion arise, these parties will try to seize State power in their own countries in order to instaurate regimes similar to the Russian one for the benefit of their indigenous bureaucracies. This has occurred in Yugoslavia, in central and southeastern Europe, and now in China.

How did things reach this pass? How did the power established by the first victorious proletarian revolution transform itself into the most effective instrument for exploiting and oppressing the masses? And how did the parties of the Third International, created to abolish exploitation and to instaurate on earth the power of workers and peasants, become the instruments of a new social formation with interests as radically opposed to those of the proletariat as had been those of the traditional bourgeoisie itself? These are the questions that all advanced workers will anxiously ask themselves, once they have understood that to see anything "socialist" in Russia is to calumniate the very word "socialism."

The October Revolution succumbed to the bureaucratic counterrevolution under the combined pressures of external and internal forces, of objective and subjective factors. They all boil down to the following idea: Between the second and third decade of this century neither the world economy nor the working class was as yet quite ripe for the total abolition of exploitation. A revolution, even a victorious one, would be overthrown if it remained isolated in a single country. It would either be overthrown from outside, through civil war and the armed intervention of other capitalist countries, or it would degenerate from within, through a change in the nature of the regime to which it had given birth.

The proletarian revolution can culminate in the instauration of socialism only if it is worldwide. This in no way implies that the revolution has to occur simultaneously in all countries. It merely means that, starting in one or more countries, the revolution must continue to spread until capitalism is exterminated all over the globe. This idea was shared by Marx and Lenin, by Trotsky and Rosa Luxemburg. It is neither a theoretician's hallucination nor a system builder's obsession. Workers' power and capitalist power are incompatible whether they confront one another in one country or in the international arena. Internationally, either the one or the other must win out. If workers' power does not win, bourgeois power will—either by the direct overthrow of the workers' power and its replacement by a capitalist government, or as the result of an internal deterioration, leading to the creation of a class regime reproducing all the fundamental features of capitalist exploitation. This inevitable deterioration of an isolated revolution is determined above all by economic factors.

Socialism is not an "ideal" society imagined by dreamy do-gooders or fanciful reformers. It is a positive, historical perspective whose possible realization is based on the development of wealth in capitalist society itself. It is precisely because society has reached such a stage in the development of its productive forces that it becomes possible first to attenuate to a great extent and then to abolish the struggle of all against all for the satisfaction of material needs. Because of these objective possibilities, socialism is no absurd dream. But these potentialities exist only when one considers the world economy as a whole.

A single country, however wealthy, would never be able to obtain such abundance for its inhabitants, even if locally the power of the capitalists were overthrown. The victory of the revolution in a single country does not abolish the relations of that country with the world economy or its dependence on it. Not only would such a country be compelled to maintain and to increase its military defense—one of the principal sources of unproductive waste in the modern world—but it would be faced with a serious economic dilemma.

In order to make economic progress, either it would have to maintain and heighten specialization in the production process (which means maintaining production geared in all important respects toward the world capitalist economy, which in turn means subordinating production indirectly, but just as effectively, to capitalism's laws and capitalism's anarchy) or the country will have to turn in the direction of autarky, even producing goods that it could obtain much more cheaply through exchange. This would mean taking a considerable step backward, economically speaking. In either case this isolated revolution would lead neither to abundance nor to a lessening of economic antagonisms between individuals and between social strata. Isolation will lead only to regression, to social poverty, to an accentuation of the struggle of all against all for the satisfaction of basic needs. This is exactly what happened in Russia.

When this struggle of all against all for the satisfaction of needs occurs in a poverty-stricken society suffering from a scarcity of goods, the inevitable result is that those who find themselves, even temporarily, in leading positions will use these positions to fulfill their own needs whenever these needs conflict with those of others. This occurs quite independently of the "honesty," rank, or other qualities of the leading personnel. Economic necessity will drive the "leaders," good or bad, honest or dishonest, in the same direction. To solve their own problems they will attempt first of all to stabilize their power. Then they will gradually seek to transform it into the rule of their own particular social stratum. Finally, they will seek to abolish every trace of democracy in social life, every possibility of criticizing themselves and their kind.

Once firmly installed in the seats of power, the new rulers will follow the path of every previous ruling class. They will have to exploit the proletariat to the full, make it constantly produce more and more, see to it that it costs less and less. This they will do under the double pressure of needing to satisfy their own needs while also having to strengthen the State in its struggles with foreign enemies. The ever-increasing exploitation of the proletariat has its inevitable corollary: the reinforcement of dictatorship and of terror. And so on. This is but a description in general terms of the real process of degeneration of the Russian Revolution.

The statement that socialism is impossible below a certain level of development of the productive forces, however fundamental it may be, is only a partial statement. It could lead one to totally wrong conclusions. It could lead one to conclude, for instance, that the instauration of a collectivist regime is by definition impossible. It is certain, for example, that no capitalist society will ever develop the productive forces to the point where a direct transition from an economy of scarcity for the vast majority to an economy of universal plenty will be possible. As Marx foresaw, between capitalist society and communist society there would be a transitional period during which the regime's form can be none other than that of the dictatorship of the proletariat.

This transitional period can point to the road toward communism if it leads to a rapid development of the productive forces and thus allows a constant improvement in the material standard of living of the masses, a progressive reduction in working hours, and thereby an improvement in their level of culture. Revolution on a world scale could achieve these ends. It would do so by suppressing the parasitic role of the exploiting classes and of their bureaucratic State machines, by abolishing military expenditures, by developing an economy freed of all the obstacles arising from private ownership and national narrowmindedness, by rationalizing and planning production on a world scale, by developing backward countries and particularly by utilizing the tremendous increase in the productivity of human labor that will come about once it has been freed from exploitation, from alienation, and from the brutalization imposed on it by capitalists and bureaucrats alike.

During the period of transition between the overthrow of the old ruling class and the achievement of a communist society two different courses are open. Either society will go forward, gradually strengthening the communist tendencies in the economy and culminating in a society of abundance — or the struggle of all against all will lead to the opposite development, to continued growth in the parasitic strata first of all, then to the development of a new exploiting class, and finally to the instauration of an entire economy based upon exploitation, an economy that reproduces in a different form all the essentials of capitalist alienation. Both possibilities exist side by side. Both are based on the state of the economy and of society as a whole, bequeathed to the revolution by capitalism itself.

But progress along one path and rejection of the other path does not depend on chance or on unknown or mysterious factors. They depend on the autonomous activity and initiative of the working masses. If, during the transitional period, the proletariat, at the head of all the exploited strata of society, proves capable of managing both the economy and the State collectively (without having to delegate these functions to "specialists," technicians, "professional revolutionaries," and other interested saviors of humanity) — if the proletariat shows itself to be mature enough to manage production and public affairs and to take active control over every sector of social life, then society will advance without difficulty toward communism. If, on the other hand, the proletariat cannot rise to these tasks, there will be an inevitable retreat back toward an exploiting type of society.

A fundamental question therefore has to be answered on the morrow of every successful revolution. Who will be the master of society once it is purged of the capitalists and their tools? The structure of the new regime, its political form, the relationship between the working class and its own leadership, the management of production, the type of system prevailing in the factories, all these are but particular aspects of this general problem.

Now, in Russia this problem was resolved quite rapidly when a new exploiting stratum, the bureaucracy, came to power. Between March and October 1917, the struggling masses had created organs that expressed their aspirations and that were to express their power. These organs, the soviets, immediately came into conflict with the provisional government, which was the instrument of the capitalist class. The Bolshevik party was the only organized group advocating the overthrow of the government and the conclusion of an immediate peace. Within six months it had acquired a majority in the soviets and was leading them toward a successful insurrection. But the result of this insurrection was the enduring establishment of the Party in the seat of political power and, through the Party and as it degenerated, of the bureaucracy.

Once the insurrection was over, the Bolshevik party showed that it conceived of the workers' government as its own government. The slogan "All Power to the Soviets" soon came to mean, in reality, "All Power to the Bolshevik Party." The soviets were quickly reduced to the role of mere organs of local administration. They retained for a while, it is true, a certain autonomy. But this was only because of the needs of the Civil War. The "dispersed" form the Civil War took on in Russia often made it difficult, if not downright impossible, for the central government to exercise authority.

This relative autonomy of the soviets was to prove quite temporary. Once normal circumstances were reestablished, the soviets were forced to become once again local executive organs, compelled to carry out without dissent the directives of the central power and of the party in command. They progressively atrophied through lack of use. The increasing antagonism between the masses and the new government found no organized channels through which it might express itself. Even when this antagonism took on a violent form (as in the Petrograd strikes of 1920-21, during the Kronstadt insurrection, during the Makhno movement), the masses of the workers opposed the Party as an unorganized mass and not through the soviets.

Why this antagonism between the Party and the class? Why this progressive atrophy of the soviets? The two questions are intimately interconnected. The answer to both is the same.

Long before it took power, the Bolshevik party contained within itself the seeds of these developments that could lead it into complete opposition to the mass of the workers. It based itself on Lenin's conception (outlined in *What Is to Be Done*) that the Party alone possessed a revolutionary consciousness (which it inculcates into the working class). The Party had been built on the idea that the masses themselves could attain merely a trade-union consciousness. It had been built of necessity under conditions of illegality as a rigid apparatus of cadre elements, carefully selecting the vanguard elements of the working class and of the intelligentsia. The Party had educated its members in the conceptions of strict discipline and in the notion that whatever others might say, the Party was always right. Once in power, the Party identified itself completely with the revolution. Its opponents, whatever ideology they might advocate or whatever tendency they might belong to, could only be "agents of the counterrevolution" as far as the Party was concerned.

From these conceptions it followed quite easily that other parties should be excluded from the soviets and made illegal. That these measures often were unavoidable cannot be disputed. But the fact remains that "political life" in the soviets was soon reduced to a monologue—or to a series of monologues—by Bolshevik representatives. Other workers, if they wished to oppose the policy of the Party, neither could organize to do so nor could they oppose the policy of the party effectively without organization.

Thus the Party very rapidly came to exercise all power, even at the lowest levels. Throughout the country it was only through the Party that one could gain access to higher positions. The immediate results were twofold. On the one hand, many Party members, knowing themselves to be uncontrolled and uncontrollable, started achieving "socialism" for themselves: They started solving their own problems by creating privileges for themselves. On the other hand, all those throughout the country who had privileges to defend—whether based on the new regime or not—now entered the Party en masse, in order to defend these privileges. Thus it came about that the Party rapidly transformed itself from an instrument of the working class into an instrument of a new privileged stratum, a stratum the Party itself was exuding from its every pore.

Confronted with these developments the working class was slow to react. Its reactions were feeble and fragmented. We are now approaching the key to the whole problem. The new duality between soviets and Party was quickly resolved in favor of the Party. The working class itself often actively assisted this evolution. Its best militants and most devoted and class-conscious offspring felt the need to give the Party everything they had and to support it through thick and thin (even when the Party was clearly opposing the will of the masses). All this proved possible because the working class, taken as a whole, and in particular its vanguard, still conceived of the problem of proletarian emancipation in terms that, however necessary they may have been at this stage, were nonetheless false.

Forgetting that "there is no supreme savior, neither God nor Caesar nor tribune," the working class saw in its own tribunes, in its own Party, the solution to the leadership problem. It believed that once it had abolished the power of the capitalists it had only to confide this leadership role to the Party to whom it had given its best people for that Party to act automatically in the class's exclusive interests.

To start with, the Party did in fact act in the interests of the working class and for rather longer than might have been anticipated. Not only was the Party the only one on the side of the workers and peasants between February and October 1917, not only was it the only one to express their interests; it was also the indispensable organ for the final crushing defeat of the capitalists, the one to whom the workers and peasants are indebted for the successful outcome of the civil war. But already, in playing this role, the Party little by little was becoming detached from the masses. It finally became an end in itself, the instrument of and the framework for all the privileged members of the new regime.

When considering the development of this new privileged stratum one must distinguish the purely political aspects, which are only its expression, from the far more important economic ones.

In a modern society the major part, and in particular the qualitatively decisive part, of production is that part carried out in factories. For a class to manage a modern society, it must actually manage the factories themselves. The factories determine the overall orientation and volume of production, the level of wages, and the tempo of work. In short, all those problems whose solution will determine in advance the direction in which society's structures will evolve will be settled in the factory.

These problems will be solved in the interests of the working class only if the workers solve them themselves. But for this, it is necessary for the proletariat as a class to be before all else master of the economy, both at the level of the general management of industry and at the level of the management of each particular enterprise. These are but two aspects of the same thing.

This management of production by the workers themselves assumes an additional importance in modern society. The entire evolution of the modern economy tends to replace the old opposition between owners and the propertyless with a new opposition between directors and executants in the productive process. If the proletariat does not immediately abolish, together with the private ownership of the means of production, the management of production as a specific function permanently carried out by a particular social stratum, it will only have cleared the ground for the emergence of a new exploiting stratum, which will arise out of the "managers" of production and out of the bureaucracies dominating economic and political life.

Now, this is exactly what happened in Russia. Having overthrown the bourgeois government, having expropriated the capitalists (often against the wishes of the Bolsheviks), having occupied the factories, the workers thought that all that was necessary was to hand over management to the government, to the Bolshevik party, and to the trade-union leaders. By doing so, the proletariat was abdicating its own essential role in the new society it was striving to create. This role was inevitably to be taken over by others.

Around the Bolshevik party in power, and under its protective wing, the new boss class gradually took shape. It slowly developed in the factories, at first disguised as directors, specialists, and technicians. This took place all the more naturally as the program of the Bolshevik party left the door open to such an evolution, and at times even actively encouraged it.

The Bolshevik party proposed certain economic measures that later formed one of the essential points in the program of the Third International. These measures consisted first of all in the expropriation of the big capitalist trusts and in the forced merger of certain smaller enterprises; second, in the essential field of the relations between the workers and the apparatus of production, the measures centered around the slogan "Workers' Control." This slogan was based on the alleged incapacity of the workers to pass directly to the management of production at factory level and above all at the level of the central management of the entire economy. "Control" was to fulfill an educative function. It was, during the transitional period, to teach the workers how to manage, and they were to be taught by ex-bosses, technicians, and production "specialists."

But "control" of production, even "workers' control" of production, does not resolve the problem of who really directs production. On the contrary, it implies quite clearly that throughout this entire period the problem of effective management was actually being resolved in quite a different way.

To say that the workers "control" production implies that they do not *manage* it. The Bolsheviks called for workers' control. They had little confidence in the workers' ability to manage production. There was a fundamental opposition of interests, at first latent, between the workers, who "control," and others, who actually manage production. This antagonism created in the production process what amounted to a duality of economic power. Like all situations of dual power, it had to be resolved quickly: Either the workers would press forward, within a short period, toward total management of production, reabsorbing in the process the "specialists," technicians, and administrators that had risen from their ranks, or the latter would finally reject a type of "control" that had become an encumbrance to them, a control that was increasingly a pure formality, and would install themselves as absolute masters over the management of production. If the State cannot tolerate a condition of dual power, the economy can tolerate it even less. The stronger of the two partners will quickly eliminate the other.

During the period preceding the expropriation of the capitalists, "workers' control" had a positive meaning. It implies the working class's invasion into the command stations of the economy. *After* the expropriation of the capitalists, such control can give way only to the complete management of the economy by the working class. Otherwise "workers' control" will merely prove to be a protective screen used to conceal the first steps of the nascent bureaucracy.

We now know that in Russia "workers' control" led precisely to this last development. The conflict between the mass of workers and the growing bureaucracy was resolved in the interests of this bureaucracy. Technicians and "specialists" from the old regime were kept on to perform "technical" tasks. But they rapidly merged with the new strata of administrators that had risen through the ranks of the Party and of the trade unions. They soon began to demand unchecked power for themselves. The "educational function" of workers' control played right into their hands. It did not help the working class at all. Instead, it laid the economic foundations for the new bureaucracy.

There is no mystery about the subsequent growth of the bureaucracy. Having dealt first with the proletariat, the bureaucracy then turned against the privileged elements in town and country (the Nepmen and the kulaks) whose privileges were based on traditional bourgeois types of exploitation. The extermination of these remnants of the old privileged strata proved quite easy for the bureaucracy. In its struggle against these elements, the bureaucracy had at its disposal even more advantages than a trust enjoys in its struggle against small, isolated businesses.

The bureaucracy embodies the natural tendency of the modern economy toward the concentration of the forces of production. It rapidly overcame the resistance of the petty capitalist and the rich peasant strata, which are hopelessly doomed to disappear even under capitalism. After a bourgeois revolution, the development of the economy itself precludes a return to feudalism. Similarly, a return to the traditional, disjointed, and anarchic forms of capitalism was no longer an option in Russia. The return to a regime of exploitation as a result of the degeneration of the revolution could only express itself in new forms, in the accession to power of a new social stratum reflecting the new economic structure, itself imposed by the natural tendency toward ever more complete concentration.

The bureaucracy rapidly proceeded to the complete statification of production and to "planning." It initiated the systematic exploitation of both the economy and of the proletariat. In the process, it proved capable of developing Russian production to a considerable extent. This development was imposed upon it by the need to increase its own unproductive consumption and especially by the need to expand its military potential.

The clear significance for the proletariat of this type of "planning" appears when we look at the real wages of the Russian worker. As a result of the October Revolution, wages had increased 10 percent between 1913 and 1928. Later on they fell to half their prerevolutionary levels, and at present they are even lower. The aforementioned development of production indeed is being held back more and more by the contradictions of the bureaucratic regime and above all by the drop in labor productivity. This is the direct result of bureaucratic overexploitation [see the Postface].

As the bureaucracy consolidated its power in Russia, the parties of the Third International underwent a comparable evolution. They became completely detached from the working class and soon lost entirely their revolutionary character. Bearing down upon them were the dual pressures of decaying capitalist society and of the centralized apparatus of the Third International, which itself reflected the bureaucratization of Russian society. The International increasingly came under the control of the Russian bureaucracy.

The "Communist" parties gradually became completely transformed. They were becoming converted into instruments of the foreign policy of the Russian bureaucracy at the same time that they were beginning to serve, in their respective countries, the interests of those broad strata of the trade-union and political bureaucracies that were emerging from within the ranks of labor. It was the crisis and decay of bourgeois society that was forcing these strata to break with capitalism and with its traditional reformist representatives.

Together with an increasing number of technicians in the bourgeois countries, these strata began to see the bureaucratic capitalist regime that had come to power in Russia as the perfect expression of their own interests and aspirations. The high point of this development was reached at the end of World War II. Taking advantage of the conditions left by the war, of the collapse of entire sections of the bourgeoisie and of the military support of the Russian bureaucracy, Communist parties took over political power in a number of European countries and set up regimes based on the Russian model.

The ideology of Stalinism today binds the ruling strata of Russia and the satellite countries with the cadres of the "Communist" parties of other countries. Stalinism represents the point of intersection of three distinct trends: the structural evolution of world capitalism, the disintegration of traditional society and the degree of political maturity of the working class.

From the economic point of view, the Stalinist bureaucracy expresses the fact that it is becoming more and more difficult to continue to produce within the outdated framework of bourgeois property relations and that the exploitation of the proletariat can be organized to infinitely greater advantage within a "nationalized" or "planned" economy.

From the social point of view, Stalinism expresses the interests of new strata, born of the concentration of capital and labor and of the disintegration of traditional social formations.

In the production process, Stalinism tends to group around itself the technicians and the bureaucrats in the economic and the administrative fields, and those responsible for "managing" the labor force, namely, the "working class's" trade-union and political cadres. Outside the production process, Stalinism exerts an irresistible attraction on declassed and lumpenized petty bourgeois elements and on "radicalized" intellectuals. These elements can become a social class again only after the old regime is overthrown (since this old regime offered them no collective prospects) and after a new regime based on privilege is instituted.

Finally, from the point of view of the labor movement in the countries where they have not yet taken power, the Stalinist parties express that particular stage of development of class consciousness where the proletariat, having perfectly well understood the need to overthrow the capitalist system of exploitation, still is prepared to entrust this task to a Party it considers its "own." The Party is entrusted with the unchecked responsibility for leading the struggle against capitalism and administering the new society.

But the labor movement will not stop forever at this particular stage of its ideological development.

The fact that the Stalinist bureaucracy is an exploiting stratum is perceived, instinctively at first, and later on more and more consciously, by a growing number of advanced workers. Despite the quite understandable absence of precise information about what is going on in the Russian orbit, it is becoming clear to many workers that the striking silence of the masses in the East reflects the deep hatred the workers there have for their jailers. Stalinist demagogy will not be able to conceal forever the monstrous terror being exerted against the masses.

It is difficult to imagine that workers there have many illusions left about a regime that exploits them—or that they will have any illusions about any other system that does not specifically express their power. In the capitalist countries, likewise, workers who have for many years followed the Stalinist parties are beginning to see that the policies of these organizations simultaneously serve the interests of the Russian bureaucracy and the interests of the local Stalinist bureaucracy, but never their own interests as workers. In France and Italy in particular, this still-confused awareness of what has gone wrong manifests itself in a progressive disaffection of the workers toward "Communist" parties.

But something else is also clear. Despite the chronic and deepening crisis of capitalism, despite the threat of a war of unprecedented destruction, the workers are not prepared to reorganize themselves along conventional lines or to follow new parties, whichever ones they may be and whatever their program may be. We have here not only an understandable sense of distrust resulting from the negative conclusions drawn from all previous experiences. We also are witnessing a demonstration of unquestionable political maturity that marks a decisive turning point in its political and ideological development. Far more profoundly than in the past—and in light of the lessons it has learned from its past experience—the working class is beginning to raise the crucial problems of how it should organize and what its program should be. These are the problems of how to organize and how to exercise power on a proletarian basis.

Proletariat and Revolution

Both in its bourgeois and in its bureaucratic forms, capitalism has created the objective premises for the proletarian revolution on a world scale. It has accumulated wealth. It has developed the forces of production. It has rationalized and organized production up to the very limits permitted by its own regime of exploitation. It has created and developed the proletariat, whom it has taught how to handle both the means of production and weapons, while at the same time imbuing it with a hatred of misery and slavery.

But capitalism has exhausted its historical role. It can go no further. It has created an international, rationalized, and planned economic structure, thus making it possible for the economy to be directed consciously and for social life to develop freely. But capitalism is incapable of achieving for itself this conscious management of the economy, for it is a system based on exploitation, oppression, and the alienation of the vast majority of humankind.

The supplanting of the traditional bourgeoisie by the totalitarian "workers' bureaucracy" in no way resolves the contradictions of the modern world. The basis for the existence and power of the old bourgeoisie and of the new bureaucracy is to be found in the total degradation and brutalization of man. Bourgeois and bureaucrats can develop the forces of production and increase or just maintain their profits and their power only by increasing their exploitation of the masses to an ever greater extent. For the working class, the accumulation of wealth and the rationalization of production simply mean the accumulation of misery and the rationalization of exploitation.

Both capitalists and bureaucrats try to convert the producer into a mere cog of their machinery. But in so doing they kill in him what they need most, productivity and creative ability. The rationalization and accentuation of exploitation bring in their wake a terrible decline in labor productivity, as may be seen especially in Russia. The waste that used to occur as a result of competition between enterprises now is produced on an infinitely vaster scale as a result of struggle on the international level. And further wastefulness occurs with each new periodic massive destruction of the productive forces, which now is taking on unprecedented proportions.

Should a Third World War lead to the unification of the world system of exploitation, the civilization and social life of humanity would be threatened with total collapse. The unlimited totalitarian domination of a single group of exploiters (whether Yankee monopolists or Russian bureaucrats) would give them free rein to plunder the earth. The fall in the productivity of labor under such a regime of ever-increasing exploitation and the complete transformation of its dominant stratum into a parasitic caste no longer having any need to develop the forces of production would lead to a massive regression in social conditions and to a prolonged setback in the development of human consciousness.

But the proletariat can still rise up and challenge capitalist and bureaucratic barbarism. Over a period of a century of capitalist development, the workers have seen their specific weight in society constantly increase. Problems are now posed in the clearest and most objective terms before the working class. This clarification of ideas demands not only a complete rejection of all regimes of exploitation, whether bourgeois or bureaucratic, but also an awareness of what methods of struggle are needed and of the objectives of working-class power. This awareness will become complete and definitive as we approach this terrifying war.

The *apparent* result of a century of workers' struggle can be summarized as follows: The working class has struggled, but it has only succeeded in placing in power a bureaucracy that exploits it as much or more than the bourgeoisie did. The *profound* result of these struggles, however, is to be found in the process of clarification that will be their consequence.

It now is objectively apparent to the workers in a material and palpable way that the goal of the socialist revolution cannot simply be the abolition of private property. This objective can be achieved by the monopolies and the bureaucracy themselves with no other result than an improvement in its methods of exploitation. The goal of the socialist revolution must be the abolition of all fixed and stable distinctions between directors and executants, in relation to both production and social life in general.

In the political sphere, the objective of the proletarian revolution can only be the destruction of the capitalist or bureaucratic State and its replacement by the power of the armed masses. Already this is no longer a State in the usual sense of the word (i.e., the State as organized coercion), and as such it will immediately begin to wither away. Likewise, the objective of the revolution in the economic sphere cannot be simply to remove the management of production from the hands of the capitalists in order to place it in those of the bureaucrats. It must organize management on a collective basis as a matter of vital concern to the entire working class. By moving in this direction, the distinction between managerial personnel and executants in the production process should start to wither away beginning on the very morrow of the revolution.

Only the proletariat, acting as a whole, can achieve the aims of the proletarian revolution. No one else can do the job for it. The working class cannot and should not entrust anyone with this task, and especially not its own "cadres." It cannot drop its own initiative and abdicate its responsibility for instaurating and managing the new society by passing the task on to anybody else. If the proletariat does not itself as a whole assume at every moment the initiative and the leadership of every aspect of social life, both during and more especially after the revolution, it will only have succeeded in changing masters. The system of exploitation will reappear, perhaps under different forms, but fundamentally with the same content.

We must now give concrete form to this general idea by providing more precise details about and by modifying the program for revolutionary power, i.e., the political and economic system implied by the dictatorship of the proletariat. Similar changes are necessary in relation to the working-class problems of how to organize and struggle under the capitalist system.

The program of the proletarian revolution cannot remain what it was before the experience of the Russian Revolution. It must take this experience into account. It must also take into account the changes that have occurred in Eastern Europe and in the other countries that entered the Russian zone of influence after World War II. It can no longer be held that the expropriation of private capitalists is equivalent to socialism—or that it is sufficient to statify and "nationalize" the economy to render exploitation impossible.

We have now clearly established that even after the expropriation of the capitalists, the development of a new exploiting stratum is quite possible—that it is, moreover, inevitable if the expropriation of the capitalists is not accompanied by the direct takeover and management of industry by the working class itself. We also have seen that statification and nationalizations, whether undertaken by the Stalinist bureaucracy (as in Russia and in the Russian zone of influence), by the Labour party bureaucracy (as in Britain), or by the capitalists themselves (as in France), far from eliminating or lessening the exploitation of the working class, only serve to unify, coordinate, rationalize, and intensify this exploitation. We also have established that economic "planning" is but a means to an end, that in and of itself it has nothing fundamentally progressive to offer the working class and that if it is carried out while the proletariat is economically and politically dispossessed of power it can only amount to the planning of exploitation itself. Finally, we have seen that neither land reform nor the "collectivization" of agriculture is incompatible with a modern, rationalized, and highly scientific exploitation of the peasantry.

We must conclude then that the expropriation of private capitalists (as expressed in statification or nationalization) is but the negative half of the proletarian revolution. Such measures can have a progressive content only if they are linked with the positive half of the program: the management of the economy by the workers. This means that the management of the economy, whether at the center or on the factory level, cannot be entrusted to a stratum of specialists, technicians, "capable people," or bureaucrats of whatever ilk.

Management must be carried out by the workers themselves. The dictatorship of the proletariat cannot be merely a political dictatorship. Above all, it

104 □ SOCIALISM OR BARBARISM

must be an economic dictatorship of the proletariat. Otherwise it will serve only as a front for the dictatorship of the bureaucracy.

Many Marxists, and Trotsky in particular, already have shown that unlike the bourgeois revolution, the proletarian revolution cannot confine itself to eliminating obstacles left over from the previous mode of production. For the success of the bourgeois revolution it was necessary—and sufficient—that the obstacles left over from the feudal regime be abolished (obstacles such as feudal corporations and monopolies, the feudal ownership of land, etc.). From that point on, capitalism built itself up and developed all by itself through the automatic process of industrial expansion. The abolition of bourgeois property, on the other hand, is the necessary—but not the sufficient—condition for the building and development of a socialist economy. After the abolition of bourgeois property, socialism can be built only in a *conscious* manner, that is to say, through the conscious actions of the masses, constantly resisting the natural tendency of the economy bequeathed by capitalism to revert to a regime of exploitation.

But there is a second and even more important distinction between the proletarian revolution and all previous ones. For the first time in history, the class taking power cannot exert this power through "delegation," it cannot entrust its power for any lengthy and enduring period of time to its representatives, to its "State," or to its "Party." The socialist economy is built up through constant, conscious action. The question is, who is this consciousness? Both historical experience as well as an analysis of the conditions for the existence of the working class and of the postrevolutionary regime point to the conclusion that this "consciousness" can only be that of the class as a whole. "Only the masses," said Lenin, "can really plan, for they alone are everywhere at once."

To avoid failure, the proletarian revolution cannot be confined to nationalizing the economy and entrusting its management to "competent people" or even to a "revolutionary Party," even if these measures contain some more or less vague idea of "workers' control." The revolution must entrust the management of the factories and the overall coordination of production to the workers themselves, to responsible workers who are checked on continually and who can always be recalled.

In politics, likewise, the dictatorship of the proletariat cannot mean the dictatorship of a single party, however proletarian and however revolutionary. The dictatorship of the proletariat means democracy for the proletariat. Every right must be granted to the workers and above all the right to form political organizations having their own specific viewpoints. It is inevitable that the representatives of the majority fraction in the mass organizations will be called upon more frequently than others to positions of responsibility. The essential thing, however, is that the entire working population should be able to monitor them constantly, to recall them, to withdraw its support from the fraction that till then was in the majority, should it so wish, and give it to another. Under these circumstances, the distinction and opposition between political organizations proper (parties) and mass organizations (soviets and factory committees) will quickly lose its significance. The perpetuation of this opposition could only be the harbinger of a degeneration of the revolution.

Right now we can only begin to trace the main lines of orientation that the working class's previous experience sets down for all future revolutions. The concrete forms of organization the working class will adopt can only be defined by the class itself. The question, for instance, of what kind of economic centralization should be combined with a certain necessary amount of decentralization can only be decided by the class itself as it comes to grips with these problems in the course of its struggle.

The problems of how the proletariat should organize and struggle within the framework of capitalism should be considered in much the same light. The conclusion that it is useless or harmful to organize the vanguard politically before the revolution begins does not follow, either from the fact that the class as a whole has to go through the experiences that will raise its consciousness and lead it to revolution or from the fact that workers' organizations have served till now as fertile breeding grounds for the bureaucracy.

It is historically indispensable to organize the advanced section of the class politically. This is based on the need to maintain and to propagate among the workers a clear understanding of the development of society and of the fundamental objectives of proletarian struggle. This must be done both through and in spite of temporary fluctuations of the working class's level of consciousness and amid local, national, and craft differences.

The organized vanguard will consider its first task to be the defense of working-class conditions and interests. It will constantly strive, however, to heighten the workers' struggles, and ultimately it will come to represent the interests of the movement as a whole during each stage of struggle.

Moreover, the objective existence of the bureaucracy as an exploiting stratum makes it obvious that the vanguard can only organize itself on the basis of an antibureaucratic ideology, on the basis of a program directed mainly against bureaucracy and its roots, and by constantly struggling against all forms of mystification and exploitation.

But from this point of view, the essential thing for a political vanguard organization to do, once it has become aware of the need to abolish the distinction in society between directors and executants, is to seek from the outset to abolish this distinction within its own ranks. This is not just a simple question of better by-laws, but involves above all raising the consciousness and developing the talents of its militants through their ongoing and permanent theoretical and practical education along these lines.

Such an organization can grow only by preparing to link up with the process by which autonomous mass organs are created. In this very limited sense, it might be correct to say that the organization represents the ideological and political leadership of the working class under the conditions extant in the present exploiting society. It is essential to add, however, that it is a "leadership" that is constantly preparing its own dissolution through its fusion with the working class's autonomous organs. This will happen as soon as the class as a whole enters the revolutionary struggle and ushers onto the historical stage the real "leadership" of humanity, which is none other than the proletarian masses themselves as a whole.

Only one force can arise today to challenge the continuing decay and increasing barbarism of all regimes based upon exploitation: that of the producing class, the socialist proletariat. Constantly increasing in numbers through the industrialization of the world economy, ever more concentrated in the process of production, trained through misery and oppression to revolt against the ruling classes, having had the chance to experience the results of its own "leadership," the working class, despite an increasing number of difficulties and obstacles, has ripened for revolution. The obstacles confronting it are not insurmountable. The whole history of the past century is there to prove that the proletariat represents, for the first time in human history, not only a class in revolt against exploitation but a class positively capable of overthrowing the exploiters and of organizing a free and humane society. Its victory, and the fate of humanity, are in its hands.

Postface

As we have already said in the "General Introduction," numerous ideas contained in this text as well as in others from the same period are clearly, as a legacy of traditional Marxism, erroneous and were to be revised later on. I will limit myself here to pointing out the principal ones and to referring to the subsequent texts where they have been criticized.

On the "deterioration of the working class's standard of living," see *MRCM I*, pp. 61-64, 70-75 [T/E: now reprinted in *CMR 2*, pp. 62-69, 77-92; see "Modern Capitalism and Revolution," volume 2 (*PSW 2*) of the present edition, points 3-9 in the first numbered section, which is entitled "A Few Important Traits of Contemporary Capitalism"] and *RR*, pp. 11-12, 31-32 [T/E: now reprinted in *EMO 2*, pp. 324-25, 357-58; points 11 and 34 of the Solidarity translation (see Appendix C; *RR* is to be included in *PSW 3*)].

On the "threat to elementary rights," see *CS II*, pp. 54-68 [T/E: now reprinted in *CS*, pp. 187-209; *CS II* appears in *PSW 2* (see the sections beginning with "The Councils: Universal Form of Organization for Social Activities" and ending with "The 'State,' 'Parties,' and 'Politics' ")], *MRCM II*, pp. 94-98 [T/E: now reprinted in *CMR 2*, pp. 120-25; see *MCR* in *PSW 2* (with the exception of the last four paragraphs, the page numbers Castoriadis cites here refer to the fourth numbered section, which is entitled "Capitalist Politics, Yesterday and Today")] and *RR*, pp. 15-17 [T/E: now reprinted in *EMO 2*, pp. 331-33; point 17 in the Solidarity translation; to be included in *PSW 3*].

On the "permanent crisis of capitalism," see *MRCM I*, pp. 59-62, 72-78 [T/E: now reprinted in *CMR 2*, pp. 59-67, 88-97; see *MCR* in *PSW 2*, points 1-4 in the first numbered section, which is entitled "A Few Important Traits of Contemporary Capitalism" and pp. 249-54], *RR*, p. 12 [T/E: now reprinted in *EMO 2*, p. 325; point 12 of the Solidarity translation; to be included in *PSW 3*], and *MTR/MRT III*, pp. 61-74 [T/E: now reprinted in *IIS*, pp. 103-17; see the sections entitled "Praxis and Project" and "The Social Roots of the Revolutionary Project" in Chapter 2 of the English translation of *IIS*].

On the prospect for a third world war, see *SIPP* and the texts that will be published in volume III, 1 [T/E: Castoriadis is referring to *CMR 1*].

On the "corruption of the labor aristocracy," see the interpretation of reformism in *PO I* and *RIB/RBI*.

On "workers' control," see *CS II* and *RIB/RBI*.

On the evolution of wages in Russia, see "La Russie après l'industrialisation," which will be published in *SB 3* of the present series. [T/E: Neither this text nor the volume it was to be contained in has ever been published.]

6
The Relations of Production in Russia

The question of the class nature of economic and hence social relations in Russia has a political importance that cannot be exaggerated. The great mystification that prevails around the allegedly "socialist" character of the Russian economy is one of the principal obstacles to the proletariat's ideological emancipation, an emancipation that is the fundamental condition for the struggle toward its social emancipation. Militants who are beginning to become aware of the counterrevolutionary character of the policies of these Communist parties in bourgeois countries are slowed down in their political development by their illusions about Russia. The policy of these Communist parties appears to them to be oriented toward the defense of Russia—which unquestionably is true—therefore as being already decided upon and, in a word, agreed to in terms of Russia's defense requirements. Even for the most highly conscious among them, the case of Stalinism always boils down to that of Russia, and in judging the latter, even if they accept a host of individual criticisms, the minds of the great majority of these militants remain clouded by the idea that the Russian economy is something essentially different than an economy of exploitation, that even if it does not represent socialism, in comparison with capitalism at least, it is progressive.

We also should point out that everything in present-day society seems to conspire to maintain them in this grand illusion. It is instructive to see the representatives of Stalinism and those of "Western" capitalism—who disagree on all other questions, who are capable even of disagreeing on whether two plus two equals four—concurring with astonishing unanimity that Russia has realized "socialism." Obviously, in their respective techniques of mystification, this axiom plays different roles: For the Stalinists, identifying Russia with socialism

Originally published as "Les Relations de production en Russie," *S. ou B.*, 2 (May 1949). Reprinted in *SB 1*, pp. 205-81, with Postface, pp. 282-83.

serves to prove the preeminence of the Russian regime, whereas for the capitalists it demonstrates the execrable character of socialism. For the Stalinists, a "socialist" label serves to camouflage and to justify the bureaucracy's abominable exploitation of the Russian proletariat, an exploitation that bourgeois ideologues, mellowed by a sudden attack of philanthropy, highlight in order to discredit the idea of socialism and of revolution. Now, without this identification, their respective tasks would be much more difficult. Nevertheless, in this work of mystification, Stalinists as well as the bourgeoisie have been aided by the Marxist or allegedly Marxist currents and ideologues who have defended and helped popularize the mythology of the "socialist bases of the Russian economy."[1] This has been done for twenty years with the aid of apparently scientific arguments that boil down essentially to two ideas:

1. Whatever is not "socialist" in the Russia economy is—in whole or in part—the process of income distribution. By way of compensation, production (as the foundation of the economy and of society) is socialist. That this distribution process is not socialist is after all normal, since in the "lower phase of communism," bourgeois right still prevails.

2. The socialist—or in any case, as Trotsky would say, "transitional"—character of production (and consequently the socialist character of the economy and the proletarian character of the State as a whole) is expressed in the State ownership of the means of production, in planning, and in the monopoly over foreign trade.

One can only be astonished when one discovers that all the empty talk of the defenders of the Russian regime reduces in the end to ideas so superficial and so foreign to Marxism, to socialism, and even to scientific analysis in general. By radically separating the realm of the production of wealth from that of its distribution, by trying to subject the latter to criticism and by trying to modify it while keeping the former intact, one descends to a level of imbecility worthy of Proudhon and Herr Eugen Dühring.[2] Likewise, to tacitly identify ownership and production, to willfully confound State ownership as such with the "socialist" character of the relations of production is merely an elaborate form of sociological cretinism.[3] This highly foreign phenomenon can only be accounted for in terms of the enormous social pressure exerted by the Stalinist bureaucracy during this whole period and to the present day. The force of these arguments lies not in their scientific value, which is nil, but in the fact that behind them is to be found the powerful social current of the worldwide Stalinist bureaucracy. In truth, these ideas hardly merit a separate refutation. An analysis of the bureaucratic economy as a whole ought to show their profoundly false character and their mystificatory signification. If, nonetheless, we examine them in themselves by way of an introduction, it is, on the one hand, because they have taken on at the present time the force of prejudices that must be uprooted before we can grapple with the real problem in a useful manner and, on the other hand, because we have wanted to profit from this examination in order to get to the bottom of certain important notions such as those of distribution, ownership, and the exact signification of the relations of production.

Production—Distribution and Ownership

Production and Distribution

Both under their vulgar form ("There are in Russia some abuses and some privileges, but on the whole it's socialism") and under their "scientific"[4] form, arguments that attempt to separate and oppose the relations of production and the relations of distribution revert to the days even before the creation of classical bourgeois economics.

The economic process forms a whole whose phases cannot be artificially separated, either in reality or in theory. Production, distribution, exchange, and consumption are integral and inseparable parts of a single process; they are moments that are mutually implied in the production and reproduction of capital. Thus, if production, in the narrow sense of the term, is the center of the economic process, it should not be forgotten that in capitalist production exchange is an integral part of the productive relation—on the one hand, because this relation is in the first place the buying and selling of labor power and because it involves the capitalist's purchase of the necessary means of production, and on the other hand because the laws of capitalist production take effect as coercive laws through the intermediaries of the market, competition, circulation—in a word, through exchange.[5] Thus, consumption itself either is an integral part of production (productive consumption) or it is, in the case of consumption that is called "unproductive," a prerequisite for all production, the inverse being equally true.[6] Thus in the end, distribution is only the reverse side of the production process, one of its subjective sides and in any case a direct resultant of the latter.

Here a longer explanation is indispensable. "Distribution" has two significations. In its current meaning, distribution is the distribution of the social product. Marx says of the latter that its forms are moments of production itself.

> If labor were not specified as wage labor, then the manner in which it shares in the [distribution of the] products [*participe à la répartition des produits*] would not appear as wages; as, for example, under slavery. . . . The relations and modes of distribution thus appear merely as the obverse of the agents of production. An individual who participates in production in the form of wage labor shares in the [distribution of the] products, in the results of production, in the form of wages. The structure of distribution is completely determined by the structure of production. Distribution is itself a product of production, not only in its object, in that only the results of production can be distributed, but also in its form, in that the specific kind of distribution in production determines the specific forms of distribution, i.e. the pattern of participation in distribution. . . .

Thus, economists such as Ricardo, who are the most frequently accused of focusing on production alone, have defined distribution as the exclusive object of economics, because they instinctively conceived the forms of distribution as the most specific expression into which the agents of production of a given society are cast.[7]

Distribution has another meaning. It is the distribution of the conditions of production.

In the shallowest conception, distribution appears as the distribution of products, and hence as further removed from and quasi-independent of production. But before distribution can be the distribution of products, it is: (1) the distribution of the instruments of production, and (2), which is a further specification of the same relation, the distribution of the members of the society among the different kinds of production. (Subsumption of the individuals under specific relations of production.) The distribution of products is evidently only a result of this distribution, which is comprised within the process of production itself and determines the structure of production. To examine production while disregarding this internal distribution within it is obviously only an empty abstraction; while conversely, the distribution of products follows by itself from this distribution which forms an original moment of production. Ricardo, whose concern was to grasp the specific social structure of modern production, and who is the economist of production *par excellence*, declares for precisely that reason that *not* production but distribution is the proper study of modern economics. This again shows the ineptitude of those economists who portray production as an eternal truth while banishing history to the realm of distribution.

The question of the relation between this production-determining distribution, and production, belongs evidently within production itself. If it is said that, since production must begin with a certain distribution of the instruments of production, it follows that distribution at least in this sense precedes and forms the presupposition of production, then the reply must be that production does indeed have its determinants and preconditions, which form its moments. At the very beginning these may appear as spontaneous, natural. But by the process of production itself they are transformed from natural into historical determinants, and if they appear to one epoch as natural presuppositions of production, they were its historic product for another. Within production itself they are constantly being changed. The application of machinery, for example, changed the distribution of instruments of production as well as of products. Modern large-scale landed property is itself the product of modern commerce and of modern industry, as well as the application of the latter to agriculture.[8]

Nevertheless, these two meanings of the word "distribution" are intimately connected with each other and obviously also with the mode of production. Capitalist distribution of the social product, which is derived from the mode of production, only serves to consolidate, enlarge, and develop the capitalist mode of distributing the conditions of production. It is the distribution of the net product among wages and surplus value that forms the basis of capitalist accumulation, which constantly reproduces at a higher and further developed stage the capitalist distribution of the conditions of production and this mode of production itself. This connection could not, at the same time, be better summed up and generalized than by Marx himself.

> The conclusion we reach is not that production, distribution, exchange and consumption are identical, but that they all form the members of a totality, distinctions within a unity. Production predominates not only over itself, in the antithetical definition of production, but over the other moments as well. The process always returns to production to begin anew. That exchange and consumption cannot be predominant is self-evident. Likewise, distribution as distribution of products; while as distribution of agents of production it is itself a moment of production. A definite production thus determines a definite consumption, distribution and exchange as well as *definite relations between these different moments*. Admittedly, however, *in its one-sided form*, production is itself determined by the other moments. For example if the market, i.e. the sphere of exchange, expands, then production grows in quantity and the divisions between its different branches become deeper. A change in distribution changes production, e.g. concentration of capital, different distribution of the population between town and country, etc. Finally, the needs of consumption determine production. Mutual interaction takes place between the different moments. This is the case with every organic whole.[9]

Consequently, when Trotsky—to say nothing of his epigones—speaks of the "bourgeois" character of distribution of the social product in Russia by contrasting it with the "socialist" character of the productive relations or of state property (!), it is just a silly little joke: The mode of distributing the social product is inseparable from the mode of production. As Marx says, it is only its reverse side: "The organization of distribution is determined entirely by the organization of production." If it is true that "an individual, who participates in production in the form of wage labor, shares in the products, in the results of production in the form of wages," it must be true conversely as well that an individual who shares in the products in the form of wages *participates in production in the form of wage labor*. And wage labor implies capital.[10] To imagine that a mode of bourgeois distribution can be grafted onto socialist relations of production is no less absurd than to imagine a feudal mode of distribution being grafted onto bourgeois relations of production (not *next* to, but *onto* these relations and *resulting* from these relations). As this example shows, this is not just an "error," it is an absurd notion, as devoid of scientific meaning as "horse-drawn airplane," for example, or "mammalian theorem."

Neither the distribution of the conditions of production nor the mode of production can be in contradiction with the distribution of the social product. If the latter has a character opposed to the first two, which are its conditions, it would burst apart immediately—as every attempt to instaurate a "socialist" method of distribution upon the basis of capitalist relations of production would immediately and unerringly burst apart.

If, therefore, the relations of distribution in Russia are not socialist, the relations of production cannot be either. This is so precisely because distribution is not autonomous but rather subordinated to production. Trotsky's epigones, in their desperate efforts to conceal the absurdity of their position, often have distorted this idea in the following manner: To try to draw conclusions about the Russian regime on the basis of the relations of distribution means to replace the analysis of the mode of production with an analysis of the mode of distribution. This deplorable sophism is worth as much as this other one: To look at one's watch to see if it is noon means to believe that its hands show the sun at its zenith. It is easy to understand that precisely because the relations of distribution are determined unambiguously by the relations of production, a society's relations of production can be defined unmistakably as long as the prevailing mode of distribution is known. Just as one can follow unerringly the sailing of a ship as long as one keeps an eye on the masts, so too can one deduce the fundamental (but supposedly unknown) structure of a regime from its mode of distributing the social product.

But here one very often hears talk of how "bourgeois right must continue to exist in the lower phase of communism" as far as distribution is concerned. This question will be treated later to the extent necessary. Nevertheless, let us say right away that no one before Trotsky had imagined that the expression "bourgeois right," employed metaphorically by Marx, could signify that the social product would be distributed according to capitalist economic laws. By the "survival of bourgeois right," Marx and the Marxists always understood the temporary survival of an inequality, not at all the maintenance and exacerbation of labor *exploitation*.

To these sophisms concerning distribution is tied another of Trotsky's ideas,[11] according to which the Russian bureaucracy has its roots not in the relations of production but solely in distribution. Although this idea will be discussed in depth when we deal with the class nature of the bureaucracy, it is necessary to say a few words right away on account of its connection with the preceding discussion. This idea could avoid appearing absurd to the extent that the Russian bureaucracy was thought to have the same amount of economic significance (or rather the same level of insignificance) as the bureaucracy of bourgeois States in the mid-nineteenth-century liberal era. At that time, it was a body that played a limited role in economic life, that could be characterized as parasitic for the same reason that prostitutes or the clergy would be; it was a body whose revenues came from levies on the income of classes that had their roots in production—the bourgeoisie, landowners, or the proletariat; it was a body that had nothing to do with production. But obviously, such a conception is no longer appropriate for the present-day capitalist bureaucracy, the State having become decades ago a vital instrument in the class-based economy and now playing an indispensable role in the coordination of production. If the present-day bureaucracy of the minister of the national economy in France is parasitic, it is so for the same reason and in the same sense as the bureaucracy of the Bank of France, of the national railroad, or of a trust is parasitic: I.e., this bureaucracy is indispensable within the framework of present-day capitalist economic relations. Obviously, any attempt to compare the Russian bureaucracy, which directs Russian production from beginning to end, to some honorable functionaries from the Victorian era can only provoke laughter, no matter how you look at it, but especially when viewed from the standpoint of their economic role. Trotsky himself refutes what he says elsewhere when he writes that "the bureaucracy has become an uncontrolled force dominating the masses,"[12] that it is "lord . . . of society,"[13] that

> the very fact of its appropriation of political power in a country
> where the principal means of production are in the hands of the
> State, creates a new and hitherto unknown relation between the
> bureaucracy and the riches of the nation. The means of production
> belong to the State. But the State, so to speak, "belongs" to the
> bureaucracy.[14]

How else could one group play a dominant role in the distribution of the social product, decide in absolute mastery how the net product, in part accumulable, in part consumable, is to be distributed, and regulate the division of the consumable portion between workers' wages and bureaucratic income if it did not predominate over the whole breadth of production itself? To distribute the product among an accumulable portion and a consumable portion means before all else to earmark [orienter] some specified portion of production for the production of the means of production and some other specified portion for the production of consumer objects; to divide consumable income into workers' wages and bureaucratic income means to earmark a portion of the production of consumer objects for the production of objects of mass consumption and another portion for the production of high-quality or luxury items. The idea that one can predominate over distribution without predominating over production is pure childishness. And how would one predominate over production if one did not predominate over the material as well as the personal conditions of production, if one did not have at one's disposal both capital and labor, the capital goods as well as the consumption fund of society?

Production and Ownership

In the "Marxist" literature concerning Russia, one encounters a double confusion. In general, forms of ownership [propriété] are identified with the relations of production. In particular, state or "nationalized" property [propriété] is thought to automatically confer a "socialist" character upon production. We need to briefly analyze these two aspects of the problem.

1. Already in Marx the obvious distinction between the "forms of ownership" and the relations of production is clearly established. Here is how he expressed himself on this subject in his famous preface to the *Critique of Political Economy*.

In the social production of their life, men enter into definite relations that are indispensable and independent of their will. . . . The sum total of these relations of production constitutes the *economic structure of society, the real foundation*, on which rises a *legal and political superstructure*. . . . At a certain stage of their development, the material productive forces of society come into conflict with the existing relations of production, or—*what is but a legal expression for the same thing*—with the property relations within which they have been at work hitherto. . . . In considering such transformations, a distinction should always be made between the material transformation of the economic conditions of production, which can be determined with the precision of natural science, and the legal, political, religious, aesthetic or philosophic—in short, *ideological* forms.[15]

The lesson of this text is clear. The relations of production are concrete social relations, relations of man with man and of class with class, as they are realized in the constant, daily production and reproduction of material life. Such is the relation between master and slave, between lord and serf. Such also is the relation between boss and worker as it is shaped in the course of capitalist production, whose immediate empirical form is the exchange of the worker's labor power for the wage paid by the capitalist, itself based upon the presupposition that the employer possesses his capital (both under its material form as well as under the form of money) and the worker possesses his labor power. In a "civilized" society, the law gives an abstract form, a juridical form to this productive relation.

In our example concerning capitalist society, the juridical form is expressed as follows. As far as the presuppositions of the productive relation are concerned, ownership of the means of production and of money is granted to the capitalist and the free disposition of his labor power is granted to the worker (i.e., slavery and serfage are abolished). As far as juridical relations themselves are concerned, they take the form of the labor-hiring contract. Ownership of capital, free disposition of the worker's own labor power, and the labor-hiring contract are the juridical form of the economic relations of capitalism.

This juridical expression covers not only the relations of production in the narrow sense of this term but also economic activity as a whole. Production, distribution, exchange, disposition of the conditions of production, appropriation of the product, and even consumption find themselves placed under the form of ownership and of bourgeois contractual law. We therefore have, on the one hand, economic reality, the relations of production, distribution, exchange, etc., and, on the other hand, the juridical form that expresses this reality in an abstract manner. Production is to ownership as economics is to law, as the actual base is to the superstructure, as reality is to ideology [see (a) in the Postface]. Forms of ownership belong to the juridical superstructure, or as Marx said, to the "ideological forms."

2. But what exactly is the function of this juridical expression? Can it be supposed that we have here a true mirror of economic realities? Only a vulgar lib-

eral, as Lenin would say—and as he actually said in a quite similar case[16]—or a hopeless mechanist could accept that they were identical. We cannot enter into an analysis here of the relations between the economic base and the juridical, political, and, in general, ideological superstructure of a society. But as concerns law itself, a few explanations are indispensable. Marx and Engels were fully aware of the distortion that economic reality undergoes when it is expressed in juridical terms. In his evaluation of Proudhon, Marx insisted that it is impossible to respond to the question "What is property?" without an analysis of the real, overall economic relations of bourgeois society.[17] Here, on the other hand, is how Engels expressed himself on this subject.

> In a modern state, law must not only correspond to the general economic condition and be its expression, but must also be an *internally coherent* expression which does not, owing to inner contradictions, reduce itself to nought. And in order to achieve this, *the faithful reflection of economic conditions suffers increasingly.*[18]

But the reason that Engels provides in order to express the more and more noticeable clash between economic reality and its juridical forms, however valuable it may be, is neither the sole nor the most important reason. The root of this problem is to be sought in what can be called the double function of law and of every superstructure. Law, like every ideological form in an exploitative society, simultaneously plays the role of the adequate form of reality as well as its mystified form. Although it is the adequate form of reality for the dominant class, for whom it expresses its historical and social interests, it is only an instrument for mystifying the rest of society. It is important to note that the flowering of these two functions of law is the fruit of just one historical development. We can say that, initially, the essential function of law was to express economic reality, as was done in the first civilized societies with a brutal frankness. The Romans did not bother to declare through the mouths of their jurists that their slaves were for them "things" and not persons. But the more the economy developed and civilization got the entire society to take an active part in social life, the more the essential function of law became not to reflect but precisely to mask economic and social reality. Let us recall the hypocrisy of bourgeois constitutions compared to the sincerity of Louis XIV proclaiming, "I am the State." Let us recall also the overt form that surplus labor had in the feudal economy (where the amount of labor the serf devoted to himself and that which he gave to his lord were two distinct matters) and the veiled form of surplus labor in capitalist production. Contemporary history offers us examples every day not only of the reality but also of the effectiveness of this camouflage; Stalinism and nazism especially are proven masters of the art of mystifying the masses both through their propagandistic slogans as well as through their legal formulas.[19]

The instance where this double function of law most easily can be detected is the domain of political law, especially constitutional law. It is well known that all modern bourgeois constitutions are based upon the "sovereignty of the people," "civil equality," etc. Both Marx and Lenin have shown too often and too fully what this signifies for us to return to it here.[20]

Nevertheless, a point present-day "Marxists" forget too easily is that Marx's analysis of the capitalist economy is based upon a similar unveiling of the mystificatory character of bourgeois civil law. Marx never would have gotten at the economic substance of capitalism if he had not cracked the forms of the bourgeois legal code. Neither "capital" nor the "proletarian" have any signification or any existence for the bourgeois jurist; there is not a single individual in capitalist society of whom it can be said juridically that he possesses only his labor power. And Marx is not simply being ironic when he remarks that by giving to the worker merely the price of his labor power and by appropriating the entire product of labor—whose value far exceeds the value of this labor power itself— the capitalist gives to the worker that which is due to him and does not steal a penny.[21] Exploitation in capitalist society will certainly remain unknown to those who limit themselves to contemplating the forms of bourgeois property ownership.

3. All these statements can be boiled down to the idea stated earlier, according to which law is the abstract expression of social reality. It is its expression— which signifies that, even under its most mystificatory forms, it preserves a connection with reality, at least in the sense that it must make possible the operation of society in the interests of the ruling class. But, inasmuch as it is its abstract expression, it is inevitably a false expression, for on the social plane every abstraction that is not known as an abstraction is a mystification.[22]

Marxism was, rightly, considered as the demolisher of abstraction in the domain of the social sciences. In this sense, its critique of juridical and economic mystifications has always been particularly violent. Thus, it is all the more astonishing that the tendency represented by Trotsky has defended for many years a particularly elaborate form of abstract juridicism in its analysis of the Russian economy. This retreat from the model of concrete economic analysis proposed by Marx and toward a formalism fascinated with "State ownership" has objectively aided the mystificatory work of the Stalinist bureaucracy and has merely given expression, on the theoretical plane, to the real crisis from which the revolutionary movement still has not extricated itself.

4. We must now give concrete form to these thoughts in the case of total statification of production.

Marx already has said that just as a man is not to be judged by what he thinks of himself, so a society is not to be judged by what it says about itself in its constitution and its laws. But this comparison can be extended still further. Just as, once one is acquainted with a man, the idea he has of himself is one essential element of his psychology that must be analyzed and connected to the rest in order to increase one's understanding of him, so also, once the actual state of a society has been analyzed, the image this society gives itself in its laws, etc., becomes an important element in achieving a more fully developed understanding of it. To use more precise language, if we have said that law is both an adequate form and a mystified form of economic reality, we must examine its two functions in the case of Russia and see how universal State ownership serves as a mask for the real relations of production as well as a convenient framework for the operation of these relations. This analysis will be taken up again at several different points, and it is really only this essay as a whole that will provide an answer to this question. But a few of the essential road markers should be set down at this time.

Until 1930, no one, in the Marxist movement at least, had ever thought that State ownership formed, as such, a basis for socialist relations of production or even was tending to become so. No one had ever thought that the "nationalization" of the means of production was equivalent to the abolition of exploitation. On the contrary, the emphasis had always been that

> neither the conversion into joint-stock companies, nor into state property deprives the productive forces of their character as capital. . . . The modern state, whatever its form, is an essentially capitalist machine; it is the state of the capitalists, the ideal collective body of all capitalists.[23]

The texts where Lenin explains that monopoly capitalism already was transformed into State capitalism during the First World War can be counted by the dozens.[24] If there is something in these formulations of Lenin's that can be reproached, it would be rather their overestimation of how fast the process of concentrating the means of production in the hands of the State would take place. For Trotsky, in 1936, State capitalism was an ideal tendency that never could be realized in capitalist society.[25] For Lenin, in 1917, it was already the reality of capitalism in his epoch.[26] Lenin certainly was mistaken about his own epoch, but these citations suffice to put an end to the stupid stories of Trotsky's epigones according to which it was a heresy from the Marxist point of view to believe in the possibility of a statification of production beyond the confines of socialism. In any case, this heresy was canonized by the First Congress of the Communist International, which proclaimed in its "Manifesto":

> The statification of economic life . . . has become an accomplished fact. There is no turning back from this fact—it is impossible to return not only to free competition, but even to the domination of trusts, syndicates, and other economic octopuses. Today the one and only issue is: Who shall henceforth be the bearer of statified production—the imperialist state or the state of the victorious proletariat?[27]

But what throws the clearest light on the question are the comparisons Lenin drew, from 1917 to 1921, between Germany, a State capitalist country according to him, and Soviet Russia, which had nationalized the principal means of production. Here is a characteristic passage.

> To make things even clearer, let us first take the most concrete example of State capitalism. Everybody knows what this example is. It is Germany. Here we have "the last word" in modern large-scale capitalist engineering and planned organization, *subordinated to Junker-bourgeois imperialism.* Cross out the words in italics, and in place of the militarist, Junker, bourgeois, imperialist *State* put *also a State*, but of a different social type, of a different class content—a

Soviet State, that is, a proletarian State, and you will have the *sum total* of the conditions necessary for socialism. . . .

At the same time socialism is inconceivable unless the proletariat is the ruler of the state. This also is A B C. And history took such an original course that it "brought forth" in 1918 two unconnected halves of socialism existing side by side like two future chickens in the single shell of international imperialism. In 1918 Germany and Russia were the embodiment of the most striking material realization of the economic, the productive, the social-economic conditions of socialism, on the one hand, and the political conditions, on the other.[28]

It becomes obvious to the reader of these texts, concerning which the Trotskyist tendency retains a curious silence, that for Lenin:

First, neither the "form of State ownership" nor statification in the profoundest sense of this term, i.e., the complete unification of the economy and its management under a single framework ("planning"), in any way settles the question of the class content of this type of economy, or consequently that of the abolition of exploitation. For Lenin, not only is statification as such not necessarily "socialist," but *nonsocialist statification represents the most crushing and the most highly perfected form of exploitation in the interest of the dominant class.*

Second, what confers upon State (or nationalized) property a socialist content, according to Lenin, is the character of its political power. Statification plus Soviet power, for Lenin, provided the basis for socialism. Statification without this power was the most perfected form of capitalist domination.

An explanation concerning this last point is necessary. Lenin's conception, which makes the character of State ownership depend upon the character of its political power, is correct but ought to be considered today, after the experience of the Russian Revolution, partial and insufficient. The character of political power is an infallible indication of the true content of "nationalized" property, but it is not its true foundation. What confers a socialist character or not upon "nationalized" property is the structure of the *relations of production*. It is from these relations that the character of political power itself—which is not the sole or even the determining factor—is derived after the revolution. Only if the revolution leads to a radical transformation of the relations of production in the factory (i.e., if it can achieve *workers' management*) will it be able to confer upon nationalized property a socialist content as well as create an *objective* and *subjective* basis for proletarian power. Soviet power, inasmuch as it is working-class power, does not live off itself; by itself it tends to degenerate, as does all State power. It can survive and consolidate itself while moving in a socialist direction only by starting off with a fundamental modification in the relations of production, i.e., by starting off with the mass of producers taking over the direction of the economy. This is precisely what did not take place in Russia.[29] The power of the soviets progressively atrophied because its root, the working-class management of production, did not exist. Thus, the Soviet State rapidly lost its proletarian character. With the economy and the State falling in this way under the absolute domination of the bureaucracy, State ownership simply became the most convenient form of universal power for this bureaucracy.

This said, let us simply recall that up until 1930 Marxists unanimously thought that the nationalization of production signified nothing by itself and that it received its true content from the character of political power. At this time, only the Stalinists had a different position. It was Trotsky who undertook to answer them, by writing:

> The socialist character of industry is determined and secured in a decisive measure by the role of the party, the voluntary internal cohesion of the proletarian vanguard, the conscious discipline of the administrators, trade-union functionaries, members of the shop nuclei, etc. If we allow that this web is weakening, disintegrating, and ripping, then it becomes absolutely self-evident that within a brief period nothing will remain of the socialist character of state industry, transport, etc.[30]

This was written in July 1928. A few months later, Trotsky wrote again:

> Is the proletarian kernel of the party, assisted by the working class, capable of triumphing over the autocracy of the party apparatus which is fusing with the state apparatus? Whoever replies in advance that it is *incapable*, thereby speaks not only of the necessity of a new party on a new foundation, but also of the necessity of a second and new proletarian revolution.[31]

As is well known, during this period Trotsky not only ruled out the possibility of a revolution in Russia—believing that a mere "reform" of the regime would be sufficient to remove the bureaucracy from power—but was resolutely against the idea of a new party, instead setting as his objective the rectification of the Russian CP.[32]

Finally, yet again in 1931, Trotsky said that the political features of power are what determines the working-class character of the Russian State.

> The recognition of the present Soviet state as a workers' state not only signifies that the bourgeoisie can conquer power only by means of an armed uprising but also that the proletariat of the USSR has not forfeited the possibility of subordinating the bureaucracy to it, of reviving the party again, and of regenerating the regime of the dictatorship—without a new revolution, with the methods and on the road of *reform*.[33]

We have provided numerous quotations at the risk of boring the reader because they reveal something carefully hidden by Trotsky's epigones. For Trotsky himself, up until 1931, the character of the Russian economy was to be defined according to the character of its State. The Russian question boiled down to the question of the character of its political power.[34] For Trotsky at this time, it was the proletarian character of political power that gave a socialist character to statified industry. Despite its bureaucratic degeneration, the proletarian character of this political power was for him guaranteed by the fact that the proletariat still could retake power and expel the bureaucracy through mere reform and without violent revolution. This criterion, we have said, is insufficient—or rather it is derivative and secondary. Nevertheless, it should be remembered that, at this time, Trotsky did not tie the question of the regime's character at all to "State ownership."[35]

It was only three years later[36] that Trotsky made an abrupt about-face, proclaiming both that (1) all reform in Russia henceforth is impossible, that only a new revolution will be able to chase the bureaucracy out and instaurate the masses in power, and that a new revolutionary party must be built, and that (2) the Russian regime continues to retain its proletarian character, as guaranteed by the nationalized ownership of the means of production. It was this position, jotted down amid innumerable contradictions in *The Revolution Betrayed*, that was from that time on the unassailable dogma of the Trotskyist tendency [see (b) in the Postface].

The hopeless absurdity of this position becomes glaringly apparent when one reflects for a moment upon the very term "nationalization." "Nationalization" and "nationalized property" are anti-Marxist and antiscientific expressions. To nationalize means to give to the nation. But what is the "nation"? The "nation" is an abstraction; in reality, the nation is torn by class antagonisms. To give to the nation really means to give to the dominant class in this nation. Consequently, explaining that property in Russia has a "socialist" or proletarian character because it is nationalized is quite simply a vicious circle, a begging of the question: Nationalized property can have a socialist content only if the dominant class is the proletariat. The Trotskyists respond to this by saying that it is a priori certain that the proletariat is the dominant class in Russia since property is nationalized. It is deplorable, but it is so. They also respond by saying that the proletariat inevitably is the dominant class in Russia, since there are no private capitalists there and since there can be no other class, save the proletariat and the capitalists, in the present epoch. Marx, it seems, said something along these lines. He died in 1883 and lies in Highgate Cemetery in London.

We have seen that the form of State ownership does not determine the relations of production but is determined by them, and that it can express very well the relations of exploitation. It remains for us now to understand why this form appears at just this precise moment in history and under just these concrete conditions. In other words, after having understood the way in which the form of State ownership is a mystified form of economic reality, we must examine why it also is its adequate form. We will deal with this problem elsewhere, when we try to define the relationship between the Russian economy and the development of world capitalism. For the moment it suffices for us to say that this form of ownership as well as the class-based "planning" it renders possible are only the supreme and ultimate expressions of modern capitalism's fundamental process— the concentration of the forces of production—a process they carry out in two ways: concentration of formal property ownership and concentration of the actual management of production.

5. We have seen that statification in no way is incompatible either with class domination over the proletariat or with exploitation, here in its most perfected

form. We can understand too—it will be shown in detail later on—that Russian "planning" has no less the same function: It expresses in a coordinated fashion the interests of the bureaucracy. This appears on the level of accumulation as well as on that of consumption, these two being, moreover, absolutely interdependent. With respect to its general orientation, the concrete development of the Russian economy under the domination of the bureaucracy differs in no way from that of a capitalist country: In place of the blind mechanism of value, it is the mechanism of the bureaucratic plan that assigns some specified portion of the forces of production to the production of the means of production and some other specified portion to the production of consumer goods. What guides the action of the bureaucracy in this domain obviously is not the "general interest" of the economy—a notion with no concrete or precise meaning—but rather its own interests. This is shown by the fact that heavy industry is oriented essentially toward the fulfillment of military needs—and, under present conditions and especially for a relatively backward country, this signifies that the entire productive sector needs to be developed; that the consumer-goods industries are oriented by the bureaucrats' consumer needs; and that, in carrying out these objectives, laborers have to produce the maximum amount and cost the minimum amount. We see therefore that in Russia, statification and planning only serve to advance the class interests of the bureaucracy and to aid in the exploitation of the proletariat, and that the essential objectives as well as the fundamental means (the exploitation of laborers) are identical to those of capitalist economies. In what respect, then, can this economy be characterized as "progressive"?

For Trotsky, the basic answer lies in a reference to the growth of Russian production. Russian production has quadrupled and quintupled in a few years, and this increase, says Trotsky, would have been impossible if private capitalism had been retained in the country. But if the progressive character of the bureaucracy follows from the fact that the latter develops the forces of production, then the following dilemma poses itself: Either the development of the forces of production, driven along by the bureaucracy, is, all things considered, a phenomenon of short duration and of limited extent, and therefore without historical importance; or, the bureaucracy is capable, in Russia (and in this case, also everywhere else), of assuring a new historical phase in the development of the forces of production.

For Trotsky, the second option of this alternative is to be categorically rejected. Not only is he convinced that the bureaucracy has no historical future, but he also states that in the case where a prolonged setback for the revolution would permit the bureaucracy to install itself in power for an enduring period of time, it "would be . . . a regime of decline, signalizing the eclipse of civilization."[37]

As for us, we agree completely with the essential content of this conception. There remains, therefore, the first option of the alternative: The development of the forces of production in Russia under the impetus of its bureaucracy is a phenomenon of short duration, limited extent, and, in short, without historical importance [see (c) in the Postface]. Indeed, this is the clear position of Trotsky, who does not stop here but instead points out—in a summary manner, to be sure—a few of the factors that already make the bureaucracy "the worst brake upon the development of the forces of production."[38]

But in this case it is obvious that every attempt to characterize the Russian economy as "progressive" automatically loses its basis. That the bureaucracy increased production between 1928 and 1940 by four or five times, while Japanese imperialism only doubled production during the same period, or the United States doubled production between 1939 and 1944, that it accomplished in twenty years what the bourgeoisie of other countries accomplished in forty or sixty certainly becomes from this moment on an extremely important phenomenon, meriting a specific analysis and explanation, but in the last analysis it does not differ qualitatively from the development of the forces of production that guaranteed capitalist exploitation for centuries and that it continues to guarantee during its period of decline.

The Relations of Production

The result of twenty years of discussion on the "Russian question" has been to throw a thickly woven veil of mystery around the notion of the relations of production in general. Those who tried to combat this conception, which makes Russia into a "workers' State" and turns its economy into a more or less socialist economy, generally have done so by starting with superstructural manifestations: counterrevolutionary character of Stalinist policy, police-state totalitarianism of the regime. On the economic level, one usually cites only the monstrous inequalities in income. All these points, which could have led to a radical revision of the current conception of the Russian regime if they had been developed appropriately, were considered in themselves, independently of all else, or erected as autonomous and ultimate criteria. This is what permitted Trotsky to triumph in these interminable discussions. He granted everything that one might desire. He just did not allow the following question to be posed: And what about the relations of production? Have they become capitalistic again? When? Are there private capitalists in Russia? His adversaries' inability to pursue the discussion on this terrain through an analysis of the class character of the relations of production in Russia permitted Trotsky to remain master of the terrain after each confrontation [see (d) in the Postface].

Trotsky easily could have been dislodged from this apparently dominant position by asking him the following question: So then, these relations of production, what are they in general? What are they in the case of Russia? For it is obvious to those who know Trotsky's work not only that he was always happy to brandish the magic weapon of the "relations of production" but also that he never went any further. Marx did not *talk about* capitalist relations of production: He analyzed them in depth for three thousand pages of *Capital*. One would seek in vain, in Trotsky's writings, for just the beginning of a similar analysis. His most extensive work in this regard, *The Revolution Betrayed*, contains, in the guise of economic analysis, only a description of the material volume of Russian production, of income inequalities, and of the struggle for productivity in Russia. The rest is sociological and political literature, very often good literature, but undermined by the lack of economic foundations, *by the lack, as a matter of fact, of an analysis of the relations of production in Russia.*

All that can be learned from Trotsky about the relations of production in general is this: (1) The relations of production are *not* the relations of distributing the social product, and (2) the relations of production have something to do with property forms. The first proposition is completely false, for the relations of production are also relations of distribution; more exactly, the distribution of the social product is a moment in the production process. The second is only partially true, for the whole question is precisely this: What is the connection between the relations of production and property forms? What is the relation between production and property, between economics and law? We have made our positions on these preliminary questions clear. We now must examine in a positive way what the relations of production are.

Several aspects of the relations of production must be logically distinguished.

Every relation of production is, in the first place and in an immediate way, an *organization* of the forces of production with a view toward the outcome of production. The forces of production are, on the one hand, labor itself, and, on the other hand, the conditions of labor, which can be reduced in the last analysis to past labor. The organization of the forces of production determines the goal of production at the same time as it is determined by it. Whether this organization of the forces of production occurs, so to speak, spontaneously and even blindly, as is the case in primitive societies, or whether it requires separate economic and social organs as is the case in advanced societies, it remains the first moment of economic life, the foundation without which there would be no production.

Likewise, however, every relation of production contains, both as presupposition and as consequence, a *distribution* of the outcome of productive activity, of the product. This distribution is necessarily determined by past and present as well as future production: At the start, there is distribution only of the product of production, and only under the form that production has given to this product; then, all distribution necessarily takes into account future production, for which it is the condition. On the other hand, the conservation, diminution, or extension of the community's existing wealth follows from the concrete ways in which products are distributed, from the fact that this distribution does or does not take into account the need to replace social reserves and worn-out tools or the need to increase them. Thus it can be said not only that all subsequent production is determined by the production that preceded it but also that future distribution is the factor determining the organization of current production.

Finally, production *qua* organization as well as production *qua* distribution are both based upon the appropriation of the conditions of production, i.e., upon the appropriation of nature, of nature as far as it is external to man's own body. This appropriation appears in a dynamic way in the power to have these conditions of production at one's disposal, whether the subject of this disposition is the community as an indistinct whole or it is the object of a monopoly run by a group, a category of people, or a social class.

Consequently, both the *organization (management)* of production itself and the *distribution* of the product are founded upon the *disposition* of the conditions of production, and there we have the general content of the relations of production. The relations of production in a given period are manifested in the *organization (management)* of cooperation between individuals with a view toward the outcome of production and in the *distribution* of this product, starting from a given mode of *disposing* of the conditions of production.[39]

But in the relations of production, what is important is not the general notion, which follows from the simple analysis of the concept of social life, and which, in this sense, is a tautology, but rather the concrete evolution of the modes of production through the history of humanity.

Thus in primitive societies, where class division usually is absent, where the methods and the objective of production as well as the rules for distribution undergo only an extremely slow process of evolution, where people are ruled much more by the things they do not work on, the organization of production and distribution seems to result blindly from tradition and to reflect passively the legacy of the social past, the decisive influence of natural surroundings, and the peculiarities of the already acquired means of production. The organization of production still is not, in reality, distinct from material productive activity itself; cooperation is regulated much more by immediate spontaneity and habits than by objective economic laws or by the conscious action of society's members. The disposition of the conditions of production, man's appropriation of his own body and of the immediately surrounding natural world seem to happen by themselves; the tribe only becomes aware of these when it is faced with external conflicts with another tribe.

The first moment in the economic process, which seems to arise as an autonomous entity and of which the primitive society attains a distinct awareness, is the moment of *distributing* the product. This moment becomes, in general terms, the subject of a specific customary regulatory process.

With the division of society into classes a fundamental reversal takes place. In slave society, the disposition of the conditions of production, of the earth, of tools, and of people becomes the monopoly of a social class, of the dominant class of slave owners. This disposition becomes the subject of an explicit social regulatory process and quickly obtains the protection afforded by social coercion as organized by the State of slave owners. Simultaneously, the organization of production, the management of the forces of production, becomes a social function exercised by the dominant class in a natural way based upon its disposition of these forces of production. If slave society makes the disposition of the conditions of production and the management of production appear as moments separated from economic life—by making the first a directly social phenomenon, by showing that even this disposition that man has over his own body as a force of production cannot be taken for granted but rather is a product of a given form of historical life, and by erecting the organization and the management of production as a social function of a specific class—in compensation, it abolishes distribution as a specific moment since, in the slave economy, distribution, *qua* distribution of the product between the dominant class and the dominated class, is buried within production itself. The distribution of the product is completely hidden within the immediate and possessive productive relationship between the master and the slave: to reserve a portion of the harvest for the seeds and another for the slaves is not a distribution of production, but rather immediately pertains to the organization of production itself. The preservation of the slave for the master does not have any economic meaning different than the preservation of livestock. As to the distribution of the product among the members of the dominant class themselves, this results, for the most part, from the initial distribution of the conditions of production, which is slowly transformed by the mechanism of exchange and by the embryonic appearance of a law of value.

In feudal society, which, in Western Europe at least, marks a period of historical regression in comparison to Greco-Roman slave society, the autonomous character of the disposition of the conditions of production is maintained. But here the function of the organization of production registers a setback. The lord acts as a manager only in an extremely vague and general sense: Once the division of labor in the estate and among the serfs is fixed, he is limited to commanding respect for himself. Likewise, the distribution of the product between lords and serfs is done, it could be said, once and for all: The serf owes some specified portion of the product, or some specified number of workdays to the lord. The static character of both the organization of production and of its distribution is only the consequence of the stationary position of the forces of production themselves during the feudal era.

In capitalist society, the different moments of the economic process reach full blossom and achieve an independent material existence. Here the disposition of the conditions of production, management and distribution, accompanied by exchange and consumption, emerge as entities capable of leading an autonomous existence, with each one becoming a specific object, a particular matter suitable for being reflected upon, a social force. But what makes the capitalists the dominant class in modern society is that, having the conditions of production at their disposal, they organize and manage production and appear as the personal and conscious agents of the distribution of the social product.

Generally, the following can be said.

1. The relations of production, in general, are defined by the mode of *managing* production (organization and cooperation of the material and personal conditions of production, definition of the goals and the methods of production), and by the mode of *distributing* the social product (which is intimately connected with management from several standpoints, and particularly from the standpoint of the distribution that results from the monopolization over the *capacity* to direct and earmark accumulation, which is interdependent with distribution). (We may add here that the relations of production are based upon *the initial distribution of the conditions of production*, the latter manifesting itself in the *exclusive disposition* over the means of production and over consumer objects. Such an exclusive right of disposition often manifests itself in juridical property forms, but it would be absurd to say that it coincides at every moment with these forms or that it is expressed there adequately and univocally (see the preceding section, point 2). One must never lose sight of the fact that this "initial" distribution of the conditions of production is constantly being reproduced, ex-

tended, and developed by the relations of production up until the moment these relations are revolutionized.)

2. *The class content* of the relations of production, founded upon the initial distribution of the conditions of production (monopolization of the means of production by a social class, constant reproduction of this monopolization), is manifested in the dominant class's management of production, and in the distribution of the social product in the dominant class's favor. The existence of surplus value or of surplus production defines neither the dominant class's character in the workings of the economy nor even the fact that the economy is based upon exploitation. But the appropriation of this surplus value by a social class by virtue of its monopoly over the material conditions of production suffices to define an economy as a class economy based upon exploitation; the ultimate destination of this surplus value, its distribution between accumulation and the dominant class's unproductive consumption, the earmarking of this accumulation itself, and the concrete mode of appropriating surplus value and distributing it among the members of the dominant class determine the specific character of the class-based economy and mark the historical differences among various dominant classes.

3. From the point of view of the exploited class, the class character of the economy is manifested in production in the narrow sense, through this class's reduction to the narrow role of executant and more generally through its human alienation, through its total subordination to the needs of the dominant class; and in distribution, through the dominant class's appropriation of the difference between the cost of the exploited class's labor power and the product of its labor.

Proletariat and Production

Before grappling with the problem of the relations of production in Russia, we must begin with a summary analysis of the relations of production in capitalist and socialist economies.

We begin first with an analysis of production in the capitalist economy in order to facilitate understanding. Indeed, to begin this analysis with an analysis of capitalism signifies, on the one hand, to begin with the known, and, on the other hand, to allow ourselves to profit directly from the analysis of the capitalist economy presented by Marx, an analysis that approached as much as was possible the ideal of a dialectical analysis of a historical phenomenon. But to these reasons pertaining to method must be added one pertaining to substance, which is by far the most important: As will be seen, bureaucratic capitalism signifies only the extreme development of the most deep-seated laws of capitalism, which leads toward the internal negation of these very laws. It therefore is impossible to grasp the essence of Russian bureaucratic capitalism without connecting our examination of the essence of this system to that of the laws that regulate traditional capitalism.

Before tackling our subject we also must briefly sketch the structure of the relations of production in a socialist society. This is necessary not only in order to dissipate the effects of Stalinist mystifications on this subject and in order to recall that socialism always has been understood in the workers' movement as something that has no connection either with Russian reality or with the idea of socialism as it is propagated by Stalinists. It is particularly indispensable because the apparent identity of certain economic forms—the absence of private property, the existence of planning, etc.—in socialism and bureaucratic capitalism makes it extremely instructive to compare these two regimes.

Capitalist Production

We have seen that the relations of production express themselves in the *management* of production and in the *distribution* of the product and that their class content follows from the fact that the *disposition* of the material conditions of production is monopolized by a social group. We must now give concrete form to this idea in the case of capitalist production.

1. In capitalist society, the fundamental relation of production is the relation between employer and worker. In what way is this relation a class-based relation? In the following way: The economic and social position of these two categories of persons who participate in production is absolutely different. This difference is a function of their different relation to the means of production. The capitalist possesses the means of production (either directly or indirectly); the worker possesses only his labor power. Unless the means of production and labor power (i.e., dead labor and living labor) are brought together, production is not possible, and neither can the capitalist do without the worker nor the worker without the capitalist so long as the latter has at his disposal the means of production. From the point of view of exchange among "independent economic units,"[40] this coming together, the cooperation of dead labor and living labor,[41] takes the economic form of the worker's sale of his labor power to the capitalist. For the worker, it makes no difference that the buyer of his labor power is an individual employer, an anonymous company, or the State. What matters to the worker is the predominant position such buyers have because they have at their disposal social capital or a portion of it, i.e., not only the means of production in the narrow sense, but even society's consumption fund and also, in the end, the power of coercion—the State. It is the possession of social capital and State power that makes the capitalist class the dominant class in bourgeois society.

Let us see in what way this domination of capital over labor is expressed in the organization of production and in the distribution of the product.

2. We know that every relation of production is, in the first place and immediately, an organization of the forces of production with a view toward the results of production. In modern society, the productive relation presents itself, therefore, as an organization of cooperation among the forces of production, capital, and labor (dead or already completed labor and living or actual, current labor), of the conditions of labor itself, or, as Marx says, of the material conditions and the personal conditions of production. Living labor is immediately represented in its human form in the proletarian. Dead labor is represented in its human form in the class of capitalists only by virtue of its having been appropriated by this class.[42] What on the technical level appears as the cooperation

of actual, current labor and matter endowed with value by already completed labor takes the form on the economic level of a relation between labor power and capital, and on the social level it takes the form of the relation between the proletariat and the capitalist class. The organization of the forces of production with a view toward the results of production, both from the standpoint of the order imposed upon living labor and upon dead labor in their unchanging relations and from the standpoint of the coordination of efforts of a multitude of proletarians engaged in production (relations among the producers themselves and relations between the producers and the instruments of production)—this organization, inasmuch as it does not result blindly from the physical or technical conditions of production, is guaranteed not by the producers themselves but by the individuals who socially personify capital, by the capitalists.[43] In this organization it makes no difference, from the point of view we are adopting here, that a series of tasks is accomplished, at lower echelons, by a specific personnel staff not belonging (formally or in reality) to the capitalist class. Likewise, it makes no difference to us at the moment that these tasks are delegated more and more to this specific personnel staff and that we have here a deep-seated tendency of capitalist production. It suffices for us to state that, at the top echelon, either the capitalists or their directly delegated representatives make these fundamental decisions, give an orientation to this organization of the forces of production, and determine for this organization its concrete goal (nature and quantity of the product) as well as the overall means of attaining this goal (relation of constant capital to variable capital, rate of accumulation). It is obvious that these ultimate decisions are not made "freely" (and this is true in many senses: the objective laws of technique, economics, and social life are imposed upon the will of the capitalist, whose choice is buffeted back and forth between narrow limits, and even within these limits it is determined in the end by the profit motive). But insofar as human activity in general plays a role in history, these ultimate decisions are the level on which is manifested the economic activity of the capitalist class. This class's economic activity can be defined as the relatively conscious expression of capital's tendency toward unlimited self-expansion.

That these relations of production are class relations is therefore expressed in a concrete and immediate way by the fact that a group—or a social class—monopolizes the organization and the management of productive activity, the others being mere executants, at various echelons, of its decisions. This signifies that the management of production will be accomplished by capitalists or by their representatives according to their interests. From the point of view of the productive relation properly called, i.e., of the relation between living labor and dead labor with a view toward the results of production, this relation is regulated by the immanent laws of capitalist production, which the individual capitalist and his "directors" give expression to on the level of consciousness. These immanent laws are the expression of the absolute domination of dead labor over living labor, of capital over the worker. They manifest themselves insofar as they tend to treat living labor itself as dead labor, as they tend to make the worker merely a material appendage of the equipment, and as they tend to erect the point of view of dead labor as the unrivaled viewpoint dominating production.

On an individual scale, this is manifested through the complete subordination of the worker to the machine vis-à-vis the movements involved as well as the pace of work. Likewise, cooperation among workers occurs by starting out from the "needs" of the mechanical complex they serve. Finally, on the social scale, the principal manifestation of this subordination is the regulation of the recruitment and employment (and unemployment) of workers according to the needs of the mechanical universe.

3. But these relations of production exhibit a second and equally important feature: They are in a mediated way relations of exchange and hence relations of distribution.

Indeed, the result of separating the producers from the instruments of production (a fundamental fact of the capitalist era) is that the producers can participate in production—and hence can share in the distribution of the results of this type of production—only on the basis of the sale of the sole productive force they have in their possession, i.e., their labor power (which is completely subordinated to dead labor, due merely to the consequences of technical developments), and therefore only on the basis of the exchange of their labor power for a portion of the results of production. The monopoly exercised by those who purchase labor power over both the means of production and society's consumption fund tends to ensure that the conditions for this exchange will be dictated by capitalists as concerns both the price of labor power as a commodity (wages) and the determinations of this commodity (length and intensity of the workday, etc.).[44]

Capitalist domination therefore is exerted equally in the domain of distribution. We must understand, though, exactly what this domination signifies and how the economic laws of capitalist society express themselves through the relationship between this society's two fundamental classes [see (e) in the Postface].

The economic laws of capitalism require the sale of labor power "based on its value." Being in effect a commodity in capitalist society, labor power has to be sold at cost. But what is its cost? Obviously, it is equivalent to the value of the products the worker consumes in order to live and to reproduce. But the value of these products is just as obviously the resultant of two factors: the value of each product taken separately and the total quantity of the products the worker consumes. The value of the labor power expended during a day can be one dollar, if the worker eats only a pound of bread, and if a pound of bread costs only a dollar. It can just as well be one dollar if the worker eats two pounds of bread, if each pound costs fifty cents. It also can be two dollars if the worker consumes two pounds of bread, with a pound costing a dollar. Under the rubric of the law of value, the economic analysis of capitalism lets us know the value of each product unit entering into the consumption pattern of the worker. It also lets us know the variations in this value. But the law of value in itself, in its immediate form, does not tell us anything, and cannot tell us anything, about the factors determining the greater or lesser quantity of products the working class consumes—what is usually called the working class's "standard of living." It is clear, however, that without an exact definition of these factors, the application of the law of value to the sale of labor power becomes completely problematic.

This question did not escape Marx's attention. He provided three responses that, while they differ, are not incompatible. The working class's standard of living, he says in the first volume of *Capital*, is determined by historical, moral, and social factors.[45] It is determined, he says in *Wages, Price, and Profit*, by the relation of forces between the proletariat and the bourgeoisie.[46] It is, he says finally in the third volume of *Capital*, determined by the internal needs of capitalist accumulation and by the inexorable tendency of the capitalist economy to reduce the paid part of the working day to the very minimum under pressure from the falling rate of profit and from the growing crisis of the capitalist system.

Among these three factors there exists, on the one hand, a logical connection and, on the other hand, a historical order. All three factors operate constantly and simultaneously during the capitalist era and are in no way external to each other. Thus, these "historical, moral, etc., factors" can be boiled down to the combined results of past class struggle and of the action of capitalism's intrinsic tendency toward an ever greater exploitation of the proletariat. The severity of the class struggle itself is determined, among other things, by the degree of society's capitalist development and so on.

It is also true, however, that the relative importance of these factors varies through the development of history. Roughly speaking, the first factor represents to some extent the legacy of the past, which tends, in an ideal schema of capitalist development, to even out everywhere due to the combined effects of the expansion of the class struggle and of the universal concentration of capital. The class struggle itself does not operate in the same way at the beginning and at the end of the capitalist era. During capitalism's "ascendant period," i.e., so long as the effects of the falling rate of profit still do not make themselves felt in a pressing manner and so long as capitalism has not yet entered its phase of organic crisis, the relation of forces between the proletariat and the bourgeoisie can have a considerable influence upon the distribution of the social product; this is the period during which the success of "minimal" struggles can have a relatively considerable and long-lasting importance. In contrast, during the period of capitalism's death agony, not only does it become impossible for the dominant class to grant any new "concessions" to the proletariat, but this dominant class is obliged by the organic crisis in its economy to take back from the working class everything it allowed to be wrung from it during the preceding period. "Reforms" of all sorts become objectively impossible; society finds itself face-to-face with the dilemma of revolution or counterrevolution, whose economic expression, from the point of view of interest to us here, is the following: domination of production by the producers or absolute determination of their standard of living according to capital's need for maximum profits. It is fascism or Stalinism that undertakes (under different frameworks, as will be seen later) to accomplish this task during the period of the exploitative society's death agony. During this period, the class struggle has much less effect upon the distribution of the social product between workers and bosses; its fundamental signification is to be found thereafter in the possibility of a complete overthrow of the system of exploitation. Its minimum outcome happens by force of circumstances to coincide with its maximum outcome; the struggle for the elementary necessities of life becomes directly the struggle for revolution and power. But as long as this revolution does not take place, it is capital's growing thirst for surplus value that determines more and more the working class's standard of living and hence the value of its labor power.

Nevertheless, these factors, taken as a whole, and the fluctuations in the value of labor power that result therefrom are of essential importance for determining historical tendencies, the lines of force of the development of living standards in a relatively long-term perspective. In a given period and for a given country, one can, as Marx says, consider the working class's standard of living, and hence the value of its labor power, as fixed.

This value, considered stable on the whole, is realized in the capitalist economy, like every other value, only through the necessary mediation of the market, of a relatively "free" market—which implies a supply and a demand for the commodity "labor power." This market not only is the necessary condition for adjusting the price of labor power to its value, it is above all the necessary condition for the notion of the "working class's standard of living" to have any signification whatsoever; otherwise, the capitalists would have the unlimited opportunity of determining this standard of living solely in accordance with the internal needs of the apparatus that produces surplus value. This limitation, moreover, is founded not so much on individual competition between sellers and buyers of labor power as on the possibility of the workers' limiting, overall and en masse, the supply of labor power at any given moment by a strike. In other words, it is the fact that the working class is not completely reduced to slavery that, as it gives an objective consistency to the notion of the "working class's standard of living," and thereby to the value of labor power, allows the law of value to be applied to the fundamental commodity in capitalist society, labor power. Just as the universal concentration and monopolization of the forces of production would render the law of value meaningless, so the complete reduction of the working class to slavery would empty the notion of "the value of labor power" of all content.

4. In conclusion, the inherent exploitation of the capitalist system is based on the fact that the producers do not have the means of production at their disposal, either individually (artisans) or collectively (socialism), and that living labor, instead of dominating dead labor, is dominated by it through the intermediary of the individuals who personify it (the capitalists). The relations of production are relations of exploitation under both their aspects: i.e., *qua* the organization of production properly called as well as *qua* the organization of distribution. Living labor is exploited by dead labor in production proper since its viewpoint is subordinated to that of dead labor and is completely dominated by the latter. In the organization of production, the proletarian is entirely dominated by capital and exists only for the latter. He is also exploited in the process of distribution, since his sharing [*participation*] in the social product is regulated

by economic laws (expressed by the employer on the level of consciousness) that define this participation, not on the basis of the value created through the power of labor, but according to the value of this labor power. These laws, which express the profound tendency of capitalist accumulation, bring the cost of producing labor power more and more down toward a "physical minimum."[47] By lowering the price of commodities necessary for the subsistence of the worker, increases in labor productivity already tend to reduce the portion of the social product distributed to the proletariat. But the expression "physical minimum" ought not to be taken in a literal sense; a "physical minimum" is, properly speaking, indefinable.[48] What should be understood by this phrase is the tendency toward reducing the relative real wages of the working class.

Socialist Production

We must now understand briefly how the fundamental productive relation takes shape in a socialist society [see (f) in the Postface].

1. In a socialist society, the relations of production are not class relations, for each individual finds himself related to the entire society—of which he is himself an active agent—and not with a specific category of individuals or social groupings endowed with economic powers of their own or having, in whole or in part, the means of production at their disposal. The differentiation of these individuals, due to the persistence of the division of labor, does not entail a class differentiation, for it does not entail different relations to the productive apparatus. If, as an individual, the laborer still is obliged to work in order to live, as a member of the commune he participates in determining the conditions of work, the orientation of production, and the compensation of labor. It goes without saying that this is possible only through the complete realization of the workers' management of production, i.e., by the abolition of the fixed and stable distinction between directors and executants in the production process.

2. The distribution of the consumable social product retains the form of exchange between labor power and a part of the product of labor. But this form has a completely inverted content, and thereby the "law of value completely changes with respect to its form and its substance," as Marx says.[49] We would say rather that this law is now completely abolished.

As Marx made clear long ago, the remuneration of labor in a socialist society can only be equal to the quantity of labor the laborer supplies to society, less a portion intended to cover society's "overhead expenses" and another portion intended for accumulation. But this already prevents us from speaking any longer in this case about the "law of value" as applied to labor power, for this law would require that the *cost* of labor power be given in exchange for this labor power, and not the value added to the product by living labor. That the relation between labor supplied to society and labor recovered by the worker in the form of consumable products is neither arbitrary nor spontaneously determined by the scope of individual needs (as in the higher phase of communism), but is rather a regulated relation, does not signify in the least that we encounter here a "different law of value."

First of all, let us inquire as to its form. We no longer have a necessary and blindly realized social law that cannot be transgressed even by the very nature of things. It is a "conscious law," i.e., a norm regulating the distribution of products that the producers impose upon themselves and upon those who are recalcitrant, a norm whose application must be supervised and whose transgression—which is always a possibility—must be punished. In capitalist society, the law of value expresses an objective economic order. In socialist society, it will be a juridical norm, a rule of law.

As to its substance, the following may be said: If the laborer is not paid the "value of his labor power" but rather in due proportion to the value he added to the product, i.e., if "the same amount of labor he has given to society in one form he receives back in another,"[50] we have here the complete reversal, the absolute negation of the law of labor value. For in this case, what is taken as the criterion for this exchange no longer is the objective cost of the exchanged product measured in labor time; what is paid to the laborer no longer is the "value of his labor power" at all but rather the value produced by his labor power. Instead of being determined by its cause (if we may call the cost of producing labor power its cause), the compensation of labor power is determined by the latter's effect. Instead of having no immediate relation to the value it produces, labor power is compensated on the basis of this value. After the fact, the compensation of labor power can appear as the exact equivalent of the "value of labor power" since, if the latter is determined by the "standard of living" of the laborer in the socialist society, the "standard of living" is determined by "wages." The laborer not being able to consume more than he receives from society, an equivalence between what he receives from society and the "cost of producing" his labor power can be established after the fact. But it is obvious that we find ourselves in this case in a vicious circle: "The application of the law of value" is reduced in this case to a simple tautology consisting of an explanation of the standard of living by "wages" and "wages" by the standard of living. Once rid of this absurdity, it becomes clear that the value produced by labor now determines "wages" and hence the standard of living itself. In other words, labor power no longer takes the form of an independent exchange value but solely the form of a use value. Its exchange is now regulated on the basis not of its cost but of its utility, expressed by its productivity.

3. One last explanation is necessary. It concerns the celebrated question of "bourgeois right in socialist society."

The principle according to which each individual in socialist society receives back from this society "in another form . . . the same amount of labor he has given to society in one form," this "equal right" was characterized by Marx as "unequal right . . . therefore as bourgeois right." Around this phrase, a system of mystifications has been built up by the Trotskyists, as well as by the advocates of the Stalinist bureaucracy, in order to prove that socialist society is founded upon inequality and *therefore* that the "inequality" existing in Russia does not demolish the "socialist" character of the relations of production in that country. We have already said that "inequality" in no way signifies "exploitation" and that in Russia, it is not the "inequality" in the compensation of labor but rather the *appropriation* of the proletarians' labor by the bureaucracy, therefore the *exploitation* of the former by the latter, that is in question. This simple remark ends the discussion on the substance of the question. Nevertheless, a more extensive examination of the problem would be profitable.

In what way, according to Marx, is socialist society's mode of compensating labor "bourgeois"? Obviously, it is so only metaphorically. If it were so literally, socialist society would be nothing more and nothing less than a society of exploitation. If society paid laborers only the "value of their labor power," and if a specific social category appropriated the difference between this value and the value of the product of labor—it is in this, as has been seen, that bourgeois distribution consists—we would find ourselves faced with a reproduction of the capitalist system. How far Marx was from such an absurdity is proved by the sentence with which he closes his exposition of "bourgeois right." In capitalist society, he says,

> the elements of production are so distributed . . . [that] the present-day distribution of the means of production results automatically. If the material conditions of production are the cooperative property of the workers themselves, then there likewise results a distribution of the means of consumption different from the present one. Vulgar socialism (and from it in turn a section of the democracy) has taken over from the bourgeois economists the consideration and treatment of distribution as independent of the mode of production and hence the presentation of socialism as turning principally on distribution.[51]

But this metaphorical expression has a deep significance. This right is a "bourgeois right" because it is an "unequal" right. It is unequal because the compensation of workers is unequal; indeed, this compensation is proportional to each person's contribution to production. This contribution is unequal because individuals are unequal, that is to say, different; if they were not unequal, they would not be distinct individuals. They are unequal both from the point of view of their capacities as well as from the point of view of their needs. Consequently, by rendering to each "the same amount of labor as society received from him," society exploits no one; but it no less allows the "natural" inequality of individuals to continue, as this results from the inequality of capacities and needs of each person. If to the unequal numbers four, six, and eight, I add equal amounts, I maintain inequality. I maintain it still more if I add to these same numbers unequal amounts proportional to their magnitude. I can achieve equality only by adding unequal amounts so that the result of their addition would be everywhere the same. But in order to do this, on the social plane, I no longer can use as my basis the value produced by labor. On this basis I never would be able to make individuals equal. There is but one basis upon which the "equalization" of individuals would be possible: It is the complete satisfaction of the needs of each person. The only point at which two individuals can become equal is the point at which both are fully satisfied. Then it can be said that "the result of the addition is everywhere the same," since we have achieved the same result everywhere: the complete satisfaction of needs. Only in the higher stage of communist society can this satisfaction of needs be obtained for its members. Till then, the inequality of individuals will continue, all the while growing progressively less marked.

Marx also expresses this idea in another, equally characteristic way: This right is bourgeois because "in its content, it is founded upon inequality, like every right."[52] By its nature, right can be exercised only when one uses an identical equivalent. Such an equivalent can be applied to individuals only through the use of an abstraction, which itself does violence to what is the particular essence of each individual, i.e., to what gives him his specific and unique characteristics.

It therefore may be easily understood that the "inequality" of which Marx speaks has nothing to do with the crass apologia the bureaucracy has tried to make with these ideas as their point of departure. Between this "inequality" and bureaucratic exploitation there is the same relation as there is between socialism and concentration camps.

Proletariat and Bureaucracy

General Characteristics

Let us now examine the fundamental relation of production in the Russian economy. This relation exhibits itself, juridically and formally, as a relation between the worker and the "State." As we know from sociology, however, the juridical "State" is an abstraction. In its social reality, the "State" is first of all the set of persons that makes up the State apparatus in all its political, administrative, military, technical, economic, and other branches. Before all else, therefore, the "State" is a bureaucracy, and the relations of the worker with the "State" are in reality relations with this bureaucracy. We have limited ourselves here to recording a fact: the stable and irremovable character of this bureaucracy as a whole. It has this character, not from an internal point of view (i.e., not from the standpoint of real or possible "purges" or of other such dangers facing the individual bureaucrat), but from the standpoint of its opposition to the whole of society, i.e., from the fact that there is straightaway a division of Russian society into two groups: those who are bureaucrats and those who are not and never will become bureaucrats. This fact, which goes hand and hand with the totalitarian structure of the State, deprives the mass of laborers of any possibility of exerting even the most minimal amount of influence over the direction of the economy and of society in general. As a result, the bureaucracy as a whole has the means of production completely at its disposal. We will have to return later to the sociological signification of this power and to the class character of the bureaucracy.

By the mere fact that a part of the population, the bureaucracy, has the means of production at its disposal, a class structure is immediately conferred upon the relations of production. In this connection, the absence of capitalistic "private property" plays no part. Having the means of production at its collective disposal, having the right to use, enjoy, and abuse these means (being able to build factories, tear them down, contract them out to foreign capitalists, having their product at its disposal, and determining how production will proceed therein), the bureaucracy plays vis-à-vis Russia's social capital the same role that the major stockholders of a joint-stock company play vis-à-vis the capital of this company.

Two social groups therefore find themselves face-to-face: the proletariat and the bureaucracy. These two groups enter into determinate economic relations as regards production. These relations are class relations insofar as the two groups' relationship to the means of production is totally different: The bureaucracy has the means of production at its disposal, the proletariat has nothing at its disposal. The bureaucracy has at its disposal not only machinery and raw materials but also the society's consumption fund. The worker consequently is obliged to "sell" his labor power to the "State," i.e., to the bureaucracy, but this sale assumes a special character, to which we will return soon. In any case, through this "sale" the indispensable coming together of the workers' living labor with dead labor (the market for which has been cornered by the bureaucracy) is achieved.

Let us examine more closely this "sale" of labor power. It is immediately evident that the possession of the means of production and the means of coercion, the factories and the State, confers upon the bureaucracy a predominant position in this "exchange" process. Just like the capitalist class, the bureaucracy dictates its conditions in the "labor contract." But the capitalists hold sway economically within very precise limits defined by the economic laws regulating the market, on the one hand, and the class struggle, on the other. Is it the same for the bureaucracy?

It clearly is not. No objective obstacle limits the bureaucracy's possibilities for exploiting the Russian proletariat. In capitalist society, Marx says, the worker is free in a juridical sense, and he adds, not without irony, in every sense of the term. This freedom is first of all the freedom of the man who is not shackled by a fortune, and as such it is equivalent, from a social point of view, to slavery, for the worker is obliged to labor to avoid starvation, to labor wherever work is given to him and under conditions imposed upon him. However, his juridical "freedom," while serving all along as an enticement into the system, is not devoid of significance, either socially or economically. It is this "freedom" that makes labor power a commodity that can, in principle, be sold or withheld (by striking), here or elsewhere (by availing oneself of the possibility of changing firms, towns, countries, etc.). This "freedom" and its consequence, the intervention of the laws of supply and demand, allow labor power to be sold under conditions not dictated exclusively by the individual capitalist or his class as a whole, but rather under conditions that are also determined to an important degree, on the one hand, by the laws and the state of the market, and, on the other hand, by the relation of forces between the classes. We have seen that during capitalism's period of decadence and organic crisis this state of things changes and that, in particular, the victory of fascism allows capital to dictate imperatively to the workers their working conditions. We will return to this question later, but it suffices for us to remark here that a large-scale, lasting victory for fascism would certainly lead not only to the transformation of the proletariat into a class of modern-day industrial slaves but also to profound structural transformations of the economy as a whole.

In any case, it can be stated that the Russian economy finds itself infinitely closer to this model than to the one of the competitive capitalist economy when it comes to the conditions for "selling" labor power. These conditions are dictated exclusively by the bureaucracy; in other words, they are determined solely by the internal need to increase the surplus value of the productive apparatus. The expression "sale" of labor power has no real content here: Without mentioning what is actually called "forced labor" in Russia, we can say that the "normal," "free" Russian laborer does not have his own labor power at his disposal in the sense that the worker in the classical capitalist economy has his labor power at his disposal. In the overwhelming majority of cases, the worker can leave neither the enterprise where he works, nor his town, nor his country. As for strikes, it is well known that the least grave consequence is deportation to a forced-labor camp. Domestic passports, labor passes, and the MVD[53] make all job transfers and changes of work impossible without the consent of the bureaucracy. The worker becomes an integral part, a piece of the equipment of the factory in which he works. He is attached to the enterprise more rigidly than is a serf to the land; he is attached to it as a screw nut is to a piece of machinery. Henceforth, the working class's standard of living can be determined—along with the value of its labor power—solely as a function of the dominant class's accumulation and unproductive consumption.

Consequently, in the "sale" of labor power, the bureaucracy unilaterally and without any possible discussion imposes its conditions. The worker cannot even formally refuse to work; he has to work under the conditions imposed upon him. Apart from this, he is sometimes "free" to starve and always "free" to choose a more interesting method of suicide.

There is therefore a class relationship in the production process, and there is exploitation as well. Moreover, this specific type of exploitation knows no objective limits. Perhaps this is what Trotsky meant when he said that "bureaucratic parasitism is not exploitation in the scientific sense of the term." For our part, we thought we knew that exploitation in the scientific sense of the term lies in the fact that a social group, by reason of its relation to the production apparatus, is in a position both to manage productive social activity and to monopolize a portion of the social product even though it does not directly participate in productive labor or else it takes a share of this product beyond the degree of its actual participation. Such was slave-based and feudal exploitation, such is capitalist exploitation. Such also is bureaucratic exploitation. Not only is it a type of exploitation in the scientific sense of the term, it is still quite simply a scientific kind of exploitation, the most scientific and the best organized kind of exploitation in history.

To note the existence of "surplus value" in general certainly does not suffice to prove the existence of exploitation, nor does it help us understand how the economic system functions. It was pointed out a long time ago that, to the extent that there will be accumulation in socialist society, there also will be "surplus value," or in any case a gap of some sort between the product of labor and the income of the laborer. What is characteristic of a system of exploitation is the use of this surplus value and the laws that regulate it. The basic problem to be studied in the Russian economy or in any class-based economy is to be found in how this surplus value is distributed into funds for accumulation and funds for the dominant class's unproductive consumption as well as in the character and orientation of this accumulation and its internal laws. But before we grapple with this problem, we ought to examine the limits of exploitation, the real rate of surplus value, and the evolution of this exploitation in Russia as well as begin to examine the laws regulating the rate of surplus value and its evolution, understanding that the definitive analysis of these laws can only be made in terms of the laws of accumulation.

The Limits of Exploitation

In formal terms it can be said that the determination of the rate of "surplus value" in Russia rests upon the arbitrary will, or rather the discretionary power, of the bureaucracy. In the classical capitalist regime, the sale of labor power is formally a contract, whether it is arrived at by individual or by collective bargaining. Behind this formal appearance we discover that neither the capitalist nor the worker is free to discuss and to set on their own the conditions for this labor contract. In fact, through this juridical formula the worker and the capitalist only give expression to economic necessities and express the law of value in a concrete way. In the bureaucratic economy, this "free" contractual form disappears: Wages are set unilaterally by the "State," i.e., by the bureaucracy. We will see that the will of the bureaucracy obviously is not "free" in this case, as nowhere else. Nevertheless, the very fact that the setting of wages and working conditions depends upon a unilateral act of the bureaucracy on the one hand enables this act to express the bureaucracy's interests in an infinitely more advantageous way, and on the other hand ensures that the objective laws regulating the determination of the rate of "surplus value" will be fundamentally altered by it.

The extent to which the bureaucracy has discretionary power over the overall determination of wages and working conditions immediately raises an important question. If we assume it tends to pursue maximum exploitation, to what extent does the bureaucracy encounter obstacles in its efforts to extort surplus value? To what extent are there limits to its activity as an exploiter?

As we have shown, the limits resulting from the application of the "law of value" in a competitive capitalist economy cannot exist in a bureaucratic economy. Within this economic framework (where there is no labor market and no opportunity for the proletariat to resist), the "value of labor power" — in short, the Russian working class's standard of living — becomes an infinitely elastic notion subject almost to the whims of the bureaucracy. This has been demonstrated in a striking manner since the inception of the "five-year plans," i.e., ever since the economy became completely bureaucratized. Despite the enormous increase in national income following the onset of industrialization, a huge drop in the masses' standard of living has come to light. This drop in working-class income obviously goes hand in hand with an increase both in accumulation and in bureaucratic income.[54]

One might suppose that there would be some inevitable "natural" limitation imposed upon bureaucratic exploitation, as dictated by a laborer's "minimum physiological" standard of living, i.e., the elementary needs of the human organism. Actually, notwithstanding its unlimited willingness to go on exploiting, the bureaucracy is constrained to allow the Russian worker two square yards of living space, a few pounds of black bread a month, and some rags of clothing as needed for the Russian climate. But this restriction does not signify much. First, this physiological limit itself is surpassed often enough, as is shown by such manifestations as prostitution among the workers, systematic stealing from the factories and everywhere else, etc. On the other hand, having at its disposal about twenty million workers in concentration camps on whom it spends practically nothing, the bureaucracy controls a considerable mass of manpower free of charge. Finally, what is most important, nothing is more elastic than the "physiological limit" of the human organism—as has been demonstrated by the recent war, even to those who might have doubted it. Experience has shown (both in the concentration camps as well as in the countries that suffered most under the occupation) how thick a man's skin is. In another connection, the high productivity of human labor does not always require recourse to a physiologically taxing reduction in the standard of living.

Another apparent limitation on the bureaucracy's efforts at exploitation seems to result from the "relative scarcity" of certain types of skilled labor. If such a limitation were real, it certainly would be obliged to take the problem of skilled labor shortages into account. Consequently, so the argument goes, it would have to regulate wages in these branches of work according to the relative shortage of these types of skilled labor. But this problem, which affects only certain types of work, will be examined later, for it directly concerns the creation of semiprivileged or privileged strata and as such it touches much more upon the question of bureaucratic income than on that of the working class's income.

The Struggle over Surplus Value

We have said that the class struggle cannot interfere directly with the setting of wages in Russia, given that the proletariat as a class has been bound from head to foot, that it is impossible to strike, etc. Nevertheless, this in no way means either that the class struggle does not exist in bureaucratic society or, in particular, that it does not have any effect upon production. But its effects here are completely different from the effects it can have in classical capitalist society.

We will limit ourselves here to two of its manifestations, which are tied, more or less indirectly, to the distribution of the social product. The first of these is theft—theft of objects directly pertaining to productive activity, theft of finished or semifinished goods, theft of raw materials or machine parts—insofar as it assumes massive proportions and insofar as a relatively large proportion of the working class has made up for their terribly inadequate wages with proceeds from the sale of such stolen objects. Unfortunately, a lack of information prevents us at this time from detailing the extent of this phenomenon and consequently its social character. However, to the degree that this phenomenon has grown to any significant extent, it obviously expresses a class reaction—subjectively justified but objectively a dead end—that tends to alter the distribution of the social product to a certain extent. It appears that this was especially the case between 1930 and 1937.[55]

The second manifestation we might mention here is an "active indifference" toward the results of production, an indifference manifested on both quantitative and qualitative levels. Production slowdowns, even when they do not take a collective, conscious, and organized form (a "work slowdown" strike), but rather retain an individual, semiconscious, sporadic, and chronic character, already are, in capitalist production, a manifestation of working-class reaction against capitalist overexploitation, a manifestation that becomes increasingly important as capitalism can react to the crisis resulting from the falling rate of profit only by increasing relative surplus value, i.e., by intensifying more and more the pace of production. For reasons to be examined later that are in part analogous and in part different, the bureaucracy is obliged to push this tendency of capitalism to the maximum in the area of production. It is therefore understandable how the overexploited proletariat's spontaneous reaction would be to slow the pace of production to the extent that police-state coercion and economic constraints (piece-rate wages) allows them to do so. The same goes for product quality. The bewildering amount of bad workmanship in Russian production, and particularly its chronic character, cannot be explained merely by the "backwardness" of the country (which might have played a role in this connection at the start, but which already before the war no longer could be seriously taken into consideration) or by bureaucratic disorder, notwithstanding the increasing scope and character of this latter phenomenon. Conscious or unconscious bad workmanship—the incidental fraud, if it may be called that, committed when it comes to the results of production—only gives material expression to the attitude of the worker who faces a form of economic production and a type of economic system he considers completely foreign and, even more than this, fundamentally hostile to his most basic interests.

It is impossible, though, to end this section without saying a few words about the more general significance of these manifestations from the historical and revolutionary point of view. While these are subjectively sound class reactions that cannot be criticized, their objectively retrograde point of view nevertheless ought to be understood in the same light as, for example, we view desperate workers in the early capitalist era smashing machines. In the long run, if the class struggle of the Soviet proletariat is not afforded a different way out, these reactions can only bring with them this class's political and social degradation and decomposition. Under the conditions of the Russian totalitarian regime, however, this different outcome obviously cannot be built upon battles that are partial with respect either to their subject or to their object (like strikes for wage demands, which have been rendered impossible under such conditions), but only upon revolutionary struggle. We will return later at great length to this objective coincidence of minimal and maximal goals, which also has become a fundamental characteristic of the proletarian struggle in capitalist countries.

These reactions lead us to raise another problem, one that is fundamental for the bureaucratic economy: the problem of the contradiction found in the very term "complete exploitation." The tendency to reduce the proletariat to a simple gear in the productive apparatus, as dictated by the falling rate of profit, can only bring along with it a terrible crisis in the productivity of human labor. The only possible result is a reduction in the volume, and a lowering of the quality, of production itself, i.e., the accentuation, to the point of paroxysm, of the crisis factors of an exploitative economy. We will merely indicate this problem here, and will examine it at great length later [see (g) in the Postface].

The Distribution of Consumable National Income

It is clearly impossible to undertake a rigorous analysis of the rate of exploitation and the rate of surplus value in the Russian economy today. Statistics concerning the income makeup and the living standards of various social groups, or statistics from which these figures could be deduced, ceased being published for the most part immediately after the five-year plans began to be written, and the bureaucracy systematically hides all the relevant data both from the Russian proletariat and from world opinion. From this fact alone we may infer on a moral basis that this exploitation is at least as grievous as it is in capitalist countries. But we can arrive at a more exact calculation of these figures based upon general data known to us that the bureaucracy cannot hide.

Indeed, we can arrive at some sure results based upon the following data: the bureaucracy's percentage of the population and the ratio of the average bureaucrat's income to that of the average laborer's income. Obviously, such a calculation can only be approximate, but as such it is indisputable. There is also another way in which the challenges and protests of Stalinists and crypto-Stalinists are inadmissible: Let them ask the Russian bureaucracy first for the publication of verified statistics on this matter. The matter can be discussed with them afterward.

Concerning first of all the bureaucracy's percentage of the population, we refer to Trotsky's calculation in *The Revolution Betrayed*.[56] Trotsky gives figures ranging between 12 and 15 percent and up to 20 percent of the whole population for the bureaucracy (state functionaries and upper-level administrators, managerial strata in firms, technicians and specialists, managerial personnel for the kolkhozy, Party personnel, Stakhanovites, non-Party activists, etc.). Trotsky's figures have never yet been contested. As Trotsky pointed out, they were calculated giving the bureaucracy the benefit of the doubt (i.e., by reducing its size) in order to avoid arguments about secondary points. We will retain the average result of these calculations, granting that the bureaucracy constitutes approximately 15 percent of the total population.

What is the average income of the laboring population? According to official Russian statistics, "the 'average' wage per person, if you join together the director of the trust and the charwoman, was," as Trotsky observes,[57]

about 2,300 rubles in 1935, and was to be in 1936 about 2,500
rubles. . . . This figure, very modest in itself, goes still lower if you
take into consideration that the rise of wages in 1936 is only a partial
compensation for the abolition of special prices on objects of
consumption, and the abolition of a series of free services. But the
principal thing is that 2,500 rubles a year, or 208 a month, is, as we
said, the *average* payment—that is, an arithmetic fiction whose
function is to mask the real and cruel inequality in the payment of
labor.

Let us pass over this repugnant hypocrisy of publishing "average wage" statistics (imagine if, in a capitalist country, the *only* statistics published concerned average individual income and then one tried to make judgments about the social situation in this country based upon this average income!) and let us retain this figure of 200 rubles a month. In reality, the minimum wage is only 110 to 115 rubles a month.[58]

What now of bureaucratic income? According to Bettelheim, "Many technicians, engineers, and factory directors are paid 2,000 to 3,000 rubles per month."[59] Speaking later on of even "higher salaries" that are, however, "less common," he cites income figures ranging from 7,000 to 16,000 rubles a month (160 times the base wage), which movie stars and popular writers can easily earn. Without going to the heights of the political bureaucracy (president and vice-presidents of the Council of the Union and the Council of Nationalities receive 25,000 rubles a month, 250 times the base wage: This would be equivalent in France to 45 million francs a year for either the president of the Republic or the president of the Chamber, if the minimum salary is 15,000 francs[60] a month; in the United States, if the minimum wage is 150 dollars a month, it would be equivalent to 450,000 dollars a year for the president. The latter, who only receives $75,000 a year, ought to envy his Russian colleague, who has an income comparatively six times higher than his. As for Mr. Vincent Auriol,[61] who receives only 6 million francs a year, i.e., 13 percent of what he would receive if the French economy were "collectivized," "planned," and "rationalized," in a word, truly progressive, he appears to be a poor relation indeed), we will confine ourselves just to deputies' pay, "which is 1,000 rubles a month, plus 150 rubles a day when meetings are held."[62] If it is assumed that there are ten days of meetings in a month, these figures yield a sum of 2,500 rubles a month, i.e., twenty-five times the lowest wage and twelve times the "theoretically average wage." According to Trotsky, average Stakhanovites earn at least 1,000 rubles a month (this is precisely why they are called "the thousands"), and some of them earn even more than 2,000 rubles a month, i.e., ten to twenty times the minimum wage.[63] Taken as a whole, these estimates are more than confirmed by the data in Kravchenko;[64] his information establishes that the highest figures given here are extremely modest and should be doubled or tripled to arrive at the truth concerning money wages. Let us emphasize, on the other hand, that we are not taking into account perquisites and indirect or "in kind" benefits granted to bureaucrats, which as such (in the form of houses, cars, services, special health care, well-stocked and even better-priced buying cooperatives) are at least as important a part of the bureaucracy's income as its cash income.

Therefore, a ratio between average working-class and bureaucratic incomes of 1 to 10 may be used as the basis of our calculations. Doing this, we really will be acting on the bureaucracy's behalf, since we will take the "average wage," as provided by Russian statistics, of 200 rubles, which includes a significant proportion of the bureaucracy's income in this index of *working-class* wage levels for 1936, and since we also will take 2,000 rubles a month (the least high figure cited by Bettelheim) as the *average* income for the bureaucracy. Indeed, we would be justified in taking 150 rubles a month as the average worker's wage (i.e., the arithmetic mean of the minimum salary of 100 rubles and the "average wage," which includes the bureaucracy's salaries as well) and at least 4,500 rubles a month as the average salary for the bureaucracy, which we arrive at if the "standard" salary of engineers, factory managers, and technicians—which Bettelheim indicates to be 2,000 to 3,000 rubles a month—is added to an equal amount of services from which the bureaucracy benefits as a result of their position, but which are not contained in their salaried income. This would yield a ratio of 1 to 30 between the average worker's wage and the average bureaucrat's salary. The ratio is almost certainly even greater. Nevertheless, we will base the calculations we make in the remainder of this essay upon these two bases, retaining only those figures that are the least damning for the bureaucracy, i.e., those based upon a ratio of 1 to 10.

If we suppose, therefore, that 15 percent of the population has an income ten times higher than the rest of the population, the ratio between the total incomes of these two strata of the population will be $15 \times 10 : 85 \times 1$, or $150 : 85$. The consumable social product is therefore distributed in this case in the following manner: 63 percent for the bureaucracy, 37 percent for the laboring population. This means that if the value of consumer products annually is some 100 billion rubles, 63 billion is consumed by the bureaucracy (which makes up 15 percent of the population), leaving 37 billion rubles worth of products for the other 85 percent.

If we now want to take as a more realistic basis for our calculations the ratio of 1 to 30 between the average worker's income and the average bureaucrat's income we arrive at some startling figures. The ratio between the total incomes of the population's two strata will be in this case $15 \times 30 : 85 \times 1$, or $450 : 85$. In this case, the consumable social product therefore will be distributed in a ratio of 84 percent for the bureaucracy and 16 percent for the laboring population. Based upon an annual production valued at 100 billion rubles, 84 billion will be consumed by the bureaucracy and 16 billion by the laboring population. Fifteen percent of the population will consume 85 percent of the consumable product, and 85 percent of the population will have the other 15 percent of this product at their disposal. We can understand therefore why Trotsky himself ended up writing, "In scope of inequality in the payment of labor, the Soviet Union has not only caught up to, but far surpassed, the capitalist countries!"[65] Still we should point out that it is not a matter of the "payment of labor"—but we will return to this.

Simple Labor and Skilled Labor

For all of Stalinism's apologists, and even for those who, like Trotsky, persisted in seeing in the structure of the bureaucratic economy a solution, perhaps an erroneous one but imposed by historical circumstances, to the problems of "the transitional economy," the distinction between simple and skilled labor, as well as the "scarcity" of the latter, serves as a convenient basis for explaining and (in the case of avowed Stalinists) justifying bureaucratic exploitation. This is also the case with Mr. Bettelheim, this discreet advocate of the bureaucracy whose arguments we will often have to check up on in the course of this chapter [see (h) in the Postface].

At the beginning of his book, *Les Problèmes théoriques et pratiques de la planification (The Theoretical and Practical Problems of Planning,* throughout which this honorable economist constantly—and consciously—oscillates between the exposition of the problems of a "purely planned economy" and those of the Russian economy), Mr. Bettelheim tells us his methodological hypothesis concerning the remuneration of labor.

> To simplify our exposition, we have hypothesized the existence of a "free market" for labor with a wage differential designed to help orient workers toward the various branches of industry and toward various skills in conformity with the exigencies of the plan.

"But nothing," he adds,

> prevents one from thinking that, at a certain stage in the development of planning, there might be a tendency toward equalization of wages, substituting vocational guidance and nonpecuniary stimulants (greater or lesser duration of the workday) for the effects of wage differentials.[66]

Thus, *in the absence of another explanation*, the reader will see in this "purely" economic goal (guiding the worker toward the various branches of production in conformity with the exigencies of the plan) *the essential cause* of the monstrous differentiation of incomes in Russia. In noting the rather unrefined subtlety of this method, we should point out what Mr. Bettelheim does not tell us. He does not say, "Here is the cause of such a differentiation in incomes." Indeed, he prefers to say nothing about the concrete causes and character of the present differentiation of incomes in Russia. This "Marxist" is delighted to talk on and on for 334 pages about all aspects of "Soviet planning" except those social aspects that relate to its class character. But as he says on the other hand, in a "purely" planned economy one should assume "a wage differential designed to help orient the workers," and, incidentally, "nothing prevents one from thinking that, at a certain stage in the development of planning," this differential might be replaced by vocational guidance, a longer or shorter workday, etc. A "scientific" foundation thus is offered straightaway to the careless reader as well as the malicious propagandist. Mr. Bettelheim has displayed to us such maliciousness himself in articles written in the *Revue Internationale* when he explained to us that the Russian bureaucracy's "privileges" resulted from the backward character of the country and, more generally, from the irrepressible economic laws governing the transitional economy.

We who, as sordid materialists, not only have this terrible deformity that keeps us from being interested in the ethereal problems of "pure planning" and "the transitional economy *überhaupt*," but also want to know about concrete social reality in Russia, have tried to deduce from Mr. Bettelheim's transcendental principles a concrete explanation for income differentiation in Russia. We may conclude that wage differentials are necessary to guide workers toward branches of production with respect to which they show themselves to be especially recalcitrant or toward skills they show themselves to be little disposed to acquire, that such manifestations are frequent and natural in a "transitional economy that has inherited a low level of productive forces," and that they can be surmounted later on with the aid of this policy of wage differentials.

Nevertheless, at first sight this picturesque description hardly appears persuasive to us and we begin to suspect in this instance too the decisive influence of "special historical reasons" (perhaps analogous to those that have guided Russian planning, as Mr. Bettelheim confesses, to set as its goal not "the attainment of maximum economic satisfaction" but "to a certain extent (?) the realization of maximum military potential"). Special historical reasons, no doubt, and, who knows, the Slavic soul might play an important part. For, after all, what can be observed in Russia is that the jobs toward which no one, in the rest of the world, would feel a particular aversion are compensated at a much higher rate: a factory manager, for example, or a president of a kolkhoz, a colonel or a general, an engineer or a director of a ministry, a State minister or a glorious deputy peoples' commissar, etc. Therefore, it remains for us only to suppose that the Russians, with their well-known masochism and their Dostoyevskian self-punishment complex, loathe pleasant, comfortable, showy (and well-paid) "travails" and are irresistibly attracted by the smell of peat, the collecting of garbage, the heat of blast furnaces and that, in order to succeed, after great difficulties, in persuading a few of them to be factory managers, for example, they had to be promised exorbitant salaries. Why not, after all? Tolstoy, was he not a pure-blooded Great Russian who himself fled his princely mansion to go die as a down-and-out character in some monastery?

But if these little jokes are not to your liking, we will be obliged to point out, at the very least:

1. That income differentiation in Russia has nothing to do with the pleasant or disagreeable character of work (to which Mr. Bettelheim clearly alludes when he speaks about "the greater or lesser duration of the workday"), but rather with the fact that jobs are paid in inverse proportion to their level of disagreeableness and arduousness;

2. That, as concerns the "shortage of skilled labor," we do not accept being referred, twenty years after planning has begun, to the "low level of productive forces inherited from the past" and that we ask at least to see how this shortage itself and the income differentiation supposedly resulting therefrom have developed over the years;

3. That we ought also to examine the general effect of wage differentials upon this shortage. In short, we refuse to be brought back from Marx to Jean-Baptiste Say, Bastiat, and the other "harmonists" and to believe that the mere existence of a given income finds its natural and necessary justification in the play of supply and demand.

The problem of the objective basis for differentiating incomes owed to labor, based upon the specific character of the work in question (i.e., the problem of variations in the price and value of labor power concretized in a specific productive activity) on the one hand, and that of the stable and permanent "recruitment" of a labor force in the various branches of production on the other hand, is raised not only in a planned economy but in every economy that presupposes an extensive social division of labor (i.e., one that has surpassed the stage of being a natural economy). We will now grapple with the general features of these two problems, beginning with their resolution in the capitalist economy, in order to examine them afterward in a socialist economy and in its antipodes, the Russian bureaucratic economy.

According to Marx, and as is well known, the law of value is applicable to the commodity "labor power" itself. Everything else being equal (for a given country, a historical period, a standard of living, etc.), the difference between the value of two specific, concrete labor powers boils down to the different "production costs" of each specific labor power. Roughly speaking, this "production cost" includes actual training expenses, which are its least important part, and *training time*, or, more exactly, the nonproductive period of time used up by the laborer in question before entering the production process. This time has to be "amortized" over the productive life of the laborer: In capitalist society, this occurs not under the rubric of "reimbursement" for educational and training expenses by the worker to his parents but rather under the rubric of reproducing the same (or another similar) type of labor power, i.e., by the fact that the laborer in turn raises children and, assuming mere reproduction, by the fact that they are raised in the same number and at the same level of skills.

Therefore, if we suppose that the price of labor power coincides with its value, we easily discover that wage differences in capitalist society vary within quite narrow limits. Indeed, let us take the two extreme cases, that of a manual laborer whose job requires no training and who begins work at age thirteen, who consequently has to amortize over the remainder of his life twelve years of unproductive living, and that of a doctor, who completes his studies at age thirty and who must amortize over the remainder of his life thirty years of unproductive living. Let us suppose that the two workers in question have to stop working at age sixty, and let us leave aside the problem of their support during the last years of their lives. If we grant, more arbitrarily, that the cost of supporting an individual during childhood and old age is the same, and taking as a unit price the cost of production of the labor power spent during a year of old age, the value of one year of labor power for the manual laborer will be $1 + 12/48$, whereas for the doctor it will go up to $1 + 30/30$. Therefore, if the law of value operates in full here, the difference in wages between the manual worker with no skills and the worker with the highest degree of skills possible will be 60/48 to

60/30, or less than double (1.25 to 2). In reality it ought to be less, for the arbitrary assumption we made in setting the "production cost" of a year of childhood as equal to a year of old age favors the skilled worker. If a smaller cost for childhood years is taken as our basis, we arrive, as can easily be seen, at an even narrower spread.

But we are leaving this factor aside in order to compensate for not having taken into account actual training expenses (education costs, books or personal tools, etc.). As we have already said, the importance of these expenses is minimal, for even in the case of the most costly training (university education) they never exceed 20 percent of the individual's total expenses.[67]

In fact, in the actual workings of capitalist society, things happen in a quite different manner: Various factors, all of them tied in point of fact to the *class structure* of this society, come into play, which here, as everywhere else, overdetermine the "pure" economy. Among the most important of these factors are:

1. The different "historically given" standards of living of diverse groups;
2. The ruling strata's conscious predilection for a pyramidal income structure arising out of work, for reasons we will analyze later;
3. Above all, the "well-to-do" classes' monopoly over education, a monopoly that expresses itself in a great number of ways, but already in its truest and most crass form it is expressed through the insurmountable difficulty of laying out an initial "capital investment" for educating or training the child of a working-class family.

Nevertheless, even within this class framework, the main trends of economic development have in the long run predominated. Wage differences between the manual proletariat and the intellectual proletariat, for example, have been considerably reduced, and, in certain cases, they even have fallen short of the differences imposed by the law of value (cf. teachers, and clerical workers in general in France). In so-called civilized countries, the general tendency is expressed through the relative superabundance of intellectual workers.

Concerning the second point, i.e., the stable recruitment of specific types of workers in different branches of production, there is no need at all to refer to a separate economic principle in order to provide an explanation: In general, we may say that the law of numbers explains as well as guarantees stable recruitment. A philistine might be surprised that there are always a sufficient number of people who "agree" to be garbage collectors, despite the distasteful character of this occupation and its lower-than-average pay; the convergence of an infinity of individual exploitative processes and alienation in capitalist society normally suffices to assure this result, which otherwise would be miraculous.

Let us assume nevertheless that an "irregularity" crops up. In principle, price mechanisms will intervene to reestablish the "normal" state of affairs: A moderate increase in wages for underpopulated branches of work will bring back the required labor power, which in turn brings about a similar drop in pay in the branch or branches that are relatively saturated. These variations will affect only the price of labor power and in no way its value because, in themselves, they in no way will modify the cost of producing this labor power. This even explains the limited character, as concerns the amount and the duration, of such price variations of labor power.

On the other hand, much more complex mechanisms come into play where the "shortage" in a specific type of labor power affects a labor force in need of greater skills, one requiring, in a word, a partial new "production" of its labor power. Additional production of such a labor force encounters other obstacles, essentially that of a preliminary expenditure of resources by people who have at their disposal neither capital nor the possibility of borrowing any. First, a larger increase in the prices of these types of labor power will see to it that a part of the demand for this type of work is eliminated and that the balance existing between supply and demand is assured. Second, considering that it is impossible for the working class to have at its own disposal the initial capital needed to achieve an additional production of skilled labor power, capitalist society will be obliged to devote an (obviously minimal) part of its surplus value to the production of this additional labor power (vocational schools, scholarships, etc.). The extremely small amount of money the bourgeoisie spends for this purpose shows the narrow character and very limited scope of such cases in a relatively developed capitalist society.

This is what is involved in the case of capitalist production. Now we must look at the problem within the framework of a socialist economy. Let us assume—as Mr. Bettelheim wants us to—that this society consciously applies the law of value and that, moreover, it does so with *its capitalist form and content* (an assumption that, as concerns the comparison with the case of Russia, favors its bureaucracy). That is to say, it gives to laborers not, as Marx said in "Critique of the Gotha Programme," an equivalent amount in another form of the labor that these laborers furnished to society less the necessary deductions (i.e., less, basically, the amounts intended for accumulation) but rather an amount equivalent to the value of their labor power, that is, as a *"pure" capitalist enterprise* pays them. (We will see later the internal contradictions involved in this solution, which, nevertheless, is Mr. Bettelheim's self-acknowledged theoretical premise.) As we saw earlier, in this instance the maximum "economically necessary" differences between salaries would be at the most 1 : 2 (in reality, as we have seen, it would be less). No factors affecting the functioning of this law would come into play: The monopoly over education would be abolished, society would have no reason to heighten the differentiation of incomes, but every reason to diminish this differentiation, and, finally, the "specific standard of living handed down from the past" among the various branches of production would not be taken into consideration (as will be seen, this did not play a role in the case of Russia, where one proceeded to create anew an elevated standard of living for privileged strata).

Now, what about the possibility of a "shortage" of labor power in certain branches of production? As we have already indicated, *it is not* a differentiation in pay that assures in capitalist society the stable recruitment of labor power in different branches in the proportions necessary for each branch. We shall review the three principal cases in which such a "shortage" can arise.

The first case concerns jobs that are particularly arduous, disagreeable, or unsafe. It does not seem to us that this case will pose a particularly difficult problem to resolve in the socialist economy. On the one hand, it is of a limited extent, and, on the other hand, the socialist economy will inherit this situation from capitalist production, in which the problem is already as a general rule resolved. In any case, society will have to offer to the laborers in these branches some sort of compensation, basically in the form of a shorter workday, and subsidiarily in the form of higher-than-average pay. Already today—in any case, in France and the United States—miners' wages are raised above the average wage for branches requiring a similar level of skills. This excess amount does not, however, surpass 50 percent of the average wage.

The second case concerns a temporary shortage that certain branches might experience on occasion, taking the form of a shortage in nonskilled labor power or, generally speaking, a shortage that can be overcome by a simple transfer of laborers without requiring a retraining of the existing labor force. Here a pecuniary "stimulant" would be indispensable for a certain period of time in order to restore balance; a reduction in the duration of work would be inconsistent in this case with the goal to be attained. But this increase would remain within narrow enough limits—variations of 10 to 20 percent being amply sufficient, as the example from the capitalist economy shows—to lead to the desired result.

There remains the third case, which is of a relatively different order, of a much more general import, and of a particular interest for the Russian example. This is the case of types of work requiring a more or less significant amount of skill. It is a problem of a different order, for we no longer are talking about the distribution of the existing labor force among various branches of production but rather of the very production of its labor power. It is a problem of a much more general import because it is closely related to the political, cultural, and human problems of transitional society. It is, finally, a problem of a particular interest for the discussion of the Russian case itself, since the most explicit justifications of the Stalinist bureaucracy its apologists offer us rest upon the celebrated "shortage of trained staff [cadres]" in Russia and in the transitional society in general.

First of all, it is more than improbable that a postrevolutionary society could find itself facing a shortage of skilled workers *for a lengthy period of time* and affecting production as a whole or a significant part of it: The least that can be said is that it is a matter here of achieving a production objective (the production of a labor force with concretely specified duties and qualifications) similar to other such objectives (production of the means of production or of subsistence, improvement of the soil, etc.). We have here a *derivative* as opposed to originary factor in production, the production of which boils down merely to an expenditure of simple, interchangeable [fongible] labor. We reject categorically and in their entirety bourgeois and fascist "arguments" (which are readily taken up again today by Stalinists) concerning the original and irreducible scarcity of advanced forms of labor, which would thus supposedly justify higher pay. We are in full accord with Marx and Lenin in saying that in present-day society there exists in profusion the raw material required for the production of all advanced forms of labor, in the form of a superabundance of individuals equipped with the necessary inclination and capacities. Starting from this base, socialist society will view the treatment of this raw material as an objective of production to be attained within the framework of its overall plan, requiring of course production expenses to be charged to society. To this objective a socialist society will have to pay particular attention and, if it can be said, give an absolute priority, once the general social, political, and cultural implications of the problem have been taken into consideration.

As concerns recruitment in these branches, the fact that the jobs in question have an increased value consequently ensures that compensation will be up to double the base wage, and the fact that, on the other hand, such jobs are much more attractive by their very nature—to say nothing of the revolution's presumed capacity to detect in the proletariat a host of capable individuals previously stifled by capitalist exploitation—amply suffices to guarantee the success of such recruitment efforts. But if we suppose that, despite everything, there is a persistent shortage in certain—or in all—professional branches, it would be completely absurd to suppose that a socialist society would be able or be willing to resolve this problem by boosting wages even higher in these branches. Such excessive pay raises would bring about no immediate results. For, as opposed to what occurs when a similar problem crops up among various branches of production—thus necessitating the transfer of all available interchangeable labor power (this transfer can be brought about, as we said, merely by varying the price of labor)—a simple labor force cannot be transformed into a skilled labor force overnight, nor even in one or two years, by the mere fact that it is offered higher pay (which indeed, in any case, it already would have been offered). Later on, we will be able to ask whether "the adjustment of supply and demand," which might bring about such an increase, is real and above all whether it is rational from the point of view of a socialist economy.

But could such overcompensation bring about the desired result in the long term? Would it not lead to a host of individuals acquiring the requisite qualifications, encouraged by the prospect of a higher income? It clearly would not. We have indicated first of all that the motives capable of encouraging individuals to acquire the skills in question exist independently of a pay increase above the standard level. It is even clearer that this—fundamentally bourgeois—procedure can only result in a skewed selection from the standpoint of qualifications: It would not be the most apt who would be directed toward the specialized branches in question but rather those who would be able to cover the initial expense.

And this leads us to the heart of the problem. The absurdity of this method, as it concerns the production of a skilled labor force, lies in the following fact: Increasing the pay of this labor force does not alter the fundamental factors involved in this problem, which remains posed in the same terms as before. This is so because for the son of the manual laborer who has the ability and the desire to become an engineer, but lacks the means, the problem is changed in no respect by the fact that he is told, "Once you are an engineer, you will have a magnificent salary." Before the infinite reservoir of human possibilities stands the dam of the lack of economic means, an impassable barrier for nine-tenths of all individuals.

It is obvious, consequently, that just as the socialist society does not rely upon the "spontaneity of the market" to take care of its other needs, this society no longer can rely on such "spontaneity" for the production of a skilled labor force. It will administer a rational plan, based upon vocational guidance and a systematic policy of selecting and developing the most apt individuals. To carry out such a policy it will require substantially fewer resources than the social expenditures that would be involved in boosting skilled worker's salaries, as can easily be ascertained.

Let us now see how the problem occurs within the framework of Russian bureaucratic society. Let us say straight off that in drawing up this antithetical parallel, our intention is not in the least to oppose Russian reality to the mirage of a "pure" society, however socialist it may be, or to provide recipes for a future socialist kitchen, but rather to lay down a barrage against the bare-faced lies of those who, positively or through a subtle combination of affirmations and omissions, of empty talk and periods of silence, try cynically and shamefully to justify bureaucratic exploitation through "Marxist" economic arguments.

First of all, what are the facts? According to the figures Mr. Bettelheim himself cites (figures that are well known from other sources and can be confirmed by a host of data from the most varied authorities), "the range of salaries" in Russia runs from 100 rubles a month at the base for the simple manual worker to 25,000 rubles for the summits of the state bureaucracy. This was so in 1936. The latter amount, indeed, absolutely is not an exception or unrelated to other incomes, since, according to Mr. Bettelheim, "many technicians, engineers and factory directors get 2,000 to 3,000 rubles per month, this being twenty to thirty times more than the poorest paid workers";[68] he also says here that other groups occupy intermediary echelons, with incomes of 7,000, 10,000, or 15,000 rubles a month.

We therefore find ourselves standing before a pyramid of incomes running from 1 to 250, if only monetary wages are taken into account. If "social" wages—which, "far from compensating for them (these inequalities), increase them, for these ("social wages") mostly benefit those who receive the highest salaries"[69]—are taken into account, the distance between the base and the summit of this income pyramid would easily double. Let us nevertheless make a present to the bureaucracy of its "social wage" and retain the *official* figure of 1 to 250, which is amply sufficient for what we are trying to prove.

What are the "objective" arguments aimed at "justifying" or "explaining" this enormous disparity?

First, the value of labor power ought to differ according to the degree of specialization. We will not belabor this point: We have just shown that a differentiation based upon the difference in value of labor power can only range within limits going at most from a single amount to double that amount. That is to say, from the point of view of the law of value as it was conceived by Marx, the higher strata of Russian society benefit from incomes of 10, 15, and up to 125 times higher than those the value of their labor power would necessitate.

Second, the incomes of "skilled workers" (from now on, we will have to put this entirely theoretical expression in quotation marks) had to be raised above their value in order to attract into these professions the workers lacking there.

But why the devil is there a dearth of these kinds of workers? On account of the arduous, unsafe, or disagreeable character of the types of jobs in question? Not at all. We have never heard anyone say that in Russia there was a lack of hands for this kind of work. If that indeed is what was lacking, the "labor camps and reeducation camps" (read: concentration camps) would be (and actually are) there to remedy the situation. In fact, the best paid jobs obviously are the least arduous, the most comfortable, and (the possibility of purges excepted) the least dangerous that can be found. No, these jobs on the whole are jobs for "trained staff," and the problem is promptly reduced by the bureaucracy and its advocates to the "shortage of trained staff." But we have shown already that faced with the possibility of a similar shortage, raising the pay of categories experiencing "scarcity" is no help at all, for it alters in no way the particulars of the problem. How else, indeed, can one explain the fact that after twenty-five years of bureaucratic power this "shortage of trained staff" persists and is becoming more marked, unless it is looked at in terms of the constant widening of income ranges and the permanent accentuation of privileges? Here is an amply sufficient illustration of what we have said about the absurdity of this procedure that supposedly is intended to mitigate the dearth of trained staff. In particular, how else can one explain the fact that, since 1940, the bureaucracy has brought back heavy tuition expenses for secondary education [see (i) in the Postface]? Even though it has adopted this policy of exorbitant income differentiation in order to "resolve the problem of a dearth of trained staff"—one knows not why this policy has been adopted (or rather one knows only too well why)—it clearly has not precluded itself (or rather it has not at all absolved itself) in the least from trying to increase, through centralized means, the production of the kinds of skilled labor power in question here. Beyond this, the bureaucracy (which by itself alone consumes at least 60 percent of Russia's national consumable income under the pretext of "mitigating the dearth of trained staff") prevents those who are the sole concrete hope for overcoming this dearth (i.e., all those who are not children of bureaucrats) from acquiring those skills about whose scarcity the bureaucracy is always bitterly complaining! Just one-tenth of the income swallowed up by the bureaucratic parasites would suffice in five years to bring forth a historically unprecedented superabundance of trained staff, *if* it were earmarked for the education of the people.

Far from remedying the dearth of trained staff, as we have said, this differentiation of incomes in reality only increases it. We encounter here the same sophism found in the problem of accumulation: The historical justification of the bureaucracy supposedly is to be found in Russia's low level of accumulation, whereas in fact the bureaucracy's unproductive consumption and its very existence are the principal brakes put on the process of accumulation. Likewise, the bureaucracy's existence and its privileges supposedly are justified by the "dearth of trained staff," when in fact this bureaucracy consciously acts to maintain this dearth! Thus the bourgeois go around all the time talking about how the capitalist regime is necessary because the workers are incapable of managing society, without adding at any point that there is no other reason for this alleged "incapacity" other than the conditions to which this system itself condemns the workers.[70]

During the first postrevolutionary years, when higher pay was offered to "specialists" and technicians, it was a matter first of all of retaining a large number of trained staff who otherwise would have tried to flee, basically for political reasons. Later on, it was a matter of a purely temporary measure intended to allow workers to learn from them[71] and to win time in order for the training of new staff to yield results. But that was thirty years ago. What we have seen since is the "self-creation" of privileges by and for the bureaucracy, the accentuation of the former, the crystallization of the latter, and the "castification" of its strata, i.e., the preservation of the socially dominant position of these strata through a de facto monopoly over education. This monopoly over education goes hand in hand with the complete concentration of political and economic power in the hands of the bureaucracy and is connected with a conscious policy oriented toward selecting a stratum of privileged people in every field. Such a stratum is economically, politically, and socially dependent upon the bureaucracy proper (a phenomenon of which the most astonishing example is the creation ex nihilo of a monstrous kolkhoz bureaucracy, once agriculture was "collectivized"). This policy was topped off with a trend toward intense stratification in every field, presented under the ideological mask of the "struggle against egalitarian cretinism."

In summary, we find ourselves faced with a differentiation of incomes absolutely without any relation either to the value of labor power furnished or to a policy "designed to orient workers toward the various branches of industry and toward various skills in conformity with the exigencies of the plan." How then can we characterize those who have recourse to economic arguments in order to justify this state of affairs? Let us say simply that with respect to bureaucratic exploitation they are playing the same role of shabby apologists as Bastiat had been able to play opposite capitalist exploitation.

It will perhaps be said that this is their right. Most incontestably so, we would respond. But in doing so, it is not their right to present themselves as "Marxists." For after all, it cannot be forgotten that arguments that justify the incomes of exploiting strata by the "scarcity" of a factor of production that these strata have at their disposal (interest by the "scarcity" of capital, ground rent by the "scarcity" of land, etc.—bureaucratic incomes by the "scarcity" of skilled labor) have always been the basis of bourgeois economists' arguments aimed at justifying exploitation.

For a revolutionary Marxist, however, these kinds of reasons do not justify anything. They do not even explain anything, for their own premises themselves demand an explanation. In allowing, for example, the "scarcity" (or the supply and demand) of cultivable land to "explain" ground rent and its fluctuations, one wonders: (1) upon what general foundations does this system regulated by supply and demand rest; what are its social and historical presuppositions; and (2), above all, why must this rent, which plays this allegedly objective role, be transformed, be "subjectivized" into the income of a social class, of the land-owners? Marx and Lenin have already observed that the "nationalization of the land," i.e., the suppression not of ground rent but of its transformation into income of a social group, is the ideal capitalist claim; indeed, it is obvious that the bourgeoisie, even if it admits in principle that ground rent acts as a means "of balancing supply and demand in the use of nature" and of eliminating from the market "nonsolvent needs," does not understand why this charge ought to benefit landowners exclusively, seeing that, for the bourgeoisie, no monopoly is justified save for the one it itself has over capital. Obviously, this ideal bourgeois claim is never lodged, for general political reasons first of all, and in particular on account of the rapid merger of the capitalist classes and landowners. All the same, this theoretical example proves that even if this "scarcity" is admitted in principle as a regulating principle of the economy—in reality, it is merely a reactionary mystification—the distribution of the revenue resulting from this "scarcity" to certain social categories in no way can be deduced therefrom. This was understood even by the "neosocialist" school, which tried to uphold both the regulative character of the "scarcity" of goods and services and, at the same time, the allotment to society of the resulting revenues.

In the case before us, none of these "explanations" concerning the "scarcity of skilled labor in Russia" either justifies or explains the bureaucracy's appropriation of the revenues allegedly resulting from it, *except if one refers to the class character of the Russian economy*, i.e., to the monopoly the bureaucracy has over the conditions of production in general, and over the production of skilled labor in particular. When the class structure of Russian society has been understood, everything is explained and everything even is "justified" in one stroke. But this justification—similar to the one that can be given historically to the capitalist regime and, in a word, even to fascism—does not go very far. It ends where the exploited class's possibility of overthrowing the exploitative regime begins—whether this regime calls itself the "French Republic" or the "Union of Soviet Socialist Republics"—a possibility whose only test is revolutionary action itself.

Notes

1. In connection with this, Trotsky has contributed the most—with no one else being his equal on account of the immense authority he enjoyed in anti-Stalinist revolutionary circles—toward maintaining this confusion within the vanguard of the working class. His erroneous analysis of Russian society continues to exert an influence that has become positively pernicious to the extent that it continues to be maintained with infinitely less seriousness and semblance of scientific underpinnings by his epigones. Let us note again the influence that certain free-lance Stalinists like Mr. Bettelheim—usually considered "Marxist," for the great amusement of future generations—exert due to the fact that they dress up their apologia for the bureaucracy in a "socialist" jargon.

2. For the reformers of the bureaucratic regime, it is a matter quite frankly of preserving the "good side" (the relations of production, which are "at bottom socialist") and of eliminating the "bad side" (unequal distribution, bureaucratic parasitism). (Cf. K. Marx, "The Poverty of Philosophy," in *MECW*, vol. 6, pp. 167ff.) Here is how Engels criticized the similar efforts of the late Herr Dühring: ". . . production wealth, the good side; . . . distribution wealth . . . the bad side, away with it! Applied to the conditions of today, this runs: The capitalist mode of production is quite good and can remain, but the capitalist mode of distribution is no good and must be abolished. Such is the nonsense which comes of writing on economics without even having grasped the con-

nection between production and distribution" (F. Engels, *Anti-Dühring. Herr Eugen Dühring's Revolution in Science*, trans. Emile Burns, ed. C. P. Dutt [New York: International Publishers, 1939], p. 206).

3. "The question of what this is could have been answered only by a critical analysis of '*political economy*,' embracing the totality of those property relationships, not in their juridical expression as relations of volition but in their *real form, that is, as relations of production*. . . . (Proudhon) entangled the totality of these economic relationships in the general notion of 'property' " (K. Marx, Letter to Johann Baptist von Schweitzer [in Berlin], London, January 24, 1865, in *The Letters of Karl Marx*, selected and trans. with explanatory notes and an intro. by Saul K. Padover [Englewood Cliffs, N.J.: Prentice-Hall, 1979], p. 192; our emphasis).

4. Trotsky, *The Revolution Betrayed*, ch. 9 (New York: Pathfinder Press, 1972).

5. "It is clear, firstly, that the exchange of activities and abilities which takes place within production itself belongs directly to production and essentially constitutes it. The same holds, secondly, for the exchange of products, insofar as that exchange is the means of finishing the product, and making it fit for direct consumption. To that extent, exchange is an act comprised within production itself. Thirdly, the so-called exchange between dealers and dealers is by its very organization entirely determined by production, as well as being itself a producing activity. . . . Exchange in all its moments thus appears as either directly comprised in production or determined by it" (K. Marx, "Introduction to the Critique of Political Economy," in *Grundrisse: Foundations of the Critique of Political Economy*, trans. Martin Nicolaus [New York: Vintage, 1973], p. 99).

6. Ibid., pp. 90-94.

7. Ibid., p. 95. (See also *Capital* [New York: International Publishers, 1967], vol. 3, pt. 7, ch. 51, pp. 878-83.)

8. Marx, *Grundrisse*, pp. 96-97.

9. Ibid., pp. 99-100.

10. K. Marx, *Capital*, vol. 2, pt. 1, ch. 1, p. 31; pt. 3, ch. 19, p. 389; vol. 3, pt. 7, ch. 48, pp. 824ff.; F. Engels, *Anti-Dühring*, pp. 294ff.

11. L. Trotsky, *In Defense of Marxism*, 2nd ed. (New York: Pathfinder Press, 1973), p. 6.

12. *The Revolution Betrayed*, p. 51.

13. Ibid., p. 113.

14. Ibid., p. 249.

15. Marx, Preface to *A Contribution to the Critique of Political Economy*, in *MESW*, pp. 182-83 (our emphasis).

16. See "The Proletarian Revolution and the Renegade Kautsky," *LSWONE*.

17. See Marx, Letter to Johann Baptist von Schweitzer, pp. 192ff.

18. Engels, "Engels to Schmidt . . .," in *MESW*, p. 697 (our emphasis).

19. Trotsky had pointed out that the Hitlerian regime had changed nothing formally in the Weimar Constitution and that "juridically" Hitler could be overthrown at any moment by a vote of the Reichstag. See *The Revolution Betrayed*, p. 270.

20. See *State and Revolution*, in *LSWONE*, "The Proletarian Revolution and the Renegade Kautsky," etc.

21. *Capital*, vol. 1, pt. 2, ch. 6, p. 193-95.

22. Cf. K. Marx, "Critique of the Gotha Programme," *MESW*, p. 325.

23. Engels, *Anti-Dühring*, p. 304.

24. Lenin, "Resolutions of the Sixth Congress of the R.S.-D.L.P.," in *LCW* (New York: International Publishers, 1932), vol. 20-1, p. 302.

25. *The Revolution Betrayed*, pp. 245-48.

26. Lenin, ibid., p. 88. See also *LCW* (Moscow: Progress Publishers, 1980), vol. 24, p. 305.

27. *Theses, Resolutions and Manifestos of the First Four Congresses of the Third International* (New York: Humanities Press, 1980), p. 30. [T/E: This paragraph, which we have altered slightly for purposes of standardization, comes from the "Manifesto of the Communist International to the Workers of the World" (written by Trotsky), March 6, 1919.]

28. Lenin, " 'Left-Wing' Childishness and the Petty Bourgeois Mentality," *LSWONE*, p. 443-44. [T/E: Castoriadis's quotation omits a parenthetical swipe Lenin made against "Menshevik blockheads."]

29. See the article, "Socialisme ou Barbarie," in the first issue of this review, pp. 34-37 [T/E: i.e., the beginning of the preceding essay].

30. L. Trotsky, *The Third International after Lenin* (New York: Pathfinder Press, 1970), p. 300.

31. L. Trotsky, Letter to Borodai, published in *New International*, 1943, p. 124 [reprinted since then as "Our Differences with the Democratic Centralists," in Max Shachtman, *The Bureaucratic Revolution: The Rise of the Stalinist State* (New York: Donald Press, 1962), p. 97].

32. See Trotsky's letter to Borodai and all his writings of this period.

33. L. Trotsky, "The Problems of Development of the USSR," in *Writings, 1930-31* (New York: Pathfinder Press, 1973), p. 225.

34. It was Max Shachtman who first showed that Trotsky had advanced his theory concerning the "socialist" character of nationalized property only after 1932 (see *New International*, 1943). It should be noted that Shachtman incorrectly characterizes the conception that Trotsky had defended till then as "Trotsky's first theory": This conception was just the Marxist movement's general conception, as we have shown, and not at all a theory of Trotsky's. But Shachtman cannot say this, for, in this case, he would have to give his own account of the problem of State capitalism.

35. Let us recall that most of Russian industry was nationalized by 1918, as were the land, the mines, transportation, the banks, etc.

36. The first signs of this switch are formulated in "The Workers' State, Thermidor and Bonapartism," *Writings, 1934-35* (New York: Pathfinder Press, 1974), pp. 166-84.

37. *In Defense of Marxism*, p. 9.

38. Ibid., p. 6. [T/E: The English text actually says ". . . on the technical and cultural development of the country."] (See *The Revolution Betrayed*.)

39. See Marx, *Capital*, vol. 3, pt. 7, ch. 48, pp. 822 and 827; ch. 51, p. 881.

40. From a formal point of view, the worker and the capitalist are included among such "independent units."

41. The expression "dead labor" must be taken in its full meaning, which concerns not only machines and raw materials but also the means of consumption that have to be put, during the period of production, at the disposal of the workers, i.e., ultimately all the conditions of production other than actual, current labor, capital without further qualifications.

42. Marx, *Capital*, vol. 3, pt. 7, ch. 48, p. 819.

43. Ibid., p. 827.

44. Ibid., p. 822.

45. *Capital*, vol. 1, pt. 2, ch. 6, pp. 170-71.

46. See also "The Poverty of Philosophy," in *MECW*, vol. 6, pp. 206ff.

47. Marx, *Capital*, vol. 3, pt. 7, ch. 50, p. 859.

48. See "The Limits of Exploitation," in "Proletariat and Bureaucracy," the second section of this essay.

49. Marx, "Critique of the Gotha Programme," in *MESW*, p. 323. [T/E: We have followed the French here. The English translation merely states that "content and form are changed."]

50. Ibid.

51. Ibid., p. 325.

52. T/E: See ibid., p. 324. We have changed the translation to fit more closely with the French, which expresses the idea that "bourgeois right" is *founded* upon inequality.

53. T/E: The MVD is the Soviet Ministry of Information, or secret police.

54. A study of the evolution of exploitation through the five-year plans will be made in another article. [T/E: The text was never published.]

55. On theft during this period, see the works of Ciliga, Victor Serge, etc.

56. *The Revolution Betrayed*, pp. 135-43.

57. Ibid., p. 124.

58. Bettelheim, *La Planification soviétique*, p. 62.

59. Ibid.

60. T/E: These are old francs, worth roughly 1 percent of a new franc.

61. T/E: Vincent Auriol (1884-1966) was president of the Fourth Republic at this time.

62. Bettelheim, ibid., p. 62.

63. *The Revolution Betrayed*, p. 125.

64. T/E: Kravchenko was a Russian bureaucrat who left the USSR and became known for his book, *I Chose Freedom* (New York: Scribner's, 1946).

65. *The Revolution Betrayed*, p. 125.

66. *Les Problèmes théoriques*, p. 3n. [T/E: The abridged English translation of this work (trans. Brian Pierce [New York: Asia Publishing House, 1959]) does not include any of the passages cited by Castoriadis in this article.]

67. We are not speaking here of occupations that have the character of an "absolute monopoly" (artists, inventors, geniuses of all kinds, etc.). We consider it to be generally accepted that in present-day society—to say nothing of a socialist society—there are a sufficient number of individuals capable of successfully performing all existing types of work.

68. *La Planification soviétique*, p. 62.

69. Ibid., p. 63.

70. We would need all the richly violent language of a Lenin responding to Kautsky in order to characterize with a minimum of justice the ventures of people like Mr. Bettelheim, who purposely gets lost in all the technical details of Russian "planning" and who cites a wealth of charts and figures in order to make himself forget and to make others forget what is, from the revolutionary Marxist point of view, the crux of the matter: What is the class significance of the monstrous disparity of incomes in Russia? But we have decided once and for all to ignore the very person of Mr. Bettelheim—we think this is the best thing that could happen to him—in order to lay hold of the thing itself.

71. Lenin, *LSW* (New York: International Publishers, 1943), vol. 7, pp. 372-76.

Postface

It is not without value to indicate a few of the ways in which the content of this article has been surpassed.

a) The idea that "production is to property . . . as reality is to ideology" obviously belongs to classical Marxism and is almost completely meaningless. See *MTR/MRT*.

b) What is said here concerning the idea of "State capitalism" in traditional Marxism, although correct, does not sufficiently accentuate the ambiguity that has always dominated the movement on this point and that has, in fact, made people think of "private property" when they were talking about "capitalism." It is on this ground that Trotskyist confusions can flourish.

c) Contrary to what was said in the essay, the Russian bureaucracy quite obviously is developing the forces of production—just as traditional capitalism as a whole also has done. This criterion, inherited from traditional Marxism, strictly has no value.

d) Trotsky's arguments will be found in "The Defense of the Soviet Republic and the Opposition" (against Louzon and Urbahns), in L. Trotsky, *Writings, 1929* (New York: Pathfinder Press, 1975), pp. 262-303; *The Soviet Union and the Fourth International* (against Urbahns, Laurat, Souvarine, and Weil; New York: Pioneer Press, 1934); "Once Again: The USSR and Its Defense" (against Craipeau and Yvon), in *Writings, 1937-38*, pp. 86-90; "Not a Workers' and Not a Bourgeois State?" (against Burnham), ibid., pp. 60-71; "Learn to Think" (against Ciliga), ibid., pp. 330-35; and, obviously, *In Defense of Marxism* (against Rizzi, Burnham, and Shachtman).

e) The theory of wages developed here is basically one that can be drawn from Marx, and as such it is false. See *DC I* and *MRCM/MCR I*.

f) Concerning the compensation of labor in a socialist society, see *CS I* and *II*.

g) Data concerning the exploitation of the proletariat in Russia obviously are those available at the time. The substance of the argument remains true, but the description of the historical trend, which still reflects the idea of growing exploitation and neglects the fundamental importance of class struggle in the determination of wages, even under totalitarian conditions, is erroneous. I will return to this at length in *La Russie après l'industrialisation* [T/E: this volume has not yet been published]. See also *RPB/PRAB*.

h) Mr. Bettelheim was at the time nearly the only advocate of the Stalinist bureaucracy to do anything other than merely repeat Stalin's speeches. Whence comes the importance that (circumstantially) was given to him in this article. Since then he has changed patrons: He now pleads for the Chinese bureaucracy, and he has even discovered that "juridical property" and "the real relations of production" must not be confounded, a discovery he attributes, moreover, to his friend Paul Sweezy (people are generous with that which does not belong to them). At the same time he has invented the existence of a "bourgeois State" (?) in Russia—which allows him, once more, to duck the problem of bureaucracy. See P. Sweezy and C. Bettelheim, *On the Transition to Socialism* (New York: Monthly Review Press, 1971), pp. 15 and 46.

i) The policy abolishing free secondary education in Russia has itself been abolished since then. This changes nothing at the core of the problem. And at the periphery, it should be pointed out that completely free education at all levels is the best way for a bureaucracy to co-opt the "best" members of the exploited strata.

7
The Exploitation of the Peasantry under Bureaucratic Capitalism

The Agrarian Problem Today

We hardly need recall how enormously important the agrarian problem is for the proletarian revolution and how the proletariat needs to rally a majority of the exploited peasant strata behind it under the banner of a socialist program. Let us simply mention the facts that highlight the importance of this problem.

Today, two centuries after the industrial revolution began, the great majority of our planet's population still makes its living by farming, and it does so under conditions that, most often, are not directly capitalist in their nature. Approximately two-thirds of the world's population makes its living in agriculture. Half continue to do so under conditions that preserve the form of individual small landholdings or even precapitalist types of property ownership, even though their content now is characterized by capital's exploitation of the peasantry.[1]

We know quite well that this fact has been used to the full in all bourgeois "refutations" of Marxism and especially in critiques of the theory of concentration. For many years bourgeois professors "proved" with as much rigor as they could muster that capital concentration in the way Marx analyzed it quite simply was impossible and would never come to pass. When, nevertheless, this concentration began to appear even to the blind, when all of the world's industry began to be dominated by a tiny number of capitalist groupings, these good men marched off to the fields and took refuge in the domain of agriculture, where one "knew nothing" of this process of concentration and where everything continued to work in its old patriarchal setting.

Originally published as "L'Exploitation de la paysannerie sous le capitalisme bureaucratique," *S. ou B.*, 4 (October 1949). Reprinted in *SB 1*, pp. 285-314, with Postface, p. 315.

We do not intend to analyze here the question of concentration in the field of agriculture. But let us mention the fundamental aspects of the problem.

1. The existence of the process of concentration in agriculture today is undeniable. That this process goes more slowly, that it appears to occur under different modalities than it does in industry are facts that follow from agriculture's specific characteristics as well as from the general evolution of the economy and from the very predominance of industrial concentration itself, as we shall see later. But these differences serve rather to confirm the law of concentration instead of contradicting it in any way. Leaving aside the smaller-scale aspects of agricultural concentration, which exist without exception in every country, let us recall simply that in the two principal economic powers in the world today, America and Russia, we can comprehend how agriculture has evolved since 1918 only if we examine how it has become concentrated.

2. Concentration is not a mechanical, automatic process. The predominance of the tendency toward concentration over what can be called the tendency toward the diffusion of capital basically is a result of the development of technique. The continual emergence of new, more profitable technical methods requiring considerable capital outlays and the employment of a relatively smaller labor force makes it hopeless for the small (industrial or agricultural) enterprise to struggle against the large one. Now, for several reasons, some of which are circumstantial and some of which are not at all so,[2] modern techniques have not been applied as rapidly in agriculture as they have been in industry. Only for the past thirty years has it been possible to say that modern methods of cultivation have begun to predominate over traditional methods. But to the extent that this is true, nothing will be able to stop any longer the industrialization of agriculture now that it has been set in motion.[3]

On the other hand, the development of capitalism in industry necessarily has had repercussions upon the movement of the agricultural population. During an initial period of time (what Marx called "primitive accumulation"), industrial capitalism brutally expropriated huge masses of peasants to create for itself an abundant source of cheap labor. During its expansionary phases, however, there were times when it still did not find any other source of manpower than the agricultural population. The worldwide exodus of peasants toward the towns continues even today, and this depopulation of the countryside has served as a powerful stimulant for extending modern techniques into agriculture.[4]

3. But the integration of agriculture into the process of concentration was carried out for a half century in a much more far-reaching manner through the gradual domination of the market by monopolies. The maintenance of the juridical form of individual ownership of land parcels and even the maintenance to a certain extent of land-parcel property as the productive unit for applying agricultural techniques is only of a relatively secondary importance once monopolies come to have complete dominance over the market and over industrial production. It is not just that agriculture is dominated by industry in both technical terms as well as economic ones, nor that its progress is determined by improvements in industrial techniques and by progress in industrial production. What is even more important is that monopolization of key sectors of the economy—and

this monopolization begins in its industrial sectors—entirely transforms the economic signification of the small enterprise. Not only is the small enterprise dominated thereafter by monopolies—which, for example, set the selling price and the purchase price of the goods it produces as well as the price of its raw materials, implements, etc.—not only is the owner of the small enterprise exploited *qua* consumer when he is obliged to contribute to the surplus profits monopolies build up, but the maintenance of the small enterprise in certain sectors of the economy—and principally in agriculture—corresponds, from the monopolies' point of view, to a profound economic necessity: In the sectors where production has not yet been completely rationalized, where risks arising from extra-economic factors continue to play an important role—and this is the case par excellence in agriculture—monopolies prefer for agriculture to be integrated in a manner that guarantees them maximum profits and a minimum of losses for as long as possible. The concrete significance of maintaining land-parcel farming in agriculture is that monopolies profit from agricultural production whenever things are going well, whereas land-parcel farmers bear pretty much by themselves the burden of any problems—whether in the form of bad harvests or overproduction.

4. Nevertheless, there is a factor that, formally, is opposed to the process of concentration in agriculture—although in reality it is only a manifestation of it—and which should not be underestimated: Using the State, capitalism consciously has intervened in the countryside in order to orient the development of rural economic and social relations in a particular direction. In several countries that already had carried out their bourgeois democratic revolution (in the traditional sense of the term), where therefore the partitioning of land and the constitution of an extremely numerous class of small landholders had taken place during a time when this transformation did not pose any significant challenge to political stability, the bourgeoisie began to see, correctly, that maintaining this class would furnish it with one of the essential bases for its continued domination. There is nothing astonishing if from then on its agrarian policy has been oriented steadfastly toward the maintenance of a "stable" economic and social structure in the area of agriculture. It is indeed one of the points upon which the relative antagonism existing within the capitalist State—which is itself the universal and abstract expression of the interests of capital and the daily interests of particular strata of capitalists—has at times been expressed most forcefully. This policy of the capitalist State has had two principal objectives: the "organization" of the peasants into corporate unions, which in the final analysis are a form of rural cartel in which the dominant role is played by its richest members, and the "protection" of the agricultural population through the protection of agricultural prices, which is merely the monopolistic principle of price fixing applied to a particular sector of the economy.

From the historical point of view, this capitalist State policy quite obviously is utopian, and, in the final analysis, it contradicts both the interests of capital and the insuperable tendencies that the overall development of economic concentration exhibits. As such, this policy is historically doomed; it certainly will not be in "agricultural corporatism" that bureaucratic capitalism will be able to find its complementary structure in agriculture. Since the beginning of the twentieth century and until today, however, this policy has been an important factor in the evolution of society. On several occasions, it has influenced the outcome of the class struggle in Europe.

It is in the light of the analysis of the exploitation of the peasantry within the framework of bureaucratic capitalism that we will be able to find the answer to the problem of the modern forms of capitalist exploitation of the peasantry. Indeed, Russian bureaucratic capitalism both prefigures the forms under which the exploitation of the peasantry will develop within the framework of total concentration and indicates the limits to this development.

The Exploitation of the Peasantry in Russia

The central feature of the exploitation of the peasantry in Russia is to be found in the tax the peasants have to pay in kind to the State. Both the required quantity of and the purchase price paid by the State for the produce delivered by the kolkhozy can vary; nonetheless, as a general rule the State levies 40 percent of the gross product, and 20 percent more must be delivered to the machine tractor stations (MTS [see (a) in the Postface]). Thus the peasantry disposes of at most only 40 percent of the gross product—and still we are dealing here with a hypothetical percentage.[5] In any case, we should not forget that from this gross produce seeds must be deducted, and sometimes livestock feed as well.

Pushing the way monopolies do business to the absolute limit, the State unilaterally and absolutely fixes the price at which it buys agricultural produce. This is how exploitation occurs. Here, for example, are the prices for a quintal of rye in 1933:[6]

	RUBLES
Delivery price to the State	6.03
Rationed price (rye flour)	25
Commercial price (rye flour)	45
Kolkhoz (open market) price (Moscow region)	58

Thus the State buys this produce from the kolkhozy at a price that is extremely lower than what it is worth. Later we will try to specify the order of magnitude of this theft. This is the first—and fundamental—feature of the bureaucratic State's exploitation of the peasantry, and as a matter of fact it is the one that likens this kind of exploitation to feudal exploitation: Peasants are "bound to the soil," the exploiting class deducts at least half of the produce, and all this is aggravated by the ever-changing conditions of production and by the ever-present possibility that the State will increase the length of the mandatory workday or deduct an even greater quantity of produce.

The second feature is to be found in the exploitation of the peasants as consumers. These peasants are exploited when they purchase manufactured goods they need for their personal consumption. This phenomenon already is well known under monopoly rule, but here it takes on unprecedented proportions on account of the State's absolute monopoly over all manufactured goods and the complete authority it has to fix the sale price of "its" products. The price of rye in 1933, just cited as an example, also can serve here as a basis for determining an order of magnitude. The State bought the quintal of rye at 6 rubles, and sold the *rationed* rye flour (i.e., the flour whose price is supposed to "protect" or "favor" the consumer) at 25 rubles a quintal. Assuming that turning rye into rye flour costs 4 rubles per quintal (66 percent of the price of the raw material; in fact, the processing costs, including loss in weight, ought to be much smaller), it "earns" 15 rubles per quintal (rate of profit: 150 percent); i.e., it takes back from urban working-class consumers 60 percent of the part of their wages they spend on rye flour. In the 25 rubles the consumer was paying for this quintal of rye flour, 10 rubles at most represented the real "cost" of the product *for the State*, and the other 15 the latter's profit pure and simple.

This example is indeed purely theoretical, for the worker never would have had the opportunity (during the various periods of time when rationing was in effect) to fully satisfy his needs with official rations; he is forced to resort either to the State "free" shops or the kolkhozniki's open market. In the first case, by paying 45 rubles a quintal for rye flour he will be exploited by the State on 80 percent of the value of his purchases, the State making a net gain of 35 rubles per quintal sold. In the second case, he would pay 58 rubles per quintal, and it would be the kolkhozniki who would "profit" from it. But again it is the State that wins, although indirectly, because the price of agricultural products on the open market has to cover a certain "overall profitability" of the agricultural enterprise. With all of its revenues (both those resulting from the deliveries to the State as well as those coming from sales on the open market), the peasant class has to be able to cover all of its basic needs: The exorbitant price of produce on the open market only helps to compensate for the spoliatory price the State gets for the purchases it makes, and the lower this last price is, the higher the prices on the open market will rise.

This example allows us to make a rough calculation of the order of magnitude of the exploitation that results from the mandatory delivery of produce at the State's spoliatory prices. Let x be the production cost of a quintal of rye; the cost of 100 quintals then will be $100x$, and this price should equal all the revenues the kolkhoz will receive from these 100 quintals. These revenues break down, according to the previously cited figures,[7] as follows: 60 quintals delivered to the State and to the MTS, at the price of 6 rubles per quintal; 15 to 20 quintals sold on the open market at 58 rubles per quintal; and 20 to 25 quintals consumed in kind. (We can account for the latter on the basis of their production cost.) Thus:

$$100x = 60.6 + 20.58 + 20x$$

which gives us $x = 19$.

The production cost per quintal of wheat, therefore, is 19 rubles. By deducting 60 percent of production at a price of 6 rubles, the State steals from the peasants the difference between the cost of 60 quintals and what they are paid for it;

this is a difference of $(60.19) - (60.6) = 1,140 - 360 = 780$. On the total value of 100 quintals, which is $19.100 = 1,900$ rubles, this spoliation surpasses 40 percent.

This spoliation is only one of the features of the bureaucracy's exploitation of the peasantry. The second one, mentioned earlier, occurs when the State sells industrial products to the peasants at marked-up prices. We have just seen that in the case of rye flour sold to urban workers, the latter are cheated on their wages on the order of 60 percent. We do not have the data that would allow us to determine the order of magnitude corresponding to the amount the peasants are cheated. There is no reason to believe, however, that it would be any smaller.

The third feature of this exploitation is to be found in the differentiation of incomes among the peasantry, whether it be between different kolkhozy or within the same kolkhoz. Although the effect and the social function of this differentiation are the same, its concrete bases vary according to the circumstances.

The fact that "millionaire" kolkhozniki exist not only is not hidden, it is triumphantly and cynically proclaimed by the bureaucracy. We must look at the economic underpinnings of this phenomenon.

To begin with, the kolkhozy are unequal in size (in comparison to the number of producers on each kolkhoz), as well as in relation to the fertility of their soil and the value of their produce.[8] There are small, medium-sized, and large kolkhozy relative to the number of members each one has. There are kolkhozy whose soil is extremely fertile, and others whose soil is average or poor. Some kolkhozy are designated to cultivate produce that is bought by the State at higher prices than other produce (for example, all nonfood crops). Some kolkhozy are served better than others by the MTS, some have a greater number of tractors at their disposal than others, and some, on the basis of previous harvests, can pay their tractor drivers and other operators better than others can. Thus, as of November 15, 1938, 5,000 MTS owed 206 million rubles to their drivers.[9] Naturally, they have abandoned the kolkhozy served by these stations. On the other hand, 0.3 percent of all kolkhozy in 1939 were millionaire kolkhozy,[10] while 6 percent of all kolkhozy were poor, with an annual income of 1,000 to 5,000 rubles. Seventy-five percent of the kolkhozy were medium-sized and have an annual income of 60,000 rubles, though this amounts to only 172 rubles per member per year! This income is dreadfully below the nominal income of the average worker.

Obviously, the varying degrees of fertility of the soil have tremendous effects on the differentiation of incomes. In 1937, 8 percent of the kolkhozy were given less than 1.5 kilos of grain per workday for each kolkhoznik, 50 percent of the kolkhozy were given up to 3 kilos, 10 percent were given 7 to 15 kilos and 0.3 percent more than 15 kilos. Thus differences in pay were greater than tenfold.

On the other hand, within the same kolkhoz extreme pay differences prevailed for different types of work and degrees of skill. Thus, the workday of an agricultural laborer is figured as half of a standard "workday," and that of a tractor driver is calculated as five workdays. Can we combine these figures with those given previously concerning pay differences for an average workday in different kolkhozy? We would reach the following monstrous conclusion: A tractor driver in a rich kolkhoz, which pays 15 kilos of grain for a workday, would earn $5 \times 15 = 75$ kilos per workday, whereas an unskilled laborer in a poor kolkhoz, which pays 1.5 kilos for a workday, would earn $.5 \times 1.5 = .75$ kilos per workday! Despite everything known about income inequalities in the Russian system, we hesitate in a case that seems like it has to be routine to grant a differentiation ranging from 1 to 100. Nevertheless, the figures are there, obstinately staring at us, and we do not know how else to interpret them.

The principal economic basis for the differentiations among the kolkhozy obviously comes from the fact that the abolition of private ownership of the soil on the juridical level has not done away with its economic manifestation, which is ground rent. It is obvious that the greater the advantages resulting from the larger size of some kolkhozy, the greater the differentiation of incomes among the different types of work (which is only the replication in the countryside of the bureaucratic regime's basic way of carrying out exploitation in the factories). There is also a mode of differentiation peculiar to agriculture that results from differential rents. Those agricultural enterprises that have the most fertile soil, that are best situated in relation to economic centers, etc., profit from these differences.[11] In the abstract, the bureaucratic State could equalize the differences resulting from these factors and distribute the burden of its exploitation uniformly over the entire peasantry. It does not do this because it pursues a conscious social policy that is consistent with both the stratification of the peasantry and the creation of a privileged stratum of peasants. This privileged stratum cannot but ally itself with the rural bureaucracy, since the basis for its comfortable status is precisely the kolkhoz system as it currently exists.

Under these conditions where the peasantry is exploited more heavily than under the *ancien régime*, we may understand how the peasantry becomes more and more disinterested in producing for the kolkhoz. Whence the tendency of the peasants to devote more and more of their time to farming their little individual plots and to furnish the minimum possible amount of work to the kolkhoz. Whence in turn the absolute necessity for the bureaucratic State to instaurate forced labor in kolkhoz production, which is its sole source of supply for agricultural produce. We will not dwell here on the concrete modes this type of forced labor takes.[12] Let us simply draw from the official information we have at our disposal an index of the amount of time the Russian peasant spends laboring on behalf of the kolkhoz and on his own behalf.

We know that before the war peasants on the kolkhozy spent 30 to 45 percent of their time farming their individual plots.[13] We also know that in 1940 the average amount of labor the peasants had to contribute to the kolkhoz was 262 workdays a year.[14] This means that at this time the kolkhoz year amounted to between 374 and 478 workdays. In 1943, when the "average contribution" had gone up to 340 workdays per kolkhoznik per year, the peasants probably had to work between 500 and 600 workdays per year. Obviously these figures only have a very limited significance since we do not know exactly what constitutes a "workday."[15] Assuming that it represents 8 hours of work, a year of 500 theoretical days thus would be equivalent to 4,000 hours, or 52 weeks of 77 hours of work!

We see that the burden of this exploitation is enormous, both from the point

166 □ THE PEASANTRY UNDER BUREAUCRATIC CAPITALISM

of view of the time worked and from that of the spoliation of the product. The result is that the amount of interest the peasants have in producing can only be nil, or even negative. Nevertheless, production must continue, it even must increase more and more. What must increase above all is production for the kolkhoz, the indispensable basis for State-run production. And since the kolkhoz peasants do not want to cooperate in production, they must be compelled to do so. Here is the real economic basis for the monstrous kolkhoz bureaucracy: the ever-greater control and coercion exercised over the mass of the peasantry in order to compel it to farm the kolkhoz, i.e., to produce for the State.

According to fairly modest estimates, 1,000,000 bureaucrats belong to this kolkhoz bureaucracy (presidents of kolkhozy, officials of all kinds, deputies, accountants, etc., not counting actual Party officials and those local authorities who live on the backs of the peasantry). We have arrived at this figure by counting four bureaucrats per kolkhoz on the average (there are about 250,000 kolkhozy in all of Russia).[16] Here is what the official Russian press says about them:

> When the annual financial reports are examined, one is struck by the obvious inflation of administrative and management expenses.
> Among the "jobs" listed on the personnel rolls are found "general cultural propagandists," "Directors of the Red Isbas" (propaganda organizations), "stewards." They have eaten up a considerable portion of the kolkhozy's revenues. . . . In 1940, in the "Power to the Soviets" kolkhoz, the administrative personnel totted up 12,287 workdays and 37 breeding workers, 9,872. In the "Dawn" kolkhoz there are only two kolkhozy brigades, but the number of foremen is as large as in a substantial-sized trust. . . . In a kolkhoz in the Kuibyshev region, of 235 members, 48 occupy administrative posts. Near the kolkhoz there is a ford; assigned to the ferryman is a "fording assistant"; besides a blacksmith there is a "blacksmith's assistant"; to the beekeeper of the kolkhoz is assigned a "hive assistant"; to the president of the kolkhoz is assigned a deputy, three accountants, three bookkeepers, two depot foremen, etc. The support for these numerous administrative organs costs too much for the kolkhoz. Sometimes, the amounts paid to the "administrators" reaches almost a quarter of the total annual workdays. This policy is bound to lower the kolkhoz peasants' earnings. Useless functionaries live off their labor. . . . The kolkhozniki expend thousands upon thousands of workdays supporting these idlers; the labor of honest kolkhozniki is depreciated.[17]

Nevertheless, the State law of April 21, 1940, decreed that, based upon the amount of land cultivated, the directors of the kolkhoz should be credited with 45 to 90 workdays per month, i.e., 540 to 1,080 workdays per year, in addition to a monthly salary of 25 to 400 rubles! This gives us a rough average of 800 workdays and 2,400 rubles per year for the bureaucrats of the kolkhoz, while, at this time, the "average contribution" for a kolkhoz peasant was 262 workdays per year with around 200 rubles in cash added to this amount. The difference between the average income of a kolkhoz peasant and a petty agrarian bureaucrat is on the order of 1 to 5, to which it must be added:

1. That the peasant "average" we are using here also conceivably includes bureaucratic income, and therefore the true average is less;
2. That this ratio involves only the incomes derived from work on the kolkhoz as such, and does not take into account income arising from individual plots; one tends to assume, though, that in this domain too the bureaucrats take care of themselves better than they do others (with the best and the largest plots, etc.);
3. That, in any case, the peasant's wages represent wages for labor performed, whereas the bureaucrats' salaries "remunerate" spying and the administration of the knout.

If we leave the realm of distribution to probe more deeply, we can establish without any difficulty that, here as everywhere else, this bureaucracy exercises an absolute dictatorship. Here is what the Russian press says about it:

A great number of kolkhoz administrative councils, or even just their presidents, violate the kolkhoz code and, without taking the opinions of the members of the kolkhoz into account, spend money right and left. *The soviet authorities and the Party organizations have grown accustomed to these infractions of the kolkhoz code. They do not see that the majority of the peasants have been ousted from the management of the kolkhoz.*[18]

. . . At present, the village soviets are often removed from the basic questions of kolkhoz business and are not interested in the most important problems of the economic and cultural life of the village. . . . Currently, it is rare for the villagers to be called together for meetings (of the soviets). The questions of village life are considered by the peasants only in exceptional instances. Making hundreds and hundreds of decisions, the soviets of the raions often forget even to bring them to the attention of the villagers who have to carry them out.[19]

These lines hardly merit any analysis. We can easily see the bureaucracy in its monstrous nakedness, barely hidden by the modest euphemisms of its own reporters (the "often" and "rarely," where one should read *always* and *never*). The traits of this agricultural bureaucracy are identical, point by point, with those of its elder sister, the bureaucracy in the factories and that of the State. The same incompetence, the same greediness, the same imbecility (these hundreds of decisions that are not even brought to the attention of those who have to carry them out, which, from the point of view of bureaucratic effectiveness, places this new "elite of humanity" beneath the level of the average warrant officer in a bourgeois army), in short, the same need to exploit the worker without limit and its indispensable corollary, the complete enslavement of the worker at every level.

The Reaction of the Peasantry

Amid this unlimited exploitation, amid the dictatorship and terror imposed upon rural workers, the new privileged strata in the villages make their profits. The immense majority of the peasantry can only hate this monstrous regime and struggle against it with all the means it has at its disposal. A study of its reactions in the face of this new mode of exploitation is of the utmost interest for revolutionary theory and politics.

Under every regime and in every era, the reaction of the exploited when faced with exploitation always begins by manifesting itself in the same way: hostility to production itself, indifference as to its results. Both within ancient slavery as well as among modern wage earners, this reaction—much more than the mode of exploitation itself—separates the results of production from the remuneration of the worker. Pay based upon output, whatever form it comes in, has been the means by which the exploiting class has tried to combat this reaction of "its" proletarians, a reaction that challenges the very existence of the exploiting society.

The distribution of the kolkhoz's agricultural produce between the State (which takes both the impersonal form of the State-collector and the embodied form of the kolkhoz bureaucracy) and the peasant-producer constitutes, as it happens in the present case, a kind of "output-based pay." For the kolkhoznik is remunerated in proportion to the harvest, and this harvest is, theoretically and at the very least partially, a function of the quantity and quality of the labor provided. Nothing perhaps illustrates the burden of this bureaucratic exploitation on the peasantry so well as the fact that, despite this link between its income and the results of kolkhoz production, the peasantry constantly and obstinately refuses to work the kolkhoz field. The introduction of forced labor in the countryside to which the bureaucracy has been obliged to resort testifies to this refusal. In its effort to evade bureaucratic exploitation to the greatest extent possible, the peasantry has found—and will continue to find for a long time—an outlet in the small, individual farming plots the bureaucracy was obliged to let them tend after it overwhelmingly won the battle for "collectivization."

The peasantry is incapable of living on the miserable income gained from its share of kolkhoz production. Since before the war it has turned toward the more and more intense cultivation of its individual plots. This phenomenon therefore has an immediate economic root cause. This root cause in no way is to be found in the "low level of the forces of production," as some have tried to make us believe, but rather in unbridled exploitation, as conducted by the bureaucracy. For this phenomenon is the direct result of the insufficient income that accrues from kolkhoz farming. It has, in addition, a social signification that must be analyzed because considerable errors have been committed on this score in the Marxist movement.

The peasants' need to devote a great deal of their time and their resources to the cultivation of individual plots results from the unprecedented exploitation with which the bureaucratic State burdens the kolkhozy. Not only does this phenomenon have nothing to do with the peasants' supposedly eternal "individualistic tendencies," but it also is not determined by the "low level of the productive forces" of Russia's agrarian economy. Even within the framework of the existing forces of production in Russia—which have proved perfectly capable of mechanizing and fertilizing the kolkhoz farms, at least to the extent necessary for their rational existence—the peasants are perfectly capable of understanding and doubtless have understood the tremendous advantages of large-scale mechanized cultivation as opposed to traditional plot farming. These advantages, however, exist only from the point of view of material productivity and are, as a consequence, wholly theoretical from the point of view of the peasant producer. The most backward, the most reactionary, the most brutish of peasants is bound to understand, after a year or two of experience, that when he farms the land by mechanized means and uses chemical fertilizers and specially bred seeds, considerably higher yields can be attained with an incomparably smaller expenditure of labor. What good are these yields, however, if the produce is seized by the exploiters? Let us assume that in working 100 days a year on the kolkhoz's land and using modern methods, 10 peasants harvest 1,000 quintals of wheat and that in devoting the same number of days to their own plot they each harvest only 30. What does this totally abstract yield matter to the peasants, what does it matter to them that in their work on the kolkhoz they each have produced 100 quintals whereas their work on the individual plot has yielded only 30, when they know that once the State's collections have been deducted, once they have made their mandatory sales to the MTS and covered the legal "remunerations" of local bureaucrats, they will receive only 20 to 25 quintals from this miraculous harvest? Under such conditions, individual plot farming still proves to be more profitable. The peasant will think, These methods are too good for me. Casting a melancholy glance toward the tractors, he will say to himself, We really could do some good work with these machines, if they left us the hell alone. And he will start to go back to his little patch of land. But he will not go away anywhere at all because he is not free to go away, because he is obliged to work on the kolkhoz unless he wants to be taken away. On the other hand, when he is working on it he will put in the minimum amount of work possible.

Thus, on the basis of the present configuration of the forces of production, bureaucratic exploitation pushes the peasants toward individual plot farming. But what is the sociological signification of this phenomenon?

We hardly need mention that objectively this is a retrograde tendency—however justified it might be from the point of view of the exploited peasants' immediate interests and even from their simple biological need for self-preservation under a regime that makes it by definition impossible to make any demands. But what we need to do here is understand its place within the development of the peasantry's social and political consciousness. To understand this problem better, we need to compare it to an analogous stage in the development of proletarian consciousness.

At the beginning of the capitalist era, the proletariat, perceiving that the introduction of mechanization signified a tremendous heightening of its exploitation, did not immediately and directly move toward revolutionary solutions, or even merely "progressive" ones. Its first reactions were for the most part retrograde and objectively reactionary: It smashed machines and wanted to go back to artisanal forms of production wherein each person was able to set himself up as a small independent producer. *Mutatis mutandis*, these responses express the same illusion that it is possible to "go back," the same search for a utopian solution as is found among the kolkhoz peasants in the turn toward individual plot farming. The working class had to endure a long and twofold period of apprenticeship: First of all, it had to learn that the introduction of capitalist machinery in production is inevitable and then that it is possible to utilize this machinery precisely for the purpose of abolishing exploitation. It is only when it understands that it is impossible to go back, and indeed that there is no need to go back in order to limit and abolish exploitation, it is only when the necessity of capitalism and the possibility of its being overturned become clearly apparent to it that it begins to take its position on the field of revolution. All things being equal, the same holds true for the peasant class as mechanization and the domination of the capitalist bureaucracy come to be introduced into agriculture.

The study of the development of the peasantry's class consciousness along these lines goes beyond the confines of our analysis. But on two fundamental points we should back up the analogy we have put forth. At the same time, this will permit us to avoid erroneous conceptions on this question that have gained currency within the revolutionary movement.

For the development of the peasantry to take place in the direction we have outlined, i.e., in a revolutionary direction, the inevitable character of its situation must first of all be demonstrated to it irrefutably. The illusory character of every attempt to "go back" must be proven to it during a trial period that is sufficiently long and relevant to the situation. This will take place only to the extent that such a return really is impossible, that is, only to the extent that the restoration of "private" capitalism is excluded as a possibility. After that, another solution, the revolutionary solution, must appear to it as possible. This implies, on the one hand, that technical progress and the development of the forces of production continue and, on the other hand, that the parasitic and useless character of the dominant class becomes plainly evident.

We will be very brief concerning the second aspect of this question. The forces of production still are continuing to develop. This is a fact, and it is no less true in agriculture than in the other branches of industry. As long as the struggle between different dominant classes goes on, these classes will be obliged to continue applying the latest production techniques—certainly in a contradictory, irrational manner and with tremendous waste, but with real results, for their very existence is at stake. And as this development occurs, the parasitic character of the ruling class can become more and more clearly evident to the producers.

On the other hand, we must insist much more strongly upon the other aspect of this problem, namely, how to demonstrate to the peasantry in practical terms the impossibility of going back, of any kind of restoration of the traditional private mode of farming the land. It is well known that Stalin gave three spectacular demonstrations of this proposition: during the first bloody battle over "collectivization" (1929), during the instauration of forced labor on the kolkhoz

(1939), and during the expropriation, through the "monetary reforms" (1947), of the savings of the well-to-do peasant strata, which they had built up during the war. Each time, the famous "struggle between private inclinations and the State-run economy" was resolved in favor of the latter.

It could not have been otherwise. In its struggle against the peasants' "individualist" reactions, the State bureaucracy has at its disposal formidable weapons on the economic, political, and social levels that put the petty producer at its mercy. Moreover, the whole dynamic of the modern economy assures for the bureaucracy, the personification of centralized capital, an inevitable victory over individual small-plot farming.

This seems obvious to a Marxist. Nevertheless, from the very first years of the Russian Revolution, Lenin developed an incorrect position on this score that, as it later was taken up by Trotsky and the Left Opposition, was a constant source of errors within the vanguard of the movement. This position constantly introduced crucial mistakes into its perspective and prevented it from correctly appreciating the nature of the Russian State.

Here is one among hundreds of Lenin's quotations that can be found to this effect.

> The dictatorship of the proletariat is the most determined and most relentless war against a *more powerful* enemy, the bourgeoisie, whose resistance has increased *tenfold* by their overthrow (even if only in a single country) and whose power lies, not only in the strength of international capital, in the strength and durability of their international connections, but also in the *force of habit*, in the strength of *small-scale production*. Unfortunately, small-scale production is still extremely widespread in the world, and small-scale production *engenders* capitalism and the bourgeoisie continually, daily, hourly, spontaneously and on a mass scale.[20]

As for Trotsky, we hardly need recall that he thought the entire history of social change in Russia since 1921, as far as this development was a function of indigenous factors, was determined by the continuous pressure exerted over the "socialist forms of State property" by the elements trying to restore private capitalism (Nepmen and kulaks). The domination of the bureaucracy was explained in the final analysis only as a point of equilibrium between the two "fundamental forces," the urban proletariat and the bourgeois elements of town and country. For Trotsky, the economic basis of this conception was to be found in Lenin's idea about how simple market production constantly and unfailingly begets capitalism.

This idea, however, is false. At the very least, it is false in its general formulation. Simple market production has existed for thousands of years, whereas capitalism has appeared only during the past few centuries. Simple market production is absolutely incapable, as such, of leading to capitalism, if its other conditions do not exist. In addition to a certain level of the forces of production, these conditions are the existence of labor power as a commodity, the possibility of privately appropriating the basic means of production, and the existence of capital (i.e., of a mass of values great enough to yield surplus value) in the form of private property. Now, these are precisely the crucial conditions for the passage from simple market production to private capitalist production—conditions that simple market production as such not only cannot automatically create but that, by the operation of its own rules, it tends to prevent from arising, as proven by the history of artisanal production in Western Europe. And these are the essential conditions lacking in Russia. Labor power no longer exists as a commodity. With respect to its employment within production, this commodity has been subjected to the State's absolute buying monopoly, for the State alone may employ "wage" labor in production.[21] It no longer is possible to appropriate for oneself the means of production, nor does there exist any longer the opportunity to amass the amount of values required to buy the machinery, raw materials, and labor power necessary to get a capitalist enterprise going. Consequently, any increase in values that an individual can, by hook or by crook, come to amass, can only be hoarded rather than productively accumulated by the individual, except within extremely narrow limits on which the State keeps close tabs.

But the idea we are criticizing here contains an even more basic error. Not only are the fundamental conditions for the passage from simple market production to private capitalist production lacking in Russia, but the dynamic features and the automatic mechanism inherent in this economy each day doom such small-scale production more and more to the advantage of centralized capital. The connections between simple market production and the birth of capitalism can be debated without end. Today we are not in the seventeenth or the eighteenth century, but smack dab in the middle of the twentieth. The capitalism we have before us is not nascent capitalism; it is a capitalism that is beginning to transcend the stage of monopolistic concentration to achieve a complete integration of production on a worldwide scale. Let us leave aside for a moment the Russian case and examine the case of a mere monopoly in an ordinary capitalist country. Suppose someone has just told us that Ford or General Motors is seriously threatened by the garage mechanics who fix cars, and that the American State does not really express the power of the Fords and the Morgans but rather an "equilibrium" between them and the thousands of garage mechanics, shoe repairers, etc. How will this joker be received?

Now, it is clear that in Russia we have not merely "a few" monopolies but one single gigantic monopoly with everything at its disposal: capital, raw materials, labor power, foreign trade. This one monopoly is above the law. It is identical with the State. It expropriates, kills, deports no matter whom no matter when, and is guided solely by the interests of a ruling stratum whose very existence is indissolubly linked to this universal monopoly. From a purely economic point of view, what is the relation of forces between this universal monopoly and any cluster of small individual producers? Is it not as clear as day that these latter are historically lost, doomed, without the least hope?

Lenin and Trotsky knew very well that if the Russian Revolution were isolated it would face mortal dangers that might end in the restoration of an exploitative regime. But they were deceiving themselves when they thought they saw the real source of this danger in the existence of millions of small indepen-dent producers, i.e., in a phenomenon that has lost its importance even in cap-italist countries. These small "independent" producers, in fact, have been an-nexed and are exploited, either directly or indirectly, by centralized capital. They did not foresee—and Trotsky refused to the end to *see*—that the real dan-ger was coming from the bureaucracy and not the kulaks, who had been used by the bureaucracy as a reserve army during the first phase of its struggle, which had been conducted against the proletariat. After its victory in this struggle—the only one of historical importance—the bureaucracy turned around against the small "independent" producers and proved with some brutality that this "independence" belonged to the nineteenth century and merely had to be bur-ied along with the horse-and-buggy and wooden plows.

All that remains to be said are a few words on the signification of the kolkhoz market from this standpoint. This market is entirely subordinated to the State-run economy, first of all by the State monopoly over the conditions of agricul-tural production (farming machinery, fertilizer, consumer products, labor time, the set price and set amount of the delivery quota for agricultural produce—in the final analysis the earth itself). Most of these factors that the State has at its complete disposal operate continuously, and thus allow the bureaucracy to keep the development of the rural economy under constant supervision. Among these factors are the set price of the delivery quota for agricultural produce, the set amount for this quota, and the price of consumer products. Other factors oper-ate over the long run and the State uses them less frequently. It can increase the amount of mandatory work time on the kolkhoz. By this means, production time at the disposition of the peasantry is limited and production time at the dis-position of the State is augmented. Finally, if driven to it by critical circum-stances, the State can recall that it is the "owner" of the land and thereby send yet another few million peasants to Siberia. Among all these factors, the one that currently is of greatest importance is its possession of extremely large stocks of agricultural produce (at least 40 percent of production). By exercising this con-trol, it can exert decisive pressure on the market.

Activity on the kolkhoz market, therefore, cannot stray beyond certain, very rigid, limits. These limits prevent it from being able to challenge anything es-sential to the bureaucratic economy. As for its social signification, it must not be forgotten that activity on this market consists of exchanges between the most privileged strata of the kolkhozy and the urban bureaucratic strata. In nearly ev-ery respect, these strata alone have at their disposal either a surplus of produce or a surplus of money, which is needed to give them a share of the market.

The Historical Signification of the Kolkhoz System

We have seen that the fundamental contradiction of every modern system of ex-ploitation is expressed with particular force within the confines of the kolkhoz economy. The exploiting bureaucracy's tendency to increase both production and exploitation to the hilt sets the producers against this system of production.

In the case of Russian agriculture, this reaction simultaneously manifests itself in the peasants' negative attitude toward kolkhoz production and in their tendency to fall back on individual small-plot farming. This double reaction tends to result in a lowering of agricultural labor productivity (or, in any case, at the current stage productivity does not increase proportionately with the amount of capital employed, with the new farming methods that have been introduced, etc.). And as a consequence, limits are placed on the amount of surplus production at the direct or indirect disposal of the bureaucracy. To this limitation the bureaucracy can only respond with bureaucratic measures in the profoundest sense of this term: police enforcement, the instauration or augmentation of forced labor, raising the rate of surplus production, the installation of a bureaucratic stratum in the kolkhozy whose function is to "direct" and to try to extract a maximum of effort from the producers.

All these measures, however, tend to have results that are contrary to those desired: Increased exploitation (brought about by raising the rate of surplus production and by adding the maintenance costs of a new stratum of unproductive bureaucrats) and the escalation of police repression only reinforce the producers' conviction that this type of production is hostile to their interests. Consequently, it diminishes their willingness to produce. On the other hand, the kolkhoz bureaucracy's unproductive consumption and the wastefulness it organically gives rise to in the sphere of production are an additional and in no way negligible cause of the limitation on surplus production at the disposal of the central bureaucracy.

To this new limitation the bureaucracy responds with more oppression, more exploitation, and so on. Thus we have an absurd spiral that is profoundly characteristic of a completely exploitative regime, which can only end in a stagnant economy.[22] It would be wrong to assume that the bureaucracy has no awareness of this process. The measures it constantly is taking against itself[23] are not just intended for the purposes of demagogy, although there is much of that to be found in them too. For the central bureaucracy not only takes into account the profound ineffectiveness of the measures it has drawn up in order to increase production. It also always tends to minimize the latitude granted, and the earnings allotted, to subordinate and peripheral strata—and such are par excellence the kolkhoz bureaucratic strata.

Here too, as in every exploitative regime, we see the same opposition between the State (the general and abstract expression of the interests of the ruling class) and the daily, immediate interests of the particular members of this class. This struggle of the bureaucracy against its most deep-seated, most ingrained traits, however, can have no decisive outcome. The unbridled exploitation practiced by the kolkhoz bureaucracy on the peasants for its own benefit is based upon the discretionary powers over these peasants that have been given to it to make them produce. Exploitation "beyond permissible limits" and discretionary powers go hand in hand. How can one limit the former without abolishing the latter? And how can one abolish the latter if coercion is the only thing capable of making the peasants work on the kolkhoz? The contradiction is inescapable. The only possible apparent solution is bureaucratic supercontrol of the bureaucracy over the bureaucracy. Here is the principal economic root cause for the all-powerful GPU.

How can we characterize the historical role of the bureaucracy in the area of agriculture? This question assumes an importance that is all the more considerable since, up till now, the bureaucracy has taken power in countries where, with the sole exception of Czechoslovakia, agriculture has constituted both the occupation of the majority of the population and the basic source of national income (Russia, the European satellite countries, China).

It may be said that this role appears to be the *realization of concentration in the domain of agriculture* up to the limits compatible with a regime that completely exploits the producers, and—going hand in hand with this first component—an enormous leap forced upon the development of the forces of production in this sector. In this very general sense, the bureaucracy merely continues to carry out the task undertaken by the capitalist bourgeoisie, which was to develop and concentrate the forces of production, and this is occurring, as it turns out, in the countries where this bourgeoisie had proven itself inadequate to the task. But the bureaucracy accomplishes this task during a specific period, that of worldwide capitalist decadence. This is a period during which the forces of production tend to develop at a slower and slower rate while the triumph of concentration is expressed quite often in indirect and roundabout ways. The influence of the general degradation of capitalism is manifested with a particular force in agriculture.[24] And it is not by accident that the upheaval brought about by the bureaucracy has been and will continue to be experienced to the most far-reaching extent in agriculture. Never did the bourgeoisie achieve so quickly the total expropriation of the great majority of the direct producers, the massive introduction of industrial processes in the area of soil cultivation, the concentration of agricultural farming units and the universal centralization of their control and management, or the exodus en masse of the peasants to urban industry. And never has the development of the forces of production been paid for with so much blood, sweat, and tears, nor has the burden of exploitation and oppression ever come crashing down on workers so heavily.

The bureaucracy brings this upheaval about through the kolkhoz form it imposes upon agrarian production. We must understand, therefore, the necessary connection between the bureaucracy and the kolkhoz system. This will allow us to give concrete shape to the idea set forth earlier that the role of the bureaucracy in agriculture is the realization of concentration up to the limits compatible with the complete exploitation of the workers.

In the industrial domain, it is impossible to set any limits on the development of concentration short of the total concentration of social capital in the hands of a single dominant group. This implies that at the present stage the management of industrial production as a whole is identical, from the economic standpoint, to the management of a single enterprise whose different production sectors are like workshops scattered over various locations. This process leading toward total concentration implies that the rationalization of the ruling class's goals has already been carried out to a tremendous degree. The basic obstacle this rationalization effort comes up against is an internal one. It derives from the fact that production relies on exploitation and that a rational organization of production by and for an exploiter class is impossible when this class estranges itself from the workers, when, in short, it is itself alienated and estranged from production.

Is this argument concerning the possibility of a total concentration of production in a system of exploitation applicable to agriculture as well? We think not. As we have already stressed, a fundamental characteristic of the kolkhoz system is the attempt to keep the producers interested to a certain degree in "collective" production; their remuneration is tied to the results of production, i.e., to the harvest. We have pointed out that a similar phenomenon may be observed in industry (piece-rate wages). In that case, however, its import is incomparably narrower. For it is infinitely more possible to establish control over both the quantity and quality of labor provided; in industry, it is thus the setting of norms and the supervision over their fulfillment that play the fundamental role. In agriculture, by way of contrast, it is nearly impossible to achieve this kind of control. Production operations take place in an extended space; a small number of producers are dispersed over a great area (instead of having a great number of them within the four walls of a shop); neither the quantity nor the quality of work and its results are immediately apparent (unlike in industry), but rather appear many months later. Finally, production does not take place under artificial, stable, and constantly identical conditions, but occurs rather under conditions that are independent of human will, unstable, and changing, and in the face of which a perpetual effort of adaptation is necessary on the part of the producer. All these factors make it practically impossible to exercise total control over agricultural labor, unless each laborer is followed by a supervisor.

Consequently, in a regime that carries exploitation to its limit and that cannot count on any sort of voluntary cooperation on the part of the workers, it is almost impossible to completely transform peasants into pure and simple wage earners. It is absolutely necessary to establish between them and the results of production some specific kind of connection. This connection must prevent them from losing complete interest in these results, while reserving for the State the main share of production, a share that can be enlarged at will.

From this point of view, the kolkhoz form, not in its secondary features but rather in that which is essential to it,[25] tends to represent the natural and organic form of peasant exploitation within the framework of bureaucratic capitalism. It is also an ultimate form of concentration and rationalization of agricultural production, compatible with the unlimited exploitation of labor.

Notes

1. This is the case for the majority of the populations of Asia, Africa, and Latin America.

2. Among the latter, one of the most important is the separation of capital and landed property.

3. In France, during the period from 1945 to 1949, the production and the importation of tractors are many times greater than they were before the war. The total number of agricultural machines in service in the countries of Western Europe (countries participating in the Marshall Plan) will increase 3.5-fold between 1948 and 1952. Concerning the new revolutionary inventions in agricultural techniques and their applications in the United States, see G. H. Fabius, "Technical Progress in Agriculture," *New International*, 1946, pp. 116-17.

4. The agricultural population's percentage of the total U.S. population went from 73 percent

in 1820 to 19 percent in 1940 (C. Clark, "Les conditions du progrès economique," *Etudes et Conjoncture. Economie mondiale*, 13 [June 1947], p. 49, and Jean Fourastié, *Le Grand Espoir du XXe siècle*, p. 77). From 1913 to 1939, the agricultural population in Russia went from 65 percent to 47 percent of the total (F. Forest, "An Analysis of Russian Economy," *New International*, February 1943, p. 57).

5. According to Peregrinus ("Les Kolkhoz pendant la guerre," *S. ou B.*, 4 [October 1949], pp. 3-18), the peasantry's share of the gross product stands at 30-35 percent. This information comes from the Soviet press itself.

6. Baykov, in *Economic Journal*, London, December 1941, cited by Forest, "Analysis of Russian Economy," *New International*, January 1943, p. 20.

7. The figures obviously are valid for one year and for one region. We are not trying to determine here with precision the rate of exploitation but rather to discover its order of magnitude.

8. See Bettelheim, *Les Problèmes théoriques et pratiques de la planification* (Paris: Librairie des Sciences Politiques et Sociales, 1946), p. 101.

9. According to *Pravda*, January 14, 1939, cited by Forest, "Analysis of Russian Economy," *New International*, January 1943, p. 21.

10. According to the official Russian sources cited by Forest, ibid.

11. "The question as to whether private property in land exists has absolutely nothing to do with the question of the formation of differential rent, which is inevitable in capitalist agriculture even on communal, State and ownerless lands." "Private property in land does not create differential rent" (Lenin, *LCW* [Moscow: Progress Publishers, 1980], vol. 5, pp. 124-25).

12. On this point, see Peregrinus, "Les Kolkhoz."

13. *Planned Economy*, of December 1938 (in Russian), cited by Forest, "Analysis of Russian Economy," p. 21.

14. According to a citation from *Bolshevik*, given by Peregrinus in his note 11.

15. Peregrinus's article shows that at harvest time it can consist of 16 hours of work!

16. L. Trotsky, *The Revolution Betrayed* (New York: Pathfinder Press, 1972), p. 137.

17. *Pravda* of March 20 and April 7, 1941, cited by G. Alexinsky, *La Russie révolutionnaire* (Paris: Librairie Armand Colin, 1947), pp. 192-93.

18. *Pravda*, March 26, 1941, cited according to Alexinsky, *La Russie révolutionnaire*, p. 192.

19. *Izvestia*, July 5, 1941, cited according to Alexinsky, ibid., pp. 193-94.

20. Lenin, "Left-Wing Communism—An Infantile Disorder," in *LSWONE*, p. 518.

21. The perspicacity of all the "leaders" of the Fourth International, assembled in a World Congress, was needed in order to discover that in Russia at the present time, "the *private* employment of wage earners is extending both in the towns and in the country, but remains restricted to the private satisfaction of needs of consumption by the privileged people and to an artisan production for the market"! "Documents and Resolutions of the Second World Congress of the Fourth International," in *Fourth International*, June 1948, p. 112. Everyone knows, indeed, the importance of extracting surplus value from domestic servants for the purposes of capital accumulation. As for artisanal production, which employs unskilled wage laborers (where? when? how?), how can one doubt the tremendous dangers which the redoubtable Efraim Efraimovich, the avaricious cobbler of Dorakinovo, with his two apprentices, represents for the State Shoe Trust?

22. If this regime were to be realized on a universal scale.

23. The texts cited here from the official Russian press and the laws analyzed in Peregrinus's article offer striking examples.

24. It is in the domain of agriculture that progress in production has been the least rapid over the past century.

25. It is obvious, for example, that the existence of individual plots farmed by kolkhozniki for their own profit is a secondary phenomenon and is in no way essential to the kolkhoz system. The appearance of this phenomenon is tied, on the one hand, to a determinate relation of forces between the bureaucracy and the peasantry (the latter's passive resistance has proved at this stage powerful enough to extract this concession from the bureaucracy), and, on the other hand, to a given level of needs for accumulation on the part of the bureaucracy. The inauguration of forced labor in the kolkhozy signified the first modification of these two factors. If other factors do not interrupt its development, as certainly will be the case, the bureaucracy will be obliged to go back on this conces-

sion and completely annex to the kolkhoz economy ground plots and the peasant labor time spent on them.

Postface

The statistical and other data on which the text relies obviously are those of the period. The substance of what is said there holds true today and has just been confirmed by the huge failure of the 1972 grain harvest. After a half century of "socialism," Russia is obliged, when faced with a catastrophe, to buy 20 million tons of wheat from the United States while capitalist countries subsidize farmers *not* to produce wheat.

a) The "machine tractor stations" mentioned in the text have since been abolished. I will come back, in *La Russie après l'industrialisation*, to the vain attempts at "reform" that the bureaucracy recurrently and repeatedly launches in order to achieve a solution to the problem of agricultural production. [T/E: This proposed third volume of *La Société bureaucratique* was never published.]

8
The Yugoslavian Bureaucracy

From 1923 until today, the workers' movement has been dominated by Stalinism. Maintaining the most highly evolved and the most combative sections of the proletariat under its influence, the policy of the Stalinist bureaucracy has been the predominant factor in the outcome of social crises over the last quarter of a century. One of the most significant manifestations of its overwhelming predominance was that during this entire period it has been impossible to reconstruct, in the face of Stalinism, a revolutionary vanguard worthy of the name, i.e., a vanguard built upon solid ideological and programmatic foundations and exercising some real influence within even a small section of the proletariat. The principal obstacle this attempt at reconstruction has run up against was the uncertainty and confusion that have prevailed concerning the nature and prospects of Stalinism itself.

At the time, uncertainty and confusion were almost inevitable. The Stalinist bureaucracy was still in a "nascent state." Its fundamental features had barely emerged from the surrounding social reality. It had achieved power only in a single country, which was completely cut off from the rest of the world; in almost all capitalist countries, Stalinist parties were still "opposition" parties. Taken together, these factors explain both why the proletariat could not free itself from the grasp of Stalinism during this period and why the vanguard itself had not

Originally published as "La Bureaucratie yougoslave," *S. ou B.*, 5-6 (March 1950). Written in collaboration with Georges Dupont. Reprinted in *SB 2*, pp. 25-152. [T/E: The present translation excerpts pp. 25-30, 82-101, 125-36, and the relevant notes from pp. 144-52. Notes 2-11 appeared as notes 49-53 and 64-68 in the 10/18 edition (*SB 2*, pp. 149-52). The Postface was added to the 1973 10/18 edition by the author. It appeared on pp. 153-56 of *SB 2* and contained an opening paragraph and nine notes, (a) - (i). The present edition translates this opening paragraph and notes (a), (b), (g), and (h) as notes (a), (b), and (c).]

come to an understanding of the nature of bureaucracy and to a definition of this phenomenon in relation to a revolutionary program.

Appearances to the contrary, the second imperialist war brought about a radical change in this state of affairs. The Stalinist bureaucracy has extended itself well beyond the borders of old Russia. It has become a dominant force. It exercises power in a dozen new countries, including both industrially developed regions (e.g., Czechoslovakia and East Germany) as well as an immense backward area (China). The absolute power of the bureaucracy, which might have appeared before as an exception or as the result of Russia's peculiarities, has shown itself to be equally possible in other locales. In most cases, Stalinist parties in bourgeois countries have undergone a vigorous development, but by the same token they have been obliged to share in the "responsibilities of power" and to assume the role of advocates for a bureaucratic society.

Through this considerable expansion Stalinism has lost virtually all of its "mystery." In looking at the masses of workers, it no longer can be denied that they have begun to experience Stalinist bureaucracy and that they are now experiencing it in a far more profound way than was possible before the war. For the present experience of Stalinism no longer has to do with its "betrayals" but rather with the very nature of bureaucracy *qua* exploiting stratum. In the areas where the Stalinist bureaucracy has taken power, proletarians have begun to understand its nature, or of necessity will come to understand it. For the proletariat in other countries, doubts on this question are tending to give way to a feeling of certainty. And this certainty is corroborated by an understanding of the attitude and the role of the Stalinist political and trade-union bureaucracy within the framework of the capitalist system. For what there is of a vanguard, all the elements needed to elaborate and propagate within the working class a clear conception of this bureaucracy and a revolutionary program with regard to this phenomenon now have been provided.

But even more than in the relations between the working class and bureaucracy, the present period of Stalinist expansion brings to light a radical change in the status of the bureaucracy itself. The bureaucracy has come out of the war infinitely stronger in the material and human potential it has at its disposal. But this expansion has brought to light with much greater clarity than before the bureaucracy's own contradictions, contradictions inherent in its nature as an exploiting stratum.

Obviously, these contradictions issue from the radical opposition between its interests and those of the proletariat. Stalinist parties are nothing without the allegiance of the working class, and consequently they are obliged to maintain and to deepen their ties with the latter, precisely in order to be able to impose on this class a policy that is hostile both to its immediate interests and to its historical interests. Thus there is an opposition that is muted at first but that can only continue by growing more pronounced.

On the surface, this opposition is suppressed when the bureaucracy seizes power. It can be said that to the extent it instaurates its absolute dictatorship, it rids itself of the need to have the allegiance of the working class. But in reality, the contradiction is only shifted to a much deeper and more important level, the economic level. There it becomes identical with the fundamental contradiction of capitalist exploitation. If, upon attaining power, the bureaucracy no longer needs the workers' political allegiance, it needs their economic allegiance even more. As political agents, the workers can be tamed by the GPU; as producers who refuse to be exploited, they are unstoppable.

At this stage, the basic contradiction between the interests of the workers and bureaucratic exploitation becomes materially evident to the proletariat. The bureaucracy's need to exploit the worker to the hilt while also getting him to produce the greatest amount possible creates an impasse that is expressed in the crisis of labor productivity. This crisis is nothing but the workers' absolute refusal as producers to maintain allegiance to a system whose exploitative character they are well aware of. The bureaucratic economy and bureaucratic society thus come face-to-face with an impasse that the bureaucracy tries to overcome by increasing exploitation—thus aggravating the very causes of the crisis—and by extending the range of its domination. The need to expand (bureaucratic imperialism) thus follows inevitably from the contradictions of the bureaucratic economy as an exploitative economy.[a]

This evolution could be factually observed over the past ten years. It has become evident that the constant exacerbation of the workers' exploitation and the inner necessity for expansion were essential traits of bureaucratic capitalism. It also has become evident that this expansion could occur only through the total bureaucratization of the countries that had been subjected to Russian domination. But this process of bureaucratization signifies not only that the contradiction we have spoken of here is becoming magnified but also that another contradiction is beginning to appear within the bureaucracy itself. Between the national and the international bases of the bureaucracy's power an opposition is becoming apparent. The bureaucracy can exist only as a worldwide class, but at the same time, in each nation it is a social class with particular interests. The bureaucracies of various countries therefore necessarily tend to oppose one another, and this opposition not only has made an appearance, but has burst out in a violent manner in the Russo-Yugoslavian crisis.[b]

The Russo-Yugoslavian Break:
An Expression of Internal Struggles within the Bureaucracy

The deep-seated reason for the Russo-Yugoslavian conflict—the opposition between the interests of these two bureaucracies—contained three key elements.

First of all, there was the Yugoslavian scheme for a federation of southern Slavs, which aimed at extending Yugoslavian domination to Bulgaria and Albania. Moscow could tolerate neither a loosening of its direct control over the Balkan economy, as would have been brought about by this scheme, nor a strengthening of the Yugoslavian bureaucracy, which already was the strongest of those in the satellite countries.

Next, there was Yugoslavia's Five-Year Plan, whose basic objective is, as we have seen,[1] to increase the country's industrial and military potential. Tito's statements to the Federal Assembly in December 1948 emphasized that Moscow was not in favor of this industrialization plan. The maintenance of Yugoslavia's prewar economic structure as a country supplying agricultural produce and raw materials (ore) to Russian industry and to that of other satellite countries (Czechoslovakia, Hungary) appears to have been what the Kremlin was demanding.

Finally, the current state of economic relations, which take the form of commercial exchanges and Russia's stake in "development" (i.e., its exploitation of the Yugoslavian economy), furnished the third motive for the Russo-Yugoslavian conflict. The Yugoslavians have become less and less disposed to paying the Kremlin the tribute satellite countries pay out through commercial treaties and "joint business ventures" with Russia.

It is really giving Tito a lot of credit to consider him the only Stalinist leader of a satellite country who has stood up to Moscow. His larger-than-life appearance on today's political screen tends to mask the fact that the Russian bureaucracy's direct emissaries have brought down members of various CPs guilty or suspected of "nationalist deviations." Need we mention Gomulka, Kostov, Rajk? Must we list the purges that have followed one after another for the past two years and have occurred on every level? Let us confine ourselves to pointing out how certain Stalinists have learned at their own expense that the "line" always passes through Moscow, whence come the solutions to each satellite country's economic and political problems.

Just as American capitalism's domination of the Western economy does not imply the disappearance of rearguard fighting by the bourgeoisies of various nations, so Russia's subjection of the "popular democracies" does not prevent some slight displays of autonomous action on the part of bureaucratic fractions from occurring at the present time. In this sense, it may be said that in its march toward world domination, Stalinism carries "Titoism" in its flanks. The relation of forces between these fractions and the Russian bureaucracy, bound up as it is with the overall international situation (i.e., with the development of the relation of forces between the two blocs), determines the outcome of these conflicts in each particular instance.

Nevertheless, we must be more explicit about these ideas, for what is involved in the Russo-Yugoslavian break is the problem of how bureaucratic States relate to each other. Indeed, this is one of the most important aspects of the development of imperialism in the present era.

Let us recall briefly the essential features of the classical analysis of imperialism, as presented by Leninism. The development of capitalism is ruled by the concentration of capital, which forces capitalism to extend its markets and bring raw materials into its production cycle. Within the framework of competitive capitalism, this kind of expansion is achieved by broadening the area of capitalist domination and through a growing international division of labor. Nevertheless, when concentration reaches the phase of monopoly control, possibilities for expansion of this kind start to give out. Indeed, monopolies create "hunting preserves" for themselves in order to produce raw materials and to dispose of finished goods. From then on, the expansion of each capitalist unit no longer is opposed merely to that of the other units, as was true during the phase of competitive capitalism; it now is faced with a quasi-absolute obstacle.

Two closely related problems are posed thereby. What will the relations between these monopolies, or between the States dominated by these monopolies, be? And what are the motive forces that oblige monopolies to pursue an expansionist policy during this period, despite the suppression of competition in the classical sense?

The theory of ultra-imperialism, as adopted by Kautsky, stated that it was possible for the various monopolies or monopolistic States to reach a "peaceful" entente. Such an entente would take the form either of an amicable division of available hunting grounds or of a peaceful consolidation of capital on a world scale.

The violent critique Lenin directed against this conception did not challenge it as an abstract possibility. In fact, one might add that global cartels, as well as the "peaceful" time intervals during which a temporary and provisional division of the world was accepted by the great imperialist powers,[2] are examples of how this possibility was partially realized. But Lenin rightly insisted that this theoretical possibility could never be realized on a universal scale and in a permanent fashion. For the sole concrete basis upon which such a division of the world or such a merger of national segments of world capital could be settled is the relation of forces between capitalist groupings.

Now, because the capitalist economies of various countries and sectors develop unevenly, because new competitors are always coming into the ring, and so on, this relation of forces is in a constant state of change. Germany, for example, was obliged by the relation of forces existing in 1919 to accept the Treaty of Versailles. But after twenty years it was able to challenge the "partitioning" that had been brought about and to call everything back into question. Consequently, only force can resolve the problem posed by the fact that from now on expansion for some can be achieved only to the detriment of others. Whence the inevitability of wars within the framework of monopoly capitalism, the imperialist (i.e., reactionary) character of these wars (during these wars it no longer is just a matter of opening new areas for the expansion of capitalist production, but of increasing the profits of one imperialist group at the expense of another), and the political attitude of revolutionary defeatism.

But, we may ask, why does capital, and more particularly monopoly capital, have this expansionist tendency? Because, says Lenin, of the monopolies' felt need to enlarge their "profits and power." We must not concentrate on the psychological aspects of the "thirst for profits" contained in this answer, or on the financial oligarchy's will to power, but rather on the very necessities of capitalist accumulation, and in the end the insoluble contradictions of monopoly capital. Here an explanation is necessary, for this question is directly related to the problem with which we are concerned.

The contradictions inherent under all forms of capitalist production are simultaneously internal and external. Their concrete expression changes, but their general content remains the same over the entire capitalist period of human history.

If capitalist production were not antagonistic in its innermost essence, if it were not based upon exploitation, not only would it be capable of boundless expansion but it would have no need of foreign territory for this expansion. Conversely, the internal contradictions of a capitalist State would lose their explosive character were it not menaced by other States: An "isolated" capitalist State could allow itself the liberty—barring a revolution—to stagnate and rot in its internal contradictions without its inability to have complete domination over production creating for it an absolute impasse.

But what really happens is the exact contrary of these two hypotheses. The struggle among monopolies and imperialist States does not cease, because, in the final analysis, their profits—and therefore the basis for accumulation—are rival shares that must be drawn from the same overall profit or worldwide surplus value. And this struggle renders accumulation indispensable, whether accumulation is oriented toward the production of the means of production or toward that of the means of destruction. The internal contradictions of each imperialist State thereby acquire a dynamic and explosive character whether they are expressed in overproduction crises, the falling rate of profit, or the crisis in labor productivity. Under one form or another, the need to break out of this impasse inevitably leads to war.

War therefore is the expression of the productive forces' tendency toward concentration, since it results from contradictions that themselves arise from the division and the opposition between different units of world capital. But it is also and at the same time one of the motive forces—in fact, the most powerful motive force—for this process of concentration.

This is so in myriad ways. The three most important are as follows: (1) the inevitable merger, first, of the various sectors of the economy, and then of economics, politics, and strategic considerations, the inevitability of which derives from the technical conditions of modern warfare itself; (2) the elimination, through war, of the so-called independence of all secondary countries and States; and finally (3) the crushing of the defeated powers and the need, in order to consolidate victory, to subject them—as well as the weakest "allies"—to total domination, which may go as far as the permanent military occupation of their countries.

Having reached this stage, the struggle among the various elements [molécules] of world capital therefore becomes both more bitter and more radical than was the case under the system of competition. Just as the competitive stage does not go on indefinitely, but reaches a first plateau of concentration that is expressed in monopoly control, so the violent struggle among monopolistic groupings and imperialist States cannot go on indefinitely under new forms that merely would repeat their previous content; each time it takes place at a higher level of concentration. Thus, the first imperialist war upset the existing relative balance among the imperialist powers or coalitions of imperialist powers. The new "partitioning" of the world formulated in the Treaty of Versailles signified, in fact, the exclusion of the defeated powers from this partitioning; the colonies and the spheres of influence of the central empires were annexed by the powers of the Entente. At least after this victory the victors had left the vanquished relatively "free and independent" at home.

In the second imperialist war, what was involved was no longer the mere "repartitioning" of colonies: The home territories and the "independent" political existence of the great imperialist countries themselves were put on the table. Hitler's "Europe" was the first rough sketch of what the victory of the Russo-American Allies was going to bring about: the direct domination of the victors over the vanquished countries from every political, economic, and ideological point of view.

The objective of the third and final[3] imperialist war that is now being prepared will be, if you will, the same as that of the second one. But this time, the objective will be achieved on a universal scale. Assuming that the revolution is put in check, the war can end only with the total worldwide domination of a single State.

This would be, if you wish, "ultra-imperialism," but with this difference: It could be implemented only by eliminating the weakest imperialist groupings through successive stages in a violent struggle. The mystification contained in Kautsky's concept of "ultra-imperialism" is to be found in the idea that a peaceful entente, an amicable, stable division of the world between imperialist States, was possible. Lenin stated that such a peaceful entente was impossible, and history has proved him right. But he was mistaken in thinking that the relations of force among imperialist States would be constantly and eternally changing, and that as a consequence imperialist wars would follow one after another up to the point of revolutionary victory without anything changing except the names of the victors and the vanquished.

Just as through competition (which culminates in concentration) one capitalist grouping asserts its ultimate supremacy over others (and this supremacy involves a relation of force that becomes more and more difficult to challenge), so through a series of wars is concentration carried out on an international level, culminating in an accumulation of power that makes it nearly impossible for there to be any subsequent "modifications" of the relations of forces. In 1913, or even in 1921 (disregarding for a moment the question of compatibility of economic and political objectives), many politico-military combinations were possible: The United States, England, France, Italy, Germany, and Japan could have formed many different varieties of alliances, but on the "technical" plane of war these combinations always had to result in two—or several—viable coalitions. If an ally or even one of the secondary States changed sides, the underlying relation of forces might be upset.

Today, Russia is the only force capable of resisting the United States. The other capitalist countries could not by themselves form a coalition against the latter: The relation of forces has become too overwhelming. What kind of "modification of the relation of forces" within the Western world can we talk about when France is only able to equip ten divisions with American-manufactured spare parts that it cannot even pay for? Let us add to this that such a coalition is ruled out in advance not only because of the economic interests involved but also because of the control the two great imperialist powers, America and Russia, have *already* exercised over the States in their respective zones. Finally, we must not forget the important role played by the United States' and Russia's monopolization of 95 percent of the crucial types of military technology and of the economic potentialities that constitute the basis for their power.

If we thus grant that the development of capitalism does not end with its monopolistic phase and that the process of concentration develops toward a higher phase characterized by the merger of capital and the State at a national level and by the worldwide domination of a single State on an international level, the question of the relations between States in the present era as well as the so-called national question are posed from a different angle than they were in 1915. We will consider briefly the broad outlines of this transformation in order to lay particular stress on the relations between bureaucratic States. The evolution of these relations since 1945 and the Russo-Yugoslavian conflict, in particular, offer a wealth of material for investigation.

1. In the present era, the economic development of traditional colonial countries and the entry of the colonial masses into action lead to a modification of the forms of imperialist domination over backward and secondary countries. The traditional form of colonialism tends to be left behind and is replaced by the formation of "nation"-States of recent vintage. On the social plane, this process is accompanied by a relative reinforcement of the local bourgeoisie or by the advent of a "national" bourgeoisie. But in reality, this formal "independence" signifies only a growing dependence on the dominant imperialist power; the true import of the phenomenon can be understood only when we see how the previously "independent" countries, including colonial imperialist powers, themselves are becoming dependent upon American imperialism. Although a very complex stratification appears in the structure of international relations and is one in which there are all kinds of intermediary forms (the relations between the United States and England, and between the latter and Nigeria, for example, offer two limiting cases of these types of relations), these differences tend to diminish more and more and to become subordinated to the fundamental opposition between a dominant imperialist State and the mass of countries that have been vassalized by it in one fashion or another. As in every other domain, the purest expression of this phenomenon is to be found in the zone of bureaucratic rule, in the absolute domination of Russia over its satellites.

2. Exploitation through capital exportation tends to be replaced by direct exploitation. The reason for this is that long-term crisis factors in the capitalist economy, as expressed in the falling rate of profit, begin to take precedence over short-term crisis factors (overproduction crises). The relative abundance of capital during the preceding period gives way to a relative shortage of capital. For, having been undermined by the crisis in labor productivity, the limited volume of overproduction is incapable of coping with both the unproductive consumption of the exploiting classes and the enormous accumulation requirements created by modern technical development. With the sole exception of the United

States (and even there we will have to make numerous reservations), the other imperialist countries not only are physically incapable of exporting capital, they are incapable even of resolving their own problems of accumulation. Therefore, exploitation of secondary countries less and less often takes the indirect form of making profits on investments and more and more often takes the direct form of one-sided levies by the dominant imperialist power on locally produced values.[4]

These general considerations provide us with a basis for resolving the particular case of the relations between Russia and its satellite States. It would be completely incorrect to consider these relations identical to the relations of classical colonialism. We are talking here not about the juridical form of this type of dependency—from this point of view, these countries have remained "independent"—but about its economic content. Exploitation in these regions occurs not through the "exportation of Russian capital" but essentially by means of a "tribute" levied by Russia, through one intermediary or another, on local production. The satellite countries do not serve as "outlets" for (nonexistent) Russian overproduction; rather, their production is directed toward plugging holes in the Russian economy, which is in a chronic state of underproduction in comparison to its needs. If we may use the term "bureaucratic imperialism" to express State capital's need for expansion while emphasizing the differences between this form of imperialism and that of finance capital, this term is applicable only insofar as Russia's relations of production are relations of exploitation expressing the most highly developed form of domination by capital over labor, and therefore only insofar as this bureaucratic system's own contradictions—and fundamentally its inability to resolve the problem of how to develop production based on the intensive exploitation of the producers—necessarily lead the regime to seek a way out of its contradictions on a worldwide level.

The form and content of a bureaucratic imperialist power's domination over its satellite countries are determined fundamentally by its own economic structure. In this sense it becomes clear that since the fundamental economic contradiction of bureaucratic capitalism is expressed through relative underproduction (and not through relative overproduction), bureaucratic capitalism is led to seek not "outlets" but rather countries to plunder. On the other hand, economic statification and planning in the dominant country imply an analogous transformation of the economies of the dominated countries. Capital's penetration into backward countries brings with it a dislocation of precapitalist relations since imperialist domination is able to exist in these countries only insofar as capitalist relations gradually start to take the place of feudal relations. This, in return, leads to a growing opposition between the new local bourgeoisie, which has been developed as a consequence of this imperialist domination, and the capitalism of the home country.

Similarly, bureaucratic imperialism's domination over other countries necessarily brings with it the elimination of traditional bourgeois relations and the creation of other kinds of relations, expressed through statification and planning, the only economic forms compatible with this kind of domination. In this sense, what has been called Russia's structural assimilation of Eastern European countries (and which does not signify juridical absorption pure and simple), i.e., the transformation of their economic structure in the direction of the structures prevailing in Russia, was for the Russian bureaucracy first and foremost an economic necessity, independent, so to speak, of political necessities and of these countries' own development. Without this transformation, it would have been impossible for Moscow to exploit these countries on a regular, ongoing basis. On the other hand, this transformation and this type of exploitation bring on the advent of new contradictions. The Russo-Yugoslavian crisis has been, up to now, the clearest expression of these new contradictions.

These contradictions express themselves in the latent or overt struggle among various national bureaucracies, and principally between the Russian bureaucracy and the bureaucracies of satellite countries.

We could say, reasoning abstractly, that just as the process of capital concentration within a system of competition is accompanied by the contrary tendency toward the "diffusion" of capital; just as international concentration of the economy and of power advances concomitantly with the forces that oppose it; just as these centrifugal forces, on the level of a national economy or of the world economy, can experience temporary periods of recovery (the law governing the process of concentration signifies only the long-term predominance of the tendency toward centralization over the contrary tendency), so also capitalism's transition to its State-bureaucratic phase signifies not the immediate disappearance on the international level of centrifugal forces and tendencies but rather their defeat over the long haul.

The basic kernel of this argument no doubt is correct, but it needs to be given concrete expression within current conditions. The advent of bureaucratic capitalism does not take place at just any moment in the history of capitalism, but rather at the precise moment when the international process of concentration has reached its penultimate stage through the division of the world into two blocs and when the supreme struggle for world domination between groupings of exploiters is about to take place. Consequently, it would be completely mistaken to expect an immediate transformation of all countries into State-bureaucratic ones, after which the struggle between these bureaucracies would lead to concentration on a world scale. Times are too ripe for such an evolution to take place. The two processes—concentration on the national level, as expressed by statification, and concentration on a world level, as expressed in the struggle for world domination—unfold concurrently, in a strictly interdependent fashion.

As a consequence, such phenomena as revolt or attempts at revolt by national bureaucracies against bureaucratic domination—in this case, the Russian bureaucracy—are natural and organic manifestations of the bureaucracy's constitution into a class in one or another country. These phenomena can occur only by way of an exception, and they are doomed more and more to remain as pure shows of resistance or muffled, behind-the-scene disagreements.

But these considerations would remain partial and abstract if we did not relate them to the question of the bureaucracy's class nature. The bourgeoisie was born and grew up as a class on a national level. It is through the constitution of the modern nation that it found its first "*Lebensraum*," and it is back within its national borders that it has to return when its crisis as a class becomes too intense for it and it is expelled from the world market. The changes that thrust a few and in the end a single bourgeoisie to a position of world domination are accompanied by profound modifications in its own economic and social structure so that it may be said that in achieving world domination the bourgeoisie itself will be transcended as a class.[5]

For the bureaucracy, in contrast, the nation is merely a formal framework without any genuine content of its own. Its economy is based not upon commercial exchanges with other nations (all of which already have been integrated through the division of labor into an international market) but rather on the authoritarian consolidation of every bureaucratic unit under the central command of one ruling bureaucracy. On the other hand, its accession to power, far from being a "purely" economic phenomenon—assuming that such phenomena have ever existed—is materially inseparable from a political and ideological struggle conducted on the world level and from a relation of forces that also exists on this same world level. It is therefore (by nature and in its opposition to the traditional bourgeoisie) an international class even before it becomes a ruling class within "national" borders. Cut off from this international bureaucratic system, only circumstantial factors could ensure its survival. Thus, for example, the Russo-Yugoslavian struggle would have been brought to an end in twenty-four hours had there not been an international situation that prevented the United States from remaining indifferent to a Russian occupation of Yugoslavia.

Let us summarize the foregoing. Russia's bureaucratic domination over its satellite countries derives from the very necessities of the Russian system of exploitation. The crisis of bureaucratic capitalism results from the crisis in labor productivity and manifests itself in the form of a chronic crisis of relative underproduction. The satellite countries are not "colonized" by Russia in the sense that they do not serve as the site to which its capital is exported or even as outlets for its overproduction; the bureaucracy uses them to make direct levies on their values in one fashion or another. For these countries, therefore, the Russian bureaucracy's exploitation must be added on top of the exploitation carried out by the "national" bureaucracy. The struggle over the division of the proceeds of exploitation in these countries is at the origin of the open or latent conflicts between these bureaucracies and the Russian bureaucracy. Insofar as the bureaucracy's international domination can take concrete form only on a local or national level through the particular power exercised by a given bureaucracy, these struggles, just like the conflicts between different fractions within a national bureaucracy, are inherent in the very nature of bureaucratic capitalism and consequently will continue to exist as long as the system of exploitation that engenders them exists. Nevertheless, as they continue they will be less and less able to take the overt form of conflict between "States," and already in the present epoch this form of conflict occurs only as the exception. The reason for this is the direct interdependence of various (technoeconomic or geographical) sectors of a bureaucratic system, which finds its parallel in the central bureaucracy's direct domination over peripheral bureaucracies and in the advanced stage the process of international capital concentration has reached, a stage that implies that a relation of forces has been established that confers an overwhelming supremacy upon the dominant pole (in this case, Russia) in relation to the secondary units (the satellite States).[6]

The basis of the Russo-Yugoslavian crisis is to be sought, therefore, in the typically interbureaucratic struggle over the division of the proceeds of exploitation. What is peculiar to this specific case of interbureaucratic conflict is a series of conjunctural factors that have made the Yugoslavian bureaucracy (rather than some other vassal bureaucracy) the lone pioneer of a revolt that has reached the point of the most clear-cut kind of political break. These conjunctural factors involve both the Yugoslavian bureaucracy's own characteristics and the international situation. A detailed analysis of these traits is only of secondary interest. Let us recall simply that of all the bureaucracies in the satellite countries the Yugoslavian bureaucracy was the only one to have seized power almost exclusively through its own efforts. It therefore had at its disposal within the country an autonomous and authentic force and thus had avoided, up to 1948, Russian control over its police and military forces and over its economy. On the other hand, only the division of the world into two blocs, the relative balance of forces between these two blocs, and Yugoslavia's geographical position at the border between these two worlds permitted Titoism not only to manifest itself but to continue to exist up till now instead of swiftly being crushed. But the balancing act between the two opposing colossi to which the Yugoslavian bureaucracy has committed itself has a very well defined historical limit: the outbreak of the third world war.[c]

The Future of Titoism

What has been said here concerning present-day imperialism, and in particular about bureaucratic imperialism, contains the answer to the problem of what the future of Titoism will be: Titoism is the highest expression of the struggle of local bureaucracies against the central bureaucracy. Titoism therefore ought to have expanded at the same rate and to the same extent that the bureaucracy attains power in new countries. But the bureaucracy is extending its power at a time when the international concentration of the forces of production directly raises the problem of world domination for the two opposing imperialist powers.

Two parallel processes are occurring. Centrifugal tendencies appear along with this extension of the bureaucracy's power. And there is an enormous growth in the central bureaucracy's strength and power, thus accelerating the process of international concentration. In historical terms, the second of these two processes is the stronger. It is the one that would triumph should the proletarian revolution fail. In the end, therefore, we may say that Titoism expresses a permanent tendency within the subordinate bureaucracies, though there is no historical chance whatsoever for it to be realized.

This may be expressed in concrete terms in the obvious statement that Yugoslavia, as an independent bureaucratic State, will be pulverized by the explosion of the third world war, and that it no longer will be able to build itself up again in the same way, whatever the outcome of this war. The condition for its present existence is the relative balance of forces existing between the Soviet Union and the United States—a balance that renders the "peaceful" interlude of the cold war equally possible. This balance will be tipped permanently to one side by the war and its effects.

It is superfluous to explain why a victorious proletarian revolution would signal the ruthless liquidation of the Titoist bureaucracy, and likewise for the Russian bureaucracy and the American trusts. It is just as easy to understand that, in case one of the two opposing imperialist powers achieved total victory, open revolts such as Tito's would become impossible; they would be wiped out swiftly if, through some miracle, they happened to make any appearance at all. There remains the question of the possible evolution of this regime from now until war breaks out. Leaving aside for the moment the absurd and ridiculous idea that this regime might evolve "progressively" toward working-class rule,[7] we ought to consider how it will fare when faced with the following real possibilities: direct integration into one or the other of the two opposing blocs or temporary consolidation of the Titoist bureaucracy as an "independent" bureaucracy.

As early as the first few months after the break between Belgrade and Moscow, the integration of Yugoslavia into the Russian bloc appeared impossible. There can be no question of a reconciliation between Tito and Stalin. On the other hand, the violent overthrow of the Titoist bureaucracy on the Cominform's behalf could not occur through an internal "revolution." No social forces in Yugoslavia want to struggle against Tito in order to bring a pro-Russian faction to power: neither the national bureaucracy, whose interests are expressed in the most direct fashion by Titoism, nor exploited urban and rural workers, who, having experienced the Yugoslavian bureaucracy, have at the same time experienced all bureaucracy, nor what remains of the well-off peasantry, who see in Tito a relatively lesser evil. The Yugoslavian supporters of the Cominform can gain recruits only among a few discontented or scheming bureaucrats for whom any action is circumscribed within very precise limits by Rankovich's vigilant police force.

The factors that preclude the possibility of Russia directly intervening in Yugoslavia at the present time or that would lead to immediate war preparations if this occurred are well known.

Likewise, we must exclude the possibility of Yugoslavia's being integrated directly into the American bloc. In theoretical terms, this integration would not necessarily mean that the Yugoslavian economy would return to the forms of property ownership and private management prevailing in the West; this eventuality would not be incompatible with the perpetuation of statist forms and bureaucratic power, provided that the bureaucracy bows to the control of American capital and allows it to share in the exploitation of the country. In the present situation, however, this kind of control and involvement is unacceptable to the Yugoslavian bureaucracy; its revolt against the Kremlin has been predicated precisely upon its will to avoid such a situation. The traditional attachments that bring Western European national capitalist groupings into amalgamation with American capital and thus make the United States' vassalization of the bourgeoisies of European countries more tolerable for the latter are the kinds of attachments that have been disrupted in Yugoslavia, and the almost complete statification of the Yugoslavian economy makes it nearly impossible for them to reappear. What counts the most is that during the current period the Yugoslavian bureaucracy has not only the will—which in the end counts for little—but also the temporary, but real, capacity to resist this process of integration.

We can gauge its capacity for resistance only after we have discussed the third possible outcome: the consolidation of the Yugoslavian bureaucracy as an "independent" bureaucracy. In the long run this "independence" is impossible for reasons that are economic and political at the same time and that are only two aspects of the same thing: Ultimately, Yugoslavia can only become a part of a larger system. On the economic level, this signifies that Yugoslavian production is not self-sufficient. Whether it goes the route of inter-State planning or the route of market-based trade, it has to tie in with the world system of production. On the political level, it will not in the long run have the strength to resist a single imperialist power dominating the whole world.

We thus are led to take up again the discussion of the theory of "socialism in one country"—or rather of bureaucratism in one country—on the much more concrete basis that the history of the last quarter century offers us. The idea that the construction of socialism in a single country is impossible no longer needs to be proved. Nevertheless, we can be much more explicit about this today than was possible in 1924 or 1927.

The criticism Trotsky leveled against the Stalinist "conception" of "socialism in one country," as correct as it was in its formal conclusion, was founded upon ideas that on the whole were mistaken in their content. The principal ideas were as follows:

1. Every country is dependent on the world economy. This dependence is *expressed directly in terms of the competitive weakness of each isolated country on the world market.*
2. The result of this dependence is the alliance of international capital and bourgeois-capitalist elements in this country, leading to the growing subordination of nationalized industry to private capital, and as a consequence, *the possible restoration of the traditional bourgeoisie.*[8]
3. Finally, the country's dependence upon the world economy would have to be expressed above all in its economic or political defeat in the struggle against its capitalist competitors and *in no case by its victory over them.*

These ideas completely fail to appreciate the lines of development of the contemporary economy, whose contradictions are situated at a much more profound level than that of the "market" and "private property." The Stalinist bureaucracy correctly responded to Trotsky that the "monopoly over foreign trade" would be able to protect an economy such as Russia's from "fluctuations in the world market" and that, sheltered by this type of monopoly control, the Russian economy would be able to develop. Only, what was able to develop and what actually did develop in this way obviously was not a socialist economy but rather a bureaucratic capitalist one. What Trotsky had underestimated in this case was how the "monopoly over foreign trade" was merely a form expressing the breakup of the traditional world market during capitalism's decadent phase. By rigorously enforcing this type of monopoly control, the Russian bureaucracy escaped the international division of labor.

Did this mean that the world economy's predominant position over a national economy had been eliminated? Certainly not. But this position of predominance no longer could express itself through the traditional expedient of "invading markets through cut-rate prices." And neither could it take the form of Russia's dependence upon the procurement of goods it was lacking. And this is due to a factor of "circumstantial" importance, i.e., the country's huge natural resources.[9]

It is obvious that in thus "departing" from the international division of labor, Russia suffered great losses from the point of view of economic profitability, and that, on the other hand, it still was confronted with an extraordinary capital shortage. But it also is obvious that the bureaucracy had to subordinate immediate economic profitability to its overall needs and interests—and in the first place to the imperatives of its existence pure and simple. The solution to the problem of capital shortages was provided by the unbridled exploitation of the masses.

Thus the possibility of "private capital penetration" into Russia, the sole plausible theoretical basis for bourgeois restoration, was eliminated at the same time. For the Russian peasant and the urban bourgeoisie, who were ruthlessly pulverized by the bureaucracy, proved incapable of resisting the State-run economy.

Russia's dependence upon the world economy eventually came to light in 1941, but not on the plane of the "world market." Rather it appeared on the plane of war. The bureaucratic economy was directly reintegrated into the international economy, this time at the level of the struggle for world domination. The Russian bureaucracy came out of this war victorious (thus proving the viability and even the superiority of bureaucratic capitalism as a system of exploitation in comparison with traditional capitalist forms), but in this way it demolished by itself the theory of "socialism in one country": The bureaucratic economy had to wage an armed struggle to preserve itself, and the postwar situation proved that the contradictions of bureaucratic capitalism lead to imperialist expansion no less than do those of finance capitalism.

This experience shows, therefore, that the question of whether it is possible for a bureaucratic economy *during a given period of time*[10] to maintain an independent existence is a concrete question whose solution depends on the configuration of basic factors in the particular situation. In the case of the Russian bureaucracy—disregarding the support the world proletariat actively granted to the Russian Revolution and to those who it wrongly believes are its inheritors—the factors that permitted its initial consolidation and development, and later allowed it to survive the war and win it, were the country's size and its natural resources, the balance of power after Versailles, and the ruthlessness of the conflict between the Western imperialist powers up to 1945. Certainly no modifications in these factors would have altered the fundamental development of the modern economy and society toward statification, but they might have changed its tempo and modalities.

We now must put this argument in concrete form for the case of Yugoslavia.

If the world were made up purely of economics, the bureaucracy in Yugoslavia would be in a desperate situation. Obviously no comparison can be made between the Yugoslavia of 1948 and the Russia of 1928, either from the point of view of their size and natural resources or from the point of view of their preexisting level of industrial development. Despite its great dependence upon the world economy, czarist Russia in 1913 was the fifth largest industrial power in the world, already possessing an extremely concentrated and modern heavy industrial base. Apart from insignificant exceptions, every kind of raw material and agricultural crop existed in this immense country. The outstanding problem was that of capital accumulation and the incorporation of modern industrial techniques. This problem could have been and was in fact resolved by the intense exploitation of the working population, since the physical and human factors for the solution to this problem were at hand.

Nothing of the sort exists in Yugoslavia. The fact that "new" natural resources now can be exploited and that certain processing industries can be created cannot mask the following obvious truth: By its limited size, its legacy of backwardness, and its inadequate natural wealth, Yugoslavia could depart from the international division of labor only by maintaining its economy at the level of absolute stagnation. Obviously this is impossible; the existence of the bureaucracy, even more than that of the bourgeoisie, is inseparable from industrial development. It is more obvious still that this kind of development will only increase its dependence upon advanced countries. It would be superfluous to recall here the enormous amount of specialization—and consequently dependence—involved in modern industry and the fact that in the capitalist era two countries alone—America and Russia—have succeeded in creating, one way or another, a production cycle that is more or less closed in upon itself (from the technical point of view and obviously not from the economic point of view).

The "industrialization" of Yugoslavia would be out of the question if this country could not find abroad both the requisite equipment and the credits to buy it. Once installed, this equipment must be kept in good repair, replaced, and expanded. For the foreseeable future, "industrialization" will never signify a diminution in the country's dependence upon the industrial nations that furnish it with equipment; it even will signify an accentuation of this dependence from a qualitative point of view.[11]

In contrast to Russia, then, Yugoslavia's dependence on the world economy manifests itself not only in a derivative and long-term way but also directly and immediately. Here it is not simply a matter of insoluble internal contradictions of an exploiting society and a defense-attack complex that drives toward the struggle for world domination; already at this time, it is impossible for Yugoslavia to escape the international division of labor. Therefore, it also is impossible for it to avoid "exchanges" with capitalist countries under the form these exchanges currently take, i.e., dependence upon American imperialism where the latter exercises absolute control. A monopoly over foreign trade could prevent this kind of integration from taking the form of "invasion by cheap goods," but it cannot serve as an obstacle to the installation of American control over the country.

But pure economics is an abstraction. Economics, politics, and strategic considerations are now integrated to such a degree that actions that are absurd from the "purely economic" point of view are an obvious necessity from the point of view of the general interests of ruling classes. Purely and straightforwardly economic criteria for judging profitability tend to be replaced more and more by the criterion of total profitability, judged in terms of the best defense of the universal interests of the exploiting class, interests that are often opposed to "maximum profit" being drawn from each particular operation and which go beyond such considerations.

Thus, in the specific case of Yugoslavia, a whole complex set of political and strategic reasons makes it absurd for the Western bloc and for the United States in particular to lay down economic conditions, even to set any sort of conditions for the aid they are granting to Tito in the form of credits or by lifting, in Yugoslavia's case, the commercial blockade they are trying to impose on the other countries in the Eastern zone. That they attempt to obtain the maximum amount of concessions from the Titoist bureaucracy is perfectly possible; that they make these concessions a *sine qua non* for their aid is absolutely precluded, given that the essential role Yugoslavia can play for the United States is to consolidate the break at a key point in the Soviet bloc and to serve as an example for the bureaucracies of other satellite countries. In light of these general factors, the few dollars that American imperialism may be able to pick up in one form or another by sharing in the exploitation of Yugoslavia are of little consequence. Aid to Yugoslavia is earmarked as part of the overhead expenses of preparing for the third world war.

It is by exploiting this situation that Tito will be able to continue his tightrope dance for as long as the cold war lasts.[c]

Notes

1. T/E: *SB 2*, pp. 65ff.

2. In the sense that this partitioning was not, over a given period of time, called into question by violent means.

3. We say "final imperialist war," and not simply the final war altogether. This war, which would culminate in the worldwide domination of a single State, would thereby lay the foundations for a worldwide concentration of capital. And via this route, it would open the way—assuming the revolution is defeated—to historical and social changes that would move further and further away from the present system. We cannot examine here what might be the motive forces and the violent

forms of struggle within the ruling class of such a society. One thing, however, is certain: There would no longer be imperialist wars in the precise scientific sense of this term.

4. Thus vanishes one of the last "progressive" economic aspects of capitalist exploitation. The intensive exploitation of colonial countries and workers in the classical period occurred through the exportation of capital, and therefore through investments that led to a certain economic development of the country in question. This development does not come to an end with the present era, but its motive force no longer is the exportation of capital from the home country.

5. This corresponds to the profound changes the structure of the system of exploitation itself would undergo should this consolidation of the world economy be achieved on a reactionary basis.

6. In a universally bureaucratic society, the chronic and latent character of these struggles would be one of the most significant expressions of its historical stagnation.

7. We will discuss this idea in the conclusion to this article. [T/E: This conclusion, entitled "Prolétariat et titisme," has not been translated for the present edition. It appears as pp. 137-43 of *SB 2*.]

8. And even, barring the possibility of a proletarian revolution, the *necessity* of this restoration.

9. The few raw materials not found in Russia (for example, rubber) and the highly specialized equipment required for certain production processes were supplied by the capitalist market, which at the time still drew a broad enough line between economic profit and political matters so as not to be bothered by the color of Russian money; on the whole, this remains true today. Russia usually made its payments by selling its own products below their international price (the famous Russian practice of "dumping"), independent of their production cost and of the country's own needs. Through all this it must not be forgotten that the value and volume of Russian trade with the bourgeois countries have decreased constantly since 1929. [T/E: In the French text, the word "dumping" appears in English.]

10. On the historical plane, we already have said that "independence" in the long run can be identical only with world domination for a single State.

11. Even if, for its current needs, it imports much more than an industrially developed country, a backward agrarian country can withstand much more easily a reduction in or a total interruption of the flow of imports by falling back on its own rudimentary forms of production. Such a withdrawal signals the death of industry in a developed country—unless this development already has grown to huge proportions.

Postface

See also the first section of the General Introduction on the evolution of the social situation in the countries occupied during the war by the German army, the factors that conditioned the extraordinary development of their Stalinist parties, notably in Yugoslavia and in Greece, the relations between these parties and the national bourgeoisie in each country, and the dynamic that led them to seize power and instaurate a bureaucratic regime in the image of the Russian regime.

a) On a number of points—the interpretation of imperialism, the prospects for a third world war, the worsening of the exploitation of the proletariat—the text naturally corresponds to my conceptions of the time, which were revised some time afterward. The same thing obviously goes for the reference to the imaginary "falling rate of profit." See the first half of the second section of the General Introduction. In particular, the question of imperialism is infinitely more complex than the text, or even "The Situation of Imperialism and Proletarian Perspectives," says. I will return to this question at length in *Le Système mondial de domination*. [T/E: The last text referred to never has been published.]

b) That bureaucratic capitalism gives birth organically, and not accidentally, to a conflict between "national" bureaucracies, and that this conflict between dominant, exploiting strata has no "progressive social content" on either side, has been demonstrated since this text was written by the evolution of relations within the Eastern bloc, and above all obviously by the head-on opposition between Russia and China. It is well known that the latter has had several brushes with armed conflict over the past ten years. Perhaps it would have been driven to the point of actual war were it not for the two adversaries' common fear of playing the cat's-paw for a third thief, the United States. We will leave it to the overly curious reader to find, at his own risk and peril, the interpretation in the various Trotskyist literatures and to decide whether a "degenerated workers' State" is more or less progressive than a "deformed workers' State" (this last pearl having been produced by Trotskyist oysters) and whether one ought to "defend unconditionally" Russia against China, the reverse or both at the same time, should the occasion arise.

c) The exploitation of the relative balance of forces between the Soviet Union and the United States sure enough has permitted the Tito regime a very long survival. This survival has gone hand in hand with Yugoslavia's increasing reinsertion into the capitalist world market, especially since 1960. Meanwhile, repeated and recurrent attempts at economic "reforms," which are aimed at reducing the irrationalities involved in the bureaucratic management of the economy by means of the injection of doses of pseudo-"market" forces and "competition," have been imposed upon the country. We will return to this in *Le Système mondial de domination*.

9
Proletarian Leadership

Revolutionary activity of the type inaugurated by Marxism is dominated by a profound antinomy that may be defined in the following terms: On the one hand, this activity is founded upon a scientific analysis of society, upon a conscious perspective on future development, and consequently upon a partial planning [*planification relative*] of its attitude toward reality; on the other hand, the most important factor, the decisive factor for this perspective and for this anticipation on the future, is the creative activity of tens of millions of people as it will blossom during and after the revolution. The revolutionary and cosmogonic character of this activity consists precisely in the fact that its content will be original and unforeseeable. It is vain to try to resolve this antinomy by suppressing one of its terms. To renounce rational, organized, and planned collective activity because the masses will resolve all problems in the process of their struggle is in fact to repudiate the "scientific" aspect, and more precisely the rational and conscious aspect of revolutionary activity; it is to sink voluntarily into a messianic mysticism. Not to recognize the original and creative character of the masses' activity or to pay it only lip service, on the other hand, amounts to laying the theoretical foundations for bureaucracy, whose ideological basis is the recognition of a "conscious" minority as the repository of historical reason.

This antinomy appears most conspicuously on the terrain where we encounter problems relating to the revolutionary program—and the question of the leadership of the proletariat (the party) and its relations with the working class is

Originally published as "La Direction prolétarienne," *S. ou B.*, 10 (July 1952). Reprinted in *EMO 1*, pp. 145-61. See also the Postface to this article, originally published as "Postface au *Parti révolutionnaire* et à *La Direction prolétarienne*," *EMO 1*, pp. 163-78. [T/E: Since the first of these two articles, "The Revolutionary Party," is not translated for this edition, we have omitted the sections of this Postface dealing with this first article. Noted in our brackets are the contents of the omitted sections.]

a programmatic question par excellence. Unquestionably, everything that could be said about the limited and unsatisfactory character of the efforts to resolve the party question made both by our group as well as by other currents during the last twenty years boils down to the impossibility of resolving this antinomy a priori. For we have here the very kind of antinomy that cannot be resolved on the theoretical level. Any attempt at a solution can lead only to mystifications, whether they are deliberate or not.

The sole theoretical "answer" that can be given consists in saying that the solution of this antinomy will develop during the course of the revolution because the creative activity of the masses is a conscious and rational type of activity, and hence is essentially homogeneous with the activity of conscious minorities acting before the revolution begins, but whose unique and irreplaceable contribution consists of an overthrow and a tremendous enlargement of the very content of this historical reason. If in this way a general basis is granted us to merge the "consciousness" of minorities with the "rudimentary" reason of the masses, if we thus may affirm that the revolution does not encounter any insoluble contradictions, we cannot, in return, pretend that we have discovered in advance the practical-concrete forms of this fusion. This theoretical "solution" does not prescribe them to us. On the contrary, it tells us that the concrete content of the revolution already outstrips every advance analysis since it consists in the positing of new forms of historical rationality.

It is therefore essential for a revolutionary organization to have a clear awareness of the problem in these terms and to make itself ready to adapt its ideology and action in the light of the perspective that results therefrom rather than trying at all costs to resolve by artificial means a question that is on the scale of the revolution and of the revolution alone. We know, indeed, in those instances in which "solutions" have been given in a different spirit, where they have led.

These remarks are in no way aimed at repudiating research and discussion, nor are they opposed to adopting provisional solutions, which are more than working hypotheses and are genuine postulates for action. To renounce these would signify the renunciation of every programmatic conception that is defined even a little bit, which amounts to saying that we should give up on all action. The importance of the preceding distinction lies in the fact it gives us a precise understanding of every a priori programmatic conception that we might elaborate and especially in the fact that it tends to educate the "conscious and organized minority" about the meaning and the historical limits of its role.

The problem is posed in relatively different terms when it is a question of the forms of organization and of the activity of this conscious minority itself. In this case, this minority has to provide itself with its own solutions. A revolutionary minority, or an isolated revolutionary militant, acts under its (his) own responsibility. Otherwise it (he) ceases to exist. We cannot claim today to have settled the question of proletarian power except in the form of a postulate, but we can and should answer the problem of our tasks and our general orientation.

Obviously, one of the most important aspects of the problem has to do with the connection between the organization and actual activity of a revolutionary minority and its ultimate point of view concerning proletarian power. The actual solutions must be in keeping with the line of development that defines our historical outlook. Later in this essay we will look at the implications of this aspect of the problem.

Leadership before and after the Revolution

The problem of revolutionary leadership [*direction*] presents itself as a knot of contradictions. The revolutionary process presents itself in the form of an indefinite number of persons engaged in an indefinite number of activities; unless we appeal to magic, it is impossible for this process to achieve its goals without a leadership in the precise sense of this term, i.e., without a central organ [*instance*] that orients and coordinates this manifold of activities, chooses the most economical means for attaining the assigned objectives, etc. On the other hand, the revolution's basic goal is the suppression of the fixed and stable distinction—and eventually of every distinction—between directors and executants. Therefore, there is a need for leadership just as there is a need for the suppression of leadership.

The final goal of the revolution does not immediately imply the suppression of the distinction between the functions of direction and execution (here we have a far-off problem that we will not consider), but it does necessarily imply the suppression of a social division of labor corresponding to these functions. If it is granted that the function of direction cannot be suppressed immediately, one readily derives the following conclusion: The proletariat itself should be its own leadership. The leadership of the class, therefore, cannot be distinct from the class itself.

But on the other hand, it is obvious that the class cannot immediately and directly be its own leadership. It is useless to debate this point since in any case the class in fact is not its own leadership and has not been in the course of its history. If, therefore, the revolutionary process begins in capitalist society, if explicit class struggle has a positive value and ought to be conducted in a permanent, ongoing fashion, it has to be a fraction of the class, a relatively distinct body, that can and should be its leadership. The leadership of the class cannot *not* be distinct from the class itself.

The solution to this contradiction is to be found in part over time, i.e., in its development. When we speak of the suppression of the distinction between directors and executants we are referring to a later stage, roughly the period following the victory of revolution. The suppression of exploitation and the development of the forces of production are indeed impossible without workers' management, and the latter is inseparable from the power of mass organs. When we speak, in contrast, of the necessity of a leadership distinct from the class, we are referring to the conditions of the present system of exploitation, under which these functions can be fulfilled only by a minority of the class.

But it also is obvious that this answer does not close the question. For the passage from one situation to the other—from the stage during which the exploited, alienated, and mystified class cannot be its own leadership to the stage during which the class necessarily directs itself—appears as, and in reality is, a leap, an absolute contradiction. This is a contradiction that, let it be said parenthetically, is no more remarkable than the revolution itself, nor than every moment during which a thing ceases to be itself in order to become another thing. It is impossible to explain in advance in theoretical terms how this passage will take place. For Marxism, it was never a question of deducing the revolution but rather of making it.

This does not mean that for us the recognition of the possibility of this passage is an act of faith. Without trying to or being able to describe the forms it might take, we think we can provide a foundation for this passage upon elements that exist now. The first and most important of these elements is the development of the consciousness and capacities of the proletariat, as it has been shaped by the very evolution of society. The second is the existence within the proletariat, long before the revolution, of strata and individuals who become aware of the goals and the means of the revolution. The third of these elements is the very action of the revolutionary leadership under the present system of exploitation, which continually has to aim at developing the proletariat's capacity for autonomous action and self-leadership.

The proletariat's passage from the position of the exploited class to the position of the dominant class corresponds to the transitional phase usually called the revolutionary period. In our definition, this period begins the moment the working class starts to form mass organs that take up positions on the field of the struggle for power; it ends the moment power has been won on a universal scale. This definition allows us to see exactly where the problem of class self-leadership is situated: certainly not before the inception of this period, nor after its end. Not beforehand, because there is no problem of class self-leadership if the class does not pose the problem itself—and it only poses it through the constitution of mass organs. Not afterward, because the reasons that previously rendered class self-leadership impossible have been suppressed by the victory of the revolution (otherwise they never would have been suppressed).

Certainly, it is during this period that the question of the relations between the proletarian leadership and the working class becomes decisive. Just as certainly, the discussion of this question serves no purpose today. The constitution of a revolutionary leadership under the present system of exploitation is in no way opposed to the suppression of every separate type of leadership during the postrevolutionary period; we think, on the contrary, that it constitutes one of its presuppositions. From this point of view, everything depends upon the spirit, the orientation, and the ideology in which this leadership is developed and educated and the manner in which it conceives its relations with the class and actualizes them. Moreover, this leadership in the prerevolutionary period is a leadership that directs only in a special sense—it proposes objectives and means, but it can impose them only through ideological struggle and its own example. In this sense, the question is not whether there should be leadership, but what its program ought to be.

During the revolutionary period, in contrast, everything takes place on the plane of the relations of force. A self-organized and coherent minority will play a very heavy role in the unfolding of events. It will be able—and who can state in advance that in certain cases it ought not?—to act on its own responsibility, imposing its point of view by means of violence. (Are there in the group some people for whom the difference between 49 percent and 51 percent is the difference between good and evil? Or who will require a panproletarian referendum in order to decide upon the insurrection?) It then would be a leadership in the full sense of the term. On the other hand, there will be the working class as a whole, organized and probably armed. If the leadership has been developed upon correct programmatic principles, if the class is sufficiently conscious and active, the revolution will signal the leadership's reabsorption into the class. In the contrary instance, and in any case if the class abdicates its responsibility—to the leadership or to whomever else—then bureaucratization or defeat is inevitable, and the question whether the new bureaucracy will be the formerly revolutionary leadership or some other group matters little. As for the leadership, it can do nothing more than educate itself and the vanguard in the spirit of developing the autonomous activity of the working class as well as its historical awareness.

Revolutionary Leadership under the Present System of Exploitation

If the problem of revolutionary leadership is posed for us as a permanent problem—which does not mean that it is always resolved, still less that it is so in an adequate manner—there are two reasons for this. On the one hand, we recognize that the class struggle is itself permanent. On the other hand—and above all—we recognize that the proletariat cannot exist and continue as a revolutionary class without conducting or constantly tending to conduct an explicit, overt struggle. In this struggle, it affirms itself as a separate class with its own historical goals, which are in fact universal ones. As is well known, the character of proletarian struggle differentiates the proletariat from the other exploited classes that have preceded it in history. Now, once this struggle becomes explicit, the problem of the leadership of this struggle is posed.

What does leadership mean? It means to decide upon the orientation as well as the methods of a collective action, of the action of a collectivity or a group. Leadership is this directing activity itself; it is also—and this is what matters here—the subject of this activity, the body or organ that brings this activity to bear. This subject can be the group or collectivity in question; it can also be a particular body, inside or outside the group, acting "by delegation" or on its own. In both cases the notion of leadership is tied to the notion of power, for the enforcement of leadership decisions can be guaranteed only through the existence of sanctions, and therefore of organized coercion.

Leadership in the full sense of the term, therefore, can be exercised only by a dominant class or portions thereof. This will be true when the proletariat is in power, and we have seen that a particular problem arises during the revolutionary period as a result of the fragmentation of power—or because of the generalized possibility of using violence—that characterizes this period.

Under such conditions, what can the leadership of an oppressed and exploited class be? Given the absolute character of violence in present-day society (and in contrast to what could occur in other times, in caste societies, for example), coercion cannot be used inside the class—unless whoever exercises this power already participates in one manner or another in the system of exploitation (as is the case with reformist or Stalinist trade unions and parties). Thus, agreement between the leadership and the class (or portions of the class) can only be based upon the class's voluntary adherence to the leadership's decisions. The sole "coercive" means at this leadership's disposal, in the wider sense of the term, is ideological coercion, i.e., struggle by means of ideas and by example.

It would be stupid to try to set limits on this struggle and on this kind of "coercion." The sole restrictions that can be put upon them concern their ideological content and, consequently, raise a different set of questions.

Under a system of exploitation, a revolutionary leadership therefore can have no other meaning than the following: a body that decides on the orientation and the methods of action of the class or portions thereof, and strives to get these methods adopted by the class through ideological struggle and exemplary action.

The question now is raised: Is such a leadership really necessary—not in the sense of directing activity, which goes without saying, but in the sense of a particular subject who directs? Cannot the class immediately and directly be its own leadership? The answer obviously is no. Under the conditions of the present system of exploitation, the class cannot in its undifferentiated totality be its own leadership. If we must, we will go over again the overwhelming set of reasons arguing for this conclusion.

This leadership cannot be thought of in any other way than as a universal, minoritarian, selective, and centralized organ. These are the classic characteristics of the party, though the name is of little importance. But the present age has added to these characteristics a new and still more basic one: The party is an organ whose form and substance are *unique*; in other words, it is the *sole* (permanent) class organ under the conditions of the present system of exploitation. There is not and cannot be a plurality of organizational forms juxtaposed to one another or superimposed upon each other. In particular, it is impossible for organizations that supposedly are trying to respond to economic problems as particular problems (trade unions) to be proletarian organs. The politico-economic organ for the struggle against exploitation is unitary and unique. In this sense, the distinction between Party and "Committees of Struggle" (or any other minoritarian organizational form of the vanguard of the working class) is concerned exclusively with the degree of clarification and organization and nothing else. The exclusive character of this directing organ is clearly apparent under the most modern conditions of the system of exploitation (bureaucratic dictatorship or war regime), conditions under which a plurality of organizational forms or forms of leadership is unthinkable. But it is obvious even under the "superannuated" conditions of the Western world. Indeed, neither from the point of view of the problems involved nor from that of the persons concerned can one try to create on a permanent basis a "factory" organization and a "political" organization separate and independent from each other. From this perspective, the distinction between the "organization of the workers" and the "organization of revolutionaries" ought to disappear along with the theoretical conception that is its root.

Constitution of a Leadership Group in the Present Period

Of the three elements required to constitute a leadership group (program, organizational form, actual basis for constituting the group), it is the last one, i.e., the existence and the present nature of a potential vanguard, that ought to be of particular concern. Unless we are mistaken, no comrade has questioned till now whether it is possible to define a program or whether there might be an organizational form corresponding to the content of this program and to the conditions of the present era. In contrast, there is a controversy not so much about the nature of the existing "vanguard" as about its historical evaluation and signification.

The concrete definition of the existing "vanguard" on which the entire group is more or less in accord is that it includes all of the workers who are conscious of the nature of capitalism and Stalinism as systems of exploitation and who refuse to prop up either one by their actions. Even more profoundly, and in particular with respect to Stalinism, these workers are calling into question the entire set of problems concerning both the goals and the means of working-class struggle. As has long been said in the group, the attitude of this vanguard is in essence negative and critical. As such, it undeniably signifies a kind of transcending. The whole question is, A transcending of what?

In our opinion, it is a transcending of the traditional meaning of "the program," of traditional organizational forms, and in particular of traditional forms of activity of "leadership groups." This is so as regards its objective value. No doubt its concrete content goes much further. Almost certainly, these workers as a whole not only reject the traditional solution to these problems but challenge the idea that there can be a general solution. In other words, it is certain that they do not believe, at the present time, in the proletariat's ability to become the dominant class.

Can we draw a conclusion about what is at the bottom of these problems? Perhaps, but then we must draw out the entire line of argument. If the workers who are relatively more conscious believe at the present time that every leadership group is sure to turn rotten, and if this by itself proves that it really is the case, the same line of argument can be used to prove that every program is a mystification or that the proletariat never will be capable of exercising real power; for that too is what workers think.

In reality, this state of consciousness and the attitude resulting from it reflect a new — and immensely positive — awareness of the bankruptcy of traditional answers, and as such they undeniably prepare the way for the future. But they equally reflect the world situation, and in particular the incredible, unprecedented pressure that the current relation of forces exerts on all individuals in society—including the members of our group. And to this extent they represent, so to speak, the pure and simple weight of historical matter, matter that indeed is rapidly becoming transformed and that before long will sink into the past.

As long as the vanguard is situated on this terrain, the question of constituting a leadership certainly cannot be posed as a practical task. We must wait for the pressure of objective conditions to put again before the most conscious workers the necessity of acting.

Role and Tasks for the Group

This does not mean at all that the group does not now have a role to play, a historically important role. At the present time, only the group can—and, unless we are mistaken, it is the only one in the world to do it—carry on with the elaboration of a revolutionary ideology, define a program, and do the work of propagating ideas and educating. These are quite valuable activities even if the results do not appear immediately. The accomplishment of these tasks is a basic presupposition for the constitution of a leadership, once the latter becomes objectively possible.

It is not difficult to comprehend these things, and it would be surprising if these points became an object of discussion on their own. If, nevertheless, they do, it is because the group is not a logical subject, because it is made up of individuals who belong to the same society we analyze so well for others, and because these individuals experience the same tremendous historical pressure as is currently bearing down so hard upon the working class and its vanguard. The great majority of the comrades in the group consciously or unconsciously share the same state of mind described earlier, and it is likely that they no longer understand very well their reasons for sticking with the group. As a consequence, their participation in the work of the group is almost nil, which threatens to make the work of the group and the group itself disappear. But this phenomenon and the conclusions following from it belong to another discussion. Even if the "party discussion" led to some conclusions about these or other kinds of tasks, there still would have to be comrades willing to sacrifice something so that these tasks, whatever they might be, could be accomplished.

Postface

Discussion of the organizational question went on, in more or less pointed fashion, during the entire history of the *S. ou B.* group. But the meaning of the two preceding texts [T/E: i.e., "The Revolutionary Party" and "Proletarian Leadership"] would remain obscure if they were not placed in the context of the discussions going on at the time they were written. In order to shed some light on them, it seems to me useful to reprint here the accompanying notes published in *S. ou B.*, 2 (May 1949) and 10 (July 1952).

Here first is the note that preceded "The Revolutionary Party" in issue 2. [T/E: A note on "La Vie de notre groupe" (The life of our group), *EMO 1*, pp. 163-73, summarizes the various positions taken by members of the group during an all-day plenary session on the question of the revolutionary party.]

Here follows the *Résolution statuaire* to which the preceding note referred. [T/E: This nine-point "Resolution on the By-Laws" appears on pp. 173-75 of *EMO 1*.]

The preceding discussion (itself the apparent culmination of discussions that in fact had begun before the group left the PCI) took place in April 1949. A little afterward, however, it was taken up again stronger than ever, reaching a climax in the spring of 1951 and concluding at least temporarily with the first scission of Claude Lefort and other comrades who shared his views (a scission that was, in fact, of short duration). The texts that entered into the discussion were "Proletarian Leadership," which is reprinted here, and "Le Prolétariat et le problème de la direction révolutionnaire," by Claude Lefort, which also was published in issue 10 of *S. ou B.* (and now reprinted in Claude Lefort, *Eléments d'une critique de la bureaucratie* [Geneva-Paris: Droz, 1971], pp. 30-38, under the title, "Le Prolétariat et sa direction"). [T/E: This article is found on pp. 59-70 of the second, revised edition of this book, published by Gallimard.]

These two texts were preceded by the following note. [T/E: This note briefly reviews the controversy and points out that other members of the group held positions different from those of Montal (Lefort) and Chaulieu (Castoriadis).]

I have briefly indicated in the *IG* (pp. 22-23 and 38-39 [T/E: General Introduction, this volume, pp. 10-11 and 21-22]) how the two texts reprinted above—the first especially, but this is also true, to a certain extent, of the "Response to Comrade Pannekoek," which can be read below [T/E: Castoriadis's "Réponse au camarade Pannekoek" (*S. ou B.*, 14 [April 1954]) has not been translated for this edition]—remained prisoners of traditional conceptions on some nonnegligible points. The decisive turn was brought about for me during the drafting of *CS I* during the winter of 1954-55; it is clearly indicated in "Workers Confront the Bureaucracy," in "Bilan, perspectives, tâches," "Bilan," *PO I* and *II* (see also *CS II*, July 1957, and *MTR/MRT III* and *IV*, October 1964 and March 1965). [T/E: Neither of the two "Bilan" articles nor *PO II* have been included in this edition. "Marxism and Revolutionary Theory" is now included in *IIS*.] I also hope that the General Introduction will help the reader to situate the question on its proper terrain.

It would be rather pointless to resume here in a detailed fashion the criticism of old texts, which already has been done, either implicitly or explicitly, in subsequent writings. I will add some new considerations in a new text on the organizational question, which will be published later. [T/E: This text never has been published.]

10
Sartre, Stalinism, and the Workers

In the spring of 1947 the Stalinist party left the government. It was forced to by the revolt of workers who no longer would swallow its "produce first" line (which brought with it more and more misery) and also by the fact that it no longer could continue playing its double game on the Indochina question. The year 1947 had been marked by great working-class struggles. The Stalinists spent the time readjusting their policies. Openly against the strikes when they began, the Stalinists later tried to curtail them from within, but the rapidly deepening rift between the Soviet Union and the United States and France's ultimate passage over to the American side obliged them to totally change their strategy and their tactics. The strikes of November-December 1947, when the general mobilization of the workers failed without the Stalinist party's for a single moment having clearly wanted, demanded, or organized it, marked the end of this painful period of readjustment. From then on, the goal of Stalinist policy in France was to sabotage the capitalist economy (especially in 1948-49), to set the population against the government's Atlanticist policy, and eventually to get ready to disrupt the rear of the American front when war breaks out.

The effectiveness of this policy is continually put into question by the inher-

Originally published as "Sartre, le stalinisme et les ouvriers," *S. ou B.*, 12 (August 1953). Reprinted in *EMO 1*, 179-243. [T/E: All citations given in the text come from Sartre's two works discussed here by Castoriadis. These are *CP*: "Les Communistes et la paix," originally in *Les Temps Modernes*, 81, 84-85, and 101 (July 1952, October-November 1952, and April 1954); reprinted in *Situations VI* (Paris: Gallimard, 1964), pp. 80-384, and translated by Martha H. Fletcher in *The Communists and the Peace* (New York: George Braziller, 1968), pp. 3-231; and *RCL*: "Réponse à Claude Lefort," originally in *Les Temps Modernes*, 89 (April 1953); reprinted in *Situations VII* (Paris: Gallimard, 1965), pp. 7-93, and translated by Philip R. Berk as "Response to Claude Lefort," in *The Communists and the Peace*, pp. 233-96. The French pagination is always cited first (we have used the *Situations* reprint for this purpose). We have often altered the available English translation.]

ent contradictions of Stalinism in general, and of its situation in France since 1947 in particular. The Stalinist party gets its strength in the first place from the allegiance of the working masses. Even if this allegiance is a given at the start, in the long run it cannot be maintained—and still less expanded and intensified— unless the facts tend to justify such allegiance and do not continually go contrary to it. The facts in this case are, namely, Stalinist policy and its effects on the workers' situation. The CP, therefore, must impose a line that serves the workers' immediate interests and has some discernible connection with their historical interests. Now, in its concrete actions, such a line does not necessarily coincide with a struggle that is anti-American before all else; it is easy to see that in most cases it differs from this struggle or is opposed to it. A strike in which wage demands are sacrificed to political imperatives rarely can expand or intensify the workers' allegiance to the CP. Still less can it do so when the workers begin to wonder whether the Stalinists' objectives or the means adopted to achieve these objectives really are their own.

At the same time, the Stalinists are obliged to conduct a "pacifist" policy that does not appeal to any class in particular and claims to be independent of their party goals. Both in phraseology and in real actions, however, their attempt to create a "National Front" tends to contradict their allegedly exclusive fidelity to the working class or to the exploited in general.

Moreover, as part of the international Stalinist bureaucracy, the Parti communiste français (PCF) not only is *not* free to act in its little game as it wishes but suffers the repercussions of what this bureaucracy does or what befalls it elsewhere. It has to make the best of changes in course that do not arise for it organically; it has to explain itself about Yugoslavia or Korea, Czechoslovakia or East Germany.

We must point out another factor in these difficulties faced by the Stalinist bureaucracy. Taken one by one, errors committed by the Stalinist leadership are accidents. As frequent and repeated occurrences, however, they become the necessary accidents of its bureaucracy.

Given the elements of this new situation, it takes no exceptional amount of perspicacity to foresee that the competency, cunning, and cynicism of the Stalinist leadership cannot prevent the working class from coming "unstuck" from the PCF. And in fact, we wrote in the very first issue of this review (March 1949):

> Since the strikes of November-December 1947, the French working-
> class movement seems to be in a period of fragmentation and
> profound discouragement. . . . A great number of workers still
> follow the main trade-union federations, but they do so without
> confidence; the workers' retreat from unions, from parties, from
> anything of an organized nature and from "politics" is a
> characteristic sign of the times. . . . A series of advanced elements
> are driven by current events and by the politics of the traditional
> working-class parties to stop and think about what is happening. . . .
> But the great majority of the working class today remains spellbound
> by the negative aspects of its situation; it is aware not only that it

cannot enter into a struggle against its political and trade-union leaders but even that it cannot enter into struggle independently of these leaders; it cannot struggle without calling upon them or in any case without being "headed up" by them.[1]

The forms this "coming unstuck" from the CP has taken are well known: It is continually losing members, losing its newspaper subscribers; it is becoming less and less capable of mobilizing workers for political or even economic struggles. That the CP and the Confédération générale du travail (CGT, General Confederation of Labor) have not lost votes in political or union elections since 1948 in no way contradicts this statement: The ties between the masses and bureaucratic organizations have been worn down to the thickness of a paper ballot. A choice in an election is always the choice of the lesser evil; the worker thinks that a collapse of the CGT would give the bosses a green light for an offensive, and the decayed state of the SFIO[2] bars any alternative when it comes to political elections.

In the all-out struggle between American imperialism and Russian imperialism, each profits from the other's contradictions and failures and tries to exploit them. The French bourgeoisie naturally rejoices each time the CP suffers a setback among the workers. But newspapers in the West also denounce the exploitation of the workers in the East, the president of General Motors declares his solidarity with the strikers in Berlin, and the director of the FBI laments the fate of Russian concentration camp prisoners. When Stalinists denounce the capitalist system, it appears less preposterous only because it is much more familiar.

It therefore was perfectly natural that Ridgway[3] would come to Paris in May 1952; that the Stalinists would urge the population to come out and boo him; that the government would forbid the demonstration; that the workers would not come out; that Pinay,[4] strengthened by this new rout of the CP, would arrest Duclos;[5] that the Politburo would flounder around about what posture to adopt next; that the protest strike would be a failure; and that the bourgeois press would headline this as a "Workers' Victory." History usually cannot be compared to a syllogism, but in this particular case there was nothing in the conclusion that was not already in the premises.

Yet what was unexpected or, if one prefers, irrational came in the form of a series of articles by Sartre. Having exhausted knowledge like Faust and wasted his youth like Caesar, he became more and more obsessed by the demon of action. Like Plato, he resolved to leave the fields of Saint-Germain for Sicily each time there was a Congress of Vienna.[6] The first "blurb" he offered for the Book of History (through the intermediary of the RDR)[7] had been turned down four years earlier. Sartre drew a lesson from this experience forthwith: In politics — on the "Left," no less than on the "Right"—what counts is not ideas but success. As he wrote so elegantly, "The true idea is an effective action" (RCL 21/245). To fill the Vel'd'Hiv',[8] to gather five million votes at election time, that's what's true, that's what's effective.

With such considerations in mind, Sartre set out to approach the Stalinists. A tall order if we recall the manner in which they had treated him till that time. But we also know that nine times out of ten an intellectual will not agree to leave his ivory tower unless he is assured of receiving a few swift kicks. He therefore went to the Peace Congress and heaped insults on his friend Camus, who was in the process of moving in the opposite direction. Passionately, he pointed out to him that they were both bourgeois, but that at least he, Sartre, "would make sure to pay for it."[9] Severely, he summoned him to look in *The Phenomenology of the Mind* to find the reasons for the preeminence of Stalinism and to come back in October.

Thereafter, things went rapidly downhill. The CP called the workers to demonstrate against Ridgway, and the workers did not budge; the People's First Elector was arrested, and the people did nothing. What had happened? Where did all this effectiveness go to? The workers had been engaging in battle for four years now every time they went on strike; but it was over vulgar little wage struggles, over economics, over the physicochemical, over mere molecules—in short, over completely uninteresting things. But this time we were smack dab in the middle of history, we were up to our necks in praxis; a political demonstration, organized by the Party of the Proletariat, had run aground; the Assistant Manager of the Party had gotten himself arrested by the cops amid the general indifference of proletarians. There is nothing dramatic about the workers' losing a strike for a nickel more an hour; after all, Sartre "will make sure to pay" for the steaks they won't be eating. But the workers' not going out on strike when Duclos is arrested merits 180 + x pages in *Les Temps Modernes*.

Having thus explained in his first article (in July 1952) how it was natural for the CP to carry out Soviet policy and for the working class to follow it since the USSR is the birthplace of the Revolution, Sartre (in his second article published four months later) then went to the heart of the matter when he gave his account of the meaning of the events that took place between May 28 and June 4. What were these events? Nothing. "*Nothing* was expected, *nothing* happened and on this nothing, Mr. Pinay has built up his vainglory" (*CP* 166/66)—and, might we think ingenuously, that this also was the basis upon which Mr. Sartre constructed his articles.

We must point out that Sartre abhors a vacuum. In *Being and Nothingness*, he interpreted sexual desire as expressing man's anguish before holes. It is well known that a hole is a nothing surrounded by something. Now, what was June 4 if not a hole in History? And as it turns out, this hole, this nothing, "frightened" him. Why? Because the working class repudiated the CP? No, the working class did nothing of the sort, for one simple reason: "On June 4th . . . *there wasn't* any working class" (*CP* 167/67). Those who are astonished that such a social cataclysm was not reported in the daily papers have not understood the subtlety of the game we are playing. There was no working class because the working class exists only inasmuch as it follows the Stalinist party: "It (the working class) cannot repudiate him (Duclos) without repudiating itself." And in this case, the working class no longer exists, there are only "individuals." "If the working class wants to detach itself from the Party, it has only one means at its disposal: to crumble into dust" (*CP* 195/88). And this is so because "the unity of the working class is its historical and mobile relationship with the collectivity, insofar as this relationship is realized by a synthetic act of unification which, by necessity, is distinguished from the mass as pure action is distinguished from passion" (*CP* 249/129). This "pure action" is the Party; "the Party is the very movement which unites the workers by carrying them along toward the seizure of power" (*CP* 249-50/130).

All this, the reader says to himself, might be true and might be false. But what is to be done right now? Well, he has a choice: First, he can wait for "one of the forthcoming issues of *Les Temps Modernes*," where Sartre's final installment will be published. If, however, his generosity, his enthusiasm, and his impatience carry him toward immediate action and prevent him from waiting for the natural outcome of this ideological constipation, he can try to draw conclusions right now from what he has read. He will do so, however, at his own risk and peril, and he cannot be advised to be too prudent. If, for example, he has deduced from the foregoing that he must sign up as quickly as possible in this Party that is "the workers' freedom," the "pure action" that "carries them along toward the seizure of power," he will show that he has not understood any of the wealth and complexity of Sartre's thought. For the latter is careful to indicate that while he does not agree with the CP (though he does not say why), it is possible to conclude agreements with the CP on precise and definite points (which ones? and who would be the second contracting party?); and, in the end, he hints that he wants "a Left that is independent and in liaison with the CP" (*CP* 252/132).

If this is the secret of the third article, it would be charitable to advise the reader that he would make better use of his money if he bought some caramels instead, just as Sartre would make better use of his time if he went to bed. For the past twenty years and in the four corners of the world people who were far more consistent than Sartre tried to lay the foundations for this independent Left in liaison with the CP. A fellow who had directed two revolutions (one of which was victorious) and who created the first proletarian army spent his last years, until the day the Stalinists assassinated him, trying to create an independent proletarian organization ready to make a united front with the CP. And, to go from the tragic to the ridiculous, let us remember that the PSU also worked "for an independent Left in liaison with the CP."[a] Why have all these attempts run aground so pitifully, one after another, whatever the strength or weakness of the CP at a given moment? Why have Trotskyists always been murdered by Stalinists, and why has the PSU been doomed to alternate between being a well-tended garden of underground "plants" and a desert of spineless cacti.[10] The length of Mr. Martinet's nose, perhaps?[11] And if it were longer? Ought we to hope that Sartre's nose will make this little affair any better?

For an "independent Left" really to take shape, lots of people—and above all workers—must join up. For them to join up with this independent Left rather than with the CP, there must be some reasons to set them against the latter. And these must be basic, fundamental reasons, not mere nuances or multiply split hairs. For today, problems are interconnected in such a fashion and people are smart enough that no halfway position will ever provide the basis for sufficient contrast or for the ideological foundations of a Left independent of the CP. Indeed, Sartre knows this since he recognizes that workers join the CP and judge it in terms of an overall appraisal of the nature of Communist parties and the USSR (we explained this to the Trotskyists as early as 1947). If the USSR actually is a workers' State and the CPs are proletarian parties, criticisms aimed at their policy become secondary and even gratuitous. And faced with such pseudodifferences, when it comes to a third world war and the atomic extermination of human kind, the worker will militate in the CP rather than waste his time with Sartre and his independent Left.

An independent organization will be able to take shape, therefore, only on the condition that it can show that the differences separating it from Stalinism are fundamental ones; i.e., they are concerned with the very nature of Stalinism, both in the USSR and elsewhere. It will be able to gain a foothold within the proletariat only through a permanent and irreconcilable struggle against the ideology and policy of Stalinism (and of the bourgeoisie, it must be added). Will it be able to be "in liaison with the CP" under such conditions? It is ridiculous even to pose the question.

We need not recall that an orientation fundamentally opposed to Stalinism is a necessary but not in the least sufficient condition for the reconstruction of the revolutionary movement. A significant proportion of the working class certainly must also achieve on its own a sufficient degree of political awareness to enable it to recognize in this ideology the explicit and consistent formulation of its own experience. The workers' "coming unstuck" from Stalinism and their refusal to participate in actions clearly or vaguely perceived as being foreign to their interests as proletarians constitute a necessary moment in this experience. It is going on right now before our very eyes. And whether or not we want it to be the case, long periods of passivity and inaction are inseparable from this experience. Is it inevitable that this experience will end up moving in a positive direction, going beyond the present situation and toward revolution? Certainly not. The inevitable has no place in history. But the role of the revolutionary is not to remain hypnotized by the ambiguity of every given historical situation. It is rather to bring out the positive signification lying potentially within each such situation and to struggle to bring it about. And in a period like the one we are now going through, this struggle begins with the reformulation of revolutionary ideology and with its propagation among the most advanced workers.

All this obviously will take a long time and is not easy. We must have patience—much patience and stubborn persistence. And there always have been and there always are a few who have dug within themselves and forged this terrible patience. They are the people who began in time, worked in the existing organizations, had their doubts, tried to interpret events step-by-step, experienced open conflict, and have had to retrench once again. Those people have paid for their knowledge of the infinite task about which Sartre speaks so cheerfully. They know about it well enough to know that most of the time one works for a far-off future that at present is still imbedded deep in the gangue of the possible and that the moments where one can finally do what one has been living a lifetime to do are rare and in no way guaranteed in advance.

But Sartre is deaf in this ear. He cannot be patient: He has no time to lose; he has just arrived; he has to redeem himself; he needs some "action" right away. And it doesn't matter what kind of action—just some effective action, any action in a grand style. He looks Lefort up and down with contempt, since the latter is happy keeping company "with other intellectuals and a few highly cultivated workers" (*RCL* 20/244). Sartre himself has to be able to harangue the crowd, to fill the Vel'd'Hiv'. And to do this, he obviously must be in "liaison with the CP." Otherwise, who will fill the Vel'd'Hiv'? In any case, not the independent Left. This allows us to predict that, unless someday or other he just drops it all, he will forget about his independent Left and his differences and will fall into line with the CP.[12]

This contradiction between defending the CP's entire line and some mysterious "differences" or the chaste desire for an independent Left is not the only one found in Sartre's articles. It has found company in the meantime when he tried to reply to Claude Lefort. In the April issue of *Les Temps Modernes*, Lefort had shown that Sartre had succeeded in providing a defense and justification for Stalinism only by constantly distorting Marxism and by relegating it to the level of a rationalistic empiricism.[b] Sartre's reply, two times longer than Lefort's criticism, is teeming with ineptitudes, nonsense, personally rude remarks, and lexical errors.[13] And above all, it appears to be an explosion of hysteria. For, in following his "proofs," we begin to notice that Sartre, seized with a curious form of syllogistic ataxia, sometimes proves too much and sometimes not enough. This impression is only reinforced when we encounter the mass of contradictions contained therein; for example: "If one wanted to expose the shameful finalism which is hidden under *all* dialectics . . ." (*RCL* 12/239); and: "Marx has allowed us to rediscover true dialectical time" (*RCL* 59/272). Does every form of the dialectic conceal a shameful finalism or does the Marxist dialectic avoid doing so?

After having spent about a dozen pages (*RCL* 15-32/241-53) speaking ironically about the proletariat's "cumulative experience," disputing whether the conditions for such an experience are given in reality, and claiming that it does not lead to the unity of the proletariat, Sartre adds coldly: "By the way, it's not that I'm against your cumulative experiences; indeed, I think that the proletariat profits from everything" (*RCL* 32/252-53).

We could easily expand this list of contradictions, but it would be shallow merely to state them. For in each there are two terms of unequal weight. This can be seen first of all just statistically. With an ardor that would make you shudder, Sartre regularly devotes five, ten, or twenty pages to demonstrating that without the Party the class would be nothing; that exploitation brutalizes, crushes, and transforms the workers into things; that they are passion and the party pure action. Then, an offhand phrase here or there tells us that the proletariat has a revolutionary nature; that it profits from everything; that it makes itself through its own daily action; that it is kept in motion through the consequences of its acts. Thus he himself shows how he believes seriously in only half of what he is saying, and how the rest is just hot air.

And yet, for once we have to take him seriously since not only does the allocation of his pages have a meaning independent of him but these theses by which he defends the bureaucracy have, above all, an objective significance and value. They have an objective significance because they overlap with a powerful social and historical current and because they have a corresponding agent present everywhere in reality. But where then will Sartre today find that other half, the autonomous action of the proletariat? And they have an objective value because he gives expression to this justification for the bureaucracy that the bureaucracy gives itself but does not itself care to express. In founding the need for the party on the fact that the workers are brutalized, the bureaucracy must feel that with friends like this idiotic fellow traveler, who needs anticommunist enemies, but he rises thereby to a position of high historical importance that he would never possess in his own right. Let us therefore take him for what he really is, a clumsy but enthusiastic apologist who is self-taught but studious, contrite but aggressive, whose words are stilted but whose tongue is nimble—in short, the prototype of the Modern Intellectual in the process of constructing, with the Materials of Reason, the Bridge of Opportunity across the Flood of History.

The Modern Intellectual's great familiarity with theory inculcates in him a realistic and salutary contempt for systematic constructions. Plato or Spinoza, Fichte or Marx tried to harmonize their philosophy with their political ideas. They were pedants, discursive upstarts. The Modern Intellectual has this in common with the practical aristocrat of old and the corner shopkeeper: He keeps theory in its place. Theory is good for musty old books, but in real life it does not serve much purpose. With this, Sartre will tell us what the proletariat and its party are, and how we can rescue "the working class, the entire French community and peace" (*CP* 152/56), without "fashioning or refashioning a theory of the proletariat" (*CP* 197/90). Such a theory, he says, appears to him to be "useless, dangerous, and even presumptuous" (*RCL* 10/237).

What is useless, dangerous, and especially presumptuous obviously is to babble along mindlessly for two hundred pages about the proletariat, the party, their relations, and so on without having any general idea about them. Here we have the attitude of a political quack. Sartre, however, is innocent of this crime that overcomes him, and he rather should be accused of not knowing what he is doing. It obviously would have been impossible for him to write everything he has written without having a theory (or many of them). In fact, Sartre not only is well stocked in proletarian theory, he has some left over to spare. He is dripping with it from head to foot. Like every theory that is not recognized as such, it is a confused and contradictory pile of prejudices, hearsay, and ill-digested ideas. Wanting to do theory does not suffice for it to be done well, but not wanting to do it leads necessarily to doing it badly.

Sartre had furnished his own proof of this a few lines earlier when he put forward the following proposition: "In my opinion, the class unceasingly makes itself, undoes itself, and remakes itself [*se fait, se défait, se refait*], which in no way means that it returns to its point of departure" (*CP* 10/237). Even the least discerning reader will have recognized here a general theoretical proposition, so general, in fact, that it goes beyond the grounds of the working class and can be applied profitably to the four elements, to various French governments, to colonial expeditions, and to raccoons.[14] Everything makes itself, undoes itself, and remakes itself unceasingly, and it rarely returns to its point of departure.

May the reader, however, be patient. We still are only on the third page of Sartre's reply. What the hell, in the remaining fifty-six pages we might just find nestled away in some small corner the specific difference between the working class and being-becoming in general. Let us look and see instead.

In his critique, Lefort had pointed out to Sartre that for Marxism there are objective factors (social-historical ones, of course) that tend to make the proletariat a revolutionary class. And he pointed out the most important ones: the concentration of the proletariat, the need to cooperate that capitalist production forces upon it, and the continuous upheaval brought about by the introduction of new techniques, which can occur only because the proletariat adapts these techniques and makes them work in practice. After having said that he has never "denied . . . the objective foundations of this class" (CP 7/235), Sartre devotes several pages of his reply to proving that there is nothing to these foundations, that such factors have no significance—unless, of course, they have the opposite effect, namely to "crush" the proletariat. Hence he goes on to prove too much, even with respect to his goal, which is the "justification" of the bureaucracy. As a consequence, he now no longer needs the proletariat, but merely the exploited in general.

First of all, let us look at the process of concentration. "Concentration only acts through milieux and existing forms" (RCL 26/248), Sartre says rather sententiously. But who said that the process of concentration acted outside of milieux and structures? Marxism has nothing to do with the concentration of asparagus, or with the concentration of people in general; it is interested in the concentration of a precise category of individuals (industrial producers), within a determinate process (the development of large-scale industry), in given places (towns and modern factories), inside a given system and during a given historical period (the capitalist system and its period of history). Does Sartre seriously believe that Tamerlane's gathering of 100,000 horsemen in the middle [milieu] of the steppes has the same effect and significance for a Marxist as Ford's gathering of 100,000 workers in the Rouge factories of Detroit? It is simply stupid to contrast the proletariat of the United States, which has not been made revolutionary by the process of concentration, to the less concentrated but more politicized French proletariat in order to prove—well, to prove what? That the process of concentration is not the sole important factor? But who said it was the only one? That concentration does not matter at all? This Sartre dares not say. Then, what?

Indeed, what allows Sartre to see in the history of the American proletariat only "the CIO's pitiful compromises" and a "growing indifference" (RCL 25/247)? What, if not his parochial horizons as a parishioner of Saint-Germain-des-Près and his deep conviction that what happens in France is the universal norm (it is well known that "insurrectionary passion" is one of those fancy Parisian commodities). This certainly is what prevents him from seeing the "growing indifference" of the French proletariat between 1921 and 1930 or between 1947 and x and the "pitiful compromises" by which its two parties "knew to stop the strikes" in June 1936,[15] or to chain them to the production lines between 1944 and 1947. If in the history of the American proletariat there are nothing but "pitiful compromises" and a "growing indifference," what explains the strength of unions there or the working class's standard of living, which is three times higher than in France? The benevolence of the big trusts, perhaps? Their "socially concerned outlook," as Parisian journalists say after a two-week transatlantic tour? And why, in the face of this growing indifference and of these unions who ask only to make pitiful compromises, do the trusts end up granting increases instead of forcing lower wages? Undoubtedly they have not been informed about the CIO and the American proletariat. That will teach them that they should subscribe to *Les Temps Modernes* instead of handsomely supporting some imposters who claim to be "labor relations"[16] experts, but who know less about such matters than Sartre.

But that is not the main point. For by means of this apparently innocent tautology—that "quantity couldn't produce social effects except within the framework of an already structured society and as a function of existing structures" (*RCL* 25/249)—a much more significant truth is disguised, namely, that structures are modified under the pressure of quantities. Structures do not exist eternally. And when they are overturned, quantitative changes play a fundamental role. Is the process of capital concentration anything other than a continual modification of the absolute and relative size of business enterprises? But while this process of concentration develops it gradually or abruptly changes a whole series of specific economic and social structures. Marx first analyzed the transition from simple cooperation to manufacturing, and then to large-scale industry and its effects on the working class at too great a length for us to have to go over it again here.

Second, let us look at the process of cooperation in the performance of work. By attributing to Lefort the idea that capitalism idyllically develops a proletariat in pure positivity (we do not know where Sartre got this), Sartre gives himself the ridiculous task of wanting to prove that "cooperation is not lived by the worker as the lucky sign of solidarity" and that instead he "experiences dependency" (*RCL* 27/249). Sartre does not even seem to suspect that this is what Lefort has been trying to get him to understand and that this is what has been said since Marx: that the process of capitalist production "unites, educates, and disciplines" the workers in the feeling of their mutual dependence and inculcates in them, whether they like it or not, both the idea that this dependence is inevitable and a rejection of the alienated form this dependence takes in the factory and in capitalist society.

Finally, let us look at the continuous upheaval brought about by the introduction of new techniques. Here Sartre is "frankly" indignant. What infamy indeed! The factory that maims the worker, the compartmentalized work that ruins the lovely "professional culture" of yesteryear along with the artisan's "intuitive understanding of the material"! To see anything in this other than destruction and abasement, one must "lack imagination" (*RCL* 29/251) as well as heart. Sartre lacks neither of these, and with his heart driving his imagination on, he describes at length the workers' "brutalization," their "psychoses," this vegetative life in which "they go home, eat dinner, yawn and go to sleep" (*RCL* 30/251).

Here we too are astonished. For Lefort has seen this life, from the workers themselves. He has seen more of this life than Sartre will see during his whole lifetime, and from closer range. Sartre has his Marx at home, with the pages cut and annotated. Has he then understood nothing of what he has seen, of what he has read? Or rather is what Sartre is expounding a new discovery that he modestly has buried between citations of Marx and references to biologists and "psychotechnicians"?

Of course not. None of this is new; everyone has known it for a long time. But what is *relatively* new is the will to see *only this* in the relationship between the proletariat and technical developments. Oh, quite relatively new, indeed. For, Sartre has a few precursors. One fine day, ten years ago, Burnham announced his great discovery: Marx was mistaken, the proletariat was becoming less and less capable of managing society, professional skills were being lost under modern capitalism, etc. Marx had conferred upon the proletariat the role of capitalism's successor, but this proletariat now has found itself incapable of fulfilling this role. Whence comes the positive historical mission of the "managers," i.e., bureaucrats.[17] Neither the premises nor the conclusions differ in Sartre's formulation except that he prefers a particular bureaucracy: that of the Stalinist party.

We will come back later on to this aspect of the question as well as to the influence of technical upheavals. But let us linger for an instant on the pedantic way in which Sartre upbraids Lefort.

> Perhaps you are dreaming of the "cultural" influence of compartmentalized work. In that case, I regret to inform you that Anglo-Saxon and German (!) investigations will destroy your pretty dream: the cultural influence of compartmentalized work is entirely negative, it has liquidated professional culture, etc. (*RCL* 30/251)

This simple statement proves that Sartre neither knows nor is capable of imagining what he is talking about. Only a fool could think that compartmentalized work might as such have a positive cultural influence, and Anglo-Saxon and German investigations are extremely useful except when one wants to prove that 2 plus 2 equals 4. Stupid remarks attributed to one's adversaries merely point to the stupid remarks one is capable of producing on one's own. Sartre does not suspect that, unlike him, not everyone is just starting to discover the working class, compartmentalized work, and so on; that there are people—like Lefort—who spend their lives reflecting on these questions; that perhaps they do not reflect upon them well but that one cannot teach them anything by telling them that the parts are contained within the whole, that a dog has four paws, and that compartmentalized work has a negative influence upon professional culture.

But does compartmentalized work have an *"entirely negative"* influence *on the working class*? Let us leave that to the Wagner of *Les Temps Modernes* and open up Marx.

After having depicted the workers during the period of small-scale artisanal production, Marx concludes,

> Medieval craftsmen therefore had an interest in their special work
> and in proficiency in it, which was capable of rising to a limited
> artistic sense. For this very reason, however, every medieval
> craftsman was completely absorbed in his work, to which he had a
> complacent servile relationship, and in which he was involved to a
> far greater extent than the modern worker, whose work is a matter of
> indifference to him.[18]

Right away we begin to breathe in different air. We feel ourselves elevated to higher levels of historical reflection. For Marx, artisanal activity and the professional culture that goes along with it allow a realization of the individual personality (the artisan is interested in his particular work), a realization that attains a historical value ("a limited artistic sense"). But the negative predominates: absorption in this particular job, a limited horizon, a kind of subordination that is not an imposed subordination but a much more serious kind of subordination since it is accepted, internalized, and valued by the individual. The professional worker wants to be a good professional, he is proud of it. From the point of view of subsequent historical developments, however, this is a foolish pride: The goal humanity ought to assign itself certainly is not to produce perfect tailors, carriage makers, or weavers. Capitalism transcends this situation. By undermining the objective bases for this charming professional culture, capitalism undoubtedly destroys personal realization within a particular job, but it does more than that: It suppresses its very meaning and demonstrates in practice to this foolish person what it is to put his pride and the meaning of his life in an activity machines can accomplish better and more quickly than he. And, by showing the accidental character of a person's connection with any particular kind of productive labor, it demonstrates better than any philosophy could that material production has no meaning by itself except as a means and that "the realm of freedom can blossom forth only with this realm of necessity as its basis and with the shortening of the working-day as its basic prerequisite." The worker rebels against being treated as an accident, and every day in modern production he learns that he can only be treated as one. He can get out of this situation only by becoming totally brutalized or by seizing hold of production and reducing it to its true signification as a type of activity that is subordinate to man. At the same time, the interchangeability of tasks shows him in practical terms that all particular modes of production can be dominated by the modern individual, whereas they, the modes of production, now predominate.

What does Sartre understand of all that? Nothing, we must think. Lefort had spoken of the interchangeability of *tasks*. Sartre responds to him that the interchangeability of *individuals* is the main cause of unemployment! Even if he were a "remarkably intelligent" (*RCL* 34/254) gentleman, he would need to know something of the things he is talking about. The interchangeability of tasks is a typical phenomenon of modern industry that makes a semiskilled machinist capable of working on practically any mass-production machine after a training session that varies from a few minutes to a few days. The technical-objective basis for this comes from the fact that the immense majority of modern machines are derivations or specialized versions of two or three general-purpose types of machinery. This is universality turned into an object—a *historical* object—and we are trying to get Sartre to understand that it entails a corollary for the subject who has invented these tools and who adapts them and utilizes them.[19]

But "remarkably intelligent" he decidedly is not. For, if he were, even in his ignorance of these matters he would not confuse the interchangeability of individuals and the interchangeability of tasks. Were each of them always to be called by the other's name he still would not have to confuse two different *aspects*, from which there arise different significations. But one does not have to mix up their names; the interchangeability of individuals exists independently of the interchangeability of tasks. Tailors, shoemakers, and schoolteachers are interchangeable within their respective corporations (interchangeability of individuals) but not with each other (the interchangeability of tasks). And it is dishonest to throw into the bargain the insinuation that Lefort sees already realized in the compartmentalized worker "the complete development of the universal concrete individual" (*RCL* 31/252) at the very point where the latter says that automation "*makes* the worker *aware* of a universality that *the abolition* of *exploitation alone could allow him* to achieve."[20]

Sartre therefore is trying to prove in a few pages that the proletariat's objective situation *cannot* have any signification. And what do we, who also are successors to Marx, want to prove? That the proletariat, placed in this situation, tends to have a common experience of this situation and that this experience is one of the moments in its constitution as a class. Now Sartre, who is just as comfortable on the terrain of philosophy as he is in the field of economics, spurns this idea: One cannot prove "the unity of the proletariat by the unity of its experience," for "the unity of its experience, when it develops progressively, presupposes the unity of the proletariat" (*RCL* 17-18/242).

This is a meaningless sentence. For what matters here is not a theory of knowledge, nor the ego as the principle of the synthetic unity of apperception. What matters is whether the workers *qua* workers tend to share a common experience, and whether in this experience that unfolds through time there is a meaningful succession, in other words, whether tomorrow merely is juxtaposed to yesterday or goes beyond it. What matters, in a word, is whether we can speak of a history of the proletariat.

Do we need to presuppose the ontological or transcendental unity of a group in order to speak of the unity of its experience? What is the experiential unity of a score of youngsters who all went to the same school and played in the same vacant lots throughout their childhood (an incomplete experience, of course)? What else but the identity of the school, of the teachers, of the neighborhood, of their age. The unity of experience, to the extent and within the limits it exists, is posited by the identity or the similarity of objective conditions in which the group finds itself placed. To say that each individual belonging to the group will perceive these conditions and express them in an experience according to the structures that are his own is true enough on the scale of an atomistic microsociology, but it becomes a source of sophisms when we consider the masses on the scale of history. If the "group" in consideration is reduced to two individuals witnessing the same brief event, it is doubtful that they even have had "the same perception" of the event (which they express in like fashion in the language of describing physical facts); each will have perceived numerous and important elements differently, and in any case the signification each will attribute to the facts will be different.

But if the group in question includes millions of individuals who, over generations, from birth to death and in every essential respect[21] face identical or similar conditions, it is a safe bet that the unity of its experience will go quite far. Common traits will emerge, gradually or by fits and starts. Each individual will tend to recognize in the other the bearer of an essentially similar experience. The unity of the experience "of the proletariat" is first of all the experiential unity of millions of individuals whom capitalism places in identical conditions, and hence it presupposes at the start only the unity of the capitalist system (of course it also presupposes that the exploited are possible subjects of experience in general—in other words, people). Undoubtedly, this is only the beginning of the story, and it takes many long years, if not centuries, for this experience shared by individuals to be recognized in a reciprocal manner, raised to the level of certitude concerning their ultimate and inexorable inclusion in a general unity [ensemble] transcending the particular individuals, and transformed from passive solidarity into collective action.

We will come back to this in an instant. All the same, the pseudodialectical circularity posited by Sartre is just a bad play on words. Capitalism creates workers and *imposes* on them a common experience; it *imposes* on them even the idea of belonging to a class. Sartre keeps on repeating that he is not a worker. But, has he never been *paid a wage or salary*? When an employer or an administrator says, "I am lowering or increasing *pay* by so much, I am increasing or reducing *working hours* by so much," what else is he doing but grabbing this mass of individuals by the scruff of the neck and yelling in their ears, "To me you're not a Smith, a Jones, or a Sartre—you are an accidental example of the category of wage earners, and if that doesn't meet with your satisfaction, here's the door." And if the wage earner finds this situation as it is presented to him intolerable, will he have to have a party membership card in his pocket or the complete works of Maurice Thorez[22] at home in order to come to the realization that those on his left side or those on his right side ought to find this situation equally intolerable, to discuss it with them and to come up with the idea of responding to it together?

In all this, does one merely experience "dependence," or is there not a *common* experience of dependence and is not a common response the only possible response? At first, the proletariat in itself is matter to be exploited by capital. This in-itself is already transcended as such as soon as exploitation is experienced, as soon as one is not limited to being exploited, but knows oneself to be exploited (and under the conditions of capitalism, one is aware of being exploited immediately as a participant in a specific social category). This experience is already a rudimentary for-itself, a for-itself that is fully acknowledged as soon as the experience no longer is passively accepted but becomes, through common action against the shared situation, an active practice, a strike, a revolt, or revolution. And henceforth the proletariat will be just that, the permanent possibility proletarians themselves possess of positing in practice their for-itself *qua* class. That under the conditions of capitalism this leads them to strive for power and to set as their goal the attainment of communism is another story; we will come back to that. But from this moment on, the truth is not that the unity of the proletariat in the process of making itself builds up the unity of its experience but rather that the history of the proletariat is the history of the efforts of these people to posit their for-itself and to seize power for themselves.

But that's no good, says Sartre. "The proletariat is crushed by a perpetual present" (*RCL* 18/242). This is mere literary phrasing. It might be true, strictly speaking, of animals but certainly not of proletarians. If it were true, it would have put an end to history (History) by now. As support for this absurd statement, Sartre cites Marx, who says, "Constant revolutionizing of production, uninterrupted disturbance of all social conditions, everlasting uncertainty and agitation distinguish the bourgeois epoch from all earlier ones. All fixed, fast-frozen relations, with their train of ancient and venerable prejudices and opinions, are swept away; all new-formed ones become antiquated before they can ossify." But Marx concluded this very same passage with a sentence Sartre glides over in silence: "All that is holy is profaned and *man is at last compelled to face with sober senses, his real conditions of life, and his relations with his kind*" (our emphasis).[23]

Sartre's quotation thus becomes a falsification of Marx. For Marx, the "constant revolutionizing" the capitalist mode of production introduces into social relations is, of course, what compels man to rid himself of the solid, the fixed, the traditional, and the holy and to face "with sober senses" the conditions of his life and his relations with others. It is what forces him to see in what is simply there something that is necessarily dedicated to destruction; it is what destroys domination exercised through what is merely inherited and thus accidental. This constant upheaval, Marx means to say, puts man through a double apprenticeship: It demolishes the mystifications that cover the reality of social relations, but also, and more profoundly still, it demonstrates the relativity of these relations and of everything given, even in reality itself. It forces man to see that reality is the (hitherto blind) product of man's action, and therefore that it can be transformed by him. And because the working class is placed at the core of this process of perpetual destruction, of permanent revolution in the reality dominating all other forms of reality—the reality of production—it tends to be a revolutionary class and a universal class.

Thus, Marx was saying that the working class experiences this perpetual upheaval, hence it is obliged to understand and transcend the relativity of the present. Sartre has him say that the working class experiences this perpetual upheaval, therefore it is dumbfounded by it. Sartre does something worse than falsify Marx: He attributes to him his own superficiality.

Sartre continues:

> How can you imagine that the new crop of workers who arose
> around 1910 are going to take up again the aristocratic (!) traditions
> of revolutionary syndicalism and of tradesmen? Change, yes;
> *historical* and cumulative change, surely not. (*RCL* 18/243; our
> emphasis)

We know what history means for Sartre: what grows slowly and surely, like a beard. The historical, therefore, would be the sedimented, the gradual, the incremental. Till now we thought that, rather than beards and public-record archives, history was made up of wars, revolutions, and atomic bombs.

But the word is unimportant, it being one of the fifty-nine unfortunate expressions found in this article. Indeed, there is historical change (in the true sense) in the proletariat, i.e., upheaval, the entrance of new strata en masse into industry, the revival of struggle after long periods of inaction. And then what? There is or is not a history of humanity, but catastrophes, wars, invasions, and revolutions do not prove the nonexistence of such a history. Those who have tried to show that there is no history in general have not, in order to prove it, had recourse to these sorts of events. Rather they have analyzed whether the various extant historical cultures might have drawn from each era different significations lacking any genuine and organic mutual connections. This enterprise, obviously, contradicts itself. Sartre might have tried to show without contradicting himself, however, that the meanings that can be extracted from each phase of the proletariat's existence are not coherent and do not mutually imply one other; to do that, he would have had to analyze at least two stages in the history of the labor movement and to show that these stages are in no way interconnected—or worse, that neither has any signification at all, that they are only chaos and incoherence.

Instead of doing that, he makes upheaval into another absolute and caricatures Marx as Cratylus caricatured Heraclitus: You will not enter even once into the same river. For "constant revolutionizing" is the upheaval brought about in the modes of production, in social relations, in organization, and in ideas—but certainly not a continuous evacuation from the factories. It never meant that at regular intervals the factories are scoured clean of their current personnel and that some individuals fallen from the sky park themselves in front of the machinery. As we explain to the young child, to salt one's meat does not mean to empty the whole saltshaker onto one's plate. Even at the times when capitalism creates an influx of new masses of people into the factories—for example in the United States between 1940 and 1945—the majority is still made up of the guys who were there before; they continue working, mixed in among the new workers.

Then, of course, there are parties. Certainly not the Absolute Party, the Idea of the Party, the One Party, Spherical and Equal to itself all round, with which Sartre conducts his business, but contingent and mortal parties, made up of perishable individuals who come from the class and return to it. In and through these parties militants are trained and educated. Not only do they live in the midst of action; they tend to reflect systematically upon the struggles they experience. Later on they pass into other organizations, bringing with them this experience and their reflections.

Already, however, we see that we have to make some generalizations: It no longer is a matter of parties as such, it is a matter of militants and more generally of the class's vanguard (about which Sartre evidently does not have a word to say), i.e., of workers who more often than others tend to participate in economic or political struggles or to initiate them, to reflect on these struggles and to think always within the context of future struggles. The working class has no memory other than that of the individuals who make it up, for it is neither a single individual nor a group with memory-saving institutions. The answer to the problem of the historical unity of proletarian action is to be found elsewhere. To the extent that something like a class "memory" exists, however, it can be located in this vanguard. "All observers noted that the young workers had almost no understanding of the strikes of 1936," Sartre says (RCL 19/243). These omniscient observers, my, aren't they insightful! It is true that before putting themselves out they could have thought about the fact that young workers today were three years old in 1936 and that since then they have had more pressing matters to attend to than to read about June 1936 in one of the few books that exist on the subject. But what would happen if a strike broke out today? During the last strike at Renault, the unions as usual acted like strike breakers (of course, with various nuances), and the workers were profoundly disgusted by them. And as the days passed, to the extent that the continuation of the strike in the four-horsepower car department raised the issue of what to do faced with the attitude of the workers as a whole, only one thing was discussed throughout the entire factory: June 1936. You do not have to be a wizard to understand that if in a department of two or three hundred workers there is some old guy who took part in such an event, he always will get a hearing from the others, conditions permitting. A worker's worklife extends over forty or fifty years: from the Commune till the First World War, from 1910 till today. In each factory, in each workshop, one can find a few workers who took part in the great struggles of the past. Here is the class's leavening, those people who vividly serve as the connection between the past and the present for their comrades. That they sometimes are 5 percent and sometimes 50 percent makes no difference. One in a thousand will suffice on a day when there is something to be done.

But this has no existence for Sartre. Where would you want him to meet up with this vanguard? What exists for him is the following dichotomy: the working class—an abstract and even imaginary entity—which is nowhere to be seen; then, the Party (Stalinist, of course), which is to be seen all the time: in its newspapers, among its militants, at meetings, and on posters and voting ballots. If you want to meet the Party, you know where to go. But no one can show you which bus to take to find "the working class"; it is a "cloud of dust." And yet this cloud of dust clusters together sometimes; at the Vel'd'Hiv' or from place de la Nation to the Bastille on May Day. There are the workers, a good number of them at least, and they are doing something together. If one looks more closely, however, one sees that they did not go there all alone: Someone has called them together, gathered them together, marshaled them, given them placards, started chants. Who? Good Lord, it's the Party. Hence we have found that long-sought-after "unity." And why stop in the middle of this road when things are going so well? Why limit oneself just to May Day? We will settle for no less than History and its magnificent vistas! What guarantees "the unity of experience" and continuity through the vicissitudes of life? The Party.

All this, which seems to Sartre at the same time both obvious and profound, cannot hold up against even the most superficial scrutiny. The Party, *insofar as* and *when it* exists, is an expression of the proletariat's continuity, not its presupposition. First of all, the adventures described as happening to the proletariat happen to the party tenfold. To be unaware of this fact, one needs to have Sartre's limited field of vision and to be as exclusively preoccupied as he is with the problems raised by his integration into Stalinism *hic et nunc* — in France and in 1953. The party — or rather parties, for *the* party is an objective and not a reality — these parties create themselves, destroy themselves, are exterminated by the police and abandoned by the class; they reappear, undergo scissions, exist in multiple copies, accuse each other of treason, change their program, turn it into a scrap of paper, revive it, have new generations of followers enter into them en masse — in a word, to take up Sartre's profound expression, they make themselves, undo themselves, and remake themselves nonstop. They are subjected to the same process of constant upheaval as the class itself, but much more intensely so because they are much more structured and clearly defined, much more "solid and fixed," and therefore much more shaken and swept up by events. The continuity that these kinds of parties can guarantee to the working class is a continuity of ten or twenty years, and each generation already has this kind of continuity for itself. The idea of the party as the guarantor of continuity, as the principle of unity in time and in space, could be debated if the party actually existed as a unity; but it does not.

Of course, however, Sartre perhaps will say that this unity is not given; that it is a task that must always be resumed. Very well then, here we have gotten out of Stalinist catholicism. And *who* should resume it? Starting from *what*? By being oriented toward *what*? Could it be, by chance, the proletarian vanguard, starting from its own experience, orienting itself toward the goals it itself is trying to define? Then everything's settled, and Sartre would have done all that scribbling for nothing. For then, he would have recognized that the party is only a moment in this long struggle in the course of which the proletariat tends both to define a historical role for itself and to realize it, and that this struggle, and not the party, is the principle of the proletariat's unity and of its history.

Were the party's unity actually to exist, however, that still would not prove at all what Sartre is trying to prove. As a matter of fact, he has transcended philosophy so completely that he keeps switching from being to the ought-to-be, from fact to value and from explanation to justification. He repeats endlessly: Since the PCF is here, that proves that it *ought* to be here. Likewise, he is hell-bent on proving against this poor Trotskyist, Mr. Germain [Ernest Mandel], that if the USSR and Stalinist policy are as they are, they are so necessarily—which is a tautology—*hence* they represent a revolutionary State and a revolutionary policy—which is silly. Germain, Malenkov, Sartre, Bourdet, Guy Mollet, Mendès-France, Bidault, Pinay, Laniel, and de Gaulle[24] are all necessarily what they are; we know it a priori and we more or less can prove it a posteriori. So what? Or is Malenkov privileged because he is in power? And what about Laniel then? Because he says that his power is based on the working class? And what about Tito then? Because Sartre, having reflected on the situation and having looked into his power base, has concluded that Malenkov speaks the truth and Tito lies? Is the contrary, then, a priori unthinkable? And to come up with that conclusion, where does he get the criteria? Not in the Party itself, of course; could the party be Reason itself, which includes within itself its own criteria? In the history and the experience of proletarian struggles? But then why can't a worker do what Sartre is doing? And why can't he arrive at the opposite conclusion?

This mediation that is the party: Who gave it the right? Why should the party by definition be the true expression of proletarian continuity and not its necessarily mystified expression, as some people maintain? Or simply one of its expressions, sometimes true, sometimes mystified? From where does it get its status as true mediation?

To that question Sartre does not hesitate to respond: from the very fact that the proletariat recognizes it as such. Come on! So now we can presuppose the unity of the proletariat and assume that the latter now possesses a criterion for the truth? No, the party unifies the proletariat, which in turn recognizes in the party its true expression. But is the proletariat, therefore, no longer crushed by a perpetual present? No, the party "makes it see" its past. But how can an amnesiac check the story he is being told about his own past?

And which proletariat? Which party? When? Where? In the end, the problem becomes easy for Sartre. At last a desire to play dollies with praxis has overtaken him; he has found before him a party that the workers "recognize" (more or less, but he tries to dodge this issue in order to simplify things for himself). Since he does not rack his brains with what goes on beyond the borders of the most beautiful realm on earth, and since he still has some time left here (whether he will become a complete Stalinist later on or will go back to his more customary pursuits), he does not seem to have an inkling that there are moments when it is necessary to choose between two opposing parties.

Workers and revolutionary militants know, however, that these are the crucial moments of action. What should have been done in 1914, for example? On the one hand, there was the party—the International—continuity itself, its functionaries, its honored leaders who had proved themselves, and the working class, which considered them its chiefs or at least did not disavow them. On the other hand, there was a band of crackpots, or at least they were considered as such by the Sartres of the time, which accused the International of being a "stinking corpse" and invited the workers to go in for some absurd and utopian ventures—like transforming the war into revolution. What should a German militant have done in 1918? A Russian militant in 1923? A Spanish militant in 1936? An East Berlin worker in 1953? Where was the unity, the mediation, the continuity during these moments that have decided decades of history? Where were the criteria?

Sartre has the correct criterion in his hip pocket: "The true idea is an effective action." Sartre undoubtedly believes he is reaching the summits of Marxism with this affirmation, but in fact he is only expressing a vulgar pragmatism that is, moreover, the organic philosophy of the bureaucracy.

For, if Marx greatly deepened the meaning of the Copernican revolution that began with Kant when he showed not only that all knowledge is knowledge for the subject, but also that this subject is a historical subject, hence essentially practical-active, he in no way intended thereby to offer up a new transcendent criterion of the truth, a new model—practice—to which what one thinks would be compared in order to see if one's thoughts were true. For practice does not include its own interpretation, it refers one toward further reflection; if reflection exists "in this world" only in connection with practice, practice has meaning only as it is related to an idea. And this movement alone is historical truth, truth as an infinite task.

All this is still abstract, of course, for society is divided into classes, and hence each has a truth and an "efficacy" of its own. The true idea is the effective one, you say? Did Hitler therefore share in the truth? Oh, he was not effective since he was overthrown. But what about beforehand? And what about Franco? And is not everything overthrown one day or another? You talk to me about Fascists and the bourgeoisie. Fine. Let's talk about Scheidemann and Noske. Here we have working-class ministers, Marxists, very effective ones: Through their praxis they proved that the German Revolution was impossible in 1919. Hence they were right? And what about Stalin when he assassinated Trotsky? His attempts failed several times; so he was not yet completely in the right. But the day Stalin achieved full revolutionary consciousness, he proved the this-worldliness of his thinking by effectively assassinating Trotsky (or perhaps the effectiveness of Trotsky's assassination plunged him into revolutionary truth? Or rather the accomplishment of the one accomplished the other?).

Within the context Sartre places it and in light of his "proof," the idea that "praxis decides" (RCL 21/244) is only the expression of the most cynical opportunism. For if praxis decides something it decides *after* the action has taken place, so much longer afterward that what has to be decided is of greater importance. Praxis will have "decided" the truth of what we are saying to each other only on the morrow of communism's complete and nondegenerable instauration over the whole planet—but then this truth will be of little interest. From 1914 to 1917 praxis decided day after day that Lenin was wrong—then everything came tumbling down: Lenin was in the right, since he made the revolution that he had predicted and called for. Was he in the right beginning October 26, 1917?

This is what people who join victorious revolutions the day after they happen think: You need to keep up with the times, it is praxis that decides. If someday a proletarian revolution seizes power in France, Sartre probably will sing its praises to the skies, the day afterward. If the role of the poet, as Rilke said, is to say what is, let us add that the role of the intellectual is to glorify it. But did Lenin, through praxis, provide the definitive demonstration of the fact that he was right? The revolution degenerated later on, and the Mensheviks who were against the revolution before it occurred thought they had proved that he was wrong since this degeneration supposedly showed that Russia was not "ripe" for socialism. Will we ever find our bearings again amid all this, guided by "the praxis that decides" and by "effective action"?

And "effective" in relation to what? Sartre dawdles around showing that the PCF is effective and forgets that judgments concerning effectiveness presuppose first of all an extrapolation through time, and then a definition of the objective in relation to which an action is or is not effective. There is someone to whom it would be as cruel to compare him as it would be to compare Beethoven to the composer of "Viens poupole,"[25] but we must do it since he fills the public arena with his cacophonous noises; this someone, who spent his life making revolutions—I mean Trotsky—wrote volume upon volume to demonstrate that Stalinist policy is not effective, that it leads to the ruin of the Soviet State and of the world proletariat, and that one day the Stalinist bureaucracy will collapse under the weight of its crimes and errors—crimes and errors committed out of necessity, no doubt, but *historically* ineffective ones. Sartre himself has decided that the bureaucracy is ever effective, that it always will be there. Were he ever to read Trotsky—or were he to "reread" him, as he loves to say with such magnanimity—he would discover perhaps that he is making a miscalculation.

But there is something more important. *We* believe that Trotsky was mistaken in thinking of the bureaucracy as ineffective, for he was judging it in relation to an objective (communism) that *is not* the bureaucracy's objective. Everything the bureaucracy does works toward suppressing the possibility of communist revolution. In doing this, however, the bureaucracy *is* effective; it is effective for itself and with regard to the objective it aims at, which is not communism but the consolidation and expansion of its power and its system of rule. And on the day of supreme effectiveness, when from the balcony of the *Red Figaro*[26] Sartre will be privileged to applaud Marshal Poppof and Maurice Thorez[27] marching down the Champs-Elysées, praxis will have decided for him that Stalinism is true and not just another way of exploiting the workers. Effectiveness is effectiveness in relation to a goal, and the goal of the worker is not that of the bureaucrat just as it is not that of the bourgeois.

But it is not the workers' allegiance to Stalinism (in France and Italy) that makes the latter into the revolutionary party (on a world scale). There is also the power Stalinism has already achieved, first of all in Russia. Sartre is constantly explaining and justifying the concrete policy of various Communist parties (we already have shown that, for him, explanation and justification are the same thing) by referring to the revolutionary character of the USSR, the fundamental assumption of its system. Thus for example, the American CP's abandonment of the antiracist struggle during the war was based upon the need "not to provide Nazi propaganda with any arguments (!)" (*CP* 90/11) while the war was on and Russia was in danger. Russia's safety is the supreme law, and that is the case because Russia *is* a workers' State. It may well be seen that if in reality Russia *is not* a workers' State, the policy of the various CPs becomes doubly reactionary, both

in its means and in its ends. One is inclined to think that Sartre would have examined more closely his assumption before going any further, especially since
this assumption is being attacked more and more every day from all sides, since
it has been attacked for years by Lefort even in his own review, since it is still
now being indirectly but clearly attacked by Péju's articles on the Slánský
trial.[28]

Are you kidding? To examine these assumptions is just "pompous and simplistic" "nitpicking." This is how Sartre rids himself of the "Russian question,"
the touchstone for understanding the problems of the workers' movement for
the past thirty years. You can state that the French workers play the cat's-paw
for the USSR, he says, only if you can "show that the Soviet leaders no longer
believe in the Russian Revolution or that they think the experience has ended in
failure. It goes without saying that even if this were true, which I strongly
doubt, proving it would not be possible at this time" (*CP* 93/13). He promises
to return to this issue "in the second installment," but he has not done so till
now, unless we take into account his discussion with the Trotskyist, Mr.
Germain. During this discussion Sartre proved that the Russian leaders are revolutionary . . . because they cannot do anything but what they are doing.

First of all, a twelve-year-old child could tell Sartre that what the Soviet leaders "believe" or do not believe has nothing to do with the matter. The exploitation of the Russian proletariat—which governs everything else—could not be
instaurated just because Russian leaders no longer believed in the revolution,
nor would it be abolished if Malenkov, struck by the hand of Grace, began to
believe in it again.

Second, Sartre's argument about how it is impossible to "prove" the contrary
is an old, well-worn argument of crypto-Stalinists. If the crypto-Stalinist is told
that the proletariat is exploited in the USSR, he does not lose his temper; he
adopts the most neutral, the most scientific voice possible, and responds that
there are no data to prove it. But then there no longer are any data to prove the
contrary either, or to believe it. Unless, of course, you belong to that category of
imbeciles defined by Lenin as those who believe others on their word—the others being in this case the Stalinist bureaucracy, armed with its propaganda.

As his argument against the Trotskyists indicates, Sartre probably would respond to this that there was a socialist revolution in October 1917, that the working class took power there, and that there has been no restoration of the bourgeoisie since then. But the question is not what happened in Russia in 1917, but
what is happening there now in 1953; it is not a matter of knowing if the Russian
working class seized power, but of whether it kept it. The assumption that it
could lose it *only* through a restoration of the classical bourgeoisie is untenable
on the theoretical plane.[29] And the quarrel over "socialism in one country" signifies that in the absence of "information" and proofs to the contrary, a Marxist
would reject a priori the idea of working-class power holding on in an isolated
country for thirty-five years—since Stalin himself "justified" the possibility of
building socialism in Russia by appealing to the country's *unique* and *exceptional*
characteristics.

But Sartre pushes this cynical attitude further than the current crop of cryptos do. In his "Response to Lefort," he severely upbraids the latter. Do you have at your disposal, he asks him, the primary source documents needed to undertake a study of the "working class" in the USSR?

> And if you do not have them, what can you say? That the worker *is* exploited in the USSR? From this standpoint, you have in mind especially the economic system. The discussion is open; but that is not what matters at this moment. That the working class (this time without quotation marks—Au.) is opposed to exploitation? Yes, *that* is our subject. But the sole proof you can furnish is that it is opposed to this exploitation because it cannot fail to be so without contradicting you. (*RCL* 79/286)

So the fact that the working class *is* exploited in the USSR relates *especially* to the economic system! This "especially" is worth its weight in existential droolings. Might it not have just the slightest relation to anything else? Within the context Sartre sets forth, we should think not. For Sartre, the fact that the economic system might be based upon the workers' exploitation has nothing to do with the rest of the issue; exploitation does not determine society; it sheds no light on its class character. In Germany the workers are blond; at Toulon they love to drink Pastis, a licorice-flavored liqueur; in Russia they are exploited. Well, what about it? Go call up an anthropologist, a public-health officer, an economist, says Sartre; it's not my business. And this after having for dozens of pages expounded the idea (which has become commonplace since Marx) that exploitation determines social reality from one end to the other, and in the very first place the immediate being of the proletariat.

Our subject, Sartre says shamelessly, is not whether the working class is exploited in Russia, but whether it *is opposed* to exploitation. As the paternalistic bourgeois proclaims: My workers are happy with their lot and know what's good for them better than troublemakers of your kind. Here again we discover how easily an individual's logical workings come unhinged when his real situation is out of kilter. For Sartre himself has explained in his previous article that the basic objective of a system of exploitation is to destroy in the exploited person his opposition to exploitation.[30] And indeed, the idea that the Russian working class would not be opposed to being exploited—having assumed this exploitation to be established—not only would prove the contrary of what Sartre wants to prove but in reality already has been *used* in order to prove its contrary. It has been used by those who maintain that Russian bureaucratic capitalism *is* barbarism since it has destroyed in Russian proletarians even the possibility of opposing their exploitation, thereby transforming them into a class of modern industrial slaves.[31]

And what kind of opposition are we talking about here? Open opposition, in broad daylight, by means of strikes, meetings, street demonstrations? All that is practically impossible under a totalitarian regime, and its absence proves nothing. Did the absence of such demonstrations under Hitler and Mussolini prove that the German or Italian proletariat gave its blessing to its exploiters? Isn't it funny how the torturer of a gagged victim responds to you: Well, you see, he's not protesting, he's really having a great time.

Might it not be a muffled, silent, everyday and multiform kind of opposition that the workers carry on against exploitation in every country and under all kinds of circumstances, when they refuse as much as possible to collaborate with their exploiters and to participate in the production process? If this opposition did not exist in Russia, why are there "economic crimes," Stakhanovism, piece-work wages, and poor workmanship in production—all of which constantly fills page after page in the Russian press? Would all that express the workers' allegiance to the system of rule that exploits them? Economic and social analysis does not have the same level of exactitude found in astronomy, but starting from the simple existence of production norms as determined by the State, we can establish from Paris that the workers are exploited and opposed to this exploitation with as much certitude as Leverrier established the existence of Neptune starting with the perturbations in the trajectory of Uranus.

Indeed, this muffled opposition is transformed into open opposition as soon as a crack develops in the shell of totalitarianism—as the latest events in East Germany and Czechoslovakia prove.

But let's do some astronomy. Let us assume that there are no hard data on what occurs in Russia. Who does not see that this fact itself, the absence of information, is itself a mine of information? Why should we have no information? Because storms have knocked out communications, or because no one in Paris understands Russian? No, it is because the Russian bureaucracy does not provide any. And why not? For military reasons? But then why do the United States, France, and England provide such information. And what, from the point of view of military security, would it have to hide? New arms, production processes, factory sites, the number of people enlisted in the military services? But we are not asking about that. If worst comes to worst, overall economic potential for coal, steel, oil, and tractor production? But that kind of stuff is published! Using published data, the American logistical services know Russia's present military strength within a range of 5 percent. What the bureaucracy tries to hide as much as it can is something else: buying power, income distribution. And those indeed are weapons of war. For in the coming war, with its social and ideological factors, truth from here on out is a weapon; and the fact that the truth is hidden signifies that it is a weapon *against* the Russian bureaucracy. Otherwise the latter would use it.

And under what conditions would data on buying power and income distribution become a weapon against the regime? If they tended to establish that there was no essential difference between this system of rule and the capitalist system as concerns the working class's situation. Hence, if the bureaucracy keeps silent about these questions, both of the following points have to be true simultaneously:

1. Income-distribution inequalities must be comparable to or worse than those existing in capitalist countries;

2. The workers' standard of living must be rising as slowly as it does in the capitalist countries, or even more slowly.

If the bureaucracy actually could show that in Russia the distribution of incomes
is more egalitarian than in the West, whether the workers' standard of living
rises there as rapidly as elsewhere, clearly that would be the only thing we would
ever hear talked about from now on. That this is not so is proven with room to
spare by the line of defense adopted by the most adept cryptos (like Charles
Bettelheim). Indeed, such people explicitly admit (as much as a crypto can do
anything explicitly) the enormous inequalities in the distribution of incomes and
the constant reduction in the working class's standard of living. They then try to
"justify" the situation, starting from the low level of the productive forces (in
1913!) and from the shortage of skilled staff (which, assuming increasing inequality, must for some unknown reasons be growing constantly worse). We have
refuted these pitiful sophisms elsewhere.[32]

Evidently, Sartre restates these sophisms, more or less correctly. "The
present form of the Russian experience" is perhaps dictated, he says, "by the vital necessity of intensifying production," of "developing the industry of production (!)," by the "mortal danger" that calls for "iron discipline" (*RCL* 77/285).
Since when is it necessary, in order to intensify production or for defensive military purposes, not to limit consumption but to annihilate the producers' level of
consumption and monstrously raise that of those who parasitically feed upon
them? And if exploitation of man by man is indispensable for the development
of production, what becomes of the prospects for socialism? Is it therefore
wrong to say that the suppression of exploitation is henceforth the condition for
the development of the forces of production, and "for the greatest force of production, the revolutionary class itself"? And what kind of "mortal danger"
starting in 1927 was more pressing than the kind that existed between 1917 and
1921, years of foreign military intervention and civil war, where democracy in
the Soviets and in the Party, for better or for worse, never ceased to function?
What kind of bureaucratic cretinism is more economically effective than planning by the masses who, as Lenin said, "alone can truly plan for they alone are
everywhere at once"?

If all that means that some combination of concrete and universal factors has
led to the installation in power of an exploiting class, the bureaucracy, and that,
by rationalizing history after the fact, we explain this installation in power as a
necessary phenomenon, fine! But to call what resulted from this "socialism" or
a "workers' State" expresses nothing other than a glorification of a fait accompli, which is typical of the contemporary intellectual.

Of course, this story about would-be missing "data" is in reality a quaint little joke. Despite what he wants us to believe, Sartre was not born yesterday and
he knows about the data that prove the exploitation of the workers and the peasants, for the bureaucracy obviously cannot organize absolute secrecy nor can it
prevent everything that leaks out about this regime from going to establish one
and the same signification. He knows very well that the pyramid of incomes in

the USSR is extremely high and that if he lived there he would be a millionaire (or purged). He is capable of solving the following simple mathematical problem: I have a hundred individuals, I take fifteen of them and give them each ten apples; if I give only one apple to the other eighty-five remaining people, how have I apportioned my apples between the fifteen and the eighty-five? He must have read, in Ciliga or in Victor Serge (who left Russia only long after the advent of the bureaucracy), the description of the condition of the working class, and that of the working-class or peasant woman, who, having been roused with immense hope during the revolutionary period, has fallen back into age-old servitude and, in her life of filth and misery, has no other outlet than to go for "many miles in worn-out shoes in dust, mud, or snow to go kneel and worship at the only church that has not been closed, which is always very remote—terribly remote." Of course, in the end, the Father of the Peoples had pity on these poor women. He opened more churches where they could go to learn the Good News—that if not Earth, at least the Kingdom of Heaven will belong to them and that in the meantime it is necessary to render unto Caesar that which is Caesar's and to turn one's check when struck. But all that undoubtedly is concerned "especially" with the system of religion—just as Moscow's haute couture exhibitions are concerned "especially" with the practices of the clothing trade, just as the concentration camps are concerned "especially" with the penal system, just as censorship and cultural cretinism are concerned "especially" with the prevailing ideological system, just as the domination and exploitation of the satellite countries are concerned "especially" with foreign affairs—in short, just as anything in particular is concerned "especially" with particularity. Show us the shameful organicist, the miserable Hegelian, the dirty determinist who would dare claim that everything can be organized around a single idea, a single principle—exploitation and alienation. Show him to us, this doubting Thomas who does not want to believe that all this proves that in Russia they are marching toward communism—even when he *is told* so!

In his article, Lefort had shown that the proletariat's development can (and, from a revolutionary perspective, should) be grasped as a history leading toward communism. We have done the same thing in this review ever since the first issue.[33] And this idea seems to be as important as it is difficult to contest. For, if there is a connection between the proletariat and communism, one must be able to find it through the various phases of the proletariat's existence in capitalist society. Hence we should be able to consider the proletariat's development as a history by taking up our position at this viewpoint.

This idea profoundly but quite understandably amazes Sartre. The idea that the workers can gripe or kick up a fuss but are incapable of seizing power themselves, and still less of managing society, is the thing that is most solidly anchored in the soul of the bourgeois and what saves him in his own eyes. And the bourgeois is perfectly correct—till now the workers still have not yet been able to do this. Sartre is bourgeois (he has repeated it often enough!). Not, as he believes, because he "lives on the income of capital." That is just a bourgeois externality, being bourgeois by accident, like being large or small, brown-haired or blond. Sartre is bourgeois because he has internalized the bourgeoisie, because he chose to be bourgeois. And he chose to be so the day he fully adopted the conviction that is constitutive of the bourgeoisie: that the workers are incapable of realizing communism. He bemoans their fate like a society lady at a charity ball. He thinks they deserve better, that they even deserve to be in power; but what do you want? The sentiments are beautiful, but nothing can be done: They are not capable of it. Someone should do them some good. If he owned a factory around 1900, Sartre would have been a paternalistic bourgeois; possessing only the rights of an author in 1953, he will be a Stalinist. These conscious feelings of self-pity for his superiority will furnish him with the gangplank allowing him to abandon the sinking bourgeois ship for the bureaucratic ship that seems to hold water well. And when he feels stricken with this abject and justified certainty, when Lefort shows him that something else besides defeats, dust, and "passion"[34] can be seen in the history of the proletariat, he will defend himself with irony. Mixing together in his confusion quotations from Marx and quotations from Lefort (to such an extent that one no longer knows whom he is making fun of), he pokes fun at "class immanentism," under which is hidden "as in all dialectics . . . a shameful finalism." The immanentism in question is, roughly speaking, the idea "that in producing capital, the proletariat produces itself as the gravedigger of capitalism" (*RCL* 11/238). "The worker produces himself while producing." All is therefore for the best, Sartre sneers; there is no more reason to complain about exploitation since it is inseparable from capitalism, which is for him the presupposition of the revolution. "If I were an up-and-coming young employer today, I would be Lefortist" (*RCL* 13/239). And he goes on to tell us that Lefort has invented the monstrous idea, viz., that in and through capitalism the working class grows as a revolutionary class, so that he can justify his future anchorage (*RCL* 13/239) in the intellectual bourgeoisie. It is vain that Lefort is "opaque," Sartre has "seen through him" immediately.

Now it is our turn to be astonished. Is Sartre himself so unaware, is what he reads—what he *cites*—of Marx so opaque to him? And if so, why the devil, instead of babbling on about the Party, doesn't he spend a month or two attending a training school of some Marxist party? It will teach him in a schematic and clear language (which later on he will be able to render opaque to his heart's content) that capitalism leads to socialism because it simultaneously develops the revolution's "objective conditions" and "subjective conditions," and in particular the proletariat as the revolutionary class. And if he thinks he is too old to enroll in a training school and that he ought to be admitted right now directly into the Central Committee, let him open first to page 763 of Chapter 32 of Volume 1 of the Samuel Moore and Edward Aveling translation of *Capital* and learn by heart the following passage. Perhaps what is said there is true, maybe not, but it is the key to understanding Marxism, a theory in vogue these days among some advanced people and even among some others.

Along with the constantly diminishing number of the magnates of capital, who usurp and monopolize all advantages of this process of transformation, grows the mass of misery, oppression, slavery, degradation, exploitation; but with this too grows the revolt of the working class, a class always increasing in numbers, and *disciplined, united, organized by the very mechanism of the process of capitalist production itself.* . . . Centralization of the means of production and socialization of labor at last reach a point where they become incompatible with their capitalist integument. This integument is burst asunder. The knell of capitalist private property sounds. The expropriators are expropriated.

And Marx himself cites, in a note, the following passage from the *Communist Manifesto*.

The advance of industry whose involuntary promoter is the bourgeoisie, replaces the isolation of the laborers, due to competition, by their revolutionary combination, due to association. . . . What the bourgeoisie . . . produces above all is its own gravediggers. . . . Of all the classes that stand face to face with the bourgeoisie today, the proletariat alone is a really revolutionary class. . . . (T)he proletariat is (Modern Industry's) special and essential product.[35]

Since he cited it, we know that Sartre read the half page preceding our quotation. In his diagonal reading of Marx he always falls upon the wrong halves. In any case, now that he can discover Marx's "immanentism" and "shameful finalism," he ought to be able to explain his own position about Marxism and stop bashing us over the head with mutilated quotations from Marx presented as arguments.

But if Sartre does not have the courage to explain his own position on Marx, he makes up for it with Engels. It is Engels, he says, who whispered these monstrosities in Lefort's ear, Engels clandestinely stricken with economism, Engels who no doubt aimed at anchoring himself in the bourgeoisie—but then, he already was solidly anchored there. In fact, he spent his whole life at the head of a factory.

It became fashionable a few years ago among amateur Marxists and semivirgins of the "Left" to oppose Engels to Marx. What they found—or what they believe they found—of the mechanistic, of the naturalistic, of the "nineteenth century" in Marxism is Engels. Marx—oh, no, Marx is just the *1844 Manuscripts* and nothing else. This attitude expresses both stupidity and cowardice. Everything Engels published during Marx's lifetime was either approved by Marx before publication—including the *Anti-Dühring*—or read by Marx, who never disavowed it. Moreover, what Engels can be reproached for *also* can be found in Marx.[36] So much for stupidity.

The cowardice lies in what these gentlemen, who protest all the while that they are not Marxists, do not dare to say (to judge by Sartre's example, do not even dare to think), namely, that one is not obliged to accept *en bloc* everything Marx might have said or written.

Engels's appearance in Sartre's discussion leads to results that are humorous

enough for us to devote a few lines to it. The quotation from Engels that is supposed to prove both his own economism and that of Lefort's at the same time
says, in brief, that the mere functioning of the law of value is sufficient to produce capitalism—which has nothing to do with what Lefort says, by near or far.
Of course, what Engels says is incorrect, and Marx showed in *Capital* that, although capitalism functions according to the law of value, the latter is not sufficient for its creation, that a violent rupture, primitive accumulation, is necessary. But Engels's mistake has nothing to do with "economism" or with the
description of exploitation "as a physico-chemical process," since, for Engels, as
for Marx, value quite obviously is a human social relation (just as much as capital is) and not a physico-chemical property of things; and, according to Marx,
the fundamental relation in capitalist society, the exploitation of labor, is based
upon the equality of exchange values.[37]

But there is something even more humorous. For this same passage by Engels
that now proves his physico-chemical ignominy was cited by Sartre in his first
article, prefixing it with a hearty approbation: "And then, *as Engels has shown
quite well . . .*"[38] It is understood that the proletariat has to be deprived of its
memory. Why, Sartre, should it be alone in its sad fate?

Let us leave aside Sartre and his amnesia and come back to serious matters. In
the passage cited, Marx describes how the process of capital concentration and
the numerical growth of the proletariat increase concomitantly. Marx obviously
was not being mechanistic; the educational process capitalism subjects the workers to was for him as important as, and even more important than, this numerical growth. An ambiguous and contradictory process, it must be said, for Marx
never saw the history of capitalism as an idyllic development of economy and
culture where one day perfectly cultivated workers peacefully—or, through an
instantaneous "revolution," cracking the shell—come to manage society. Capitalism imposes on the proletariat "misery, oppression, degradation" at the same
time as it "disciplines it, unites it, and organizes it"; the two aspects reciprocally
condition each other, and it is the two of them together that are the source of
revolution—or barbarism. Marx never saw this process of development as a lin-
ear ascent. In a passage whose capacity for historical anticipation is almost
frightening, he described how proletarian revolutions

> interrupt themselves continuously in their own course . . . recoil ever
> and anon from the indefinite prodigiousness of their own aims, until
> a situation has been created which makes all turning back
> impossible.[39]

A century has elapsed since then. What Marx anticipated so brilliantly can
now be studied in its actual—but not fully accomplished—development. And
this actual development has added to the process an element Marx did not take
into account, at least not in the way in which it came about: the properly *political* evolution of the proletariat. The proletariat has created various forms of organization—parties, communes, trade unions, soviets. It has followed organizations of varying ideologies, specifically Marxist, anarchist, reformist, Leninist,

Stalinist. These organizational forms have collapsed or been emptied of their substance: Political parties have disappeared or have committed "betrayal." All things considered, the history of the labor movement appears first of all as a series of—external or internal—defeats. Should not all of this put into question the prospect of revolution? Can we find a meaning or direction for all this? Can we speak of a process or of a history—or is it all nothing but accident, error, and illusion, a tale full of sound and fury, signifying nothing?

One can respond that these defeats are due to a relation of forces between the bourgeoisie and the proletariat that so far has been unfavorable. If that is so, why should it be favorable in the future? And how can one not see that this relation of forces in the first place involves the working class? In 1918 the German bourgeoisie did not exist, so to speak; the French bourgeoisie in 1936 was almost nothing. In these two cases—we could cite many others—it is the working class's own parties that have massacred it or stopped it along the way. Why have these parties acted in such a way?

To this the Trotskyists respond with two words: betrayal and errors. Childish words, of course. We then would have a century during which the leaders the proletariat gave itself committed betrayals or made mistakes—at least at the decisive moments, the only ones that count. And why would they continually have committed betrayals or made mistakes? Is it a divine curse? And why should this curse be removed in the future?

Lenin provided more reliable answers about reformism and Trotsky did the same for Stalinism. One can say, if one wants, that reformism or Stalinism "makes mistakes [se trompent]" or "commits betrayals" but that would be just a shorthand answer. In reality, reformist or Stalinist politics should be explained by sociological factors. Lenin interprets reformism based upon the labor aristocracy and the political and trade-union bureaucracy, combined with the objective possibility of reforms during the time when imperialism enjoyed a period of prosperity. Trotsky explained Stalinist politics as the politics of a bureaucratic stratum that has usurped power in the first workers' State.

Here we have hold of a solid method of explanation. Indeed, the policies of these organizations certainly have been adapted to the interests of the social strata dominating them. These strata themselves correspond to easily describable phenomena and phases of the capitalist economy.

This explanation, however, is insufficient. It leaves out the principal interested party: the proletariat. For we are asking not only why reformist or Stalinist leaders adopt the policies they adopt but also why the proletariat follows these leaders. We cannot say simply that they *deceive [trompent] the proletariat*, for one cannot be fooled with nothing—not for long, anyhow. And, from the practical point of view, we would stumble back onto the same question: Why won't the proletariat be deceived forever?

Perhaps this is the explanation: The proletariat follows these leaders because up to a certain point and for a certain amount of time it adheres to their policies and their ideology. Why does it adhere to them? Because these policies and ideologies partially express its attitude; because they constitute the proletariat's concrete responses to the situation in which it finds itself vis-à-vis the bourgeoi-

sie during a given stage as well as the provisional definitions of its goal, moments
in this process of searching for the concrete form of its emancipation in which
capitalism constantly reimmerses it. Why does it one day stop adhering to these
policies and ideologies? Sometimes because all struggle becomes impossible and
simply stops; most often because the concrete situation has changed or because
the previous ideological formula has been outstripped, or both at once.

But can we speak of "moments in a process of searching" and of "outstripping" when we refer to the proletariat? Are we not the victims of language?
Does not this process of searching, this outstripping, presuppose a subject in the
proper sense of this term? Does not such a subject refer to logical structures and
uniform criteria? And does it not persist through time, and is it not therefore endowed with "memory"?

The answer might appear paradoxical. It is, in fact, banal. Because the proletariat is objective it is a possible subject. We have already seen that the unity of
the proletariat as a subject—as an experience and as a criterion—is posited first
by the objective conditions of capitalism, and then by the workers' reaction
against these conditions. Likewise, the unity of the history of the proletariat as
a series of significations finds an objective expression in current social reality.
The proletariat has no need to recall previous struggles, for the results of these
struggles are there, already incorporated in its present situation. The results of
its past activity have become an integral part of its current experience, perceptible in the present with no need to have recourse to reflection on the past. In
this sense, each great action by the proletariat tends to outstrip the preceding
ones because it contains them in its current object, social reality, which itself has
been fashioned by previous struggles.

The proletariat has no need of memory to draw the lesson that comes out of
the failure of reformism. It has this lesson there before it: Here is what capitalism can furnish through some peaceful reforms, here is the measly 5 percent
more that it still might eventually furnish. In order to arrive at the distinction
between property forms and the actual relations of production—the understanding of the kind of exploitation found in bureaucratically administered statification—and in order to reject the vision of party dictatorship as a dictatorship over
the proletariat rather than of the proletariat, the Russian proletariat does not
need to relive the history of the degeneration of the October Revolution, to read
Trotsky or even *Socialisme ou Barbarie*. Higher forms of class consciousness are
potentially there, before it, as the negative side of its past action; they necessarily will become explicit the day it takes up the struggle again.[40]

Each party expresses at a given moment of its existence a necessary stage in
the proletariat's development. Is it worth the trouble to add that it does not at
all follow from this fact that you always have to support the strongest "working-
class" party in the country in which you happen to find yourself? Only someone
with the soul of a lackey or a parliamentarian would draw such a conclusion.

Before closing, let us give Sartre the floor one more time: All this is arbitrary, he
says; it's just your interpretation, your opinion; and if you find a meaning in the
history of the proletariat, it is because you started off by deciding that there was

one. You reconstruct the history of the proletariat like a dialectic, and you forget that the truth of a dialectical movement is proved either because one is in praxis or because one finds oneself placed at the end of history.

All this is indeed our opinion. What else is there? That it is not arbitrary results from the fact that it is one of two possible opinions. The other—yours or that of Camus, that of Malenkov or of McCarthy—consists in not finding a meaning in the history of the proletariat, because you have started off by deciding that there cannot be one. We reconstruct the history of the proletariat like a dialectic because it is the only way to understand something or to do something. And your dilemma about praxis and the end of history proves once again that you do not know what you are talking about. For to be in praxis means precisely to posit the end of history—of this history here—as a project of action and, starting from a possible meaning contained in the present, to maintain a practical perspective that in turn illuminates this meaning.

However that may be, henceforth it is not with Sartre but only about Sartre that we can now debate.[41,d]

Notes

1. Marc Foucault, "1948," *S. ou B.*, 1 (March 1949), p. 60.

2. T/E: The SFIO was the Section française de l'Internationale ouvrière, founded in 1904. A majority of socialists split from the SFIO at the 1920 Congress of Tours to form the Section française de l'Internationale communiste (SFIC), later the PCF. The SFIO was in the government with the PCF and the MRP in 1946-47, and with the MRP and liberals after the exclusion of the PCF (1947-50), thereafter entering into opposition. It is the forerunner of the present Parti socialiste (PS).

3. T/E: General Matthew Ridgway (b. 1895) was at this time just beginning his tour as the Supreme Commander of Allied forces in Europe. The background of the Ridgway affair and of the subsequent controversy between Sartre and Lefort, along with Castoriadis's contribution, is discussed in Arthur Hirsh's *The French New Left: An Intellectual History from Sartre to Gorz* (Boston: South End Press, 1981), pp. 46-49 and 113.

4. T/E: Antoine Pinay (b. 1891) was president of the Council at this time.

5. T/E: Jacques Duclos (1896-1975), a PCF Politburo member, was president of the Party's parliamentary group at this time.

6. T/E: Les près de Saint-Germain (the fields of St. Germain) plays on the name of a well-known church in Paris's Latin Quarter, Saint-Germain des près (St. Germain of the Fields). The references to Sicily and Vienna allude to Sartre's cutting short his vacation to go to the World Peace Congress, as he describes in *CP*.

7. T/E: The RDR was the Rassemblement Démocratique et Révolutionnaire, a postwar French political party organized by David Rousset, Sartre, and others in 1947. It was noncommunist, but advocated an alliance with the PCF.

8. T/E: The Vélodrome d'Hiver was a bicycle race track in Paris often used for holding political meetings.

9. On this day, the infant mortality rate went down in working-class neighborhoods of Paris. [T/E: Castoriadis is poking fun at Sartre's citation of French infant mortality statistics, broken down by class (*CP* 147/52).]

10. T/E: Literally, "a flotilla of submarines and a flock of seagulls" ("la flotille de sous-marins, et la bande de mauviettes"). The word "submarine" can also mean an unseen supporter of an opposing group (here the PCF), and "seagull" can have the connotation of a (spineless) coward (reformist socialists).

11. T/E: Gilles Martinet (b. 1916) is a left-wing Parisian journalist and was at the time director of *France-Observateur*. In note (i) of the "Postface à *La Bureaucratie yougoslave*" (*SB 2*, p. 156),

Castoriadis says Martinet was the "Captain Nemo" of the "PSU, a Stalinist minisubmarine of the era." The mention of his nose here relates to Sartre's reference to Pascal's discussion (in the *Pensées*) of the effect of the length of Cleopatra's nose on history. Sartre speaks of the length of Stalin's nose.

12. This does not necessarily imply that he will become a member of the CP: Sartre is much more profitable for the CP by not being a member of the Party: "Given that an independent person, like Sartre, himself also recognizes etc." Obviously the CP would prefer Bouvil or Louison Bobet, who are much more popular, but one doesn't always have a choice. [T/E: Louison Bobet (1925-83) was a celebrated victor in the Tour de France bicycle race. Bouvil was a popular French comedian of the time.]

13. "Man is object . . . of the sun, of a dog" (*RCL* 35/255).ᶜ Developing "the industry of production" (*RCL* 77/285). The universal is that which "embraces an entire collection" (*RCL* 38/257). "The relations of production remain individuals" (*RCL* 11/238).

14. T/E: The addition of "raccoons" here parallels a poem by Jacques Prévert, *Inventère*, which consists of an inventory of unrelated items; each stanza ends with "raccoons."

15. T/E: In June 1936, Maurice Thorez, secretary-general of the French Communist party, coined the phrase that "one must know to stop a strike" at a certain point and reap the rewards negotiated. Some take this "wisdom" as an example of the CP's fear of potentially revolutionary movements over which it does not exercise full control.

16. T/E: The term "labor relations" appears in English in the original.

17. James Burnham, *The Managerial Revolution* (Bloomington: Indiana University Press, 1973), pp. 49-53.

18. Marx and Engels, "The German Ideology," in *MECW*, vol. 5, p. 66.

19. An outstanding development of this idea will be found in P. Romano's and R. Stone's *L'Ouvrier américain*, published in *Socialisme ou Barbarie*, 1-8 (March 1949-January 1952). [T/E: These articles are a translation from the original pamphlet, *The American Worker* (1947; reprint, Detroit: Bewick Editions, 1972), which consisted of Romano's "Life in the Factory" and Ria Stone's (i.e., Grace Lee—now Boggs) "The Reconstruction of Society."]

20. T/E: "Le Marxisme et Sartre," in *Les Temps Modernes*, 89 (April 1953), p. 1552; reprinted in *Eléments d'une critique de la bureaucratie* (Geneva and Paris: Droz, 1971), p. 67. This article was not reprinted in the 1979 edition.

21. Here, of course, we are making a choice. We are deciding that to be an industrial wage earner is an essential relation whereas having cousins or not is not.

22. T/E: Maurice Thorez (1900-64) was the secretary-general of the PCF from 1930 to 1964.

23. T/E: Marx and Engels, "The Communist Manifesto," in *MESW*, p. 38.

24. T/E: Germain is the pseudonym of the Trotskyist Ernest Mandel. Malenkov (b. 1902) was Stalin's designated successor. Claude Bourdet was a supporter of the PCF. Guy Mollet (1905-75), secretary-general of the SFIO, was a deputy to the National Assembly at this time who brokered his party's participation in coalition governments. Pierre Mendès-France (1907-82), who belonged to several moderate left parties in his career, was another Assembly deputy at this time. Georges Bidault (1899-1983) was the minister of foreign affairs in many Fourth Republic cabinets. Pinay is mentioned in note 4, this chapter. Joseph Laniel (1889-1975) had just been chosen as president of the Council.

25. T/E: "Viens poupole," which translates roughly as "Come, my darling" was an undistinguished but popular song of the day.

26. T/E: *Le Figaro* is now, and was at the time of Castoriadis's writing, an extremely conservative daily Parisian newspaper.

27. T/E: "Marshal Poppof" stands for an imaginary Russian military leader. Thorez is mentioned in notes 15 and 22, this chapter.

28. T/E: Rudolf Slánský, a member of the Central Committee of the Czechoslovakian CP, was arrested in November 1951, as head of a "conspiracy"; he was executed the next year. His son and namesake is now a prominent Czechoslovakian dissident. "Péju's articles on the Slánský trial" refer to a series of articles written by Marcel Péju in *Les Temps Modernes*.

29. In any case, it can be discussed, it has been discussed, and it eventually was abandoned by its fiercest advocate, Trotsky himself, who wrote a few months before his death that in case the world revolution is defeated, the forms barbarism will take have been foreshadowed by fascism, on

the one hand, and by the degeneration of the Soviet State on the other (*In Defense of Marxism* [New York: Pathfinder Press, 1973], p. 31).

30. An ideal objective, of course, which a system of exploitation can realize only in a fragmentary and temporary fashion.

31. This is more or less the position of Georges Munis in France and much more clearly of Shachtman in the United States. [T/E: Munis was a Spanish Trotskyist revolutionary living in France at the time.]

32. "Les Relations de production en Russie," *S. ou B.*, 2 (May 1949), pp. 1-66. [T/E: Translated for this volume as "The Relations of Production in Russia."]

33. *S. ou B.*, 1 (March 1949), p. 23-46. [T/E: See "Bureaucracy and Proletariat" in the translation of *SB* in this volume.]

34. This expression is a stroke of genius. Not on Sartre's part, but on the part of every exploitative class that has existed or ever could exist. The worker *is* "passion," for he *has to be* "passion." What is the *ideal* object of exploitation? A purely *passive* object. It is only a *purely* passive object that cannot be exploited; slaves, not cows, workers, not machines, produce surplus value. Therein begins the tragedy of the exploiters.

35. T/E: Marx and Engels, "The Communist Manifesto," in *MESW*, pp. 46, 44.

36. One example among several: the passages in the preface to *Capital* where Marx talks about "society's natural law of evolution," or else where he compares economic analysis to chemical analysis.

37. Sartre's misadventures can be explained in part by his gross ignorance of political economy. He must be reading *Capital* as a historico-philosophical novel desperately fleeing before its essence, namely, the idea that at a given stage philosophy has to become economics or else be doomed to sink into abstraction. The passages in his first article where he comes to grips with the question of wages are particularly entertaining. They recall the critic of whom Kant said that he would have read Euclid as a drawing manual.

38. *Les Temps Modernes*, July 1952, p. 45. [T/E: *CP* 145/50.]

39. T/E: "The Eighteenth Brumaire of Louis Bonaparte," Marx and Engels, *MESW*, p. 100.

40. In this sense, Lefort's statement, "There is no objective factor that would guarantee the proletariat's progress," is incorrect—unless the entire emphasis is placed on the word "guarantee," in which case it can be true for everything historical, and thus of little interest. Sartre does not linger over this; everything is guaranteed for Thorez, he has his insurance policy in his back pocket.

41. Henceforth: for this is what Sartre wrote a few years earlier: "It is not our fault if the CP no longer is a revolutionary party. True, today in France one can hardly reach the laboring classes except through it. But only loose thinking can identify their cause with the CP's." And again: "Nazism was a mystification; Gaullism is another, Catholicism is a third. At the present there can be no doubt that French communism is a fourth." "Qu'est-ce que la littérature?" (*Les Temps Modernes*, 22 [July 1947], pp. 93 and 107. [T/E: *What Is Literature?*, trans. Bernard Frechtman (New York: Harper & Row, 1965), pp. 259, 279. We have altered the translation of the first passage.])

a) We're talking about the PSU of that era, which bears little relation to the one of today. [T/E: The PSU is the *Parti socialiste unifié*. See note 11, this chapter, for another reference to the PSU.]

b) "Le Marxisme et Sartre," now reprinted in Lefort, *Elements*, pp. 59-79 [T/E: see note 20, this chapter, for full reference].

c) At issue here was a vague recollection of Marx, who wrote right in the *1844 Manuscripts*: "To be objective, natural and sensuous, and at the same time to have object, nature and sense outside oneself, or oneself to be object, nature and sense for a third party, is one and the same thing. . . . The sun is the *object* of the plant—an indispensable object to it, confirming its life—just as the plant is an object of the sun, being an *expression* of the life-awakening power of the sun, of the sun's *objective* essential power" ("Economic and Philosophic Manuscripts of 1844," *MECW*, vol. 3, pp. 336-37). But, while understandable within the context of a Hegelo-naturalistic metaphysics such as the *1844 Manuscripts* ("*Man* is directly a *natural being*," Marx wrote a few lines before the passage just quoted), such statements are meaningless in a philosophy of the *cogito* and of absolute freedom (where the "party" has taken the role of consciousness), such as the one that underlies the texts of Sartre discussed here—and all the other ones, too.

d) This text might seem unfair to certain people who know Sartre only through certain positions he has taken after May 1968. Alas, a May 1968 does not suffice to change a person. Here is what Sartre declared a few months ago (*Actuel*, 28 [February 1973], p. 77: "I am of course opposed to everything that might resemble the Moscow Trials. But revolution implies violence and the existence of a more radical party that imposes its will to the detriment of other, more conciliatory groups. Can one conceive of Algerian independence without the elimination of the MNA by the FLN? And how can one reproach the FLN for its violence, after being daily confronted for years with the repression of the French army, with its torture and its massacres? It is inevitable that the revolutionary party might just as well happen to strike out at some of its own members. I believe that we have here a historical necessity and nothing can be done about it. Find me a means of escaping this necessity and I will subscribe to it immediately. But I don't see one." —*Actuel*: "Must one take this position so quickly? One can pose this problem before the revolution and seek to escape from this necessity." —Sartre: "That won't do much good. During the revolution each person is determined by the revolution itself. At the very most there may be some heroes who are capable of intervening to have democratic debate respected between the revolutionary forces and to have free discussion maintained. Nothing more can be said or wished for."

This text needs no comment. Let us say simply that the Maoizing Sartre remains faithful to the Stalinizing Sartre. There still is the adoration of the fait accompli ("historical necessity"—which no longer would be historical necessity if a "hero" appeared). He still justifies in advance all the crimes a bureaucratic dictatorship is capable of committing (and, "of course" the noble soul is opposed to such crimes *once they have taken place*, when nothing can be done) through the most pitiful sophisms (because the French army was repressive, revolutionaries ought to exterminate each other: but did Stalin's lawyers say anything different when they invoked the danger of nazism in order to justify the Moscow trials?). Here we have the same justification as before, and it still serves the same function.

11
The Bureaucracy after the Death of Stalin

The changes that have taken place in the USSR and in its satellite countries since Stalin's death are important both in themselves and for an understanding of the bureaucratic regime. By posing the formidable problem of who should succeed him, the death of the personage who had been for the past twenty-five years both the undisputed incarnation of the power of the Russian bureaucracy and the despot dreaded and hated by his own class necessarily had to cause a stir within ruling circles and ran the risk of touching off interclique struggles that had been held in check till that point by the absolute power of a single person. In itself, however, his death was not sufficient to determine any changes in domestic and foreign policy. If such changes have come, it is the objective situation in Russia and in its satellite countries that has necessitated them more and more. Stalin's death undoubtedly helped them along, for the singular individual who had incarnated the previous orientation has now disappeared, and the process of petrification of groups and policies that had accompanied the last years of his reign has now been halted. Undoubtedly too, this death must have accentuated these changes and compressed them in time, insofar as the new leadership team tries to draw from it all the advantages that might promote its consolidation of power.

We hardly need recall how the events of the last six months have confirmed the class character of the Russian regime, of which Stalin's personal power was the expression and in no way the foundation. Reactionary journalists are at it once again with their "Red Czar." The struggles of the Diadochis around the succession of Stalin might, if they became extremely violent, promote the explo-

Originally published as "La Situation internationale," in *S. ou B.*, 12 (August 1953). Written in collaboration with Claude Lefort. Reprinted as "La Bureaucratie après la mort de Staline," in *SB 2*, pp. 157-88.

sion of a working-class revolution in Russia, but this is an extremely unlikely prospect right now. By themselves, these struggles could never lead to the collapse of a regime representing twenty to thirty million privileged, oppressive bureaucrats.

Changes in the USSR

Let us recall the most significant measures taken since Stalin's death. They all seem to go in the same direction, a softening of the dictatorship: (1) amnesty; (2) an end to the doctors' conspiracy; (3) lowered prices; and (4) the purge of the Ukrainian CP.

As for the amnesty, we cannot determine its extent from the text authorizing it, for we need to know both the number of persons in prison and the manner in which it will be administered. Nonetheless, it is likely that this amnesty is appreciably broader than all previous ones. We must note that it excludes political offenses (what are called "counterrevolutionary" crimes) meriting sentences of more than five years, but we should also point out that this type of offense can be interpreted in a number of ways. It is not out of the question for political offenses to be dealt with under common law, and in this sense they will benefit from the amnesty all the same; but it is likely that confusions about such offenses will operate in the opposite direction too, for numerous "economic" mistakes that ought in principal to be erased might have been or can be considered counterrevolutionary: Is the worker who has been sentenced for having "sabotaged" production, damaged work materials, or refused to follow orders an "economic" criminal or a counterrevolutionary? This equivocation appears quite clearly in the proviso thrown in about thefts of State property, which can cover very different offenses and by itself should restrict the category of amnesties for economic crimes. Finally, it is not out of the question that Article 8 (which allows for criminal penalities to be replaced with disciplinary sanctions in the case of an economic offense) will make it possible to ease the administrative system of rule in the factories. On the whole, "common law offenders" surely will be affected by this amnesty, but its effect upon other categories of detainees cannot be estimated. The state of ignorance in which we find ourselves can be measured by the differences in interpretation to which these measures have given rise: While *Le Monde* assumes that they will affect at the most a few thousand or dozens of thousands of persons, *The Economist* talks of many hundreds of thousands, and *L'Observateur* (Alexander Werth) of at least one and a half million people.

The rehabilitation of the doctors arrested at the end of Stalin's reign and the measures accompanying this action have a more precise meaning, thereby leading us to admit that the amnesty has a certain value. For a conspiracy charge to be set aside and judicial "errors" to be denounced explicitly is in itself unprecedented. Furthermore, the large-scale publicity given to this event indicates the leadership's desire to affirm that a radical change has taken place in domestic policy. The leadership has seized the occasion to officially condemn racial discrimination and to proclaim the rights of citizens as guaranteed in principle by the Constitution. The *Pravda* article announcing the doctors' rehabilitation insists too strongly on the respect for legality that should animate public life in the USSR and the rights of particular strata of the population (kolkhozniki and intellectuals) for this action to be simply a matter of ritual demagogy. Moreover, the setting aside of the conspiracy charge has been accompanied by a purge of the Ministry of Security, which, if it corresponds to a settlement of the struggle between cliques, also should show the public the limitations placed on the power of the police.

An anxiousness to return to more flexible methods of dictatorship is apparent in the way another issue has been handled: The purge of the Ukrainian Communist party and the removal of its First Secretary, Melnikov, has been accompanied by criticism of the way he applied national and cultural policy; the leadership of the Ukrainian Party is reproached for having subjected the country to Russian domination by placing individuals from other regions in all key posts and by trying to impose upon it Russian culture and language. The same misfortune just came down on the leadership of the Lithuanian Party.

Finally, arising in this climate of detente, the lowering of prices is also a sign of the government's new preoccupations. This drop certainly was not the first (but rather the sixth); nevertheless, it is more extensive than the preceding ones. The prices of a whole series of necessities have been lowered by 10 to 15 percent; price reductions reach 40 percent for vegetables; 50 percent for potatoes; 60 percent for fruits. At the same time, a vast campaign to benefit the people's welfare, to construct workers' housing, and to improve consumption occupies the front pages of *Izvestia*.

These measures have gone hand in hand with upheavals in ruling circles. This is an expression of the struggle between bureaucratic cliques triggered by Stalin's death.

During an initial phase, this struggle—already manifest in the previously mentioned purges of national CPs—was to remain indecisive and had to end in a temporary compromise. This is shown first by the Ignatiev affair: Ignatiev, who was removed for having hatched the fake doctors' conspiracy, was minister of state security—till March 7, the date his ministry was attached to the Ministry of the Interior, held by Beria; he had been designated on March 6 as one of three new secretaries and on March 14, when the exact composition of the Secretariat was announced, as one of its five members. That is to say, the decision to eliminate him was not made immediately after Stalin's death and probably was the object of a deal among the new leaders.

Therefore, there was an initial, uncertain phase of negotiations culminating in a division of responsibilities among the new leaders. This idea is confirmed by many facts. First, there was the recovery of key posts—interior, the army, and foreign affairs—by three men who had seen themselves removed from real control five years before: Beria, Bulganin, and Molotov. Then, the Politburo was reconstituted with former members like Mikoyan, Kaganovich, and Voroshilov at the sides of the aforementioned three men, and Malenkov. The reconstitution of the Politburo is particularly significant: It had been replaced last autumn by a

Presidium of thirty-six members clearly favorable to Malenkov, since the latter directed the unit charged with making nominations to the Central Committee and therefore could count on men loyal to the Presidium. Now, this large organ, where the authority of former Politburo members could easily be scaled down, was suppressed immediately upon Stalin's death. While it had been created by the Party Congress, the Central Committee was not even given the opportunity to decide whether it should be abolished.

This phase came to a close with the arrest of Beria, who was accused of being a foreign imperialist agent. It is still hard to know whether this elimination of "Number 2" is merely a decisive episode in Malenkov's ascent toward a Stalinist-type of absolute personal power or whether it expresses something more, namely, a political struggle between two bureaucratic factions, and, to this extent, whether it is calling back into question changes that have taken place or whether it is changing their practical effect. Several indications tend to make us think that the second interpretation is the more plausible one. Malenkov was very closely associated with the State leadership during the final phase of Stalin's reign, whereas Beria was kept in the background; we therefore might be able to establish a connection between the latter's return and the policy changes that have occurred since March. Likewise, the character of the accusations brought against Beria—as opposed to those brought in March against Ignatiev, who was accused at the time of incompetency—is vintage Stalinism and reintroduces straightaway the atmosphere of the years of the great trials, even though this arrest allegedly is directed against the excessive powers of the police. And *Pravda*'s repeated affirmations of the preeminence of collective leadership and the pernicious character of personal power recall too vividly the proclamations Stalin made, so long as he himself had not yet become a person, for us to attach any great importance to them. We must recall, nevertheless, that in a bureaucratic regime a leader and his fate are not tied to a policy or its success, and that Malenkov very well might shoot Beria and then apply his policies.

The real question does not involve writing a novel about the bureaucratic leadership but rather is about seeking the motives that underlie the antagonisms among leadership groups and the present transformations of domestic policy. Before answering this question we must set aside any simplistic interpretation that would fail to take into account the bureaucratic class's stability and would make one faction of the bureaucracy or another the representative of the interests of another class, the proletariat or the peasantry. Through their resistance to exploitation, the proletariat, like the peasantry, may well pose problems for the government and in this way give rise to disagreements among groups of bureaucrats over the most effective leadership methods to be employed, but only indirectly do they influence State policy, which always represents the interests of the dominant stratum.

Political differences can be interpreted only within the framework of the bureaucracy. But this statement does not necessarily signify that we must search for the source of these variations in the opposition between distinct social strata of the bureaucracy. This search, which for years has satisfied the imagination of former Mensheviks employed by the bourgeois press, is based upon a confusion between the bourgeoisie and the bureaucracy, between the classical mode of capitalist exploitation and collective, planned capitalism. Whereas it is meaningful in the first case to relate, for example, a certain policy to distinct industrial groups (the sector of light industry being able to be more interested in granting concessions to the proletariat than the sector of heavy industry or in conducting a conciliatory diplomatic strategy in some particular part of the world in order to preserve its particular markets), it is more than doubtful that such a relation could be established in a society where competition cannot be expressed on the economic level. A social group such as technicians or factory directors may very well possess certain characteristics that set them apart from the army, for example, but these common characteristics that are based on the similarity of their functions do not overlap with a clearly defined economic interest that could be represented in a national or international policy. Competition between bureaucrats, which exists here just as necessarily as it does in every other exploitative class, most likely follows more along the lines of local association and personal rivalries rather than along the lines of the objective structure of the system of production. In short, it is a struggle of cliques, not a rivalry between clearly constituted social strata seeking to appropriate for themselves a larger part of the surplus value that has been snatched from the hands of the proletariat.

This evaluation of the bureaucracy allows us to reject the fantastic hypotheses about a struggle that is supposed to have taken place between the Party, the army, the police, and administrators and technicians, and about an alleged reallocation of power between the Party (Malenkov), the police (Beria), and the army (Bulganin). Indeed, the Party obviously does not constitute a distinct group but is represented rather in all social sectors; were one to claim that the Party membership of generals and factory directors does not give them any real power, that would signify precisely that the line of demarcation is to be drawn not horizontally between these allegedly adversarial groups but vertically between the middle and upper levels of the bureaucracy, the latter being torn only by a conflict among cliques and not because it reproduces the differences among entire strata of society.

No matter how the situation turns out, the hypothesis proves particularly fragile when it is applied to the latest changes in the State leadership. How can one speak, as was done in the press, of a victory for the army or a return of the generals when the army's representative in the Secretariat is Bulganin, who always was considered by the military an outsider delegated by the Party to watch over them? (And at the same time, a certain number of small but significant facts point in the opposite direction: the absence of the generals from the official tribune during the May Day review; the replacement of military people by civilians in key diplomatic posts in Austria and Germany.) How, on the other hand, can one insist on a victory for the police when this victory—if it exists— is acquired at the cost of a large purge in the security services, beginning with that of its minister, Ignatiev; and even as the amnesty and the proclamation of individual rights tend to diminish its hold on society? And how again can the recent annihilation of Beria be interpreted within this framework?

The main thing, after all, is not to know the details of the personality struggles and inter clique rivalries that Stalin's death has brought into broad daylight, but to appraise correctly the import of the domestic changes that have occurred and to understand their causes. Till now these changes appeared to be going in the direction of a softening of the dictatorship. We must add immediately to this idea two details that limit its import tremendously: First, the extent to which this softening actually is being put into effect is not known (there is nothing to keep us from thinking that in reality it amounts to very little), and second, whether it will last also is not known (the Beria affair seems to indicate rather that it will not, irrespective of Beria's personal fate). But that does not prevent these measures from expressing beyond all doubt that real factors are pushing toward a softening of the dictatorship. What are these factors and how far can they go?

It would be a mistake to identify the Russian bureaucratic regime with the Stalinist police dictatorship. A system never is to be defined starting from its political regime. In theory, it is not inevitable that the stage of capitalism we call bureaucratic capitalism—in order to account for the novel character of its dominant stratum—be associated always and everywhere with a totalitarian policy of terror in the style of the one to which Stalin lent his name. We can even imagine that a total Labourite victory in England, accompanied by complete nationalization of production and fully integrated planning, would not immediately and completely abolish "democratic" English institutions and "liberal" mores. This hypothetical example, however, does not signify that a political regime can assume widely diverse forms in a bureaucratic system. The statification of the economy and the concentration of political power accompanying it go hand in hand with a tendency to control *all* sectors of social life. And this bureaucratic mind-set encourages the institution of strict discipline over individual behavior and thought.

Up to what point does State control exercise and even require violence? *This* question does not mechanically depend upon economic structure, but also depends upon historical factors (origins of the bureaucracy, the international situation, etc.). In the case of the Russian bureaucracy, which came into existence by forging for itself its own economic bases, terror was a means of imposing class unity, utilizing the war of all against all to benefit the functioning of the whole. The great Terror certainly had already come to an end before the last war with the final elimination of all political opponents and with the economic consolidation of the regime. But public life continued to be subjected to dictatorial arbitrariness; while the proletariat was crushed purely and simply under the burden of exploitation, the bureaucrats themselves, whatever their social position, did not obtain the kind of personal security that the consolidation of the economic system should have brought them. We may ask whether, in the long run, this situation has not become less and less compatible with the aspirations of the majority of the bureaucracy. It seems that the privileges the latter have won little by little—which allow an individual from birth onward to occupy a high-level place in society (thanks to the advantages enjoyed by his family, his inheritance, and the education he is sure to receive)—were completely insufficient so long as the Terror burdened each bureaucrat with the threat of being physically or socially eliminated.

It is logical, therefore, for the bureaucracy to exert pressure against its own higher-ups in order to obtain some guarantees concerning the personal fate of each bureaucrat and the power to enjoy his privileges in complete security. This assumes not only that the bureaucracy has entered a new phase in its development but that it is more and more conscious of it: First privileges had to be created, completely built into society, and its position as dominant class had to be guaranteed on the social level against the country's other classes, the proletariat and the peasantry; then it actually had to begin thinking of itself as a bureaucracy by divine right and to settle down comfortably in good conscience, in order to demand for itself an inviolable status — which means that the party ought to exist for the bureaucracy and not the bureaucracy for the party. On the other hand, that the very nature of the bureaucratic economy and society dictates a total centralization of power and necessarily tends to give it a totalitarian, dictatorial character shows us a profound contradiction in this system of rule analogous to the contradiction that leads to the ruination of parliamentary democracy in the final phase of monopoly capitalism. But the struggle between those who socially embody the two poles of this contradiction is not necessarily resolved always and everywhere in the same fashion. And it is particularly clear that during the phase in which the centralizing pole has been extremely weakened by the death of the singular individual who for so long personified it, the internal struggles among his successors led them to make large concessions on this level, granting a caricature of habeas corpus to their liege men through the intermediary of articles in *Pravda*.

But we can see a second factor at work in these measures as well as in the recent concessions on the masses' standard of living, whether these concessions are apparent or real: This is the need to attenuate the fundamental social contradiction of this system of rule, the workers' opposition to the regime. Russia's low labor productivity results from the workers' nonallegiance to a system of production that cheats them as well as from a miserable standard of living combined with terror. The resulting permanent economic crisis becomes much more serious as the technical and economic level of the country rises. Canals can be dug with concentration camp prisoners controlled by the whip as long as some of their skin is left on. But modern industry requires that the worker maintain at least partial allegiance to his job, and this allegiance cannot be obtained by terror pure and simple; to obtain it, he must be given some interest in the economic results of production. Under the pressure of workers' struggles, American capitalism has been resolutely engaged upon this course for a long time, though in the final analysis this has not lessened the burden of the workers' alienation. We must think that Russian workers' opposition to production has become sufficiently strong so as to oblige the bureaucracy to initiate some specific concessions.

Changes in the domestic field of Russian policy appear, therefore, as a response to the growing pressure of the regime's contradictions. We will see that this idea is singularly reinforced when we examine the changes that have occurred in the foreign policy of the USSR and in the policy of the satellite countries.

All of Russia's foreign policy gestures since Stalin's death have gone in the same direction: They have been designed to create the impression that the USSR no longer seeks to intensify the cold war but wants rather to attenuate it. While Westerners feverishly and confusedly have continued to seek an unobtainable policy, Moscow seemed to be taking the initiative once again in its operations, acting simultaneously and in a concerted manner in all four corners of the earth, in Korea and in Germany, proclaiming its peaceful intentions and sending Soviet sailors to visit the Eiffel Tower. What is the meaning of this turnabout? Is it simply a question of propagandistic or tactical maneuvers, or is it rather a reorientation of its long-term policy? If it is the latter, what are the causes of this reorientation, how far can it go, and what might its effects on the Western bloc itself be? And finally, whether it is intending to accentuate the contradictions between America and its allies or in any case ends up accentuating them, insofar as this turnabout inevitably has some effects on the strategy of the Western bloc, a third question arises: How far can these contradictions develop, and what effect do these contradictions have on each another?

Let us take up again our first question: What is the extent of the Russian reversal? We should point out first of all that it is limited. Despite its violent diplomacy, the USSR had not sought to unleash war; it now seems clear that the USSR did not count on an American counteroffensive when it began the Korean conflict. Since then, its line certainly has been to give nothing away, but it is also designed to preserve the status quo and nothing else. The systematic search for a compromise, therefore, is not a political about-face.

True, the search for an armistice in Korea has led the Sino-Koreans to give in on a series of points that have, on the local scale, a certain importance (the methods for exchanging prisoners will allow them to get their hands back on only a small percentage of their former troops). But for all that, these points are secondary when one considers the international context of this Stalinist initiative. In fact, this initiative is advantageous. The Korean operation has proved unprofitable: It required a costly military effort on China's part at a time when the latter should have been tackling the crucial problem of building an industrial infrastructure for itself and consolidating the new social regime; in any case, a Chinese military victory had become impossible and the pursuit of it could only have led to a generalization of the war. In proposing peace, the Chinese and the Russians have nothing to lose right now; on the other hand, they sow confusion among their adversaries, divide the United Nations and South Korea, the United States and the English, and weaken the American war effort.

By itself, therefore, the Korean turnabout would not be sufficient to prove a new policy of compromise. But we know that a whole series of diplomatic gestures are heading in the same direction: in Austria and in Germany, the nomination of civil commissioners and the lifting of the Iron Curtain; the renunciation of economic demands upon Turkey; the reestablishment of diplomatic ties with Yugoslavia; the proposal to renew commercial relations with Western Europe (to which is added a change in tone of Russian diplomacy). This new attitude has not been expressed till now by any concrete measures, and, to take an example, the refusal to resume negotiations on Austria on any other bases than those of Potsdam might make one think that the USSR was seeking more a detente than a settlement of European disputes.

The new policy of the East Berlin government nevertheless has shed new light upon Russian tactics. The halt to the policy of collectivization and industrialization "at all costs," the explicit recognition of the hostility of the population and its exodus to the West, the assurances given to the peasants and to the middle classes, the decision to reinstate the properties of those who had been expropriated and those who had fled, the pure and simple capitulation to the Evangelical church (which had been designated enemy number one)—all these measures cannot be interpreted merely as tactical gestures. Far from that, the concessions we mention here are so important that they force us to ask ourselves about the motives behind Stalinist strategy.

And in that case we must recognize that the USSR is in the process of responding to an unprecedented crisis in its bloc, a crisis with many features, both social and economic, as revealed by recent events in Hungary, but especially in Germany and in Czechoslovakia. In these two countries, the local bureaucracy has proven incapable of securing its own power. The difficulty in both cases comes from the fact that Stalinism has run up against an advanced proletariat endowed with a tradition of struggle that knew how to digest quickly the experience of bureaucratic exploitation. The Czechoslovakian strikes and especially the movements in Berlin and Magdeburg have proved that the unification of the Eastern European front is far from complete. It is likely, therefore, that the preoccupation with consolidating the dictatorship in these countries and with building up at the same time an economy of the same type as that of the USSR has been a decisive factor in the policy of detente.

In these regions, which are the most industrialized in central Europe, the bureaucracy has not succeeded in liquidating proletarian resistance: The reduction in the standard of living, the extension of the workday, and the acceleration of the work pace appear as what they are—overexploitation—to a proletariat that is not one step out of serfdom but instead already has behind it a long history of resistance and struggle within the capitalist system. To this it must be added that this proletariat does not feel that it has been crushed by a revolutionary defeat as the Russian workers might have felt when the Stalinist dictatorship came crashing down upon them: Even though they did not oppose the instauration of popular democracy, and even though they supported it at the outset, the German and Czechoslovakian workers did not manufacture it themselves, and they perceive much more clearly that it is foreign to them and that they are its victims.

These factors have found their highest expression in East Germany during the June days.

Faced with these growing difficulties on the home front, and wanting at the same time to create the most favorable impact upon West Germany, the Stalinists had taken a series of measures to promote detente as early as May. What appears most strikingly in these measures is the thoroughly *anti-working-class* character of the bureaucratic regime. Indeed, these detente measures were addressed to all the strata of the population: peasants, shopkeepers, refugees, the bourgeoisie, priests—all social categories except one, the workers. They had not been forgotten, for it was they who would have to cover the costs of the operation, to compensate the bureaucracy for what it otherwise would have lost by making concessions to other strata of the population.

The production plan had been revised in a way that increased the production of consumer goods at the expense of the production of equipment; at the same time, however, production norms were "voluntarily" increased by 10 percent, which amounted in fact to a much larger reduction in wages (P. Grousset, *L'Observateur politique, économique et littéraire*, June 25, 1953, p. 11).

We know very well how the working class manifested its reaction: The partial strikes of June 15 and 16 were transformed on June 17 into a powerful revolt embracing most of the great industrial centers of Eastern Germany. In East Berlin, the demonstrators took over the streets the morning of June 17; in other towns, they even seized governmental buildings. Elsewhere we will provide a more thorough study of the origins of the movement and its consequences.[a] Let us mention here the most important points that emerge from these events.

1. Without the intervention of the Russian army, it is likely that the German Stalinist government would have been overthrown. Its own leadership was dislocated, demoralized, and unable to act. Its own police force either had abandoned it or was lying low. The Russian tanks did not have to do battle, for their mere arrival was a reminder that, until further notice, East Germany is a part of the Russian Empire. Except for the likely repercussions of a working-class revolt within the Russian army, this fact shows both the indestructible power of the proletariat and the limitations on potential movements so long as the system of exploitation remains secure at the world's two opposing poles, the Soviet Union and the United States.

2. The experience of Stalinist bureaucratism as merely a new form of exploitation is an established fact for the industrial proletariat of the satellite countries. Through a number of signs, the workers' opposition to the bureaucratic regimes of the satellite countries was already well known, but now the two terms of this opposition have been made clearly distinct.

3. The concessions that the East German Stalinist bureaucracy has been obliged to undertake in order to forestall events in Hungary and Czechoslovakia contain a fundamental lesson for the workers of these countries: *Resistance and struggle pay off.* We cannot insist too strongly on the literally revolutionary significance of this conclusion, which the workers of these countries already have drawn and which is without doubt in the process of spreading throughout the entire Soviet glacis.

And yet, if working-class opposition succeeds in expressing itself and putting the stability of a new regime in peril here and there it is also because the leadership strata are not unified and because they have come up against considerable difficulties in erecting or consolidating their economic structure. These difficulties already existed due to the mere fact that the requirements of accumulation involve sacrifices on the part of all strata of the population and that the USSR cannot meet all the investment demands coming in simultaneously from China, Romania, Poland, Czechoslovakia, etc. But they also have been added to by the policy of the USSR which, after a period of outright pillaging in Europe, never has attempted to share the burden of industrialization; on the contrary, it has always accorded itself substantial advantages in its dealings with its satellites. If one part of the bureaucratic leadership is so strongly tied to the USSR that it can do nothing but enforce its policy no matter what the circumstances, another part, at least, and in particular the largest strata on which it relies, cannot help but be sensitive to the USSR's privileges and can accept the sacrifices imposed on their countries only grudgingly. The open scission with Tito and the various oppositions that have been punished with purges and spectacular trials reveal the battle going on within the national bureaucracies, a battle that probably has not ended. Finally, the proximity of the Western armies and the prospect of a war that might challenge the present regimes and reestablish the status quo ante have fed the hope and resistance of the middle-class people remaining in these countries, who have not yet forgotten their old privileges.

All these factors, which conspire to make the European satellites particularly vulnerable elements of the Russian defense system, suffice to make it clear why it would be advantageous to have a period of respite capable of leading to a reestablishment of authority. And the persistence with which Eastern diplomacy is seeking trade with Western Europe (whatever might be the tactical value of these postures in relation to the contradictions that exist within the Western bloc) confirms that the USSR is desirous of easing its immediate economic difficulties.

Our intention, as we have said already, is not to indulge in unverifiable conjectures; we cannot estimate at the present time the extent of the contradictions in the Russian bloc and calculate, as a consequence, how far the USSR might go under their impetus. Let us be content to note that some of these contradictions cannot be overcome absolutely and that the response it has begun to provide for them can exacerbate them. The most interesting example is the turnabout effected in Germany: Its consequences already are highly significant, and—if it continues—they will become even more so. In this case, we have seen both a working-class revolt and a collapse of the CP. These two events, which obviously are connected, are to a certain extent an initial response to the Kremlin's new policy. And this initial response already is upsetting the givens upon which this new policy was based.

America and the Contradictions of the Western Bloc

It would be artificial to try to describe Russian policy and the difficulties to which it is responding and which it encounters without speaking of their relation to Western policy.

What is remarkable, till now, is the extreme confusion found in U.S. policy.

This confusion has only been reinforced by the new Russian initiatives; indeed, it has been perceptible for several years now and—independent of the latest international events—it corresponds to a crisis in the whole of American society. The boom in the forces of production and in technical development and the disorder in the struggle between monopolies, the anxiousness about organizing the allied bloc strategically and the blindness of its position of economic dominance that destroys the cohesiveness of this bloc, the will to make war against the USSR and the retreat before the concomitant financial costs, the divvying up of State power between military-industrial clans who achieve predominance by turns, the extreme corruption of officeholders and government functionaries, and the hysteria of large sections of the petty bourgeoisie, who have replaced the lynching of Negroes with the struggle against communism, together make of American society, in the absence of a political expression of the proletariat, a broken-down imperialist power that still has found neither the conditions nor the means to produce *a policy*.

Confining ourselves to the last few months, it is only too easy to emphasize the disarray that the USSR's peace offensive has provoked. Eisenhower's speech last April, described as historic by all the Western press, is a hastily drawn-up propaganda tract that merely responds to the concern that nothing be said that implies either peace or war. And yet at the same time he finds himself partially contradicted by John Foster Dulles's threatening statements. While *Le Monde* periodically announces that the president-general is taking the reins of power back into his own hands, all his gestures reveal his weakness. He puts the pressure on for the military-credits vote, but that does not keep them from being partially reduced. He proclaims his loyalty to the European alliance, but names Radford in the place of Bradley. While responding to Taft, he shows that he is concerned above all with handling him with kid gloves, and he reaffirms his opposition to China's admission to the United Nations. He opens up the possibility of a four-power conference after the Bermuda meeting, but again lets Dulles rule this conference out by setting conditions that in fact render it impossible. Finally, after having warned youth against the inquisitional methods some people are trying to introduce into the United States, he takes special care to say that his speech was not aimed at McCarthy and he refuses to pardon the Rosenbergs.

In the absence of a concerted policy on the part of its government, the United States nevertheless has a strong reaction on the economic level—and will have an even stronger reaction if the Russian policy of detente is borne out. The beginning of the recession, reported in the last issue of *Socialisme ou Barbarie*, could have dangerous consequences, and could grow and dislocate the Western economy. Everything depends on whether such a situation would promote a return to a New Deal type of policy or the rise of a McCarthyite fascism, as seems more likely. In the latter case, however, it is doubtful whether aggressive U.S. policy will bring the majority of the Western camp in its wake so much as it will signify a slowdown or a discontinuation of credits for Europe. Nevertheless, the United States' ability to maintain relative cohesion in the Western bloc does not depend on its internal economic and political development alone, but also on that of the Eastern bloc, on the latter's capacity to overcome its difficulties in part and to interest Western Europe in international detente and in commercial exchanges. At present, the clearest thing is that the United States, comfortably settled into its cold war and at the same time feeling incapable of developing it into a successful hot war, is not interested in detente.

The English and the French, in contrast, do have an interest in detente. The entire difficulty there, however, stems from the fact that it is impossible for them to make policy independent of the United States, though pure and simple dependence in the long run would be disastrous.

The English reaction to the Russian reversal is dictated by this double requirement: at the same time to keep its distance from the United States, pushing for detente, and yet not to provoke any scission with the latter since the situation does not allow for the existence of a third international force. On the economic level, England is very desirous of resuming commercial links with the East, and it keeps violating American trade restrictions, as the celebrated affair of the English delivering goods to China has shown. If the Battle Act were discontinued or eased up, such commerce might permit the exportation of raw materials, machine tools, and certain manufactured products for which the Eastern bloc has the greatest need. We must not exaggerate its importance, however. The Geneva Conference's allowances for East-West trade were very modest (3 percent of world commerce); even if these exchanges were enlarged, they could not reach prewar levels because the structure of Eastern European countries has been modified and Westerners no longer can count on receiving massive exports of grains at low prices (the domestic market now absorbing a much larger proportion of agricultural produce than before).

The pursuit of trade with the East, therefore, is not an end in itself for the English: It is also a means of putting pressure on the Americans, whose ruthless protectionism the English are less and less willing to put up with. The aggressive tone of Butler, the chancellor of the exchequer, recently has shown that the English will not hesitate to resort to a certain amount of extortion in order to force the Americans to ease up on their economic policy. Economic blackmail is much easier to conduct when it supports the political interests of Great Britain, which does not want war at any price, conscious as it is that it then would be in danger of losing for good its rank as a great power.

While England, unlike the United States, has a bourgeoisie conscious of its interests and a government with a political line, the objective situation hems it in with difficulties it cannot master. The danger of an economic crisis in the United States directly affects it too; as was seen at the beginning of the Russian turnabout, the London Stock Exchange remains particularly sensitive to the threat of detente (in 1938, a 4 percent drop in American production brought about a 41 percent fall in English exports and a 50 percent fall in the trading of the sterling area with the dollar area). Although economic interdependence between the two powers has been considerably reduced, it still is substantial enough for a downturn in the United States to have appreciable repercussions in Great Britain. Whatever England's interest in detente, we must note that on this point intercapitalist contradictions still make a coherent strategy difficult to achieve and autonomous activity impossible.

What is true for England is truer for France, which is even more interested in seeing that the cold war does not develop into open conflict and yet is extremely dependent upon the United States. We need only note that French capitalism suffers its contradictions from one day to the next without trying to overcome them or even to transpose them into a coherent political language. The persistence of inflation, growing unemployment, and the worsening of the Indochina conflict have led to a total crisis for the regime. This is expressed in concrete terms by the fact that it has been impossible to form a government. The Russian turnabout has had some repercussions on the French bourgeoisie, as testified to by Mendès-France's bid for power, which would have been unthinkable in a different international climate.[b]

Were this bid to be taken up again when circumstances would allow it, it would not signify that the possibilities for a third force have grown appreciably larger. There is no need for us to note that the English did not relish the idea of a Mendès government and that the Conservatives openly condemned it, seeing it as a leftist Bevanism.[1] The rapprochement of the French with England runs up against the latter's traditionally isolationist policy toward Europe.

Contradictions in the Western bloc, contradictions in the Eastern bloc, the inability of each to take full advantage of the other's difficulties because of its own difficulties; and the proletariat: a force whose actions neither system can predict, but one which, when it enters onto the scene, upsets all the schemes of the exploiters—such are the characteristics of the situation that we have tried to bring out. This situation is not entirely new. We do not think any more today than yesterday that a comprehensive settlement of East-West conflicts might be in the offing. Russia does not have free rein with the German bureaucracy any more than the United States does with Syngman Rhee; and for both adversaries a genuine compromise would only make their domestic problems even worse. We do not believe any more today than yesterday that the proletariat is completely dominated on an international scale. And yet the last few months have taught us that the development of contradictions in the two blocs may not be leading toward war as quickly as we had thought. We have learned that the proletariat can benefit from these contradictions and, before the war starts, begin to join together again upon autonomous bases.

Notes

1. T/E: Aneurin Bevan (1897-1960) was a left-wing Labour MP who rose from being a mineworkers' agent to a minister of health, and then labour, in wartime and postwar British Cabinets (1941-51).

a) See the articles by A. Vega and Hugo Bell in issue 13 of *S. ou B.* (January 1954); see also B. Sarel, *La Classe ouvrière d'Allemagne orientale* (Paris: Ed. ouvrières, 1958).

b) We are referring to Mendès-France's first bid to become the president of the Council (beginning in the summer of 1953), which failed. [T/E: The Conseil de la République was at the time the upper chamber of the French Parliament.]

12
The Situation of Imperialism and Proletarian Perspectives

The analysis of the current world situation, as presented in this review since its first issue,[1] can be summarized in the following manner: The fundamental characteristic of the contemporary era is the struggle between the American bloc and the Russian bloc for the domination and the exploitation of the world; this struggle has its source in the inexorable necessity that drives the ruling class in each bloc—the American trusts and the Russian bureaucracy—to enlarge its profits and its power, to assure for itself the exploitation of all humanity, to guarantee its predominant position against every form of foreign attack and any kind of domestic uprising. There is little chance that the proletariat might, by a revolution that would forestall war, overthrow the exploiting regimes of East and West, and therefore it is extremely probable that the struggle between the two blocs will culminate in a third world war. This war would accelerate tremendously the ripening of the conditions for revolution; the prospects for revolution are intimately tied to those for war. The period that separates us from war, whether short or long, ought to be used profitably for the construction of a vanguard organization, which is indispensable if the revolutionary possibilities that will arise from the war are to be realized. This construction ought to begin with an ideological and programmatic rearmament, for without this nothing lasting can be built up.

The events that have followed one after the other since the beginning of 1953 seem to put this outlook into question. The slowdown in American rearmament; the changes in Russia following the death of Stalin; the new Russian attitude toward its relations with the United States and the resumption of stalled negotiations (Germany), the sudden culmination of another set of negotiations that had

Originally published as "Situation de l'impérialisme et perspectives du prolétariat," *S. ou B.*, 14 (April 1954). Reprinted in *CMR 1*, pp. 379-440.

made no headway for a long time (Korea), or some new overtures for discussion (Indochina); finally, the revolt of the East German proletariat in June and the French strikes of August—these events incontestably form a whole whose signification at first sight seems to be the following: a slowdown of the race toward war, the attempt by both blocs to stabilize their relations, and the working class's reentrance onto the scene. To stop at this point, however, would be to replace the careful analysis of the present system of exploitation and of the proletariat with hasty conclusions and mere impressions; it would fail to draw from these events the lessons they contain, replacing Marxist criticism with a meteorology of political atmospheric conditions, a field in which the Trotskyists have become such successful specialists. We must, on the contrary, profit from this "turn of events," whether they are apparent or real, in order to pose even more sharply the problems facing us and to explore more fully what may still be unclear.

What has provoked these changes? Where can they lead to? Is there a real slowdown in the race toward war? Have the prospects for war been modified by it? In any case, what exactly does it signify? What is the underlying driving force of the struggle between the two blocs? Can their attempt to stabilize their relations succeed? What mode of coexistence can they achieve so long as war does not break out? What can the working class do during this period? What tasks are posed for the vanguard? These are questions to which we can give a response here. It cannot be done in a serious fashion, however, unless we reconsider certain theoretical points and review the development of the situation that preceded the events of the past year.

Imperialism and War

The Driving Forces behind Imperialist War

Lenin's concept of imperialist-era wars starts with an analysis of imperialism as a particular stage of capitalism. Imperialism is the era in which, on the one hand, the capitalist economy and capitalist society are dominated by monopolies, and where, on the other hand, the partitioning of the world among monopolies and the States they dominate already has been achieved. Monopolies no longer find any open spaces for expansion, no new countries to expand into—as was possible throughout the nineteenth century. Their tendency to increase their profits and power can only lead them toward a violent struggle for a new partitioning of the world in which each hopes to enlarge the sphere under its direct exploitation.

What Does Expansionism Mean for the Exploiting Classes?

For the monopoly groups that dominate the opposing imperialist States, to enlarge their sphere of exploitation means to enlarge directly their profits and their power; to obtain raw materials cheaply or to export capital means to appropriate for themselves the colonial proletariat's surplus value instead of leaving it for competitors. Colonial surplus value indeed has no special odor that as such attracts imperialists, and Lenin expressly says that the latter are interested just as much in annexing industrial territories.[2] In this struggle to enlarge profits, the *possible* sources of raw materials preoccupy the imperialists' attention practically as much as the *real* sources;[3] and territories having no direct economic interest are fought over fiercely on account of their strategic interest,[4] for being powerful is not an end in itself but rather is the sole means in the capitalist world, where "all contradictions can be resolved only by force,"[5] of regulating the partitioning of the world's surplus value among the exploiters.

If we try to systematize the economic factors that explain the tendency of capitalist countries to dominate as extensive a zone as possible, we come up with the following three ideas:

1. Capital from the imperialist countries tends to bring under its exploitation the greatest possible amount of man power, and in particular that of the backward countries, where the rate of exploitation tends to be the highest. The utilization of this man power can involve the exportation of capital from imperialist countries to the dominated country, but that is not indispensable;
2. In moving into primary-product countries (whether agricultural or mining related), capital from the imperialist country appropriates for itself the ground rent related to these types of production, which otherwise would be paid to other strata or to other countries;
3. By extending the zone under its political and economic control, capital from the imperialist country enlarges the market it is "protecting" and reserving for itself. In this way, it is able to exploit monopolistically the nonproletarian strata of the population.[6]

It is easy to see that these three ideas boil down to a single one, namely, the imperialist country's *direct exploitation* of as large a zone as possible.

Imperialism Does Not Necessarily Imply a Private Form of Capitalism

We can ask ourselves: Are not these characteristics already those of capitalism in general? Why throw monopolies into the definition of imperialism?

The answer is that these characteristics are not necessarily those of competitive capitalism, at least if the latter is defined rigorously. For in the case of competitive capitalism, the capital of each country finds itself competing with the entire world market, which does not differ in substance from its national market. If this hypothesis is taken in its full rigor, we see that there is no advantage in reserving a zone of exploitation of one's own, since "market protection" does not exist in such a system, since capital can be invested in whatever countries have the highest profit rate, etc.

True, such a form of competitive capitalism is a theoretical schema that still is less of a reality on the international level than on the national level. True, the factors mentioned earlier as determining imperialist expansion have operated in modern history for a long time before the domination of monopolies. It nevertheless remains the case that the ascendancy of monopolies gives to these factors the force of necessity, indissolubly links them to the deep structure of monopoly capitalism, and makes essential what was heretofore accidental.[7] Territorial expansion has a meaning for competitive capitalism insofar as it deviates from its concept, for monopoly capitalism insofar as it realizes it.

But if imperialist expansion is the necessary expression of an economy in which the process of capital concentration has arrived at the stage of monopoly domination, this is true a fortiori for an economy in which this process of concentration has arrived at its natural limit, domination "by a single capitalist or group of capitalists" (Marx). In other words, imperialist expansion is even more necessary for a totally concentrated economy, for a bureaucratic capitalist one. For the exploiting class of such an economic system, the tendency toward the direct exploitation of as extended a sphere as possible appears with the same degree of necessity as is the case with monopolies, and it boils down to the same three elements we analyzed. That they are realized through different modes (for example, capital exportation plays a much more restricted role and acts in a different way than is the case with monopoly domination) is the result of the differences separating bureaucratic capitalism from monopoly capitalism, but at bottom this changes nothing.

We must strongly emphasize that the imperialistic features of capital are not tied to "private" or "State" ownership of the means of production, or to the existence of a "free" or "planned" market. In reserving for themselves a market, monopolies reserve for themselves the possibility of exploiting (as consumers or as "independent" producers) the nonproletarian strata of a country, but the same process takes place if, instead of monopolies, there is an exploiting bureaucracy; in other words, this bureaucracy also can *exploit*, but only on the condition that it *dominates*. And Lenin's conception, which we summarized, has nothing to do with the theory of "outlets" or the "need to realize surplus value," as the eclectic interpretations sometimes put forth by certain Stalinists or Trotskyists would have us believe; these conceptions are based implicitly upon Rosa Luxemburg's theory of accumulation, which is erroneous. Unfortunately, it is impossible for us to go into this point at length here. It is important, nevertheless, to say a word about the tendency of Stalinists and Trotskyists to resort to an unconscious form of Luxemburgism. Rosa's theory of accumulation implies that imperialist expansion springs from the inability of market capitalism to realize its surplus value at home; it therefore can be made to imply that imperialist expansion springs from the existence of a market and its anarchy, and therefore that statification and planning ipso facto render imperialism inconceivable. All that is completely foreign to the conception developed by Lenin, who saw in German imperialism (in 1918!) an "organized and planned State capitalism." And it expresses the same mystification as the idea that statification automatically abolishes classes and exploitation. Russia cannot be imperialist, they say, because it has no unemployment to export. As for man power to import (or to exploit wherever it is found), they do not say a word.

The imperialist peace separating the two wars (both of which may also be termed "imperialist") rests upon a balance of forces between imperialist groups or States, and it is the rupture of this balance of forces that touches off war, not a crisis or an "economic impasse" as such; the latter can play a role either by modifying the preexisting balance or by increasing the number of risks an imperialist group is willing to accept in entering into war, but it is not the cause of war, whose underlying motives exist on a permanent basis. These motives can be neutralized only temporarily by the existence of a balance of forces.

Why Is It Necessary to Enlarge Profits and Impossible to Come to a Permanent Entente?

But whence comes the tendency of monopolies to enlarge without limit their profits and their power? And why could not an amicable arrangement between monopolies for the concerted pillaging of the earth be established and imposed forever (what Kautsky called "ultra-imperialism")? These two questions allow of only one answer.

Clearly, as we already have recalled, being powerful is not an end in itself but rather the sole means in the capitalist universe of safeguarding and enlarging profits. But in the monopolies' tendency toward enlarging profits, what matters is not the psychological impulse, the "unlimited thirst for profit" (although the latter exists and is one of the foundations of capitalist society). Profit is, in its turn, the condition for the capitalist's survival. Statically, what the capitalist makes is capital, but dynamically, capital is only accumulated profit, and it is the expansion of his capital, the accumulation of profit that alone can perpetuate the capitalist's existence. This is clear under competitive capitalism; the capitalist who does not accumulate a sufficient amount is ousted by his competitors, and what allows him to accumulate a sufficient amount is not bourgeois asceticism but a larger volume of profits. The era of monopolies puts an end (in its essentials) to competition between enterprises of the same sector within a country, whether through the emergence of a monopoly in the real sense of the term (a single capitalist or group of capitalists who from then on dominate the sector) or by a cartel or an understanding between several enterprises still in existence (which already assumes, in most instances, a limited number of competitors). Nevertheless, this era is far from ending the struggle between capitalists. The struggle continues on the international level, where the emergence of a genuine monopoly is, for several reasons, the exception; it ceases to exist only with the erection of international cartels, in other words, with the compromises that mark off the respective spheres of exploitation of national monopolies.

Such compromises, however, are in essence temporary. As Lenin showed in his refutation of Kautsky on "ultra-imperialism,"[8] the basis for these compromises is the relation of forces between the participants at the moment the compromise is reached. But this relation of forces is perpetually evolving; those who have gained the advantage through this evolution will put the compromise back into question by demanding a new, more favorable partitioning, and as each revision makes the position of the strongest even stronger, it is bound to happen that a moment will come when the others repudiate this revision, for in the long run it can only lead to their total ouster. Ultimately, a settlement can only come about through force: economic war or total war.

Thus, no compromise can last forever, and everybody knows it. All anyone can do is prepare for the moment when it will be put back into question through peaceful means or through violence; and all anyone can do to prepare for it is to accumulate and increase one's economic strength and overall power from here on out.

The struggle between capitalists and groups of capitalists goes on. The need to accumulate and the need to increase profits does not let up. The areas they control and the populations they exploit continue to be controlled and exploited. All this continues to the same extent as, and even more so than, under competitive capitalism. It continues even more so, for now the struggle ceases to be merely an economic one. Each "temporary stabilization," each economic compromise, each period of peace is utilized by each side only as a new plateau, another stepping-stone allowing it to recuperate, consolidate, extend, and organize its forces with an eye toward a subsequent attack. Since these forces grow at unequal rates among the various adversaries, a moment comes when the preceding period of "stabilization" crumbles. And then it starts all over again.

Imperialist War Is a Stage in the Process of Worldwide Concentration

But does this struggle start again and again, ad infinitum? And in particular, does it always start over again in the same fashion? Can we say that as long as the revolution is not victorious, "*an indefinite number* of imperialist wars" and "*an indefinite number* of new partitionings of the world" will follow one after the other? Does not each war permanently eliminate a whole batch of competitors — just as each crisis permanently eliminates a whole batch of capitalists — and does not each war create a situation that is, in part, irreversible?

Yes, certainly. And we must now add to Lenin's conception — which till this point we have merely been summarizing — by examining the profound transformation of imperialism that itself has been brought about by imperialist wars and by taking into account the very effects of the process we have just described. Through these wars there is a progressive elimination of competitors and domination by an increasingly limited number of imperialist States; a profound transformation of imperialism therefore takes place. Every compromise, every peace treaty can be put back into question — this "putting back into question" being war itself. But from war there emerge situations that no longer can be put back into question: There are ultimate defeats and unassailable accumulations of power. It no longer is just a matter of dividing up colonies and backward regions. What is now at stake is domination over imperialist countries by other, incomparably stronger imperialist countries. And as long as the proletarian revolution does not intervene, this process must end in the domination of the world by a single imperialist State, a single group of exploiters, not through a peaceful entente between various States, but through violent struggle and through the extermination or submission of the weakest.

We therefore must deepen Lenin's definition and see in the wars of the imperialist era decisive moments in the process of worldwide capital and power concentration, not simply some struggles for new partitionings of the world, but advancement toward the all-embracing domination of a single exploiting group. And clearly in this sense we have not had "a number of imperialist wars" but rather each war has represented—or will represent—a very distinct step in this process of worldwide concentration.[9] It will be useful to shed more light on this conception with a short historical review.

The Russo-American Struggle for World Domination

The First and Second World Wars

The First World War aimed at a new partitioning of the world, and it was able to realize its objective. The imperialist powers of the Entente stripped the central empires of their colonies and zones of influence, gave their will the force of international law through the Treaty of Versailles, and established upon their victory a new relation of forces that in its turn guaranteed the results of this victory.

An illusory guarantee. Twenty years later, Germany, which had been crushed in 1918, recovered enough of its strength to put everything back into question, crushing France in its turn and conquering Europe. Germany's conquest and organization of Europe as well as the requirement of "unconditional capitulation" showed that this Second World War no longer aimed at just a new "partitioning of the world" but the total extermination of one of the two opposing camps. Its objective was the domination of the world by a single imperialist bloc.

But this objective of exclusive world domination could not be realized. War was waged against Germany. In hindsight, this can only seem to be a misunderstanding or an anachronism. For, while in Europe the relation of forces was changing rapidly and spectacularly in favor of Germany and against France and England beginning in 1933, it was changing much more thoroughly on the world scale against the European imperialist powers and in favor of America and Russia, which already in 1939 were the sole serious candidates for world domination. (It may appear that in saying today that from 1939 on, Russia was, with the United States, "the sole serious candidate for world domination," we merely have twenty-twenty hindsight. However, from 1939 on, Russia had, with an industrial base second only to that of the United States, a population greater than America's and more than double that of the "great" German Reich. Above all, it had a social system that, far from being especially fragile, as both the bourgeoisie and Trotskyists thought, was much more solid and effective than that of its adversaries. Indeed, its strength was multiplied by its ability to create social and political currents in bourgeois countries, which were both deeply rooted in national life and fiercely pro-Russian. This never was the case with any "classical" imperialist country.)

The Second World War, therefore, posed in reality the problem of world domination, but it was not able to resolve it. Its outcome lay in the elimination of the secondary candidates—Italy, France, Japan, England, Germany—who were decisively reduced to the role of clients of American imperialism. Left face-to-face were the two true protagonists, Russia and the United States.

The Character of the Second World "Peace"

From this fact it follows directly that World War II could not end in a genuine compromise, even a temporary one. The First World War aimed at settling the relations between Germany and the powers of the Entente; with Germany vanquished, the English and French could dictate the "compromise" they wanted (not without considerable internal frictions, it is true), consolidate the relation of forces resulting from the German defeat, and make the Treaty of Versailles incontrovertible for a certain period of time. Nothing like this came out of the Second World War. One could impose all the conditions upon Germany that one could imagine — so what! There was no difficulty in that; the difficulty lay rather in finding a solution to the problem of Russo-American relations. These relations, however, were not discussed during the war; neither of the two adversaries had acquired through force the possibility of imposing its will on the other. The test remained to be done; for a whole series of reasons, the true test, which would have been the prolongation of the war as a Russo-American war, did not take place. This is why, even if the interlude between the Second and Third World War proves in the end to be much longer than the one separating the First from the Second, its character will be completely different. There will be no temporary stabilization, no compromise established upon a clearly defined relation of forces, demonstrated by a clear show of arms and consolidated to a even greater degree by the provisions of the compromise itself. Rather, there will be a series of transitory *modi vivendi*, changing along with the perpetually fluctuating relations of force, the highly unstable balance that rests upon the presumed equality of the adversaries' forces. It also will be extremely difficult to settle points of dispute left over by the war because of uncertainty over the amount of pressure each can exert upon the other in order to force it to back down.

An Indefinite Period of Equilibrium between the Two Blocs Is Impossible

But if the war that ended in 1945 could not establish the objective bases for such a compromise, might not a series of frictions, partial conflicts, tentative efforts, and negotiations establish it? In the absence of an incontestable superiority of one over the other resulting from a military victory, could not the mutual recognition of a presumed balance of forces lead to a settlement?

In the abstract, such a settlement is not inconceivable. It could take the form of a rigorous separation of the world into two zones, one dominated by America, the other by Russia. Each of the adversaries would commit itself in actual practice not to go beyond its own boundaries, or to intervene in one fashion or another in the other's zone; obviously, there must not be any territories omitted from this partitioning, for their subsequent fate could put everything back into question. Yet it is clear that such a situation could only be temporary and that eventually it would lead again to open conflict as soon as the real or presumed balance of forces was upset.

To see this, it suffices to examine the real bases of the balance of forces between the Russian bloc and the American bloc. In doing this, we will be able to understand how rapidly they are, by their very nature, changing and how far they are from being capable of supporting a lasting settlement of Russo-American relations.

Factors Involved in the Russo-American Balance of Forces

On the strictly economic plane, first of all, industrial production in the Russian bloc represents at the present time about a quarter of world production. The American bloc, therefore, should enjoy a position of overwhelming superiority (on the order of three to one). Two factors, however, tremendously limit the import of this statement even if they do not cancel it out entirely. The Russian bureaucracy totally controls what happens in its zone, American imperialism can do so only in part; it does not at the present time have English production at its disposal in the way Moscow can have Czechoslovakian production at its disposal. In short, the struggle is above all a struggle between the Russian bloc and the United States, not between the Russian bloc and "the rest of the world." On the other hand, the Russian bureaucracy can gear—and certainly it does gear—its production toward military production much more than Yankee imperialists can do at the present time. With production equal to half of American production, Russia can be stronger if it devotes to armaments a percentage of its production twice as high as the percentage the United States devotes to its weaponry. Despite that, America's potentialities could get the upper hand, if given enough time. But nothing guarantees that it will be given the requisite amount of time.

Till now the United States' economic superiority has not appeared as an unchallengeable superiority of attack power. It appears all the same as technical advancement in the field of armaments—especially in the field of atomic weapons.

In modern warfare, however, the true relation of forces goes beyond the economic and technical level and includes political and social factors that, till now, undoubtedly have operated in favor of the Russian bureaucracy. The latter has the opportunity to utilize large sections of the proletariat of Western countries in its war efforts and to profit from social crisis in the homelands of its adversaries, whereas it is impossible for these adversaries to intervene actively in the Russian bureaucracy's own domestic crises.

Finally, the decisive relation of forces is not the one that will exist at the moment war breaks out but rather the one that will be brought about by the outbreak of war itself; specifically, real Russian strength is not Russia's present strength but the strength it would have at its disposal if, after the first few months of war, it occupied, as is likely, continental Europe and the most important territories of Asia; the eight hundred million people of the Eastern bloc could then become sixteen hundred million, and the Americans would find themselves in the company of Perón and Malan.[10]

Perpetual Modification of These Factors

We have here a static image of the most important factors whose resultant currently determines the relation of forces between the two blocs and its presumed balance. We can see right away, however, that by their very nature these factors are in a perpetual state of change and that the resulting balance can only be extremely fragile.

Thus one may ask, What is more solidly established than the superiority of American industrial strength over Russian industrial strength? However, the fact that Russian production is developing at a much more rapid pace than American production constantly alters the relation of forces. It is merely a platitude to say that if these different paces of development are maintained, Russian production would one day surpass American production; but we must also be aware how relatively short this space of time is. Within eleven years a quantity that increases 10 percent a year catches up with a quantity that is initially twice as large, but that increases only 3 percent; it catches up with a quadruple of the first quantity within twenty-two years.[11]

Likewise, America's technical prowess today is unquestionably superior to Russia's level, but the Russian level may grow more rapidly. Very complex factors—and not all of them are rational—are at work here. There is, however, a decisive one favoring the Russians. Simply put, it is their ability to profit from the technical advances of the Americans themselves. Even with a less effective spy network, the Russians still would learn something from the Americans, the inverse not being, we assume, true. In addition, military techniques are indissolubly linked with overall production techniques; as long as the whole of American production is not hidden under the fedora of the FBI, the Russians will profit directly from the majority of American technical improvements, and indirectly from almost all of them. Indeed, we hardly need recall how the Russians' discovery (or copying) first of the atomic bomb and then of the hydrogen bomb has demonstrated either the absurdity of the idea of their permanent and congenital technical inferiority or else the futility of American counterespionage efforts, and probably both at the same time.

Within this framework, the immutable givens of geography lose the meaning they once had. The advantages Russia reaped from its central position facing the majority of this hemisphere now can be seriously challenged by developments in aviation and atomic weaponry. Conversely, these developments have already destroyed the isolation of the United States.

It Is Impossible for Moscow and Washington to Have
Total Control over their Power Base, the Proletariat

Even more changeable and fluid than these advancements in technique are the political and social relations within each of the blocs, which themselves are a determining factor in the relation of forces. One of the United States' fundamental weaknesses is its inability to bring about—and even to conceive of—a rational organization of its own bloc; but whatever this organization or rather disorganization may be, it is constantly evolving (frictions with England and France, the stalemate over the creation of the European Defense Community [EDC], Iran, Egypt, etc). Conversely, one might think that the Kremlin bureaucracy's domination over its zone was indisputable; in reality, for their being so bottled up, the contradictions are all the more violent, as the Yugoslavian case and the Berlin revolt have demonstrated in different ways. One of the Russian bureaucracy's principal assets, the strength of Stalinist parties in certain Western bloc countries, is far from being given once and for all; this power is attacked frontally by the bourgeoisie and undermined by the proletariat's mistrust or by its increasing demystification.

Certainly, this is the most profound and in the last analysis the most important factor in the whole situation. All things considered, neither American imperialism nor the Russian bureaucracy has absolute control over its own domain; neither of them constitutes a system of exploitation capable of achieving rational social relations, for it is precisely such relations that would imply the abolition of exploitation. The dominant class in each bloc has to lead the struggle against its external enemy; it also and above all has to lead the struggle on its own domestic front in order to be able to assure for itself its domination over its own society, for at every instant this domination is being put back into question, either implicitly or explicitly. Moscow's or Washington's sole force is the Russian or American proletariat. But this force does not in reality belong to them. They have to usurp it. They can succeed in appropriating it for themselves only through a combination of cunning and violence, deceit and oppression, corruption and exploitation. At the same time that they appropriate this force it becomes even more profoundly alienated from them. As they extort still more surplus value from the workers they line them up even more profoundly against the system that exploits them, and each time they beat down a revolt they set forth, without knowing it, a premise for the revolution.

The situation of the ruling class in the American bloc as well as in the Russian bloc can only be understood in the light of this permanent double struggle: against the foreign enemy and against the domestic enemy. And each of these struggles acquires its full significance and all its acuity only because the other one exists at the same time; the ruling class capable of resolving its domestic problems and really dominating its society would be able, at that moment, to wipe out its foreign adversary almost without difficulty. Conversely, the bloc capable of exterminating its foreign adversary would be able to face its domestic contradictions in a totally different manner; at that moment, these contradictions would lose their virulence and it could simply let them go on rotting indefinitely. But obviously the ruling class cannot achieve this first solution — resolving the internal contradictions of its society — for that would signify it has been abolished as a dominant class; only a society without exploitation and without oppression can be organized on a rational basis. There remains for it only the second path: trying to suppress the external enemy. Here we have, in the last analysis, the underlying motive force behind the struggle between the two blocs and the most important factor in this struggle; of all the factors making their relation of forces unstable, this one is the most independent. And, as far as the exploiters are concerned, its reactions are the least susceptible to prediction.

Relationship between the Class Struggle and the Race toward War

But cannot the class struggle within each bloc slow down the race toward war by obliging the imperialist powers to take into account the reactions of the exploited? Cannot it even go further and, by means of a revolution "preceding" this war, abolish the system of exploitation and thus war itself?

We have said in this review[12] that the inability of each of the blocs to surmount its internal contradictions—and the latter all follow in the last analysis from the proletariat's resistance to its being exploited—has conditioned the turnabout in their policy in 1952-53. But this interpretation has nothing to do with the idea that an "accretion" of resistance to oppression on the proletariat's part can postpone imperialist conflict indefinitely. This idea, which serves as the foundation for the reformist conception that working-class "pressure" might be capable of preventing war indefinitely (a conception taken up on occasion by the Trotskyists), is a mystification. Indeed, it is one thing to say that given such circumstances the imperialist powers' inability to completely dominate their societies has obliged them to take a step backward on the road toward war (which happened in 1952-53), and it is another thing to say that such a situation could last indefinitely. That would assume that class war can remain indefinitely in a state of equilibrium on the point of a knife. The fact that they have been obliged to take a step backward at the first stage means that the imperialist powers are actively preparing to totally foist themselves upon the proletariat during a second or third stage. Both the analysis and the experience of a century of working-class struggles show that the class struggle in capitalist society can only end in working-class defeat or in revolution.

The second possibility, therefore, remains to be examined: that a revolution previous to the war suppresses the prospects for this war. Certainly any forecast we might make here does not involve matters of principle. On the basis of an a priori analysis, we cannot conclude that revolution is a certainty or declare it absolutely impossible. But the examination of the concrete historical situation shows that a revolution previous to war is extremely improbable.

Indeed, the two fundamental presuppositions for a victorious revolution will be given on a world scale only when there is war: These are the ideological maturation of the proletariat and the crisis in the exploiters' apparatus of domination and repression. The situation with respect to these two factors is inversely symmetrical in the two halves of the world: In the West, the exploiters' apparatus of domination would not present an insurmountable obstacle to the proletariat taking action, but it is paralyzed by ideological factors, as a matter of fact by the existence and influence of a working-class bureaucracy. In the East, the exploitative nature of the bureaucracy offers no mystery for the populations of that area, but its totalitarian dictatorship makes it practically impossible for them to organize and act. War will bring about some radical changes as well as the following situation: in the West, demystification of the role of the bureaucracy; in the East, the knocking over of the apparatus of domination and repression—and this under conditions in which their respective populations are universally armed.

The most important thing, however, is that war alone can bring about these conditions in a relatively synchronized manner on a world scale. And it is really the world scale that matters. Let us assume that the conditions for revolution have come together in a given country—which is neither impossible nor even improbable. Who does not see that one or the other of the two blocs or both at the same time would intervene immediately in order to crush this revolution—in other words, that civil war would be transformed rapidly into an imperialist war? Who can think that the Americans or the Russians would allow a proletarian revolution to take power and hold onto it in France, in Italy, or in Germany? Such a revolution would trigger an immediate and probably simultaneous intervention. This intervention could be held in check only if the revolution spread to other countries, and principally to Russia and to the United States. Each bloc's attempt to intervene in movements taking place on its adversary's turf would rapidly turn the situation into a general conflagration, and this conflagration alone would tend in return to create the conditions for a general revolution. It is therefore possible for war and revolution to be closely woven together from the outset, but it is highly improbable for the revolution, spreading like wildfire over the planet, to overthrow the power of the exploiters without further ado.

These last considerations show that the class struggle can in an extreme case accelerate war rather than slow it down. But at a deeper level it remains true that, independent of its "conjunctural" effect upon the relations of the two blocs (in one sense or the other of this word), the class struggle is in the last analysis both the condition for and the driving force behind their struggle, and the most important factor in the instability of their relation of forces. It also is the factor that makes it impossible for the Russians as well as for the Americans to establish and maintain a rational strategy and policy toward their adversary.

It Is Impossible for the Exploiting Classes to Have a Rational Strategy

The same factors that tend more and more to give to strategy a predominant place in the life of contemporary society also are tending to take away its rational bases. To see this we need only compare the nature of strategy in the modern world with that of past centuries.

Back then, strategy was the art of the most effective utilization of exclusively military forces available over a critical and limited period of time, the time of war itself. The industrialization of war and its corollary, the militarization of society, have, as is well known now, made war total in a twofold sense. It is total, first of all, "in space" in the sense that it concerns social activity as a whole, from production to ideology. But it is also—and here we have a feature that usually is less emphasized—total "in time" in the sense that neither are the forces to be utilized thought of any longer as given—they are conceived rather as something that can and should change in terms of changes in strategy—nor is the period covered by this strategy limited any longer by "war" in the narrow sense of the term, for now this period encompasses all of the future. Strategy therefore becomes the art of developing on a permanent basis and in the most effective manner a society's entire set of forces with a view toward conducting total war against another society that proceeds in the same manner.

The repercussions of such a modification of strategy are enormous. The instrument of war formerly was the army, a tool that could be improved, that had to be utilized according to particular rules following from its very nature and its mission, but about it, one knew, in the final analysis, virtually everything concerning its value and what could be expected of it. Today the instrument of war is society as a whole, and social contradictions and the fluidity of social relations have suddenly been transposed into the very center of strategic concerns. Formerly, technique certainly was evolving, but it followed a pace that today seems little different from immobility. Today weapons are outmoded even before their prototype can be tested, but at the same time their perfection also requires research and development stretching over years, and this research and development phase has to be planned in advance too. In short, strategy today involves the total control of social activities and planning of these activities over the span of many long years. This means, first of all, that politics, strategy, and economics are tending to become identical with each other; this also means that a country's strategic orientation as well as the actual application of its strategy in practice become determining factors in the development of society.

Hence, whereas strategy formerly was limited in its rationality only by a certain unforeseeability of natural conditions (which now has been almost completely eliminated) or else by one's adversary's strategy (which, since it tended to be rational itself, was similar to one's own strategy and therefore its reactions could be reckoned upon and integrated as one element of the overall situation), today it suffers a loss of internal rationality, for its very own instrument is itself tending to elude its control. Control used to be possible insofar as the instrument of war—the army—was isolated from the society from which it came, insofar also as one worked on the basis of the same techniques over dozens of years. This no longer is possible today, for neither of the adversaries can exert total control over its own society nor can either foresee the developments in its own techniques. We must conclude from this that there is an insuperable tendency within each bloc to increase the rational basis of its strategy by increasing the degree of control it has over society and society's development. But insofar as, deep down, this tendency is held in check—even if it ends up asserting itself in an external, superficial way—the strategy of each bloc, like its policy, can only end up being simultaneously incomplete and modified under the constant pressure of factors that are in fact external to it, i.e., empirical.

Let us sum up. A stabilization of relations between the two blocs is impossible. It is impossible even in the sense of a "temporary stabilization," i.e., in the sense of a settlement that cannot be brought back into question for a certain amount of time. Conjunctural compromises, on the other hand, whether they are implicit or explicit, are possible and even likely, based upon a given configuration of the relation of forces. Their duration can be short or long, their extent broad or narrow, but in any event they are essentially transitory, for they can rest only upon the relation of forces at a given moment, and this relation is by its very nature unstable and shifting. Nothing more can be said in advance.

The history of the last few years, and particularly that of 1953, amply shows this.

Russo-American Relations, 1945-52

The period from 1945 to 1948 was the period of final crystallization of the two blocs and their geographic delimitation. In Europe as well as in Asia, the war had left behind economic, social, and political chaos. The "zones of influence" defined at Yalta and at Potsdam could be clear-cut on the map, they could define the limits of the armies' advances, but from the social and political point of view, this influence had to be given a concrete content, and that could be done only through the instauration and consolidation of bureaucratic rule in the countries of the Eastern zone, of the traditional bourgeoisie in Western countries. This instauration, in its turn, could not take place automatically; both the Russians as well as the Americans had to intervene in the political life of these countries, they had to support the elements that were favorable to them and attack the others. Moreover, as each imperialist power's influence (which was uncertain at the outset in its own zone) began to penetrate into the opposing zone and as the Russians had the opportunity of using the Communist party to influence French politics and the Americans were able to use bourgeois or reformist parties to influence Czech or Polish politics, the struggle between the two blocs during this period was bound to take on the aspect of a specifically social and political struggle, with each bloc trying to exterminate its adversary's partisans in its own zone and to push forward its own partisans in the other's zone.

This process reached a broad plateau in 1947-48; the failure of the November-December 1947 strikes in France, the March events in Prague, then the Italian elections in May 1948 brought about the consolidation of Russian or American power in the most disputed countries; and the American intervention in Greece starting in 1947 left little doubt as to the fate of this country (where civil war, nevertheless, only came to an end two years later, in August 1949). A certain sealing off of these two blocs was thus achieved. Indeed, this sealing-off process presupposed above all the economic consolidation of each of the two regimes in its own zone, and in return, the conclusion of this sealing-off process has reinforced economic consolidation.[13]

This sealing-off process, however, was quite relative. Indeed, it was relative in several ways. First of all, the Russian bureaucracy was still able to act within certain important capitalist countries (France and Italy) through its intermediary, the Stalinist parties. Inversely, as the case of Yugoslavia has shown, bureaucratic domination was not always without its own fissures. In the second place, this sealing-off process corresponded, in the cases of Germany or Korea, to an artificial carving up of the countries in question and gave rise to frictions and repeated conflicts (the Berlin blockade). Finally, in the case of countries like Indochina or China, armed conflict continued and seemed to be the only way of settling their fate.

One might have thought at this time that on the basis of this sealing-off process, even if it was relative, a stabilization of relations between the two blocs could ensue and might endure. This is what superficially appeared to be happening from 1948 to 1950. Beginning in 1949, however, the bases for this state of equilibrium that, with some difficulty, seemed to have been established, threatened to collapse, first of all because of the Stalinist conquest of China, then because of the explosion of the Russian atomic bomb. These two events constituted a radical reduction in American strength; the first, by adding five hundred million people to the Russian bloc and by showing that, in case of war, the United States risked losing all of continental Asia; the second, by annihilating the atomic monopoly of the United States, which, till that point, had relied upon this monopoly to counterbalance Russia's superiority in "classical" arms.

The American response to the conquest of China was the so-called North Atlantic Treaty, signed in April 1949. Formally speaking, this treaty brought about nothing new: It consecrated American hegemony, which had been a fact since 1942, and defined an "unattackable" zone whose boundaries had long been known. The treaty could acquire concrete meaning only through the rearmament of the countries that were its signatories and through the definition of a coherent and rational strategy. If there was the least doubt about this at the start, it was dispelled with the explosion of the Russian atomic bomb in the summer of 1949. The latter event showed that the Russians would have to be confronted, if need be, on the actual plane of total war, and not on the imaginary plane of a push-button war; the number of buttons continued to multiply, but henceforth they could be pushed on both sides of the Iron Curtain.

It was one thing, however, to establish this fact and to draw from it the conclusion that total rearmament was necessary and another thing to define in precise and concrete terms, within the given conditions of the American "coalition," a strategy that was at the same time both realizable and effective. This task was then and remains, as we shall see, impossible for the American bloc to achieve. In any event, the "classical" rearmament that was intended to compensate for the loss of America's atomic monopoly actually began in the spring of 1950.

The contradictions and the internal weakness of the American bloc were brought to the fore in June 1950, when the North Koreans invaded South Korea. Once again it was proved that, while the Russians always could act through surrogates and utilize the potential of the regions they controlled, the Americans were only capable of equipping puppet regimes that give way at the first tremor. At the same time, the Americans were obliged, lest they suffer a complete moral collapse of their coalition, to intervene with their own forces and to fight a ground battle within the limits set by their adversary. They were losing this battle for quite a period of time, and they were able to fight their way back only by engaging in an all-out classical war and by sending in their best available troops.

By brutally pushing the Americans back to around the 38th parallel, the Chinese counterintervention demonstrated that, whatever American potentialities might be in a future war or on *Kriegspiel* boards, these potentialities could be measured quite accurately against their adversary's potentialities in the only war that by definition mattered, war today on the field of battle set by one's adversary. It also demonstrated how limited are the number of possible ways the world can be divided up: Neither of the adversaries can accept a loss of ground, however small it might be. In 1952, it quickly became clear that the Korean War was coming to an impasse; each of the adversaries was ready to increase its efforts and bring in still more forces to avoid pulling back. The real dilemma was posed as follows: generalization of the war or a halt to it.

This was not some abstract dilemma but rather a dilemma between two real tendencies, at least on the side of American imperialism. The MacArthur episode showed this. The policy he represented came from the recognition of the very obvious fact that on the military level there could be no solution to the Korean War if the Americans did not utilize all the means they had at their disposal to attack the source of their adversary's sources of strength, in other words, if, to begin with, they did not bomb Manchuria. That this would have set off a massive counterresponse from the Chinese leading to a generalization of the war was almost certain, and it was on this point that MacArthur's narrow military logic turned into mere stupidity, given the concrete conditions of the time. Moreover, Truman's recall of MacArthur demonstrated at the same time that American imperialism still was not ready for a generalization of the war and even that the Western rearmament effort was in the process of going through a profound crisis. Under the pressure of economic and social contradictions, this crisis in the American bloc has given rise, since 1952, to a relative turnabout in the situation. This relative reversal was to revolve even further in 1953 when it was revealed that the Russian bloc was going through just as profound a crisis.

"Appeasement"

The Crisis of Western Rearmament

As soon as it became fully apparent that the war in Korea had reached a military impasse, opposition to this war rapidly began to grow in the United States. The absurdity of a situation in which conscripts were being killed for no reason and with no result became glaringly apparent to the popular masses, and the absurdity of taking on a growing burden of seemingly useless military expenditures also was becoming apparent to the masses as well as to the American petty bourgeoisie and even to large sectors of the bourgeoisie. It is well known that this change in public opinion played a determining role in the Republican victory of November 1952.

This factor takes on its full weight when we examine the internal inconsistency of rearmament policy as it has been conceived and applied since 1950-51. What was it aiming at? Was it to make real preparations for war, even in the American journalists' civilized sense of a showdown[14]—to show your cards—so that the West, armed to the teeth, could finally say to the Russians: "Commit suicide or be killed"? Obviously, such a line would imply rearmament on a completely different scale, involving a total mobilization of the economy and the population for war. Beyond the political impossibility of putting such a policy in force, it obviously would be a direct invitation for the Russians to attack right away, before those preparations had gone too far.

The only objective the Western general staffs at the present time say they are seriously considering is a certain kind of "defensive security." And this by itself points to all the Western bloc's contradictions as well as to its impotence, for, on the plane of total war, an effective defense cannot be developed without the means for an effective offense, and if the latter cannot be provided, the former no longer can be realized. On the plane of limited wars (like that of Korea), being "on the defensive" places the Americans in a position of permanent inferiority, since their adversary always is being left the choice of the time, the place, the terrain, and the extent of the conflict. This second point is obvious, but we must consider the first one more closely.

The important features of the strategic situation from the Americans' point of view are as follows. The Russians have at their disposal a significant ground force (on the order of 150 to 200 divisions), to which must be added the armies of the European satellite countries and the Chinese army. These forces could easily be doubled or tripled in a few weeks preceding and following the outbreak of war. Moreover, their emplacement near Western Europe, the Near and Far East, and Southeast Asia gives them virtual domination over these regions, where a third of the world's population is found along with what there is of industry in the Western bloc besides American industry and of important raw materials (oil, rubber, tin, etc.). The forces the American bloc can have at its immediate disposal against the Russians are incomparably smaller (about fifty divisions at the most), and the principal reservoir thereof (the United States) is far from the main theaters of operation. Under these conditions, the Russians' occupation of these regions is practically assured in case of war, and the advantage the latter thus would gain in a drawn-out war would be, so to speak, unbeatable.

America's atomic monopoly could balance out the situation since, if the United States could deliver a blow of atomic destruction on Russian territory, the essential forces of the Eastern bloc would collapse on their foundations long before the resources of the occupied continents could be put to use. In a brief atomic war, the advantages to the Russians of possessing the world's most important regions would disappear.

But when the Russians themselves also got their own atomic bomb the two adversaries were placed in virtually the same situation. A certain American superiority might persist from the standpoint of the quantity and quality of their bombs as well as from the standpoint of delivery (meaning, of course, delivery on the heads of the Russians). Nothing prevents the United States from now on being threatened with receiving a few blows too instead of just dealing them out. War becomes long again; the immediate stakes (Europe and Asia) regain all of their importance; so does their defense. This is what has led to Western rearmament since the beginning of 1950.

What could be the goal of this rearmament effort? It was out of the question to create an equality of forces capable of preventing the Russians from immediately occupying vulnerable regions. The figures put forth at the time by the

Western general staffs as their goal (creation of some thirty divisions in Europe) indicated that it was a question of outfitting a mere protective force intended to buy enough time for a partial mobilization of the European countries and of the United States.

This objective clearly was inadequate. Faced with the Russian army, these "protective" forces protected nothing at all and seemed merely to promise a new Dunkirk. Assuming there was time for it to take place, the "mobilization" of countries like France or Italy, where a third to a half of the population would be likely to fight for the Russians rather than against them, makes no sense. In the United States, mobilization always could take place by the time the Russians arrived at Gibraltar; this mobilization does not need "protective" forces but rather delaying actions. But at the same time this inadequate rearmament effort was intolerable; the West's plans were, as *Le Monde* said with disarming moderation, "ridiculously exaggerated." This inadequate rearmament effort overwhelmed the economy of the United States' satellites and created a growing reaction in the United States itself; it proved simultaneously effective at lining up these populations against their governments and ineffective at "stopping the Russians."

To the internal contradictions of this rearmament policy was added the growing reaction of the United States' largest satellite countries, and in the first place, England.

Once the alarm of the Korean War and the intervention of the Chinese stopped sounding and once they had made certain that the Russians were not at all in the immediate future aiming at a generalization of the war but rather were continuing their strategy of limited attacks on points where they had significant advantages, the European capitalists found the burden of rearmament intolerable. These economic difficulties can be appreciated fully only when seen in connection with one of the situation's fundamental and permanent factors, the contradiction of the rearmament policy now seen from the standpoint of the United States' European satellites: the fundamental divergence between the war aims of the various European bourgeoisies and those of American imperialism. For the latter, the goal of a war would be the extermination of Russia; for the former it would be to avoid being occupied. As a consequence, the entire American strategy, in its substance, has to be oriented toward the periphery. It uses Europe as a "glacis" upon which to fight and from which to fall back in order to win time.

For the American general staff, Europe's usefulness lies in the delaying actions that can be fought from there; then it will be a matter above all of preventing the Russians from utilizing Europe's industrial and human potential or what will remain of this potential. For the European general staffs, it can only be a matter of defending territories. No matter what the scenario, this defensive approach probably is utopian. But from now on, in any case, it involves a military effort that a tottering European capitalism is totally incapable of providing. Unable to achieve what it needs in order to maintain an autonomous existence (i.e., total rearmament, which, however, would precipitate war), European capitalism is organically led toward the twin utopia of international appeasement and reliance on the United States' total nuclear supremacy (which is supposed to hold the Russians back through fear of reprisals).

In short, since the second half of 1952 the West has been forced to betray the fact that it was incapable of sustaining a generalized war, that it was likewise incapable of increasing its military potential at the same pace and that it wanted to get out of the impasse in Korea. This was confirmed by Eisenhower's electoral victory in November 1952. And the first budget he presented to Congress (February 1953) included a reduction in military credits compared with the amount projected by the Truman administration, which themselves already had been scaled down from the initial plans.

At this very moment, Stalin's death allowed the crisis within the Russian bureaucracy to express itself overtly.

The Crisis of the Russian Bloc

In October 1952, the Nineteenth Congress of the Communist party was held in Moscow. Beyond the ostentatious designation of Malenkov as the regime's heir apparent, this Congress basically did not lead to any new direction for Russian policy. This policy remained just as it was when it was defined in 1947-48: emphasis on "capitalist encirclement," exclusion of any idea of a possible compromise with the West, and internal economic development centered on rearmament and heavy industry.

Stalin's death set loose an extremely brutal change in this orientation. From March to June 1953, new measures followed one upon another: a one-sixth lowering of prices, official proclamations about the priority to be given henceforth to consumer industries, amnesty, affirmation of the Soviet citizen's individual rights and liberties. On the international plane, initiatives were taken to bring a conclusion to the Korean negotiations, and a number of diplomatic and commercial gestures of conciliation were made toward Western countries.

This set of events raises several questions. Up to what point are these changes real, and up to what point do they merely express a mystificatory demagogy for domestic consumption within Russia and a temporary diplomatic maneuver for foreign consumption aimed at winning time? What is the underlying reason for these changes and what are the limits? These questions are closely connected. We can respond to them only by considering the Russian bloc and its bureaucracy as a whole.

To what extent are the internal changes that have taken place real? Who benefits from the amnesty? Has there actually been a lowering of prices or is it merely a ploy? And if they actually have been lowered, to what extent have they been lowered? In other words, how much did the consumer gain? Have the promises about emphasizing the consumer-goods industries been kept? How far has this change gone? Of course, it is impossible to answer these questions even with a modicum of precision if we start with primary source data since what we know about Russia is only what the Russian bureaucracy wants to tell us; as a rule, it will say only what "confirms" what it elsewhere claims it is doing. Only by indirect reasoning can we attempt to get a fix on the real character of these measures.

It seems there is an element of reality in these disputed "reforms." First of all, this is because it is much more difficult—and it would be an extreme blunder—to lie totally about clear-cut measures. "The standard of living is increasing 5 percent per year" is the kind of statement no one can totally refute by mere individual experience. If in contrast it is said, "The price of bread sold in cooperatives is going down from 12 to 10 rubles, that of shoes from 330 to 275," it would be surprising—unless one was aiming at inciting the population—for it all to be untrue. Things may happen (and they always do) that greatly reduce the significance of the change (for example, bread might become darker, shoes might disappear for a few months from the stores, etc.), but it would be difficult for there to be nothing to it at all. Likewise, insofar as they constitute a numerous group, and thus insofar as their relatives and acquaintances constitute a considerable proportion of the population, the promise to free all nonpolitical detainees sentenced to less than a certain number of years has to be accompanied by a certain number of actual releases, if only to create among those who do not see their friends and loved ones return the impression that they belong to a "special" category.

Other, apparently more "substantial," data lead us in the same direction, but they raise some questions of interpretation. In the trade agreements with countries from the American bloc, which have increased in number over the past year, the Russians are now including many more consumer articles than heretofore was the case. They thus are trying to improve the supply of these articles in Russia. But to what extent are these articles intended to go to workers rather than to the privileged strata of the country? On the other hand, according to official Russian statistics, the number of workers jumped an unprecedented amount in 1953; taking into account other possible factors for this change, we may conclude that around a million concentration camp prisoners now are counted among the paid work force. But does that mean that they actually have been freed? We must recall in this connection that it is practically impossible to find them again in Russian population statistics.

But the most important thing in judging what is of importance—the overall situation of the Russian bloc—is not the reality of reforms but the fact that they have been proclaimed at all. Even if all this is just a matter of demagogy pure and simple, the simple fact that the Russian bureaucracy has been obliged to have recourse to such demagogy has a fundamental significance. We have here something new. Obviously not the recourse to demagogy in itself. From its very beginning the bureaucracy has not been able to exist without mystification. Abroad, the emphasis has always been on the absolute degree of well-being achieved till that time; we were told how the Russian worker has been freed from exploitation. Domestically, the emphasis has always been on improvements in "tomorrow's" standard of living—once industrialization has been achieved; once the first, then the second, then the third plan has been carried out; once the Stalinist transformation of nature has been effectuated, etc. "Tomorrow there will be free lunches," Stalin almost had written in his text for the Nineteenth Party Congress. The radical change is that now Malenkov is obliged to say, "Today we will eat a little better," and that he has been forced to recognize at least implicitly that till now the worker has been sacrificed completely and that the situation requires some immediate improvements.

Even if the change is only apparent, then, to a certain degree it is real; even if the bureaucracy does not grant all that it promises, it is obliged to say that it will grant something right away. And this by itself points to the origin of the factors that have determined this turnabout. The first and most fundamental factor undoubtedly is the growing reaction among the working population against the overexploitation and oppression to which they have been subjected. Under the conditions of totalitarian terror prevailing in Russia, this reaction cannot be expressed in the same way in which it is expressed in a "democratic" country, but this in no way means that it cannot be expressed at all. There is nothing to prevent strikes from exploding from time to time in some town or factory, collective movements of protest from taking place in some workshop—all of these manifestations being ones about which, by definition, we can know nothing. On the other hand, there are not only overt and explicit manifestations of the class struggle that the bureaucracy is obliged to take into account; it is even more affected by the daily, muted struggle within production itself: noncooperation, workers' resistance to production as it becomes materialized in such phenomena as absenteeism, shoddy workmanship, damaged machinery, a reduction of work effort to the very minimum, etc. The bureaucracy reacts at once to all this by employing classical capitalist methods: increased mechanization of production, piecework or other forms of output-based wages, and fines, but also by means it has created, which are its original contribution to the history of labor exploitation, e.g., Stakhanovism, proliferation of supervisory positions, "criminal" penalties inflicted upon recalcitrant workers ("economic crimes"). That none of these counterresponses is permanently effective is quite obvious, for the worker's allegiance to the production process will be won only on the day exploitation is abolished. It therefore is extremely likely that in the face of a growing crisis in labor productivity, in the face of the workers' ever-firmer refusal to cooperate in the production process, the bureaucracy has been led to make concessions, to concede a certain improvement in living standards and to throw in the towel on "economic crimes" (the amnesty).

To this reason we may add two others. First, there is the reaction of the lower and middle strata of the bureaucracy itself against the regime's excesses of terror. Once firmly installed in power and decked out with privileges, the large mass of bureaucrats must aspire to enjoy these privileges in peace and not under the constant threat of a purge or disgrace; the bureaucracy as a whole without doubt exerts constant pressure against those who hold power at the summits so as to normalize political and legal relations within the bureaucracy and to guarantee to each loyal and moderately qualified bureaucrat the enjoyment of his position and a normal career. This pressure is bound to become objectively stronger as the bureaucracy becomes more stabilized in its dominant position and subjectively stronger as the bureaucrat feels less and less like a usurper of power and more and more like a ruler by divine right.

The arbitrariness of the 1935-40 purges could be accepted by the bureaucrats to the extent that they themselves had arrived in their place by a similar arbitrariness and very often, as it happened, by the occurrence of a previous purge. But more and more the bureaucracy is made up of people who are where they are by virtue of normal developments, or because their fathers were bureaucrats already. These bureaucrats very probably think it is the Politburo that owes its existence to them and not they who owe their existence to the Politburo. And their reaction against the total arbitrariness of the supreme authorities gradually has to assert itself.

Finally, there are the difficulties the Russian bureaucracy encounters in its effort to integrate and assimilate the satellite countries. These difficulties are themselves of three different orders. In the first place, there are the temporary difficulties inherent in the process of converting countries of a classical capitalist or backward structure to a bureaucratic structure: resistance from peasants, the expropriated petty bourgeoisie, and middle-level functionaries of the old bourgeois society; the difficulties of creating in a short time a totally centralized economy from the top down in countries that are, generally speaking, the most backward. In the second place, there are the underlying contradictions inherent in the bureaucratic capitalist regime itself: first of all, the reaction of the workers, who are mystified at the beginning by "nationalizations," "popular" power, the construction of "socialism," etc., but who gradually discover behind this mask the hideous and well-known face of exploitation and oppression. In the last place, there are the "autonomistic" tendencies of national bureaucracies. Certainly these tendencies vary in their intensity from country to country and according to the concrete conditions present. In some cases, at least, they have been able to continue growing, but only insofar as, from the outset, these national bureaucracies relied only indirectly upon the Red Army or received only the indirect support of Moscow, and only insofar as, eight years later, they have been able to establish an economic base of their own and to gain some stability for themselves on the national level.

All these factors, of course, act upon each other too: Along with their exploitation by their own "national" bureaucracy, the satellite countries are subjected to additional exploitation by the Russian bureaucracy. The more intense this latter exploitation is, the more difficult it is (everything else being equal) for the national bureaucracy to extract from "its" workers and peasants the surplus value that is to revert to it; thus, the more it has to turn against them, and the more their reactions do or can become violent. Just as a colonial bourgeoisie lines up against the dominant imperialist power, a satellite bureaucracy has its own economic reasons for lining up against the dominant bureaucracy and for trying to limit the latter's additional exploitation of the country. But in the case of a "communist" national bureaucracy, its fate is inexorably tied up with the fate of the Russian bureaucracy to an even greater degree than the fate of a colonial bourgeoisie is tied up with the fate of the bourgeoisie of the imperialist power that dominates it.

But all these factors, it rightly can be said, have existed and have been in effect for a long time. Why have the changes that they had to entail appeared all of a sudden and so abruptly? And why in 1953?

First of all, not only is it likely that the reactions mentioned here had to continue to grow in intensity, but also that their rate of growth had to increase much more rapidly in the course of the last few years. Let us consider first the workers' attitude toward exploitation. During the first five-year plans (before 1940), the mystification of the plans conceivably played well with a large proportion of the workers: Industrialization was under way, one had to go without for a period of time in order to build factories. Then the war came and half of what had been built up was destroyed. One had to rebuild. But in 1950, the regime officially proclaimed that reconstruction was complete. It would be silly to attach any special importance to this date and to this proclamation, but for the last few years it certainly must have been impossible to continue mystifying the population with the same old arguments. By presenting war as more or less imminent, not only was it shown all the more clearly that the population's standard of living was to a certain extent a function of a given level of armaments and therefore of a political orientation that could be changed, but it also looked like they would have to start the whole thing over again: tightening their belts to build factories that once again would be destroyed, and then tightening their belts another notch to rebuild them again. The "joyful tomorrows" kept being put off, without any material necessity now being able to justify their postponement. Likewise, in the satellite countries, a few years after the old capitalist class was totally expropriated—this having been accomplished around 1948-49—a phase of rapid reawakening had to start up. Indeed, we have already indicated the reasons that make us believe that, for the Russian bureaucracy, daring to stand up against the Politburo had to be a relatively new phenomenon, and the same goes for the bureaucracy of certain satellite countries.

Another factor whose impact also increases with time gradually changes the meaning of working-class reactions and the importance the regime is obliged to attribute to them. This factor involves the advances production itself is undergoing, in particular the phenomena of industrialization and modernization. To use a crude but clear example, one can get a canal dug by brandishing a whip but one cannot get electronic calculators built in the same way. The increasing mechanization of production in no way signifies the total elimination of the human element, and there is a point at which the kind of collaboration in the production process that can be assured by material or economic coercion in its harshest form no longer suffices, for the nature of the products and of the production methods has changed. At this point, the regime—whether Russian or American—is obliged for a while to make real concessions to the worker.

This consideration holds equally well for the mass of the bureaucracy. The bureaucracy ensures the coordination of production, but only terror ensures the coordination of the bureaucracy. The resulting wastefulness is immense. Limiting bureaucratic waste while also maintaining the bureaucracy as the managing authority of the production process cannot be achieved without restoring to the bureaucrats a minimum of freedom and security.

Concessions within the system therefore sooner or later became inevitable. The workers had to be given something real. Squeezed more and more between Moscow's requirements and the resistance of the population, the bureaucracy's position in the satellite countries had to be alleviated a little—under penalty of encouraging the "Titoist" tendencies always potentially present within these bureaucracies. Finally, the summit of the bureaucracy had to make a few concessions to the very class from which it arises and of which it is the expression.

All this also necessarily has implied a turnabout on the international level. Limited as these concessions were, any real concessions on the masses' standard of living entailed a reorientation of production. And they were possible only at the expense of a real reduction in the level of armaments; such a reduction would be absurd without an effort to reduce international tension and to come to some form of *modus vivendi* with the West.

Perhaps the change would have taken place under Stalin if he had lived longer; perhaps it would have taken place earlier if power had changed hands sooner. These speculations are not of interest. What is important is to understand that the underlying factors determining this turnabout already had been in operation for some time. In a regime of total absolutism, it is understandable that a change in direction takes place at the point where the person of the despot changes, even if this change had become necessary a long time before. In this sense, the reigns of absolute monarchs often have marked off distinct periods; the team exercising power becomes sclerotic, and the successor, even if he is closely associated with this team, often has a less remote view of reality. To all this is added the need of Malenkov's team to consolidate not only the regime in general but its own power against rival bureaucratic groups, through measures that create for it a certain amount of popularity.

Perspectives

Possibilities for a Russo-American Compromise

We have seen that a genuine, even a temporary, stabilization of relations between the two blocs was impossible. At the same time, their situation at present prevents and will continue for some time to prevent the Russians as well as the Americans from returning to accelerated war preparations. "Appeasement" therefore will go on—obviously no one can say for how long. The question whether it will be crowned by an agreement or formal compromise on the two main points of conflict (Indochina and Germany) offers little interest in itself. In any case, even if such a compromise came about, it would endure only as long as the relation of forces that was its basis. Technical or social developments could put it back into question at any instant, just as the overall international situation could. This relation of forces is what matters, not its juridico-diplomatic expression on a scrap of paper. But since the discussions and palavers about this topic have taken center stage over the past year, since they are an instrument of mystification used by both the Stalinists and the bourgeoisie, it is worth the effort to examine the chances for such a compromise.

For several reasons the chances are extremely thin. First of all, taken separately, neither the problem of Indochina nor that of Germany can have a "halfway" solution; the partitioning of Vietnam is impossible, the scuttling of the

Vietminh is as unacceptable for the Russians as "free" elections are for the West. The unification of Germany would imply for the Russians the loss of their zone while it is doubtful that the "neutralization" of the country (which is unacceptable both to the Americans and to German capitalists) would be sufficient to get them to agree. A combined solution to the two problems hardly seems feasible. The evacuation of Indochina, combined with the rearmament of a unified Germany, would provoke a deep political crisis in France and probably also in England, while the opposite solution—Russia's abandonment of Indochina in return for a neutralization of Germany—would meet with the opposition of German capitalism. Indeed, neither of these formulas would be acceptable to the Russians, who hold a third of Germany and the certainty of victory in Indochina and have no reason to sacrifice one for the other.

The incessant modification of the situation—not after the conclusion of an agreement, but before it is concluded and during the negotiations themselves—is another important factor. The Vietminh's redoubled efforts in light of the Geneva Conference, the Americans' intensive use of thermonuclear explosions, and the hardening of their position following the success of these explosions abundantly illustrate this factor. The actual givens for the negotiations thus are constantly being altered. Moreover, the idea that more such changes might occur in the near future renders all genuine negotiations nearly impossible, since it suggests that by waiting one might obtain better terms. The example of the EDC is typical in this regard; the Russians expect French opposition to the treaty to render a vote on it impossible, and all their "proposals" are aimed at nothing but reinforcing this opposition until this treaty is rejected—in which case their previous proposals obviously would become null and void, and they would be able to negotiate from a new, more advantageous position.

It is therefore likely that we will witness a prolongation of the present situation rather than a temporary "settlement" of relations between the two blocs. The diplomatic chitchat will continue to roll along the surface while the real factors resolve the problems in question, whether it is a matter of Indochina or of German rearmament.

The solution probably will be given "by itself"; the Vietminh will control Indochina more and more, the Americans will rearm Germany, if not through the EDC, then under another form. It would be incorrect, however, to conclude that such a "solution" is a real solution, for a Stalinist victory in Indochina, German rearmament, or both at once would constitute in themselves new factors that would engender other changes in the situation. It is even possible that they will mark the end of the present period of "appeasement."

The Present Situation of the Two Blocs

We still are not at that point. The internal contradictions analyzed here, which have forced the slowdown in the race toward war, continue to operate in the same direction and will continue to do so in the immediate future.

The factors we have analyzed in the Eastern bloc are in their very essence permanent and ongoing. But their acuity and above all the manner in which the bureaucracy can respond to them vary. There is a limit to the concessions the Russian bureaucracy, pressed by its need to accumulate, to build up arms and to take care of its own unproductive consumption, can make to the proletariat. At the same time, these concessions have a double edge. In certain cases they can result in increased working-class demands. Indeed, in general they serve as an example to workers in Russian bloc countries (e.g., East Germany), and they lead directly to the idea that resistance to exploitation is profitable. Certainly, one day or another these factors will lead the Russian bureaucracy to reverse its policy. In the meantime, as long as it is obliged to drop some ballast on the domestic side and as long as the Eastern bloc's own development permits it to do so, by necessity it will have to limit its arms buildup and conduct a foreign policy that corresponds to such a limitation.

This tendency is reinforced within the Eastern bloc by the economic problems posed by China. For the Chinese bureaucracy, the rapid industrialization of the country is a question of life or death; its primary need is accumulation, not an arms buildup. Only through rapid industrialization can the Chinese bureaucracy annihilate the bourgeoisie economically (after having done so politically), subjugate the peasantry, and strive to limit Russian tutelage. The economic aid Moscow can furnish to China obviously is disproportional to this huge country's capital needs, which can only be satisfied through a kind of primitive accumulation similar to what took place in Russia between 1927 and 1940 and whose active phase still has not begun. Therefore the Chinese bureaucracy, too, probably will attempt to avoid foreign entanglements for a while.

The situation within the Eastern bloc also will ensure for some time the continuation of the present policy. Reductions in armament expenditures, begun in 1953, are becoming even more marked and no doubt will continue. In any big country today, it is not politically possible to force upon the population a reduction of its standard of living in order to finance an arms buildup. It is even more clear that the lowering of tensions in Russo-American relations magnifies conflicts within the Atlantic "coalition"; the French bourgeoisie's growing opposition to Bonn's German rearmament policy (now that the "Cossack obsession" has subsided) is the most striking example of this tendency.

Of course, beneath the apparent "stability" of economic and political relations within the Western bloc, the factors that prepare new crises are always at work, and thus mark out the limits of the present situation. We need only recall that Western capitalism still has not been able to resolve either the problem of economic fluctuations ("crises") or the problem of the relations between the various national economies.[15] And the slowdown in rearmament runs the risk of raising these problems again in a more aggravated manner. The recession that has been growing since the summer of 1953 in the United States shows that American capitalism has gotten out of the problems raised by military spending increases only to enter into other problems created by the lowering of these expenditures. And the aggravation of the dollar-shortage problems of other countries (which first of all runs the risk of bringing on a recession, and then the reduction of military expenditures abroad) again postpones the prospect of reestablishing the convertibility of currencies and free trade between capitalist countries. None of these problems is organically insoluble for these exploiters, but their solution is possible only at the price of a structural transformation—suppression of the market economy, complete integration of the economy of the satellite countries into that of the United States—the political and social conditions for which are still far from being established. Further crises will be required in order to establish them.

Working-Class Struggles: The Bureaucratic Parties and the Vanguard

Elsewhere we have shown the importance of the change in international circumstances in launching working-class struggles in 1953.[16] We can limit ourselves here to stating that the conditions favorable to these struggles still exist and will without doubt exist in the coming period: The lessening of international tensions will continue in effect and will make it nearly impossible for either side to exploit these working-class battles for political purposes. The concessions Eastern European regimes can grant, while insufficient to blunt the workers' demands, are just enough to teach them that active opposition to exploitation alone can improve their lot. This has long been known in Western Europe, and the problem that presents itself is how to constitute a working-class leadership group independent of the bureaucracy. This is the question to which the following pages are devoted. It would be impossible to answer this question, however, without a preliminary analysis of the policy of the bureaucratic parties, both Stalinist and reformist, as well as an analysis of the ideological development of the vanguard of the working class.

From 1948 to 1953, the attitude of bureaucratic organizations was fundamentally determined by the ongoing effort to use the sectors of the working class over which they had control for their own immediate political ends. The proletariat was mobilized and its struggles were directed—either actively or passively—merely in order to serve the political maneuvers of the Stalinists or the reformists.

The Stalinists, for example, tried to get the workers to strike against Ridgway, independent of any other considerations—so independent of everything else that it was absurd. This failed attempt has used up for good the Stalinist's influence with the proletariat, thus wasting the capital Stalinism might have used more profitably on another occasion and in the longer term. It also ended up taking away from these very demonstrations all of their effectiveness, since in the end the workers, even Stalinist workers, no longer bothered to participate in them at all. It even let the bourgeoisie profit from the situation inasmuch as the failure of such attempts furnished the bourgeoisie with a proof—and the bourgeois press and bourgeois governments made ample use of such proof—of Stalinism's inability to mobilize the masses around its political slogans and allowed the bourgeoisie to go on the offensive with much greater assurance. The extremism of the Stalinists on "political" questions was combined with its strike-breaking attitude when it came to economic questions. While no effort was spared when it came to a strike on the Atlantic Treaty, a strike on working-class economic demands was carefully sabotaged by commission or omission.

They did this to give assurances of social tranquillity to the middle classes and to the "neutralist" faction of employers whom they wanted to win over to a policy of "national independence." They also sabotaged strikes on account of the bureaucracy's growing inability to have bureaucratic control over struggles waged by workers who were less and less willing to accept its tutelage.

This attitude had its counterpart in the attitude of reformist bureaucrats. For them it was a matter before all else of defending the regime, of protecting the bosses as much as they could and of opposing Stalinists and any movements where the latter played an active role, even when the character of the demands in these movements could not easily be reproached. Under the combined influence of these factors, the reformist leaders in France staged from 1948 to 1953 one of the purest performances of strike breaking in their history, however rich in examples of this kind their history is; they were transformed into paid agents—in the ordinary, material meaning of this phrase—of the French bosses and of American agencies.

Thus, the policy of both sets of bureaucratic organizations objectively ended up making working-class struggles impossible since it created and constantly renewed divisions within the working class. And these divisions were along lines that were fundamentally foreign to its basic interests. It sufficed, in short, for the Stalinist organization to initiate a movement or participate in it for the reformists to sabotage it, and vice versa.

This policy has been catastrophic for working-class struggles right now, but it has had a profoundly positive result for the long term. It has been the principal factor in helping to demystify workers about these organizations, since day after day it has demonstrated to them that such organizations have nothing to do with the proletariat's interests; they pay no attention to these interests for they pursue rather their own policies. The nature of bureaucratic organizations thus was unmasked in the eyes of large sections of the working-class masses—and no longer, as was the case before, just in the eyes of a small minority of workers in the vanguard. The immediate corollary of this consciousness raising has been the rapid drop in the bureaucratic organizations' influence over the working class, which manifests itself less through lowered vote totals in political and union elections or even through drops in union membership enrollment than through the workers' refusal to follow the bureaucracy into action.

We have said that this policy was leading to absurd results even from the bureaucracy's own point of view (this is clear in the Stalinists' case as well as in the case of the reformists). The principal result was precisely this drop in influence. One could have said that it would have been more "intelligent" for the Stalinists not to have pushed too hard in this direction, not to throw away their influence over the working class like this. But that is just an abstract argument that assumes there is a general staff that decides the best tactics to follow independent of all pressure and of the entire chain of actual events.

Now, the Stalinist leadership here is the executant in France of Moscow's world policy. Its orientation is determined by the general needs of the Russian bloc and not by a concern to increase its influence within the proletariat to the maximum extent; the latter is only one of the elements entering into its considerations, and it is not the principal one. In any case, during the present period of time the Stalinist bureaucracy could come to power in France only by the force of Russian arms and never by a national coup d'Etat. In formulating its strategy, therefore, it can attribute to the proletariat only a secondary role of clearly secondary importance: to create a permanent diversion on the Western capitalist class's home front and to aid, through guerrilla operations (in the proper sense of this term), the advance of Russian divisions when war does come. In a period of growing international tensions, like that of 1948-52, it was out of the question for the Stalinist leadership to "capitalize" any further in France. Instead, it had to expend its capital. If, in the end, there was war, it would be imperative for this leadership to use its potentialities as intensively as possible. And if a compromise should be achieved, one would have time to reconsider things and to recuperate the forces expended during this period. Even within the confines of this outlook, which is basically correct from its own standpoint, the Stalinist leadership showed it was not above committing errors, and in particular the typically bureaucratic mistake of underestimating the workers' level of awareness and the extent of its real (and not merely its electoral) loss of influence over them. But this does not at all change the fact that its orientation was strictly imposed upon it by the overall situation and by the trend toward war. The same thing holds, *mutatis mutandis*, for the leadership of reformist groups, in France as well as in countries (like England or West Germany) where it practically has a monopoly over working-class "representation."

From this point of view, recent changes might mean that the bureaucratic organizations henceforth have much more latitude in their game, since their masters will not force them in the coming period to subordinate everything else to mobilizing the workers on political issues for the benefit of one bloc or the other. One might infer from this, as a first approximation, that the Stalinists' and reformists' main efforts during the present, open period would be to win back their influence over the proletariat. And to do this, they would have only one means: to follow a "correct" attitude on economic demands, to try to appear in reality and not just in their statements as the "best defenders of working-class interests."

This argument, however, is not worth very much. For, a number of factors — some of which are circumstantial, others permanent and deep-rooted — extremely reduce the bureaucratic organizations' margin for free action, even in the coming period. And in particular, these factors make it extremely unlikely that a change in their attitude toward working-class struggles would be profitable for them.

This is clearly the case with the Stalinists. First of all, the CP certainly will continue to try to play its role on the bourgeois political chessboard. The lessening of international tensions has not signified and will not signify the end of the integration of France and of the other Western European countries into the American bloc. But it will signify a renewed influence for those sections of the French bourgeoisie (and their political spokespeople) that would like to lessen this degree of integration. Therefore, it will reinforce at the same time the CP's attempts to drive a wedge into Franco-U.S. relations and to reinforce the "neutralist" wing of the French bourgeoisie. It even will give a certain real basis to such attempts.[17]

From what is apparently a completely different angle, we see that it is still possible that the CP will be led to oppose the working class's economic demands. Yesterday it did so in order to struggle for "peace"; today it may do so in order not to disturb it.

But this factor is neither the most deep-seated nor the most important. The example of the Stalinists' sabotage of the Renault strike in September 1953 suffices to point this out.[18] How can this sabotage be explained? If things got going at Renault, it was very likely that the movement would spread to all metal workers. With millions of public-service workers already on strike, this development might have led the Stalinists much further than they wanted to go. At a subsequent stage it could pose for them a catastrophic dilemma: to be out front in their opposition to the extension, deepening, and continuation of the strike — thus showing their true character on an unprecedented scale — or else to start an all-out battle in France, sure in advance that they would lose it at a moment not of their own choosing, when, on the contrary, their overall policy worldwide was heading in the opposite direction. Their control of Renault, the strategic point, allowed them to forestall such a development. But they barely got out of it by the skin of their teeth. This example is instructive, for it contains all the elements of the present situation. Every working-class struggle that reaches a certain size (and thus every working-class struggle that would have the chance to be effective, even from the narrowest economic point of view) would pose the same problem for the Stalinists and would probably give rise on their part to the same counterresponse: sabotaging the strike, quietly if possible, out front, if necessary.

This factor is closely related to another, even more important one. It has not always been impossible for the bureaucracy to direct effective working-class struggles through its own methods, but this is becoming more and more the case. To the extent the workers become aware of the bureaucracy's true character or just begin distrusting it, it becomes increasingly important for them to lead these struggles by themselves. In practice this often even becomes a condition for their participation or their active support.

Indeed, this profound scission between the bureaucratic "leaders" and the working-class masses also is becoming clear on the level of formulating demands. Here the bureaucracy, for reasons that are organically related to it, inevitably will support, for instance, a hierarchy of wages, even though class-conscious workers more and more are tending to line up against such a divisive system. Thus, even if the bureaucracy wanted to play the role of an "effective" leader of labor struggles, to an increasing degree the workers' growing awareness prevents this from happening.

As for the reformists, in France at least their case offers no interest. Their weakness and rottenness are such that in the main they can do no more than continue to play the same old role of scabs and strike breakers that they have played up till now. The case of the English Labour party, or of German social democracy is different, but in the last analysis they meet the same deep-seated contradictions in their relations with the proletariat as those we have just analyzed for the Stalinists.

It is therefore likely that the masses' will to struggle will encounter in the coming period the same degree of overt or underhanded opposition on the part of the bureaucracies. Under such conditions, the role of the vanguard of the working class assumes utmost practical importance. And we should not hide the fact that we discover here the difficulties that the resumption of the workers' movement will encounter.

There exists in France a stratum of workers (certainly a minority, but in no way negligible) that has become aware of the problem of bureaucracy. For them, Stalinism's character as alien and hostile to the proletariat is clear for the same reason that reformism's total integration into the bourgeois system is clear. But in addition, criticism of the mystification of Stalinism has gone hand in hand for them (how could it be otherwise?) with a crisis in the traditional objectives and program of the revolutionary movement, and even of the very notion of a revolutionary workers' organization. Indeed, understanding the exploitative and oppressive character of the Russian State, for example, was bound to bring with it a questioning of traditional notions of what the objectives of the revolution should be: In brief, to recognize that Russia is not a workers' State means to recognize that the nationalization of factories and the dictatorship of a party that claims to be working class is not sufficient to change the deep-seated nature of an exploitative society. Likewise, to understand that reformist trade unions are not by accident but by nature serving capitalism and that the Stalinist trade unions are serving Russia means one understands that the trade-union form of organization is no longer a working-class form of organization.

But to grasp what the ends and means of the working-class movement are *not* does not yet mean that one understands what in reality and affirmatively they are. Therefore, at the same time that this vanguard is clear about the character of the bureaucracy, there is a crisis over the most fundamental programmatic notions, and therefore also the temporary impossibility of engaging in systematic, organized action. To this is added a doubt about the proletariat's historical capacity to abolish exploitation and to instaurate a classless society. This doubt has been nourished by the defeat of previous revolutions, by the degeneration of the Russian revolution, and quite particularly by the events of the last five years, where both the mystification of the working-class masses by Stalinism and its own demoralization, inaction, and apathy have created in those who belong to this vanguard a certain distrust about the capacity of the working class as a whole to understand and to struggle. For the most part, the result has been a refusal on the part of the members of this vanguard to organize themselves and to act. Sometimes their refusal is even fiercer than that of the masses.

What changes have recent events brought to this situation?

First of all, the ideological obstacles that prevent this vanguard from getting organized and acting evidently have not been eliminated. No more today than before does the objective situation contain the elements that would allow these workers to define for themselves a clear program or to form a proletarian organization.

If somehow spontaneous class action should arise, the problem will be greatly altered. Certain questions (for example: What should the form of organization be? Who should lead these struggles? What should their objectives be?) will be raised immediately by the actual situation itself, even if at the outset in a very narrow form. The most active elements within the class will be led to try to give a practical answer to these questions. They thus will be led to define for themselves the appropriate organizational forms and objectives of action, even if these definitions do not immediately yield a coherent and systematic whole. The working class's reentry into struggle will restore the vanguard's confidence in the working class's capacities, and this, in conjunction with the experience the vanguard has already had of the bureaucracy, will point the vanguard down the path toward a positive solution of the problem of working-class organizational forms, namely, the path toward the autonomous organization of the proletariat and the leadership of the workers by the workers themselves. In this atmosphere, the vanguard will be put back in touch with Marxist thought and ideology, and a process of fusion would take place between it and militants or revolutionary Marxist groups.

Conversely, to the extent that these revolutionary groups will be capable of actually establishing a political presence in events, of helping the vanguard to draw lessons and to generalize from its experience, the development of this experience will be tremendously accelerated. This is why at the present time it is literally of tremendous importance that there be a political rallying point and a revolutionary crystallization of the vanguard. Its absence will weigh heavily on the subsequent development of events.

Starting right now, revolutionary militants can bring to the vanguard of the working class important contributions not only on the ideological and political planes but also on the concrete plane of struggle in the factories. Of course, at the outset only the vanguard itself, and later on only the entire working class, can furnish a definitive solution to these problems. And every solution brought in from the outside that would not correspond to the working class's own experience and deep-seated aspirations would have no echo and no effectiveness. But to the extent that these militants have elaborated these contributions beginning not from personal whims or a priori schemata, but from the working-class experience of the past few years, they will quickly be able to join with the vanguard based in the factories. And conversely, their analysis of the content of workers' demands, forms of struggle, and organizational forms can help to accelerate the crystallization of spontaneous movements in the factories.

Notes

1. See the articles "Socialisme ou Barbarie" (no. 1 [March 1949]), "1948" (ibid.), "La Consolidation temporaire du capitalisme mondial" (no. 3 [July 1949]), "La Guerre et la perspective révolutionnaire" (no. 9 [April 1952]) and the "Notes" on the international situation in nos. 2 (May 1949), 3 (July 1949), 4 (October 1949), 7 (August 1951), 8 (January 1952), 11 (November 1952), 12 (August 1953). [See *SB 1*, and *CMR 1*. T/E: Only the first article appears in the present edition.]

2. See Lenin, "Imperialism, the Highest Stage of Capitalism," in *LSWONE*, p. 235. Obviously, this means that imperialism is not interested *exclusively* in colonial territories; it might be interested in these territories in particular if man power can be exploited there the most intensely (see point 1 in the next paragraph).

3. Ibid., p. 229.

4. Ibid., p. 235.

5. Ibid., p. 239.

6. Proletarian strata, too, of course; but strictly speaking, this aspect is one of the factors that determines the particular rate of exploitation, about which we spoke under the first point.

7. From the narrowly economic point of view, and within the schema of competitive capitalism, the nation is an accident. Everything in this case of economic significance for the nation (geographic boundaries, consumer habits, the rootedness of manpower) is, from the economic point of view, inorganic, imposed by nature or inherited from history. Under monopoly capitalism, in contrast, the nation acquires its own economic meaning: It is the domain of direct exploitation for a group of monopolies, a market under its exclusive control.

8. "Imperialism," p. 256.

9. We have spoken here of the connection between war and the process of concentration only from one viewpoint, the international one. There is a connection from another viewpoint, the "national" viewpoint, which is just as deep-seated and significant; in other words, the conduct of and even the mere preparation for war are powerful levers for capital and power concentration within a country or within a bloc. This will become clear in reading the pages that follow.

10. T/E: Daniel François Malan (1874-1959) was prime minister of South Africa beginning in 1948. He applied a policy of strict apartheid. Perón, of course, is the Argentinian dictator, Juan Perón.

11. Three and ten percent are the percentages generally thought to be the average annual production increases for the United States and Russia, respectively.

12. See the "Note sur la situation internationale," in no. 12 of this review (August 1953), pp. 48-59. [Reprinted in *SB 2*, pp. 157-87. T/E: *Not* included in the present edition.]

13. See the article, "La Consolidation temporaire du capitalisme mondial," in *S. ou B.*, 3 (July 1949). [Now reprinted in *CMR 1*, pp. 217ff. T/E: *Not* included in the present edition. This article was signed by Pierre Chaulieu, i.e., Castoriadis.]

14. T/E: The phrase appears in English in the original French text.

15. That is to say, the decomposition of the traditional world market, which has manifested itself in import quotas and state control over foreign trade, control over foreign currency exchanges and nonconvertibility between different currencies, and, since the war, in the "dollar problem" (generalized shortage of dollars—which have become the international means of payment for most capitalist countries—and limitations on the importation of American products).

16. Issue 13 of *S. ou B.* (January 1954) is devoted almost entirely to the analysis of working-class struggles of 1953 in Germany and France.

17. In a January issue of *Le Monde*, Mr. Duverger alluded sympathetically to the prospect of a government to which the CP would lend its "support without participation." The bases for a compromise that might lead to this possibility are not hard to discern: retreat from Indochina and rejection of the EDC would be swapped for "social peace." That this prospect cannot be fulfilled does not prevent the CP from being able to exert real pressure on the politics of the French bourgeoisie and from taking many steps to join up with the latter. [T/E: Maurice Duverger, *Le Monde*, "Une Majorité de rechange?", February 2, 1954, p. 1.]

18. See "La Grève chez Renault," by Daniel Mothé in *S. ou B.*, 13 (January 1954), pp. 34-45.

13
On the Content of Socialism, I

From the Critique of Bureaucracy
to the Idea of the Proletariat's Autonomy

The ideas set forth in this discussion perhaps will be understood more readily if we retrace the route that has led us to them. Indeed, we started off from positions in which a militant worker or a Marxist inevitably places himself at a certain stage in his development and therefore positions everyone we are addressing has shared at one time or another. And if the conceptions set forth here have any value at all, their development cannot be the result of chance or personal traits but ought to embody an objective logic at work. Providing a description of this development, therefore, can only increase the reader's understanding of the end result and make it easier for him to check it against his experience.[1]

Like a host of other militants in the vanguard, we began with the discovery that the traditional large "working-class" organizations no longer have a revolutionary Marxist politics nor do they represent any longer the interests of the proletariat. The Marxist arrives at this conclusion by comparing the activity of these "socialist" (reformist) or "communist" (Stalinist) organizations with his own theory. He sees the so-called Socialist parties participating in bourgeois governments, actively repressing strikes or movements of colonial peoples, and championing the defense of the capitalist fatherland while neglecting even to make reference to a socialist system of rule. He sees the Stalinist "Communist" parties sometimes carrying out this same opportunistic policy of collaborating with the bourgeoisie and sometimes an "extremist" policy, a violent adventur-

Originally published as "Sur le contenu du socialisme," *S. ou B.*, 17 (July 1955). Reprinted in *CS*, pp. 67-102. Preceding the article was the following note: "This article opens up a discussion on programmatic problems, which will be continued in forthcoming issues of *Socialisme ou Barbarie*."

ism unrelated to a consistent revolutionary strategy. The class-conscious worker makes the same discoveries on the level of his working-class experience. He sees the socialists squandering their energies trying to moderate his class's economic demands, to make any effective action aimed at satisfying these demands impossible, and to substitute interminable discussions with the boss or the State for the strike. He sees the Stalinists at certain times strictly forbidding strikes (as was the case from 1945 to 1947) and even trying to curtail them through violence[2] or frustrating them underhandedly[3] and at other times trying to horsewhip workers into a strike they do not want because they perceive that it is alien to their interests (as in 1951-52, with the "anti-American" strikes). Outside the factory, he also sees the Socialists and the Communists participate in capitalist governments without it changing his lot one bit, and he sees them join forces, in 1936 as well as in 1945, when his class is ready to act and the regime has its back against the wall, in order to stop the movement and save this regime, proclaiming that one must "know to end a strike" and that one must "produce first and make economic demands later."

Once they have established this radical opposition between the attitude of the traditional organizations and a revolutionary Marxist politics expressing the immediate and historical interests of the proletariat, both the Marxist and the class-conscious worker might then think that these organizations "err" [se trompent] or that they "are betraying us." But to the extent that they reflect on the situation, and discover for themselves that reformists and Stalinists behave the same way day after day, that they always and everywhere have behaved in this way, in the past, today, here, and everywhere else, they begin to see that to speak of "betrayal" or "mistakes" does not make any sense. It could be a question of "mistakes" only if these parties pursued the goals of the proletarian revolution with inadequate means, but these means, applied in a coherent and systematic fashion for several dozen years, show simply that the goals of these organizations are not our goals, that they express interests other than those of the proletariat. Once this is understood, saying that they "are betraying us" makes no sense. If, in order to sell his junk, a merchant tells me some load of crap and tries to persuade me that it is in my interest to buy it, I can say that he is trying to deceive me [il me trompe] but not that he is betraying me. Likewise, the Socialist or Stalinist party, in trying to persuade the proletariat that it represents its interests, is trying to deceive it but is not betraying it; they betrayed it once and for all a long time ago, and since then they are not traitors to the working class but consistent and faithful servants of other interests. What we need to do is determine whose interests they serve.

Indeed, this policy does not merely appear consistent in its means or in its results. It is embodied in the leadership stratum of these organizations or trade unions. The militant quickly learns the hard way that this stratum is irremovable, that it survives all defeats, and that it perpetuates itself through co-optation. Whether the internal organization of these groups is "democratic" (as is the case with the reformists) or dictatorial (as is the case with the Stalinists), the mass of militants have absolutely no influence over its orientation, which is determined without further appeal by a bureaucracy whose stability is never put into question; for even when the leadership core should happen to be replaced, it is replaced for the benefit of another, no less bureaucratic group.

At this point, the Marxist and the class-conscious worker are almost bound to collide with Trotskyism.[4] Indeed, Trotskyism has offered a permanent, step-by-step critique of reformist and Stalinist politics for the past quarter century, showing that the defeats of the workers' movement—Germany, 1923; China, 1925-27; England, 1926; Germany, 1933; Austria, 1934; France, 1936; Spain, 1936-38; France and Italy, 1945-47; etc.—are due to the policies of the traditional organizations, and that these policies have constantly been in breach of Marxism. At the same time, Trotskyism[5] offers an explanation of the policies of these parties, starting from a sociological analysis of their makeup. For reformism, it takes up again the interpretation provided by Lenin: The reformism of the socialists expresses the interests of a labor aristocracy (since imperialist surplus profits allow the latter to be "corrupted" by higher wages) and of a trade-union and political bureaucracy. As for Stalinism, its policy serves the Russian bureaucracy, this parasitic and privileged stratum that has usurped power in the first workers' State, thanks to the backward character of the country and the setback suffered by the world revolution after 1923.

We began our critical work, even back when we were within the Trotskyist movement, with this problem of Stalinist bureaucracy. Why we began with that problem in particular needs no long involved explanations. Whereas the problem of reformism seemed to be settled by history, at least on the theoretical level, as it became more and more an overt defender of the capitalist system,[6] on the most crucial problem of all, that of Stalinism—which is *the* contemporary problem par excellence and which in practice weighs on us more heavily than the first—the history of our times has disproved again and again both the Trotskyist viewpoint and the forecasts that have been derived from it. For Trotsky, Stalinist policy is to be explained by the interests of the Russian bureaucracy, a product of the degeneration of the October Revolution. This bureaucracy has no "reality of its own," historically speaking; it is only an "accident," the product of the constantly upset balance between the two fundamental forces of modern society, capitalism and the proletariat. Even in Russia it is based upon the "conquests of October," which had provided socialist bases for the country's economy (nationalization, planning, monopoly over foreign trade, etc.) and upon the perpetuation of capitalism in the rest of the world; for the restoration of private property in Russia would signify the overthrow of the bureaucracy and help bring about the return of the capitalists, whereas the spread of the revolution worldwide would destroy Russia's isolation—the economic and political result of which was the bureaucracy—and would give rise to a new revolutionary explosion of the Russian proletariat, who would chase off these usurpers. Hence the necessarily empirical character of Stalinist politics, which is obliged to waver between two adversaries and makes its objective the utopian maintenance of the status quo; it even is obliged thereby to sabotage every proletarian movement any time the latter endangers the capitalist system and to overcompensate as well for the results of these acts of sabotage with extreme violence every time reactionaries, encouraged by the demoralization of the proletariat, try to set up a dictatorship and prepare a capitalist crusade against "the remnants of the October conquests." Thus, Stalinist parties are condemned to fluctuate between "extremist" adventurism and opportunism.

But neither can these parties nor the Russian bureaucracy remain hanging indefinitely in midair like this. In the absence of a revolution, Trotsky said, the Stalinist parties would become more and more like the reformist parties and more and more attached to the bourgeois order, while the Russian bureaucracy would be overthrown with or without foreign intervention so as to bring about a restoration of capitalism.

Trotsky had tied this prognostication to the outcome of the Second World War. As is well known, this war disproved it in the most glaring terms. The Trotskyist leadership made itself look ridiculous by stating that it was just a matter of time. But it had become apparent to us, even before the war ended, that it was not and could not have been a question of some kind of time lag, but rather of the *direction* of history, and that Trotsky's entire edifice was, down to its very foundations, mythological.

The Russian bureaucracy underwent the critical test of the war and showed it had as much cohesiveness as any other dominant class. If the Russian regime admitted of some contradictions, it also exhibited a degree of stability no less than that of the American or German regime. The Stalinist parties did not go over to the side of the bourgeois order. They have continued to follow Russian policy faithfully (apart, of course, from individual defections, as take place in all parties): They are partisans of national defense in countries allied to the USSR, adversaries of this kind of defense in countries that are enemies of the USSR (we include here the French CP's series of turnabouts in 1939, 1941, and 1947). Finally, the most important and extraordinary thing was that the Stalinist bureaucracy extended its power into other countries; whether it imposed its power on behalf of the Russian army, as in most of the satellite countries of Central Europe and the Balkans, or had complete domination over a confused mass movement, as in Yugoslavia (or later on in China and in Vietnam), it instaurated in these countries regimes that were in every respect similar to the Russian regime (taking into account, of course, local conditions). It obviously was ridiculous to describe these regimes as degenerated workers' States.[7]

From then on, therefore, we were obliged to look into what gave such stability and opportunities for expansion to the Stalinist bureaucracy, both in Russia and elsewhere. To do this, we had to resume the analysis of Russia's economic and social system of rule. Once rid of the Trotskyist outlook, it was easy to see, using the basic categories of Marxism, that Russian society is divided into classes, among which the two fundamental ones are the bureaucracy and the proletariat. The bureaucracy there plays the role of the dominant, exploiting class in the full sense of the term. It is not merely that it is a privileged class and that its unproductive consumption absorbs a part of the social product comparable to (and probably greater than) that absorbed by the unproductive consumption of the bourgeoisie in private capitalist countries. It also has sovereign control over how the total social product will be used. It does this first of all by determining how the total social product will be distributed among wages and surplus value (at the same time that it tries to dictate to the workers the lowest wages possible and to extract from them the greatest amount of labor possible), next by determining how this surplus value will be distributed between its own unproductive consumption and new investments, and finally by determining how these investments will be distributed among the various sectors of production.

But the bureaucracy can control how the social product will be utilized only because it controls production. Because it *manages* production at the factory level, it always can make the workers produce more for the same wage; because it manages production on the societal level, it can decide to manufacture cannons and silk rather than housing and cotton. We discover, therefore, that the essence, the foundation, of its bureaucratic domination over Russian society comes from the fact that it has dominance within the relations of production; at the same time, we discover that this same function always has been the basis for the domination of one class over society. In other words, at every instant the actual essence of class relations in production is the antagonistic division of those who participate in the production process into two fixed and stable categories, directors and executants. Everything else is concerned with the sociological and juridical mechanisms that guarantee the stability of the managerial stratum; that is how it is with feudal ownership of the land, capitalist private property, or this strange form of private, nonpersonal property ownership that characterizes present-day capitalism; that is how it is in Russia with the "Communist Party," the totalitarian dictatorship by the organ that expresses the bureaucracy's general interests and that ensures that the members of the ruling class are recruited through co-optation on the scale of society as a whole.[8]

It follows that planning and the nationalization of the means of production in no way resolve the problem of the class character of the economy, nor do they signify the abolition of exploitation; of course, they entail the abolition of the former dominant classes, but they do not answer the fundamental problem of who now will direct production and how. If a new stratum of individuals takes over this function of direction, "all the old rubbish" Marx spoke about will quickly reappear, for this stratum will use its managerial position to create privileges for itself, it will reinforce its monopoly over managerial functions, in this way tending to make its domination more complete and more difficult to put into question; it will tend to assure the transmission of these privileges to its successors, etc.

For Trotsky, the bureaucracy is not a ruling class since bureaucratic privileges cannot be transmitted by inheritance. But in dealing with this argument, we need only recall (1) that hereditary transmission is in no way an element necessary to establish the category of "ruling class," and (2) that, moreover, it is obvious how, in Russia, membership in the bureaucracy (not, of course, in some particular bureaucratic post) can be passed down; a measure such as the abolition of free secondary education (laid down in 1936) suffices to set up an inexorable sociological mechanism assuring that only the children of bureaucrats will be able to enter into the career of being a bureaucrat. That, in addition, the bureaucracy might want to try (using educational grants or aptitude tests "based upon merit alone") to bring in talented people from the proletariat or the peasantry not only does not contradict but even confirms its character as an exploiting class: Similar mechanisms have always existed in capitalist countries, and their social function is to reinvigorate the ruling stratum with new blood, to mitigate in part the irrationalities resulting from the hereditary character of managerial functions, and to emasculate the exploited classes by corrupting their most gifted members.

It is easy to see that it is not a question here of a problem particular to Russia or to the 1920s. For the same problem is posed in every modern society, even apart from the proletarian revolution; it is just another expression of the process of concentration of the forces of production. What, indeed, creates the *objective* possibility for a bureaucratic degeneration of the revolution? It is the inexorable movement of the modern economy, under the pressure of technique, toward the more and more intense concentration of capital and power, the incompatibility of the actual degree of development of the forces of production with private property and the market as the way in which business enterprises are integrated. This movement is expressed in a host of structural transformations in Western capitalist countries, though we cannot dwell upon that right now. We need only recall that they are socially incarnated in a new bureaucracy, an economic bureaucracy as well as a work-place bureaucracy. Now, by making a *tabula rasa* of private property, of the market, etc., revolution *can*—if it stops at that point—make the route of total bureaucratic concentration easier. We see, therefore, that, far from being deprived of its own reality, bureaucracy personifies the final stage of capitalist development.

Since then it has become obvious that the program of the socialist revolution and the proletariat's objective no longer could be merely the suppression of private property, the nationalization of the means of production and planning, but rather *workers' management* of the economy and of power. Returning to the degeneration of the Russian Revolution, we established that on the economic level the Bolshevik party had as its program not *workers' management* but *workers' control*. This was because the Party, which did not think the revolution could immediately be a socialist revolution, did not even pose for itself the task of expropriating the capitalists, and therefore thought that this latter class would remain as managers in the workplace. Under such conditions, the function of workers' control would be to prevent the capitalists from organizing to sabotage production, to get control over their profits and over the disposition of the product, and to set up a "school" of management for the workers. But this sociological monstrosity of a country where the proletariat exercises its dictatorship through the instrument of the soviets and of the Bolshevik party, and where the capitalists keep their property and continue to direct their enterprises, could not last; where the capitalists had not fled, they were expelled by the workers, who then took over the management of these enterprises.

This first experience of workers' management only lasted a short time; we cannot go into an analysis here of this period of the Russian Revolution (which is quite obscure and about which few sources exist),[a] or of the factors that determined the rapid changeover of power in the factories into the hands of a new managerial stratum. Among these factors are the backward state of the country, the proletariat's numerical and cultural weakness, the dilapidated condition of the productive apparatus, the long civil war with its unprecedented violence, and the international isolation of the revolution. There is one factor whose effect during this period we wish to emphasize: In its actions, the Bolshevik party's policy was systematically opposed to workers' management and tended from the start to set up its own apparatus for directing production, solely responsible to the central power, i.e., in the last analysis, to the Party. This was done in the name of efficiency and the overriding necessities brought on by the civil war. Whether this policy was the most effective one even in the short term is open to question; in any case, in the long run it laid the foundations for bureaucracy.

If the management [*direction*] of the economy thus eluded the proletariat, Lenin thought the essential thing was for the power of the soviets to preserve for the workers at least the leadership [*direction*] of the State. On the other hand, he thought that by participating in the management of the economy through work-ers' control, trade unions, and so on, the working class would gradually "learn" to manage. Nevertheless, a series of events that cannot be retraced here, but that were inevitable, quickly made the Bolshevik party's domination over the soviets irreversible. From this point onward, the proletarian character of the whole sys-tem hinged on the proletarian character of the Bolshevik party. We could easily show that under such conditions the Party, a highly centralized minority with monopoly control over the exercise of power, no longer would be able to pre-serve even its proletarian character (in the strong sense of this term), and that it was bound to separate itself from the class from which it had arisen. But there is no need to go as far as that. In 1923, "the Party numbered 50,000 workers and 300,000 functionaries in its total of 350,000 members. It no longer was a work-ers' party but a party of workers-turned-functionaries."[9] Bringing together the "elite" of the proletariat, the Party had been led to install this elite in the com-mand posts of the economy and the State; hence this elite had to be accountable only to the Party, i.e., to itself. The working class's "apprenticeship" in man-agement merely signified that a certain number of workers, who were learning managerial techniques, left the rank and file and passed over to the side of the new bureaucracy. As people's social existence determines their consciousness, the Party members were going to act from then on, not according to the Bolshe-vik program, but in terms of their concrete situation as privileged managers of the economy and the State. The trick has been played, the revolution has died, and if there is something to be surprised about, it is rather how long it took for the bureaucracy to consolidate its power.[10]

The conclusions that follow from this brief analysis are clear: The program of the socialist revolution can be nothing other than *workers' management*. Workers' management of power, i.e., the power of the masses' autonomous organizations (soviets or councils); workers' management of the economy, i.e., the producers' direction of production, also organized in soviet-style organs. The proletariat's objective cannot be nationalization and planning without anything more, be-cause that would signify that the domination of society would be handed over to a new stratum of rulers and exploiters; it cannot be achieved by handing over power to a party, however revolutionary and however proletarian this party might be at the outset, because this party inevitably will tend to exercise this power on its own behalf and will be used as the nucleus for the crystallization of a new ruling stratum. Indeed, in our time the problem of the division of society into classes appears more and more in its most direct and naked form, and stripped of all juridical cover, as the problem of the division of society into directors and executants. The proletarian revolution carries out its historical program only insofar as it tends from the very beginning to abolish this division by reabsorbing every particular managerial stratum and by *collectivizing*, or more exactly by *completely socializing*, the functions of direction. The problem of the proletariat's historical capacity to achieve a classless society is not the problem of its capacity to physically overthrow the exploiters who are in power (of this there is no doubt); it is rather the problem of how to positively organize a collective, socialized management of production and power. From then on it becomes obvious that the realization of socialism on the proletariat's behalf by any party or bureaucracy whatsoever is an absurdity, a contradiction in terms, a square circle, an underwater bird; socialism is nothing but the masses' conscious and perpetual self-managerial activity. It becomes equally obvious that socialism cannot be "objectively" inscribed, not even halfway, in any law or constitution, in the nationalization of the means of production, or in planning, nor even in a "law" instaurating workers' management: If the working class cannot manage, no law can give it the power to do so, and if it does manage, such a "law" would merely ratify this existing state of affairs.

Thus, beginning with a critique of the bureaucracy, we have succeeded in formulating a positive conception of the content of socialism; briefly speaking, "socialism in all its aspects does not signify anything other than worker's management of society," and "the working class can free itself only by achieving power for itself." The proletariat can carry out the socialist revolution only if it acts autonomously, i.e., if it finds in itself both the will and the consciousness for the necessary transformation of society. Socialism can be neither the fated result of historical development, a violation of history by a party of supermen, nor still the application of a program derived from a theory that is true in itself. Rather, it is the unleashing of the free creative activity of the oppressed masses. Such an unleashing of free creative activity is made *possible* by historical development, and the action of a party based on *this* theory can *facilitate* it to a tremendous degree.

Henceforth it is indispensable to develop on every level the consequences of this idea.

Marxism and the Idea of the Proletariat's Autonomy

We must say right off that there is nothing essentially new about this conception. Its meaning is the same as Marx's celebrated formulation "The emancipation of the workers must be conquered by the workers themselves."[11] It was expressed likewise by Trotsky: "Socialism, as opposed to capitalism, consciously builds itself up." It would be only too easy to pile up quotations of this kind.

What is new is the will and ability to take this idea in total seriousness while drawing out the theoretical as well as the practical implications. This could not be done till now, either by us or by the great founders of Marxism. For, on the one hand, the necessary historical experience was lacking; the preceding analysis shows the tremendous importance the degeneration of the Russian Revolution possesses for the clarification of the problem of workers' power. And on the other hand, and at a deeper level, revolutionary theory and practice in an exploiting society are subjected to a crucial contradiction that results from the fact that they belong to this society they are trying to abolish. This contradiction is expressed in an infinite number of ways.

Only one of these ways is of interest to us here. To be revolutionary signifies both to think that only the masses in struggle can resolve the problem of socialism and not to fold one's arms for all that; it means to think that the essential content of the revolution will be given by the masses' creative, original, and unforeseeable activity, and to act oneself, beginning with a rational analysis of the present and with a perspective that anticipates the future.[12] In the last analysis, it means to postulate that the revolution will signify an overthrow and a tremendous enlargement of our present form of rationality and to utilize this same rationality in order to anticipate the content of the revolution.

How this contradiction is relatively resolved and relatively posed anew at each stage of the workers' movement up to the ultimate victory of the revolution, cannot detain us here; this is the whole problem of the concrete dialectic of the historical development of the proletariat's revolutionary action and of revolutionary theory. At this time we need only establish that there is an intrinsic difficulty in developing a revolutionary theory and practice in an exploiting society, and that, insofar as he wants to overcome this difficulty, the theoretician—and, likewise indeed, the militant—risks falling back unconsciously on the terrain of bourgeois thought, and more generally on the terrain of the type of thought that issues from an alienated society and that has dominated humanity for millennia. Thus, in the face of the problems posed by the new historical situation, the theoretician often will be led to "reduce the unknown to the known," for that is what theoretical activity today consists of. He thereby either cannot see that it is a question of a new type of problem or, even if he does see that, he can only apply to it solutions inherited from the past. Nevertheless, the factors whose revolutionary importance he has just recognized or even discovered—modern technique and the activity of the proletariat—tend not only to create new kinds of solutions but to destroy the very terms in which problems previously had been posed. From then on, solutions of the traditional type provided by the theoretician will not simply be inadequate; insofar as they are adopted (which implies that the proletariat too remains under the hold of received ideas) they objectively will be the instrument for maintaining the proletariat within the framework of exploitation, although perhaps under a different form.

Marx was aware of this problem. His refusal of "utopian" socialism and his statement that "every step of real movement is more important than a dozen programs" express precisely his distrust of "bookish" solutions, since the latter are always separate from the living development of history. Nevertheless, there remains in Marxism a significant share (which has kept on growing in succeeding generations of Marxists) of a bourgeois or "traditional" ideological legacy. To this extent, there is an ambiguity in theoretical Marxism, an ambiguity that has played an important historical role; the exploiting society thereby has been able to exert its influence on the proletariat movement from within. The case analyzed earlier, where the Bolshevik party in Russia applied traditionally effective solutions to the problem of how to direct production, offers a dramatic illustration of this process; traditional solutions have been effective in the sense that they effectively have brought back the traditional state of affairs or have led to the restoration of exploitation under new forms. Later we will come upon other important instances of bourgeois ideas surviving within Marxism. It is useful nevertheless to discuss now an example that will bring to light what we are trying to say.

How will labor be remunerated in a socialist economy? It is well known that in the "Critique of the Gotha Programme," where he distinguishes the organizational form of this postrevolutionary society (the "lower stage of communism") from communism itself (where the principle "from each according to his abilities, to each according to his needs" would reign), Marx spoke of the "bourgeois right" that would prevail during this phase. He understood by that equal pay for an equal quantity and quality of labor—which can mean unequal pay for different individuals.[13]

How can this principle be justified? One begins with the basic characteristics of the socialist economy, namely that, on the one hand, this economy is still an economy of scarcity where, consequently, it is essential that the production efforts of society's members be pushed to the maximum; and on the other hand, that people still are dominated by the "egoistic" mentality inherited from the preceding society and maintained by this state of scarcity. The greatest amount of effort in production therefore is required at the same time that this society needs to struggle against the "natural" tendency to shirk work that still exists at this stage. It will be said, therefore, that it is necessary, if one wants to avoid disorder and famine, to make the remuneration of labor proportional to the quality and quantity of the labor provided, measured, for example, by the number of pieces manufactured, the number of hours in attendance, etc., which naturally leads to zero remuneration for zero work and in the same stroke settles the problem of one's obligation to work. In short, one ends up with some sort of "output-based wage."[14] Depending on how clever one is, one will reconcile this conclusion, with greater or lesser ease, with the harsh criticism to which this form of wage payment has been subjected when it is applied within the capitalist system.

Doing this, one will have purely and simply forgotten that the problem no longer can be posed in these terms: Both modern technique and the forms of association among workers that socialism implies render it null and void. Whether it is a matter of working on an assembly line or of piecework on "individual" machines, the individual laborer's work pace is dictated by the work pace of the unit to which he belongs—automatically and "physically" in the case of assembly work, indirectly and "socially" in piecework on a machine, but always in a manner that is imposed upon him. Consequently, it no longer is a problem of individual output.[15] It is a problem of the work pace of a given unit of workers (which in the final analysis is the factory unit), and this pace can be determined only by this unit of workers itself. The problem of *remuneration* therefore comes down to a *management* problem, for once a general wage is established, the concrete rate of remuneration (the wage-output ratio) will be determined by determining the pace of work; the latter in its turn leads us to the heart of the problem of management as the problem that concretely concerns the producers as a whole (who, in one form or another, will have to determine that such and such a production pace on one line of a given type is equivalent as an expenditure of labor to another production pace on another line of another type, and this will have to done between various shops in the same factory as well as between a variety of factories, etc.).

Let us recall, if need be, that in no way does this signify that the problem necessarily becomes any easier to solve. Maybe even the contrary is the case. But finally it has been posed in correct terms. Mistakes made while trying to solve this problem might be fruitful for the development of socialism, and the successive elimination of such mistakes would allow us to arrive at *the* solution. As long as it is posited in the form of an "output-based wage" or "bourgeois right," however, we remain situated directly on the terrain of an exploiting society.

Certainly, the problem in its traditional form still can exist in "backward sectors"—though this does not necessarily mean that one should provide a "backward" solution. But whatever the solution might be in such a case, what we are trying to say is that historical developments tend to change both the form and the content of the problem.

But what is essential is to analyze both the mechanism and the mistake. Faced with a problem bequeathed by the bourgeois era one reasons like a bourgeois. One reasons like a bourgeois first of all in that one sets up an abstract and universal rule—this being the only form in which problems can be solved in an alienated society—forgetting that "law is like an ignorant and crude man" who always repeats the same thing[16] and that a socialist solution can only be socialist if it is a concrete solution that involves the permanent participation of the organized unit of workers in determining this solution. One also reasons like a bourgeois in that an alienated society is obliged to resort to abstract universal rules, because otherwise it could not be *stable* and because it is incapable of taking concrete cases into consideration on their own. It has neither the institutions nor the point of view necessary for this, whereas a socialist society, which creates precisely the organs that can take every concrete case into consideration, can have as its law only the perpetual determining activity of these organs.

One is reasoning like the bourgeois in that one accepts the bourgeois idea (and here one is correctly reflecting the real situation in bourgeois society) that individual interest is the supreme motive of human activity. Thus, for the bourgeois mentality of English "neosocialists," man in socialist society continues to be, before all else, an *economic man*, and society therefore ought to be regulated starting out from this idea. Thus transposing at once both the problems of capitalism and bourgeois behavior onto the new society, they are in essence preoccupied by the problem of incentives (earnings that stimulate the worker)[17] and forget that already in capitalist society what makes the worker work are not incentives but the control of his work by other people and by the machines themselves. The idea of *economic man* has been created by bourgeois society in its image; to be quite exact, in the image of the bourgeois and certainly not in the image of the worker. The workers act like "economic men" only when they are obliged to do so, i.e., vis-à-vis the bourgeois (who thus makes money off of their piecework), but certainly not among themselves (as can be seen during strikes, and also in their attitudes toward their families; otherwise, workers would have ceased to exist a long time ago). That it may be said that they act in this way toward what "belongs" to them (family, class, etc.) is fine, for we are saying precisely that they will act in this way toward everything when everything "belongs" to them. And to claim that the family is visible and here whereas "everything" is an abstraction again would be a misunderstanding, for the everything we are talking about is concrete, it begins with the other workers in the shop, the factory, etc.

Workers' Management of Production

A society without exploitation is conceivable, we have seen, if the management of production no longer is localized in a social category, in other words, if the *structural* division of society into directors and executants is abolished. Likewise we have seen that the solution to the problem thus posed can be given only by the proletariat itself. It is not only that no solution would be of any value, and simply could not even be carried out if it were not reinvented by the masses in an autonomous manner, nor is it that the problem posed exists on a scale that renders the active cooperation of millions of individuals indispensable to its solution. It is that by its very nature the solution to the problem of workers' management cannot be fitted into a formula, or, as we have said already, it is that the only genuine law socialist society acknowledges is the perpetual determining activity of the masses' organs of management.

The reflections that follow, therefore, aim not at "resolving" the problem of workers' management theoretically—which once again would be a contradiction in terms—but rather at clarifying the givens of the problem. We aim only at dispelling misunderstandings and widely held prejudices by showing how the problem of management is *not* posed and how it *is* posed.

If one thinks the basic task of the revolution is a negative task, the abolition of private property (which actually can be achieved by decree), one may think of the revolution as centered on the "taking of power" and therefore as a *moment* (which may last a few days and, if need be, can be followed by a few months or years of civil war) when the workers seize power and expropriate de facto and de jure the factory owners. And in this case, one actually will be led to grant a prime importance to the "taking of power" and to an organ constructed exclusively with this end in view.

That in fact is how things happen during a bourgeois revolution. The new society is prepared for completely within the old one; manufacturing concentrates employers and workers, the rent peasants pay to landed property owners is stripped of every economic function as these proprietors are stripped of every social function. Only a feudal shell remains around this society that is in fact bourgeois. A Bastille is demolished, a few heads cut off, a night falls in August, some elected officials (many of whom are lawyers) draft some constitutions, some laws, and some decrees—and the trick is played. The revolution is over, a historical period is closed, another is opened. True, a civil war may follow: The drafting of new codes will take a few years, the structure of the administration as well as that of the army will undergo significant changes. But the essence of the revolution is over before the revolution begins.

Indeed, the bourgeois revolution is only pure negation as concerns the area of economics. It is based upon what already is there, it limits itself to erecting into law a state of fact by abolishing a superstructure that in itself already is unreal. Its limited constructions affect only this superstructure; the economic base takes care of itself. Whether this occurs before or after the bourgeois revolution, once established in the economic sector, capitalism spreads by the force of its own laws over the terrain of simple commercial production that it discovers lying stretched out before it.

There is no relationship between this process and that of the socialist revolution. The latter is not a simple negation of certain aspects of the order that preceded it; it is essentially *positive*. It has to construct its regime—constructing not factories but new relations of production for which the development of capitalism furnishes merely the presuppositions. We will be able to see this better by rereading the passage where Marx describes the "Historical Tendency of Capitalist Accumulation." Please excuse us for citing a long passage.

As soon as the capitalist mode of production stands on its own feet, then the further socialization of labor and further transformation of the land and other means of production into socially exploited and, therefore, common means of production, as well as the further expropriation of private proprietors, takes a new form. That which is now to be expropriated is no longer the laborer working for himself, but the capitalist exploiting many laborers. This expropriation is accomplished by the action of the immanent laws of capitalistic production itself, by the centralization of capital. One capitalist always kills many. Hand in hand with this centralization, or this expropriation of many capitalists by few develop, on an ever-extending scale, the co-operative form of the labor-process, the conscious technical application of science, the methodical cultivation of the soil, the transformation of the instruments of labor into instruments of labor only usable in common, the economizing of all means of production by their use as the means of production of combined, socialized labor, the entanglement of all peoples in the net of the world-market, and with this, the international character of the capitalistic regime. Along with the constantly diminishing number of the magnates of capital, who usurp and monopolize all advantages of this process of transformation, grows the mass of misery, oppression, slavery, degradation, exploitation; but with this too grows the revolt of the working-class, a class always increasing in numbers, and disciplined, united, organized by the very mechanism of the process of capitalist production itself. The monopoly of capital becomes a fetter upon the mode of production, which has sprung up and flourished along with, and under it. Centralization of the means of production and socialization of labor at last reach a point where they become incompatible with their capitalist integument. This integument is burst asunder. The knell of capitalist private property sounds. The expropriators are expropriated.[18]

What in fact exists of the new society at the moment when the "capitalist integument is burst asunder"? All its premises: a society composed almost entirely of proletarians, the "rational application of science in industry," and also, given the degree of concentration of business enterprises this passage presupposes, the separation of property ownership from the actual functions of directing production. But where can we find already realized in this society socialist relations of production, as bourgeois relations of production were in "feudal" society?

Now, it is obvious that these new relations of production cannot be *merely* those realized in the "socialization of the labor process," the cooperation of thousands of individuals within the great industrial units of production. For these are the relations of production *typical* of a highly developed form of *capitalism*.

The "socialization of the labor process" as it takes place in the capitalist economy is the premise of socialism in that it abolishes anarchy, isolation, dispersion, etc. But it is in no way socialism's "prefiguration" or "embryo," in that it is an *antagonistic* form of socialization; i.e., it reproduces and deepens the division between the mass of executants and a stratum of directors. At the same time the producers are subjected to a collective form of discipline, the conditions of production are standardized among various sectors and localities, and production tasks become interchangeable, we notice at the other pole not only a decreasing number of capitalists in a more and more parasitic role but also the constitution of a separate apparatus for directing production. Now, socialist relations of production are those types of relations that preclude the separate existence of a fixed and stable stratum of directors of production. We see, therefore, that the point of departure for realizing such relations can be only the destruction of the power of the bourgeoisie or the bureaucracy. The capitalist transformation of society *ends* with the bourgeois revolution; the socialist transformation of society *begins* with the proletarian revolution.

Modern developments themselves have abolished the aspects of the problem of management that once were considered decisive. On the one hand, managerial labor itself has become a form of wage labor, as Engels already pointed out; on the other hand, it has become itself a *collective labor of execution*.[19] The "tasks" involved in the organization of labor, which formerly fell to the boss, assisted by a few technicians, now are performed by offices bringing together hundreds or thousands of persons, who themselves work as salaried, compartmentalized executants. The other group of traditional managerial tasks, which basically involve integrating the enterprise into the economy as a whole (in particular, those involving market "analysis" or having a "flair" for the market—which pertain to the nature, quality, and price of manufactured goods in demand, modifications in the scale of production, etc.), already has been transformed in its very nature with the advent of monopolies. The way this group of tasks is accomplished has been transformed too, since its basics are now carried out by a collective apparatus that canvasses the market, surveys consumer tastes, sells the product, etc. All this already has happened under monopoly capitalism. When private property gives way to State-run property, as in [total] bureaucratic capitalism, a central apparatus for coordinating the functioning of enterprises takes the place both of the market as "regulator" and of the apparatuses belonging to each enterprise; this is the central planning bureaucracy, the economic "necessity" for which should issue, according to its defenders, directly from these functions of coordination.

There is no point in discussing this sophism. Let us simply note in passing that the advocates of the bureaucracy demonstrate, in a first move, that one can do without bosses since one can make the economy function according to a plan and, in a second move, that for the plan to function, it has need of bosses of a different kind. For—and here is what interests us—the problem of how to coordinate the activity of enterprises and sectors of production after the market has been abolished, in other words, the problem of planning, already has been virtually abolished by advancements in modern techniques. Leontief's method,[20] even in its present form,[21] removes all "political" or "economic" meaning from the problem of how to coordinate various sectors or various enterprises, for it allows us to determine the consequences for a entire set of sectors, regions, and enterprises once we have settled upon the desired volume of production of end-use articles. At the same time, it allows us a large degree of flexibility, for this method makes it possible, if we want to modify the plan while work is in progress, to draw out immediately the practical implications of such a change. Combined with other modern methods,[22] it allows us both to choose the optimal methods for achieving our overall objectives, once they are settled upon, and to define these methods in detail for the entire economy. Briefly speaking, all of the "planning activity" of the Russian bureaucracy, for example, could be transferred at this point to an electronic calculator.

The problem, therefore, appears only at the two extremes of economic activity: at the most specific level (how to translate the production goal of a particular factory into the production goals to be carried out by each group of workers in the shops of this factory) and at the universal level (how to determine the production goals for end-use goods of the entire economy).

In both cases, the problem exists only because technique (in the broad sense of this term) develops—and it will develop even more in a socialist society. Indeed, it is clear that with an unchanging set of techniques the type of solution (if not the solutions themselves, whose exact terms will vary if, for example, there is accumulation) would be given once and for all, and that it would be merely a matter of allocating tasks within a shop (perfectly compatible with the possibility of interchangeable producers being able to switch between different jobs) or of determining the end-use products. The incessant modification of the different possible ways of carrying out production along with the incessant modification of final objectives will create the terrain on which collective management will work itself out.

Alienation in Capitalist Society

By alienation—a characteristic moment of every class society, but one that appears to an incomparably greater extent and depth in capitalist society—we mean to say that the products of man's activity (whether we are talking about objects or institutions) take on an independent social existence opposite him. Instead of being dominated by him, these products dominate him. Alienation is that which is opposed to man's free creativity in the world created by man; it is not an independent historical principle having its own source. It is the objectification of human activity insofar as it escapes its author without its author being able to escape it. Every form of alienation is a form of human objectification; i.e., it has its source in human activity (there are no "secret forces" in history, any more than there is a cunning of reason in natural economic laws). But not every form of objectification is necessarily a form of alienation insofar as it can be consciously taken up again, reaffirmed or destroyed. As soon as it is posited, every product of human activity (even a purely internal attitude) "escapes its author" and even leads an existence independent of that author. We cannot act as if we have not uttered some particular word, but we can cease to be determined by it. The past life of every individual is its objectification till today; but he is not necessarily and exhaustively alienated from it, his future is not permanently dominated by his past. Socialism will be the abolition of alienation in that it will permit the perpetual, conscious recovery without violent conflict of the socially given, in that it will restore people's domination over the products of their activity. Capitalist society is an alienated society in that its transformations take place independently of people's will and consciousness (including those of the dominant class), according to quasi-"laws" that express objective structures independent of their control.

What interests us here is not to describe how alienation is produced in the form of alienation in capitalist society (which would involve an analysis of the birth of capitalism as well as of its functioning) but to show the concrete manifestations of this alienation in various spheres of social activity as well as their intimate unity.

Only to the extent that we grasp the content of socialism as the proletariat's autonomy, as free creative activity determining itself, as workers' management in all domains, can we grasp the essence of man's alienation in capitalist society. Indeed, it is not by accident that "enlightened" members of the bourgeoisie as well as reformist and Stalinist bureaucrats want to reduce the evils of capitalism to essentially economic evils, and, on the economic level, to exploitation in the form of an unequal distribution of national income. To the extent that their critique of capitalism is extended to other domains it again will take for its point of departure this unequal distribution of income, and it will consist basically of variations on the theme of the corrupting influence of money. If they look at the family or the sexual question, they will talk about how poverty makes prostitutes, about the young girl sold to the rich old man, about domestic problems that are the result of economic misery. If they look at culture, they will talk about venality, about obstacles put in the way of talented but underprivileged people, and about illiteracy. Certainly, all that is true, and important. But it only touches the surface of the problem, and those who talk only in this way regard man solely as a consumer and, by pretending to satisfy him on this level, they tend to reduce him to his (direct or sublimated) physical functions of digestion. But for man, what is at stake is not "ingestion"[23] pure and simple; rather it is a matter of self-expression and self-creation, and not only in the economic domain, but in all domains.

In class society, conflict is not expressed simply in the area of distribution, in the form of exploitation and limitations on consumption. This is only one aspect of the conflict and not the most important one. Its fundamental feature is to be found in the limitations placed on man's human role in the domain of production; eventually, these limitations go so far as an attempt to abolish this role completely. It is to be found in the fact that man is expropriated, both individually and collectively, from having command over his own activity. By his enslavement to the machine, and through the machine, to an abstract, foreign, and hostile will, man is deprived of the true content of his human activity, the conscious transformation of the natural world. It constantly inhibits his deep-seated tendency to realize himself in the object. The true signification of this situation is not only that the producers live it as an absolute misfortune, as a permanent mutilation; it is that this situation creates at the profoundest level of production a perpetual conflict, which explodes at least on occasion; it also is that it makes for huge wastefulness—in comparison to which the wastefulness involved in crises of overproduction is probably negligible—both through the producers' positive opposition to a system they reject and through the lost opportunities that result from neutralizing the inventiveness and creativity of millions of individuals. Beyond these features, we must ask ourselves to what extent the further development of capitalist production is possible, even "technically," if the direct producer continues to be kept in the compartmentalized state in which he currently resides.

But alienation in capitalist society is not simply economic. It not only manifests itself in connection with material life. It also affects in a fundamental way both man's sexual and his cultural functions.

Indeed, society exists only insofar as there exists an organization of production and reproduction of the life of individuals and of the species—therefore an organization of economic and sexual relations—and only insofar as this organization ceases to be simply instinctual and becomes conscious—therefore only insofar as it includes the moment of culture.

As Marx said, "A bee puts to shame many an architect in the construction of her cells. But what distinguishes the worst architect from the best of bees is this, that the architect raises his structure in imagination before he erects it in reality."[24] Technique and consciousness obviously go hand in hand: An instrument is a materialized and operative signification, or better yet a mediation between a deliberate intention and a still-ideal goal.

What is said in this quotation from Marx about the fabrication of bees' honeycombs can be said as well about their "social" organization. As technique represents a rationalization of relations with the natural world, social organization represents a rationalization of the relations between individuals of a group. Beehive organization is a nonconscious form of rationalization, but tribal organization is a conscious one; the primitive can describe it and he can deny it (by transgressing it). Rationalization in this context obviously does not mean "our" rationalization. At one stage and in a given context, both magic and cannibalism represent rationalizations (without quotation marks).

If, therefore, a social organization is antagonistic, it will tend to be so both on the level of production and on the sexual and cultural planes as well. It is wrong to think that conflict in the domain of production "creates" or "determines" a secondary or derivative conflict on other planes; the structures of class domination impose themselves right away on all three levels at once and are impossible and inconceivable outside of this simultaneity, of this equivalence. Exploitation, for example, can be guaranteed only if the producers are expropriated from the management of production, but this expropriation both presupposes that the producers tend to be separated from the *ability* to manage—and therefore from culture—and reproduces this separation on an larger scale. Likewise, a society in which the fundamental interhuman relations are relations of domination presupposes and at the same time engenders an alienating organization of sexual relations, namely, an organization that creates in individuals deep-seated inhibitions that tend to make them accept authority, etc.[25]

Indeed, there obviously is a dialectical equivalence between social structures and the "psychological" structures of individuals. From his first steps in life the individual is subjected to a constant set of pressures aimed at imposing on him a given attitude toward work, sex, ideas, at cheating him out of [*frustrer*] the natural objects of his activity and at inhibiting him by making him interiorize and value this process of frustration. Class society can exist only insofar as it succeeds to a large extent in enforcing this acceptance. This is why the conflict is not a purely external conflict, but is transposed into the hearts of individuals themselves. This antagonistic social structure corresponds to an antagonistic structure within individuals, each perpetually reproducing itself by means of the other.

The point of these considerations is not only to emphasize the moment of identity in the essence of the relations of domination as they take place in the capitalist factory, in the patriarchal family, or in authoritarian teaching and "aristocratic" culture. It is to point out that the socialist revolution necessarily will have to embrace all domains in their entirety, and this must be done not in some unforeseeable future and "by increments," but rather from the outset. Certainly it has to begin in a certain fashion, which can be nothing other than the destruction of the power of the exploiters by the power of the armed masses and the instauration of workers' management in production. But it will have to grapple immediately with the reconstruction of other social activities, under penalty of death. We will try to show this by looking at what kind of relations the proletariat, once in power, will entertain with culture.

The antagonistic structure of cultural relations in present-day society is expressed also (but in no way exclusively) by the radical division between manual and intellectual labor. The result is that the immense majority of humanity is totally separated from culture as *activity* and shares [*participe*] in only an infinitesimal fraction of the fruits of culture. On the other hand, the division of society into directors and executants becomes more and more homologous to the division between manual labor and intellectual labor (all management jobs being some form of intellectual labor and all manual jobs being some form of labor that consists of the execution of tasks).[26] Workers' management is possible, therefore, only if from the outset it starts moving in the direction of overcoming this division, in particular with respect to intellectual labor as it relates to the production process. This implies in turn that the proletariat will begin to appropriate culture for itself. Certainly not as ready-made culture, as the assimilation of the "results" of historically extant culture. Beyond a certain point, such an assimilation is both impossible in the immediate future and superfluous (as concerns what is of interest to us here). Rather as appropriation of activity, as recovery of the cultural function itself and as a radical change in the producing masses' relation to intellectual work. Only as this change takes hold will workers' management become irreversible.

Notes

1. Insofar as this introduction gives a brief summary of the analysis of various problems already treated in this review, we have taken the liberty of referring the reader to the corresponding articles published in *S. ou B.*

2. The April 1947 strike at Renault, the first great postwar working-class explosion in France, was able to take place only after the workers fought physically with Stalinist union officials.

3. See in *S. ou B.*, 13 (January 1954), pp. 34-46, the detailed description of the way in which the Stalinists were able to "scuttle" the August 1953 strike at Renault without overtly opposing it.

4. Or with other, essentially similar currents (Bordigism, for example).

5. Among its serious representatives, which nearly amounts to just Trotsky himself. Present-day Trotskyists, knocked about by reality as no ideological current has ever been knocked about before, have reached such a degree of political and ideological decomposition that nothing precise can be said about them at all.

6. In the last analysis, our ultimate conception of working-class bureaucracy leads to a revision of the traditional Leninist conception of reformism. But we cannot dwell here on this question.

7. See the "Lettre ouverte aux militants du PCI" in *S. ou B.*, 1 (March 1949), pp. 90-101. [T/E: This article, "Open Letter to PCI Militants," is reprinted in *SB 1*, pp. 185-204, but is not included in the present edition.]

8. See "The Relations of Production in Russia."

9. Victor Serge, *Russia Twenty Years After*, trans. Max Shachtman (New York: Hillman-Curl, 1937), p. 150.

10. See the editorial in *S. ou B.*, 1 (March 1949), pp. 27ff. [T/E: Reprinted in *SB 1*, pp. 139-84 and translated in this volume as "Socialism or Barbarism."]

11. T/E: From the "Provisional Rules" written by Marx and adopted by the First International, in *The First International and After*, vol. 3 of Karl Marx, *Political Writings*, ed. David Fernbach (London: Penguin/New Left Books, 1974), p. 82.

12. See "La Direction prolétarienne," in *S. ou B.*, 10 (July 1952), pp. 10-17. [T/E: Reprinted in *EMO 1*, pp. 145-62 and included in this volume as "Proletarian Leadership."]

13. We have shown elsewhere that the amount of inequality would be extremely limited. See *DC*, *S. ou B.*, 13 (January 1954), pp. 66-69. [T/E: Not included in this present edition or in the 10/18 edition. It was to be included in the volume entitled *La Dynamique du capitalisme*, which never was published.]

14. Obviously the term is not being utilized here with the exact technical meaning it currently possesses.

15. Cf. the selections of *Tribune Ouvrière* published in this issue of *S. ou B.*, 17 (July 1955).

16. Plato, *The Statesman*, 294 b-c. [T/E: We have simply translated Castoriadis's French.]

17. T/E: The word "incentives" appears in English in the original French text, followed by a parenthetical explanation in French.

18. *Capital* (New York: International Publishers, 1967), vol. 1, pp. 762-63.

19. See the article by Philippe Guillaume, "*Machinisme et prolétariat*," in *S. ou B.*, 7 (August 1951), in particular, pp. 59ff.

20. We have set forth a few of this method's basic concepts in *DC*, published in *S. ou B.*, 12 (August 1953), pp. 17ff. See also Leontief et al., *Studies in the Structure of American Economy* (1953; reprint, Armonk, N.Y.: Sharpe, 1976).

21. This is an important reservation, for the practical applications of this method hardly have been developed at all till now, for obvious reasons.

22. See Tjalling Koopmans, *Activity Analysis of Production & Allocation* (1951; reprint, New Haven, Conn.: Yale University Press, 1972).

23. T/E: When Castoriadis criticizes the consumeristic aspects of an emphasis on "digestion" and "ingestion," we should keep in mind the etymologically related French word for (workers') "management": *gestion (ouvrière)*.

24. *Capital*, vol. 1, p. 178.

25. On the profound relation between class structures and the patriarchal regulation of sexual relations, see the writings of W. Reich: *The Sexual Revolution* (New York: Farrar, Strauss, & Giroux, 1974), *Character Analysis* (New York: Farrar, Strauss, & Giroux, 1972), and *The Function of the Orgasm* (New York: Farrar, Strauss, & Giroux, 1973). In the last of these see the analysis of the neurotic structure of the fascist individual (section 3 of ch. 6: "Fascist Irrationalism").

26. Between these two is situated the category of labor consisting of the execution of intellectual tasks, which is becoming more and more important. We will talk about this at the conclusion of this essay.

a) See now "*Le Rôle de l'idéologie bolchevique*" in *EMO 2*, pp. 385-416, and the Brinton text cited therein. [T/E: Castoriadis's article is to be included in a proposed third volume of this edition as "The Role of Bolshevik Ideology in the Birth of the Bureaucracy." See Appendix C for previously published translations; see also Maurice Brinton, *Bolsheviks & Worker's Control* (London: Solidarity, 1970; Detroit: Black & Red, 1975).]

Appendixes

Appendix A:
Table of Contents of Volume 3

Appendix B:
10/18 Texts Omitted from
Political and Social Writings, volumes 1-3
(arranged by volume)

EMO 1, 383-408	"Bilan, perspectives, tâches" (1957).
EMO 1, 409-44	"Comment lutter?" (1958).
EMO 2, 89-116	"Bilan" (1958).
EMO 2, 117-21	"Note sur Lukács et Rosa Luxembourg" (1958).
EMO 2, 189-248*	"Prolétariat et organisation, II" (1959).
CMR 1, 11-14	"Note liminaire" (1978).
CMR 1, 15-118	"La Crise du capitalisme mondial et l'intervention du parti dans les luttes" (1947): sections not included in *PSW 1*.
CMR 1, 119-37	"La Situation du prolétariat et les tâches des révolutionnaires" (1948).
CMR 1, 139-216	"Rapport politique pour le Ve Congrès du P.C.I." (1948).
CMR 1, 217-80	"La Consolidation temporaire du capitalisme mondial" (1949).
CMR 1, 281-342	"Notes sur la situation internationale" (1949-52).
CMR 1, 343-62	"La Guerre et la perspective révolutionnaire" (1952).
CMR 1, 363-73	"La Politique du bloc occidental" (1954).
CMR 1, 375-77	"1953 et les luttes ouvrières" (1954).
CMR 2, 11-39	"Les Classes sociales et M. Touraine" (1959).
CMR 2, 40-46	"Les Elections anglaises" (1959).
CMR 2, 279-86	"Fissures dans le bloc occidental" (1963).
CMR 2, 287-91	"Quelques remarques sur *Riches et Pauvres en Amérique*" (1964).
CS, 47-65	"Sur le programme socialiste" (1952).
CS, 223-60*	"Ce que signifie le socialisme" (1961).
CS, 261-99	"Discussion avec des militants du P.S.U." (1974).
SF, 13-14	"Note liminaire" (1979).
SF, 15-51	"La Situation française et la politique du P.C.I." (1947).
SF, 53-88	"Mendès-France: Velléités d'indépendance et tentative de rafistolage" (1954).
SF, 89-95	"Les Elections françaises" (1956).
SF, 97-104	"La Situation française" (1957).
SF, 105-39	"Perspectives de la crise française" (1958).
SF, 141-49	"Tract diffusé le 27 Mai par le groupe *Pouvoir Ouvrier*" (1958).
SF, 151-64	"Crise du gaullisme et crise de la 'gauche'" (1961).
SF, 237-58*	"La Gauche et la France en 1978" (1977).
SF, 295-314	"De la langue de bois à la langue de caoutchouc" (1978).

*See Appendix C for available English-language versions.

Appendix C:
Previous English-Language Versions of 10/18 Texts
(arranged by volume)

SB 1, 139-83*   "Socialism Reaffirmed" ("Socialisme ou Barbarie," 1949), London: Bob Pennington, no date (a typescript version is in T/E's possession); also as the inaugural *Solidarity Pamphlet*, 1961.

EMO 1, 11-120**   "On the History of the Workers' Movement" ("La Question de l'histoire du mouvement ouvrier," 1973), trans. Brian Singer and Patricia Tummons, *Telos*, 30 (Winter 1976-77), pp. 3-42.

EMO 2, 123-87*   "Working Class Consciousness" ("Prolétariat et organisation I," 1959), trans. Maurice Brinton, *Solidarity*, 2:3, pp. 23ff. Reprinted in 5:12, pp. 9ff.

EMO 2, 189-249***   "Proletariat and Organization, II" ("Prolétariat et organisation II," 1959), unpublished draft translation by Pierre Lanneret, Daryl Van Fleet, and Sandie Van Fleet, in author's and T/E's possession.

EMO 2, 249-53*   "What Is Important" ("Ce qui est important," 1959), trans. Tom McLaughlin, *Catalyst*, 13 (Spring 1979), pp. 91-94.

EMO 2, 307-65**   "Redefining Revolution" ("Recommencer la révolution," 1963), trans. Maurice Brinton, *Solidarity Pamphlet* 44 (no date).

EMO 2, 385-416**   "From Bolshevism to the Bureaucracy" ("Le rôle de l'idéologie bolchevique dans la naissance de la bureaucratie," 1964), trans. Maurice Brinton, *Solidarity Pamphlet* 24 (no date); reprinted in *Our Generation*, 12 (Fall 1977), pp. 43-54.

EMO 2, 427-44** "Hierarchy of Salaries and Incomes" ("La Hiérarchie des salaires et des revenus," 1974), excerpted trans. by Tom McLaughlin and Peter Royle, *Catalyst*, 13 (Spring 1979), pp. 95-104; previous translation by Tom McLaughlin in *The Red Menace*, 3 (Winter 1977).

CMR 2, 47-203* "Modern Capitalism and Revolution" ("Le Mouvement révolutionnaire sous le capitalisme moderne," 1959-61), *Modern Capitalism and Revolution. A Solidarity Book*, trans. Maurice Brinton. 2nd ed. (London: Solidarity, 1974), pp. 15-95; previous *Solidarity* translations, 1963 and 1965. The 1963, 1965, and 1974 versions contain new material, written in English in 1963 and 1965; the 1979 French version contains new material not included in earlier versions of *MCR*.

CMR 2, 205-22* "Appendix: The 'Falling Rate of Profit' " and "Appendix to APPENDIX!" (originally written in English in 1965; subsequent French trans. by Cornelius Castoriadis as "Appendices à la première édition anglaise du MRCM"), *Modern Capitalism and Revolution. A Solidarity Book*, pp. 96-101 and 102; the 1979 French edition of the Appendixes contains a number of clarifications of the earlier, English-language versions.

CMR 2, 223-58* "Author's Introduction to the 1974 English Edition" (originally written in English; subsequent French trans. by Castoriadis as "Introduction à la deuxième édition anglaise du MRCM," 1974), *Modern Capitalism and Revolution. A Solidarity Book*, pp. 1-11.

CMR 2, 293-316** "The Crisis of Modern Society" (lecture delivered in English in 1965; subsequent French trans. by Castoriadis as "La Crise de la société moderne"), *Solidarity Pamphlet* 23 (no date).

CS, 11-43** "Socialism and Autonomous Society" ("Introduction. Socialisme et société autonome," 1979), trans. David J. Parent, *Telos*, 43 (Spring 1980), pp. 91-105.

CS, 103-221* *Workers' Councils and the Economics of a Self-Managed Society* ("Sur le contenu du socialisme, II," 1957), trans. Maurice Brinton (London: Solidarity, 1972; reprint, Philadelphia Solidarity, 1974, and as a Wooden Shoe Pamphlet, 1984).

CS, 223-60***   "Socialism and Capitalism" (originally written in English; subsequent French trans. by Castoriadis as "Ce que signifie le socialisme," 1961), *International Socialism*, 4 (Spring 1961), pp. 20-27; reprinted with publisher's introduction in slightly altered form as "The Meaning of Socialism," *Solidarity Pamphlet* 6 (1961). The December 1969 and July 1972 *Solidarity* reprints each contain additional introductory material.

CS, 367-441**   "The Hungarian Source" (unauthorized editing of original English-language version by Paul Piccone; subsequent French trans. Maurice Luciani as "La Source hongroise"; preedited original now lost), *Telos*, 29 (Fall 1976), pp. 4-22.

SF, 165-221**   "The Anticipated Revolution" ("La Révolution anticipée," 1968), unpublished draft translation by Basil Druitt with corrections by Castoriadis is in author's and T/E's possession.

SF, 223-35**   "The Diversionists" and "Reply to André Gorz" ("Les Divertisseurs," 1977), trans. Dorothy Gehrke, *Telos*, 33 (Fall 1977), pp. 102-6 and 108-9.

SF, 237-58***   "The French Left" ("La Gauche et la France en 1978," 1977), trans. Bart Grahl, Susan Wheeler, Dorothy Gehrke, Bob D'Amico, Bill Hamilton, and John Fekete, *Telos*, 34 (Winter 1977-78), pp. 49-73.

SF, 259-294**   "The French Communist Party: A Critical Anatomy" ("L'Evolution du P.C.F.," 1977), trans. Adrienne Foulke, *Dissent*, Summer 1979, pp. 315-25.

*A version is included in *PSW 1* or *2*.
**Planned for *PSW 3*.
***Not included in the present translation series.

Appendix D:
Non-10/18 Writings of Cornelius Castoriadis in English

1958   "The Marxist Organization Today" (unauthorized editing of
            original text, now lost), in Grace Lee (Boggs), Pierre Chaulieu
            (Castoriadis) and J. R. Johnson (C. L. R. James), *Facing
            Reality* (Detroit: Correspondence, 1958), pp. 90-102? (reprint,
            Detroit, Bewick, 1974).

1961   "Socialism or Barbarism" (statement originally written in
            English for a May 1961 international "conference of
            revolutionary socialists" held in Paris), *Solidarity Pamphlet* 11,
            intro. dated May 1969.

1966   "The Fate of Marxism" (from *MTR*; now in *IIS* [French ed.],
            pp. 13-20), trans. Maurice Brinton, *Solidarity*, 4 (August
            1966), pp. 15ff; later reprinted by Solidarity (Clydeside), and
            then as *A* (London) *Solidarity Pamphlet* (no date). (New
            English translation in *IIS*.)

1971   "History and Revolution" (from *MTR*; now in *IIS* [French
            ed.], pp. 21-56), trans. Maurice Brinton, *Solidarity Pamphlet*
            38, intro. dated August 1971. (New English translation in
            IIS.)

1973   "Revolutionary Perspectives Today" (lecture delivered in
            English by the author to the London Solidarity group on
            February 10, 1973); a copy of Solidarity's unpublished
            transcription is in author's and T/E's possession.

1975   "An Interview with C. Castoriadis" (from January 26, 1974,
            APL interview), trans. Bart Grahl and David Pugh, *Telos*, 23
            (Spring 1975), pp. 131-55.

1977   "Listen, Psychiatrist" (from *MTR*; now in *IIS* [French ed.], pp. 126-30), trans. Maurice Brinton, *Solidarity for Workers' Power*, 8 (August 8, 1977), pp. 19-23, with a *Solidarity* postscript. (New English translation in *IIS*.)

1978a   "History as Creation" (from *MTR*; now in *IIS* [French ed.], pp. 56-84, trans. Maurice Brinton, *Solidarity Pamphlet* 54, intro. dated July 1978. (Also: "Continuation of *History as Creation*," pp. 84-124, 125 and 130 of *IIS* [French ed.].) Brinton's unpublished final draft translation is in author's and T/E's possession. (New English translation of both parts in *IIS*.)

1978b   "From Marx to Aristotle, from Aristotle to Us" (a previous English translation of "Valeur, égalité, justice, politique . . ."), trans. Andrew Arato, *Social Research*, 45 (Winter 1978), pp. 667-738. (New translation in *CL*.)

1978c   "The Social Regime in Russia" (November 18, 1977, "introductory report to the fourth and last day of the seminar . . . that took place in Venice in the framework of the second anniversary of dissidence in Eastern European countries"), trans. David J. Parent, *Telos*, 38 (Winter 1978-79), pp. 32-47.

1980   "Facing the War" (*Libre* 8 [1980]), pp. 217-50; reprinted in *Devant la guerre*, vol. 1, 2nd ed., pp. 13-46), trans. Joe Light, *Telos*, 46 (Winter 1980-81), pp. 43-61.

1981a   "From Ecology to Autonomy" (Castoriadis's presentation and remarks from *De l'écologie à l'autonomie*), trans. Alastair Davidson, *Thesis 11*, 3 (1981), pp. 8-22, intro. Paul Breines, p. 7.

1981b   Interview (October 4, 1981), in *Psych-Critique*, 2 (1982), pp. 3-8.

1982a   "The Impossibility of Reforms in the Soviet Union" (*Devant la guerre*, vol. 1, 2nd ed. pp. 171-82), trans. Jim Asker, *Thesis 11*, 4 (1982), pp. 26-31.

1982b   "The Toughest and Most Fragile of Regimes" (discussion on Poland in *Espirt*, 3 [1979] with Paul Thibaud), trans. David Berger, *Telos*, 51 (Spring 1982), pp. 186-90.

1982c   "The Crisis of Western Societies" (*Politique Internationale*, 15 [Spring 1982]), trans. David J. Parent, *Telos*, 53 (Fall 1982), pp. 17-28.

1982d   "*Facing the War* and *The Socio-Economic Roots of Re-Armament*: A Rejoinder" (reply written in English), *Telos*, 53 (Fall 1982), pp. 192-97.

1983a   "The Destinies of Totalitarianism" (article originally written in English), *Salmagundi*, 60 (Spring-Summer 1983), pp. 107-22. (Now in *DH*.)

1983b   "The Greek *Polis* and the Creation of Democracy" (lecture delivered in English to a Hannah Arendt Memorial Symposium in Political Philosophy conducted by the Philosophy Department of the New School for Social Research), *Graduate Faculty Philosophy Journal*, 9 (Fall 1983), pp. 79-115. (Now in *DH*.)

1984a   "The Imaginary Institution of Society" (*IIS* [French ed.], pp. 162-63, 175-204 and 311-24), trans. Brian Singer, in *The Structural Allegory: Reconstructive Encounters with the New French Thought*, ed. John Fekete, intro. Brian Singer (Minneapolis: University of Minnesota Press, 1984), pp. 6-45.

1984b   "The Imaginary: Creation in the Social-Historical Domain" (presentation in English to the Stanford International Symposium), in *Disorder and Order*, ed. Paisley Livingston. Stanford Literature Studies 1 (Saratoga: Anma Libri, 1984), pp. 146-61. (Now in *DH*.)

1984c   *Crossroads in the Labyrinth* (*Les Carrefours du labyrinthe*), trans. Martin H. Ryle and Kate Soper (Cambridge: MIT Press; Brighton: Harvester Press, 1984).

1984d   "Marx Today: An Interview" (March 23, 1983 *Lutter* interview), trans. Franco Schiavoni, *Thesis 11*, 8 (1984), pp. 124-32. (Now in *DH*.)

1984e   "Defending the West" (February 26, 1983, essay originally published in *Le Monde*), trans. Alfred J. MacAdam, *Partisan Review*, 51 (1984), pp. 375-79. (Now in *DH* as "Quelle Europe? Quelles menaces? Quelle défense?" Castoriadis has called this title "misleading" and the translation "particularly bad"; his letter of protest to *Partisan Review* concerning this unauthorized translation was never published.)

1985   "Reflections on 'Rationality' and 'Development,'" trans. John Murphy, *Thesis 11*, 9 (1985), pp. 18-36. (Now in *DH*.)

1986   "The Nature and Value of Equality," trans. David Ames Curtis, *Philosophy and Social Criticism*, 11 (Fall 1986), pp. 373-90. A listing of "errata" should appear in a forthcoming issue. (Now in *DH*.)

1987a   *The Imaginary Institution of Society*, trans. Kathleen Blamey (Cambridge: MIT Press; Oxford: Polity Press, 1987).

1987b   "Primary Institution of Society and Secondary Institutions" (translation of 1985 lecture, "Institution première de la société et institutions secondes"), trans. David Ames Curtis, forthcoming in *Free Associations*, a London psychoanalytic journal.

1987c   "Cold War Fictions" (translation of letter to Professor Otto, editor of *Sozialwissenschaftliche Literatur Wissenschaft*, concerning Otto's review of *Devant la guerre*), *Solidarity Journal*, 14 (Summer 1987), pp. 14-15.

1988a   "The Gorbachev Interlude," *New Politics*, 1 (New Series, Winter 1988), pp. 60-79.

1988b   "The Movements of the Sixties" (translation of 1986 *Pouvoir* article), *Thesis 11*, forthcoming.

Appendix E:
Non-10/18 Writings of Cornelius Castoriadis in French

1949	"Les Bouches inutiles," *S. ou B.*, 1 (March 1949), pp. 104ff. (Written under the pseudonym Pierre Chaulieu.)
1953	"Sur la dynamique du capitalisme (I)," *S. ou B.*, 12 (August 1953), pp. 1-22. (Written under the pseudonym Pierre Chaulieu.)
1954	"Sur la dynamique du capitalisme (II)," *S. ou B.*, 13 (January 1954), pp. 60-81. (Written under the pseudonym Pierre Chaulieu.)
1964a*	"Marxisme et théorie révolutionnaire (I)," *S. ou B.*, 36 (April 1964), pp. 1-25. (Written under the pseudonym Paul Cardan. Reprinted in *IIS*.)
1964b*	"Marxisme et théorie révolutionnaire (II)," *S. ou B.*, 37 (July 1964), pp. 18-54. (Written under the pseudonym Paul Cardan. Reprinted in *IIS*.)
1964c*	"Marxisme et théorie révolutionnaire (III)," *S. ou B.*, 38 (October 1964), pp. 44-86. (Written under the pseudonym Paul Cardan. Reprinted in *IIS*.)
1965a*	"Marxisme et théorie révolutionnaire (IV)," *S. ou B.*, 39 (March 1965), pp. 16-66. (Written under the pseudonym Paul Cardan. Reprinted in *IIS*.)
1965b*	"Marxisme et théorie révolutionnaire (V)," *S. ou B.*, 40 (June 1965), pp. 37-71. (Written under the pseudonym Paul Cardan. Reprinted in *IIS*.)
1968*	"Epilégomènes à une théorie de l'âme que l'on a pu présenter comme science," *L'Inconscient*, 8 (October 1968), pp. 47-87. (Reprinted in *CL*.)

1971*   "Le Dicible et l'indicible," *L'Arc*, 46 (1971), pp. 67-79.
             (Reprinted in *CL*.)
1973a*   "Technique" *Encyclopaedia Universalis*, 15 (March 1973).
             (Reprinted in *CL*.)
1973b*   "Le Monde morcelé," *Textures*, 4-5 (1972), pp. 3-40.
             Enlarged version published as "Science moderne et
             interrogation philosophique," *Encyclopaedia Universalis*, 17
             (November 1973). (Reprinted in *CL*.)
1974*   "Entretien avec Cornelius Castoriadis" (interview conducted
             by members of APL—Agence de Presse Libération/Analyse
             et Popularisation des Luttes—on January 26, 1974);
             roneotyped and distributed by La Librairie des Deux
             Mondes, Paris.
1975a*   *L'Institution imaginaire de la société* (Paris: Editions du Seuil,
             1975), with author's preface. (Includes *MTR* as pp. 13-230.)
1975b*   "Valeur, égalité, justice, politique: de Marx à Aristote et
             d'Aristote à nous," *Textures*, 12-13 (1975), pp. 3-66.
             (Reprinted in *CL*.)
1977*   "La Psychanalyse, projet et élucidation," *Topique*, 19 (April
             1977), pp. 25-75. (Reprinted in *CL*.)
1978a*   *Les Carrefours du labyrinthe* (Paris: Editions du Seuil, 1978),
             with author's preface.
1978b*   "Le Régime social de la Russie" (presented at an October
             1977 colloquium in Venice on Eastern European dissidence),
             Esprit, July-August 1978, pp. 6-23; and as pamphlet no. 2 of
             the *Les Cahiers du Vent de Ch'min* series (Saint-Denis: Les
             Cahiers du Vent de Ch'min, no date). (Reprinted in *DH*.)
1978c   "La Découverte de l'imagination," *Libre*, 3 (1978), pp.
             155-89, with author's preface, pp. 151-55. (Reprinted in
             DH.)
1979a   "L'Industrie du vide" (reply to Pierre Vidal-Naquet and
             Bernard-Henri Lévy), *Le Nouvel Observateur* (July 9, 1979);
             reprinted in *Quaderni di storia*, 11 (January 1980), pp. 322-29,
             with the letters to the editor of Vidal-Naquet (June 18 and
             25, 1979), pp. 315-17 and 319-21, and Lévy (June 18, 1979),
             pp. 317-19. (Reprinted in *DH*.)
1979b   "Entretien avec Cornelius Castoriadis (I): Illusion du système,
             illusion de la spécialization," "Entretien avec Cornelius
             Castoriadis (II): La Barbarie, c'est l'absence de productivité
             historique," and "Entretien avec Cornelius Castoriadis (III):
             Une Interrogation sans fin" (July 1, 1979), *Esprit*,
             September-October 1979, pp. 29-33, 131-33 and 242-48.
             (Reprinted in *DH*.)

1980** Devant la guerre, vol. 1: Les Réalités, 1st ed. (Paris: Fayard, 1980; 2nd ed. rev., 1981), with author's foreword. First chapter was originally published in Libre, 8 (1980), pp. 217-50.

1981a** De l'écologie à l'autonomie (presentations by Castoriadis and Daniel Cohn-Bendit to a 1980 conference of 1,000 environmental activists in Louvain, Belgium), with a preface (Paris: Editions du Seuil, 1981).

1981b "Illusions ne pas garder," Libération, December 21, 1981, p. 9. (Reprinted in DH.)

1982a** "Nature et valeur de l'égalité" (September 28, 1981, lecture presented at the twenty-eighth Rencontres Internationales de Genève) in L'Exigence d'égalité (Neuchâtel: Editions de la Baconnière, 1982), pp. 15-34, with introduction by Giovanni Busino, pp. 11-14. Other comments by Castoriadis on pp. 70-72, 87-88, 97-98, 116-17. (Reprinted in DH.)

1982b* "La Crise des sociétés occidentales," Politique Internationale, 15 (Spring 1982), pp. 131-47.

1982c* "Le Plus Dur et le plus fragile des régimes" (February 3, 1982, discussion concerning Poland with Paul Thibaud), Esprit, March 1982, pp. 140-46. (Reprinted in DH.)

1982d "Institution de la société et religion," Esprit, May 1982, and reprinted in Mélanges Jacques Ellul (Paris: PUF, 1983), pp. 3-17. (Reprinted in DH.)

1982e "Le Régime russe se succédera à lui-même," Libération, November 12, 1982, p. 16. (Reprinted in DH.)

1983a "Pologne, notre défaite," introduction to Banque d'Images pour la Pologne (Paris: Limage 2, 1983), pp. 7-13. (Reprinted in DH.)

1983b* "Quelle Europe? Quelles menaces? Quelle défense?" Le Monde, February 26, 1983, in abridged form; the complete text is in Europe en formation, 252 (April-June 1983), pp. 18-22. (Reprinted in full in DH.)

1983c* "Marx aujourd'hui" (March 23, 1983, interview), Lutter, 5 (May-August 1983), pp. 15-18. (Reprinted in DH.)

1983d "La Contingence dans les affaires humaines" (debate between Castoriadis and René Girard, June 13, 1983, at a Cerisy Colloquium), L'Auto-organisation. De la physique au politique, ed. Paul Dumouchel and Jean-Pierre Dupuy (Paris: Editions du Seuil, 1983), pp. 282-301; preceded by a "présentation," p. 281.

1983e	"La Logique des magmas et la question de l'autonomie" (presented at a Cerisy Colloquium), *L'Auto-organisation. De la physique au politique*, pp. 421-43; preceded by a "présentation" (pp. 415-16) and "Questions à Cornelius Castoriadis" (pp. 417-20) by Michel Gutsatz, and followed by a *Débat* (pp. 444-52). (Reprinted in *DH*.)
1984	Interview, November 21, 1983, published in *Synapse*, 1 (January 1984), pp. 50-56; entitled "Psychanalyse et société II" in *DH*.
1985	"Institution première de la société et institutions secondes" (lecture presented on December 15, 1985, the sixth day of a conference entitled "Psychanalyse et approche familiale systematique"), *Y-a-t-il une théorie de l'institution?* (Paris: Centre d'étude de la famille, 1985), pp. 105-21.
1986a**	*Domaines de l'homme: Les carrefours du labyrinthe II* (Paris: Editions du Seuil, 1986), with author's preface. This volume also includes five articles never before published in French or English—we provide titles from *DH*: "Transition" (November 30, 1978, interview with the "leftist" Italian monthly, *Metropoli*); "Tiers Monde, tiers-mondisme, démocratie" (January 24, 1985, contribution to a colloquium entitled "Le Tiers-mondisme en question," organized by *Liberté sans frontières*); "La 'Gauche' en 1985" (March 24, 1985, interview in writing for the Rio de Janiero *Jornal do Brasil*); "Cinq ans après" (author's preface to the Polish ed. of *Devant la guerre*, dated May 5, 1985); and "Portée ontologique de l'histoire de la science" (lecture delivered on several different occasions, dated December 9, 1985); in addition, there are three articles originally published in English that have been translated into French by the author or by Zoé Castoriadis: see 1981b, 1983a, and 1983b in Appendix D.
1986b	"La *Polis* grecque et la création de la démocratie" (French translation by Pierre-Emmanuel Dauzat of 1983 English text, "The Greek Polis and the Creation of Democracy"), excerpted in *Le Débat*, 38 (January 1986), pp. 126-44. (Reprinted in *DH*.)
1986c	"Les Mouvements des années soixante," *Pouvoirs*, 39 (1986), pp. 107-16.
1986d	"L'Etat du sujet aujourd'hui," *Topique*, 38 (November 1986), pp. 7-39.
1987a	"Notations sur le racisme," *Connexions*, 48 (January 1987), pp. 107-18.

1987b   "Cette course absurde vers le nouveau pour le nouveau" (interview no. 5 in a series entitled "La Mort des avant-gardes?"), *L'Evenément du jeudi*, August 20-26, 1987, pp. 80-82.

1987c   "Les Intellectuels et l'histoire," *Lettre Internationale*, 15 (December 1987), pp. 14-16.

1987d   "L'Improbable Gorbatchev et ses impossibles réformes," *Libération*, December 9-11, 1987.

1988   "Une Exigence politique et humaine" (interview), *Alternatives Economiques*, 53 (January 1988), pp. 26-28.

*A complete English version exists; see Appendix D.
**A partial English version exists; see Appendix D.

Appendix F:
English-Language Critical Assessments of and Responses to Castoriadis

1958a   "Facing Reality—1958" and "Readers from All Walks of Life Hail New Publication" (reviews of *Facing Reality*, a book that included an unauthorized editing of Pierre Chaulieu's—i.e. Castoriadis's—contribution), *Correspondence*, June 1958, p. 1S.

1958b   "French Crisis Speeds Plans for New Workers Paper" (summary of Chaulieu's article in the July 1958 issue of *S. ou B.*), *Correspondence*, July 1958.

1966   George Lichtheim, "Bureaucracy and Totalitarianism," in his *Marxism in Modern France* (New York: Columbia University Press, 1966), pp. 182-92.

1971a   Allen Binstock, "*Socialisme ou Barbarie*." M.A. thesis, University of Wisconsin, 1971.

1971b   Bob Potter, "*History and Revolution*: A Critique of Cardan's Critique," (*Solidarity*) *Discussion Bulletin No. 1*, no date (1971?), pp. 1-5.

1971c   Maurice Brinton, "*History and Revolution*: On Unhistorical Materialism," (*Solidarity*) *Discussion Bulletin No. 1*, no date (1971?), pp. 6-14.

1975a   Mark Poster, "*Socialisme ou Barbarie*," in the "Stalinism and the Existentialists" section of his *Existential Marxism in Postwar France* (Princeton: Princeton University Press, 1975), pp. 202-5.

1975b   Richard Gombin, *The Origins of Modern Leftism*, trans. Michael K. Perl (London: Penguin, 1975), pp. 32-39, 94-95, and 98-105.

| 1975c | Dick Howard, "Introduction to Castoriadis," *Telos*, 23 (Spring 1975), pp. 117-31. |

1975c — Dick Howard, "Introduction to Castoriadis," *Telos*, 23 (Spring 1975), pp. 117-31.

1976 — Claude Lefort, "An Interview with Claude Lefort" (April 19, 1975, interview originally published in *Anti-Mythes*, no. 14; contains many references to Castoriadis), trans. Dorothy Gehrke and Brian Singer, in *Telos*, 30 (Winter 1976-77), pp. 173-92.

1977a — Dick Howard, "Ontology and the Political Project," in *The Marxian Legacy* (London: Macmillan Press, 1977; University of Minnesota Press reprint forthcoming), pp. 262-301. (A new concluding chapter will include discussion of Castoriadis's work of the last decade.)

1977b — André Liebich, "*Socialisme ou barbarie*: A Radical Critique of Bureaucracy," *Our Generation*, 12 (Fall 1977), pp. 55-62.

1979a — Gregory Renault, "From Bureaucracy to *L'Imaginaire*," *Catalyst*, 13 (Spring 1979), pp. 72-90.

1979b — Gregory Renault, "Major Works of Cornelius Castoriadis," *Catalyst*, 13 (Spring 1979), pp. 105-10.

1979c — Brian Singer, "The Early Castoriadis: Socialism, Barbarism and the Bureaucratic Thread," *Canadian Journal of Political and Social Theory*, 3 (Fall 1979), pp. 35-56.

1980 — Brian Singer, "The Later Castoriadis: Institutions under Interrogation," *Canadian Journal of Political and Social Theory*, 4 (Winter 1980), pp. 75-101.

1981 — Arthur Hirsh, "Castoriadis and *Socialisme ou Barbarie*," in *The French New Left: An Intellectual History from Sartre to Gorz* (Boston: South End Press, 1981), pp. 108-37.

1982a — John B. Thompson, "Ideology and the Social Imaginary," *Theory and Society*, 1982, pp. 659-681. Revised version in his *Studies in the Theory of Ideology* (Cambridge: Polity Press, 1984).

1982b — Gabor T. Ritterspoon, "Facing the War Psychosis," *Telos*, 51 (Spring 1982), pp. 22-31.

1982c — Andrew Arato and Jean Cohen, "The Peace Movement and Western European Sovereignty," *Telos*, 51 (Spring 1982), pp. 158-70 (see especially pp. 164 and 170).

1982d — Jean Cohen, "Between Crisis Management and Social Movements: The Place of Institutional Reforms," *Telos*, 52 (Summer 1982), pp. 21-40 (see especially pp. 35-37).

1982e — Andrew Arato and Jean Cohen, "Reply to Our Non-Critics," *Telos*, 53 (Fall 1982), pp. 188-92.

1982f — Victor Zaslavsky, "Reply to Castoriadis," *Telos*, 53 (Fall 1982), pp. 198-201.

1982g — Paul Piccone, "On Social Movements, Non-Liberals and Castoriadis," *Telos*, 53 (Fall 1982), pp. 201-8.

1984a   *"Crossroads in the Labyrinth"* (review), *Bloomsbury Review*, June-July 1984, p. 28.

1984b   Robert D'Amico, "Cornelius Castoriadis, *Crossroads in the Labyrinth"* (review), *Telos*, 60 (Summer 1984), pp. 193-200.

1985a   Stephen Rousseas, *"Crossraods in the Labyrinth"* (review), *Transaction Society*, January-February, 1985, pp. 85-86.

1985b   Joel Whitebook, "Cornelius Castoriadis, *Crossroads in the Labyrinth"* (reply to D'Amico's review), *Telos*, 63 (Spring 1985), pp. 228-39.

1985c   Robert D'Amico, "Deconstructing D'Amico, or Why Joel Whitebook Is So Upset" (reply to Whitebook's reply), *Telos*, 64 (Summer 1985), pp. 153-59.

1986   Sunil Khilnani, "The Fact of Creation" (review of *Domaines de l'homme*), *Times Literary Supplement*, December 12, 1986, p. 1404.

1987a   Martin Thom, "Under the Volcano" (review of *The Imaginary Institution of Society*), *New Statesman*, September 11, 1987.

1987b   Sunil Khilnani, "Politics of Honour," *New Society*, October 16, 1987, pp. 15-17.

Appendix G:
General Plan of Publication for 10/18 Volumes

The "general plan of publication" for the 10/18 series underwent several revisions during the course of this six-year publication project (1973-79). At first, Castoriadis envisioned a twelve-volume series. By 1975, two volumes were grouped together as one (*IIS*) and published by a different publisher (Le Seuil). Names of volumes were changed and the order was rearranged. Two volumes have never been published at all. In the end, eight volumes were published through 10/18. We provide at the end of this Appendix an English translation of the last version of this "General Plan," as it appeared in *SF*, pp. 11-12 (1979).

We should also note the reasons why Castoriadis's *S. ou B.* articles and other texts were arranged as they were in this series. Basically, he was trying to bring some order and coherence to a multivolume, multiyear publishing effort that was still being defined. We quote from a passage we have eliminated from the "Author's Preface" that elaborates his thinking on this issue.

> The grouping of texts posed some difficult problems, given that many of them, including some of the most important ones, extended beyond any particular subject. A merely chronological ordering of texts, which would have had the advantage of allowing a clear understanding of the evolution of the ideas, would have entailed, at the same time, a considerable dispersion of writings related to a particular theme, and would have made the drafting of a critical commentary nearly impossible. I have therefore regrouped the texts according to the main themes contained therein while preserving chronological order within each grouping; but the reader ought to recall, however, that this grouping allows of a significant degree of arbitrariness and that the cross-references littered throughout the notes were unavoidable. The inconveniences of the solution chosen will be mitigated in part, I hope, by the general plan of publication,

outlined below, and by the introduction placed at the beginning of
this first volume, which aims to present the basic ideas in their
temporal evolution and their logical interconnection. (Avertissement,
SB 1, pp. 5-6)

Not being faced with the same difficulties as Castoriadis, we have merely
grouped the texts selected for the present edition in chronological order and divided them into three volumes.

General Plan of Publication

  I. Bureaucratic Society
     1. The Relations of Production in Russia
     2. The Revolution against the Bureaucracy
     3. Postindustrial Russia*
  II. The Dynamic of Capitalism*
 III. Modern Capitalism and Revolution
     1. Imperialism and War
     2. The Revolutionary Movement in the Age of Modern Capitalism
 IV. The Content of Socialism
  V. The Experience of the Workers' Movement
     1. How to Struggle
     2. Proletariat and Organization
 VI. The Imaginary Institution of Society
     1. Marxism and Revolutionary Theory
     2. The Social Imaginary and the Institution
VII. French Society

*These two volumes have not yet appeared.

Appendix H:
Identification of Pseudonymous Authors

Cardan, Paul	Cornelius Castoriadis as author of his later French writings in *S. ou B.* (beginning with no. 27 [April 1959]) and of his English-language writings published in *Solidarity*.
Chaulieu, Pierre	Cornelius Castoriadis as *S. ou B.* editor/author.
Coudray, Jean-Marc	Cornelius Castoriadis as author of "La Révolution anticipée," in *Mai 1968: La Brèche* (Paris: Editions Fayard, 1968; later reprinted in *SF*, pp. 165-221).
Forest, F.	Raya Dunayevskaya
Germain, E.	Ernest Mandel
Johnson, J. R.	C. L. R. James
Montal, Claude	Claude Lefort
Stone, Ria*	Grace C. Lee (now Boggs)

*Despite assertions to the contrary by Claude Lefort (see "An Interview with Claude Lefort," 1976 in Appendix F, p. 117) and by André Liebich (see 1977b in Appendix F, p. 61, n. 17), Ria Stone was the pseudonym for Grace (Lee) Boggs, not Raya Dunayevskaya. Liebich notes, "In Lefort's interview . . . he states that Castoriadis's close entente with Rya [sic] Stone first led him to believe that there were not only political divergences but a profound opposition of thought between himself and Castoriadis." So much for this analysis of bad influences, given this incorrect identification. (Castoriadis clearly identifies Stone as Lee/Boggs in a parenthetical addition to the 1979 reprint of his Preface, included in this volume.)

Appendix I:
Glossary

We present here a small number of French words and their English equivalents, which might be of interest to the scholar. Given the absence of any significant translation complications, the text itself can stand on its own for the general reader without requiring special explanations, with the following few exceptions.

Unlike Castoriadis's later writings, the texts translated here contain few specialized terms and neologisms peculiar to the author's writings of this period. The only technical terms that appear in these texts come from the fields of philosophy, sociology, and economics (and often directly from Marx's writings). We usually have provided the standard translation term in these cases. A few terms found in the "General Introduction" do derive from his later writings and we have noted them here.

à-être	*having-to-be*. A technical term in *IIS*, which appears here only in the "General Introduction." We have followed the *IIS* translation.
autogestion	*self-management*.
cadre	*cadre* (of a party), *trained staff* (of an enterprise).
décollement	*coming unstuck*. A term *S. ou B.* tried to popularize that was used to describe the process whereby the proletariat was freeing itself from the hold of the CP.
dépasser	*to outstrip, overcome, overtake, surmount*. Unlike Alan Sheridan-Smith's translation of Sartre's *Critique of Dialectical Reason*, we have only rarely used "to transcend."

direction	*direction* (as opposed to execution), *leadership* (of a political party, State etc.), (the) *management* (of an enterprise, etc.).
dirigeant	*director* (as opposed to executant), *leader* or *ruler* (of a political party, State, etc.), *manager* (of an enterprise, etc.).
entreprise	*enterprise* (in Eastern or Western countries), *business*, *business enterprise*, *company*, or *firm* (in Western countries exclusively).
étatisation	*statification* (complete nationalization).
executant	*executant* (of tasks prescribed by a separate stratum of directors or managers in traditional or bureaucratic capitalism).
execution	*execution, carrying out* (of prescribed tasks). Opposed (in traditional or bureaucratic capitalism) to the functions of *direction*.
faire	*making/doing*. A technical term in *CL* and *IIS* that appears here only in the "General Introduction"; we have followed the *CL* translation.
fusion	*merger* or *fusion* (of economic sectors, units, or strata).
gestion	*management* (the act of managing). Also: *gestion ouvrière* ("workers' management") and *gestionnaire*, which we have usually translated as "self-managerial" (as in "self-managerial activity").
instauration	*instauration* (act of instituting or establishing something anew or for the first time). According to the *Oxford English Dictionary*, we are reviving (reinstaurating?) a now-obsolete meaning of a seventeenth-century English word. We do so because this term is so important for Castoriadis's thoughts on creation and institutionalization, especially in *IIS*. The more contemporary meaning, "the act of restoring" or "restoration"—with all of its political overtones—is exactly the opposite of what is meant here. Thus also, "to instaurate," etc.
parcellaire	*compartmentalized* (labor). We have used "compartmentalized worker" (and "compartmentalization") instead of Marx's "detail worker" or *Teilarbeiter*, since the word "detail" is not "detailed" enough, if you will, to describe "a laborer who all his life performs one and the same simple operation [and thus] converts his whole body into the automatic, specialized implement of that operation" (*Capital*, vol. 1, pt. 7, sec. 2, p. 339). Our phrase is not completely adequate, either.
propriété	*ownership* or *property*.

signification   *signification*. Another term that is developed more fully in *IIS* and in other later writings. "Meaning" has been used on occasion, as well as "significance" when the context suggested it.

technique   *technique*. The Greek *techné*, or "know-how" in the broadest sense, as Castoriadis says at one point. Contrasted with "technology," with its socially instituted *logos*—the specific set of techniques chosen by, and used in, a given society. This distinction is clearly made in the "Socialism Is the Transformation of Work" section of *CS II*.

Bibliography

Bibliography

Alexinsky, Grégoire. *La Russie révolutionnaire*. Paris: Librairie Armand Colin, 1947.

Bettelheim, Charles. *La Planification soviétique*. Paris: Librairie des Sciences Politiques et Sociales, 1946.

_____. *Les Problèmes théoriques et pratiques de la planification*. Paris: Presses Universitaires de France, 1946.

Bettelheim, Charles, and Paul M. Sweezy. *On the Transition to Socialism*. New York: Monthly Review Press, 1971.

Brinton, Maurice. *The Bolsheviks & Workers' Control*. London: Solidarity, 1970; Detroit: Red & Black, 1975.

Burnham, James. *The Managerial Revolution*. 1941. Reprint. Bloomington: Indiana University Press, 1960.

Clark, C. "Les Conditions du progrès economique." In *Etudes et Conjoncture. Economie mondiale*, 13 (June 1947), pp. 45-134.

Engels, Frederick. *Anti-Dühring. Herr Eugen Dühring's Revolution in Science*, trans. Emile Burns, ed. C. P. Dutt. New York: International Publishers, 1939.

_____. "Engels to C. Schmidt in Berlin, London, October 27, 1890." In *MESW*, pp. 694-99.

Fabius, G. H. "Technical Progress in Agriculture." *New International*, 1946, pp. 116-17.

Forest, F. "An Analysis of Russian Economy." Parts 2 and 3. *New International*, January and February, 1943, pp. 17-22 and 52-57.

Foucault, Marc. "1948." *S. ou B.*, 1 (March 1949), pp. 47-61.

Fourastié, Jean. *Le Grand Espoir du XXᵉ siècle*. 1949. New Ed. Paris: Gallimard, 1971.

Fourth International. "Documents and Resolutions of the Second World Congress of the Fourth International." *Fourth International*, June 1948, pp. 111ff.

Grousset, P. "Ce qui s'est passé réellement en Allemagne orientale." *L'Observateur politique, économique et littéraire*, 163 (June 25, 1953), pp. 11-14.

Guillaume, Philippe. "Machinisme et prolétariat." *S. ou B.*, 17 (August 1950), pp. 46-66.

Koopmans, Tjalling. *Activity Analysis of Production & Allocation*. 1951. Reprint. New Haven, Conn.: Yale University Press, 1972.

Lefort, Claude. "Le Marxisme et Sartre." *Les Temps Modernes*, 89 (April 1953), pp. 1541-70; reprinted in *Eléments d'une critique de la bureaucratie*. Geneva-Paris: Droz, 1971, pp. 59-79.

_____. "Le Prolétariat et le problème de la direction révolutionnaire." *S. ou B.*, 10 (July 1952), pp. 18-27. Reprinted as "Le Prolétariat et sa direction." In *Eléments d'une critique de la bureaucratie*. 2nd ed. Paris: Gallimard, 1979, pp. 59-70.

Lenin, V. I. "The Agrarian Question and the 'Critics' of Marx." In *LCW*, vol. 5. Moscow: Progress Publishers, 1980.

_____. "Imperialism, the Highest Stage of Capitalism." In *LSWONE*, pp. 169-263.

_____. " 'Left-Wing' Childishness and the Petty Bourgeois Mentality." In *LSWONE*, pp. 432-55.

_____. " 'Left-Wing' Communism—an Infantile Disorder." In *LSWONE*, pp. 506-91.

_____. "The Proletarian Revolution and the Renegade Kautsky." In *LSWONE*, pp. 468-75.

_____. "Resolutions of the Sixth Congress of the R.S.-D.L.P." In *LCW*, vol. 20-1. New York: International Publishers, 1932.

_____. *The State and Revolution*. In *LSWONE*, pp. 264-357.

_____. *What Is to Be Done*. New York: International Publishers, 1969.

Leontief, W., et al. *Studies in the Structure of American Economy*. 1953. Reprint. Armonk, N.Y.: Sharpe, 1976.

Marx, Karl. *Capital*. 3 Vols. New York: International Publishers, 1967.

_____. "Critique of the Gotha Programme." In *MESW*, pp. 315-55.

_____. "Economic and Philosophic Manuscripts of 1844." In *MECW*, vol. 3, pp. 229-346.

_____. "The Eighteenth Brumaire of Louis Bonaparte." In *MESW*, pp. 95-180.

_____. "Introduction to *The Critique of Political Economy*." In *Grundrisse: Foundations of the Critique of Political Economy*, trans. Martin Nicolaus. New York: Vintage, 1973.

_____. Letter to Johann Baptist Schweitzer (in Berlin), London, January 24, 1865. In *The Letters of Karl Marx*, selected and trans. with explanatory notes and an intro. by Saul K. Padover. Englewood Cliffs, N.J.: Prentice-Hall, 1979.

_____. "The Poverty of Philosophy." In *MECW*, vol. 6, pp. 105-212.

_____. Preface to *A Contribution to the Critique of Political Economy*. In *MESW*, pp. 181-85.

_____. "Provisional Rules." In *The First International and After*. Vol. 3 of K. Marx, *Political Writings*, ed. David Fernbach. London: Penguin/New Left Books, 1974.

_____. *Wages, Price, and Profit*. In *MESW*, pp. 186-229.

Marx, Karl, and Frederick Engels. "The German Ideology." In *MECW*, vol. 5, pp. 19-539.

_____. "Manifesto of the Communist Party." In *MESW*, pp. 35-63.

Mothé, Daniel. "La Grève chez Renault." *S. ou B.*, 13 (January 1954), pp. 34-45.

Peregrinus. "Les Kolkhoz pendant la guerre." Translated from the German by Pierre Chaulieu (Cornelius Castoriadis). *S. ou B.*, 4 (October 1949), pp. 3-18.

Reich, Wilhelm. *Character Analysis*. 1948. New trans. Vincent R. Carafagno. New York: Farrar, Strauss & Giroux, 1972.

_____. *The Function of the Orgasm*. 1942. New trans. Vincent R. Carafagno. New York: Farrar, Strauss & Giroux, 1973.

_____. *The Sexual Revolution*. 1945. Trans. Therese Pol. Reprint. New York: Farrar, Strauss & Giroux, 1974.

Romano, Paul. "Life in the Factory." In Paul Romano and Ria Stone, *The American Worker*. 1947. Reprint. Detroit: Bewick Editions, 1972.

Sarel, Beno. *La Classe ouvrière d'Allemagne orientale*. Paris: Editions ouvrières, 1958.

Sartre, J.-P. *Being and Nothingness*, trans. Hazel Barnes. New York: Washington Square Press, 1966.

_____. "The Communists and the Peace," trans. Martha H. Fletcher. In *The Communists and the Peace*. New York: George Braziller, 1968.

_____. "Reply to Lefort," trans. Philip R. Berk. In *The Communists and the Peace*. New York: George Braziller, 1968.

_____. Sartre parle des maos." *Actuel*, 28 (February 1973), pp. 73-77.

_____. *What Is Literature?*, trans. Bernard Frechtman. New York: Harper & Row, 1965.

Serge, Victor. *Russia Twenty Years After*, trans. Max Shachtman. New York: Hillman-Curl, 1937.

Stone, Ria. "The Reconstruction of Society." In Paul Romano and Ria Stone, *The American Worker*. 1947. Reprint. Detroit: Bewick Editions, 1972.

Trotsky, Leon. "The Defense of the Soviet Republic and the Opposition." In *Writings, 1929*. New York: Pathfinder Press, 1975.

_____. *In Defense of Marxism*. 2nd ed. New York: Pathfinder Press, 1973.

_____. "Learn to Think." In *Writings, 1937-38*. New York: Pathfinder Press, 1976.

_____. Letter to Borodai, published in *New International* (1943). Reprinted as "Our Differences with the Democratic Centralists," in Max Shachtman, *The Bureaucratic Revolution. The Rise of the Stalinist State*. New York: Donald Press, 1962.

_____. "Manifesto of the Communist International to the Workers of the World." In *Theses, Resolutions and Manifestos of the First Four Congresses of the Third International*, trans. Alix Holt and Barbara Hessel, ed. Alan Adler. New York: Humanities Press, 1980, pp. 27-35.

_____. "Not a Workers' and Not a Bourgeois State?" In *Writings, 1937-38*. New York: Pathfinder Press, 1976.

_____. "Once Again: The USSR and Its Defense." In *Writings, 1937-38*. New York: Pathfinder Press, 1976.

_____. "The Permanent Revolution." In *The Permanent Revolution & Results and Prospects*. New York: Pathfinder Press, 1970.

_____. "The Problems of Development of the USSR." In *Writings 1930-31*. New York: Pathfinder Press, 1973.

_____. *The Revolution Betrayed*. New York: Pathfinder Press, 1972.

_____. *The Soviet Union and the Fourth International*. New York: Pioneer Press, 1934.

_____. *The Third International after Lenin*. New York: Pathfinder Press, 1970.

_____. *The Transitional Program for Socialist Revolution*, trans. Max Eastman. 2nd ed. New York: Pathfinder Press, 1974.

_____. "The Workers' State, Thermidor and Bonapartism." In *Writings, 1934-35*. New York: Pathfinder Press, 1974.

V. W. "Stakhanovisme et mouchardage." *S. ou B.*, 3 (July 1949), pp. 82-87.

Index

INDEX

Cornelius Castoriadis, who has been teaching at the Ecole des hautes etudes en sciences sociales since 1980, is a practicing psychoanalyst living in Paris. Born in Constantinople in 1922, he studied law, economics, and political science at the University of Athens. After participating in the underground movement against the Nazi Occupation in Greece (1941-45) and against the Greek Communist Party, Castoriadis moved to Paris after World War II, and in 1949 he founded the revolutionary group and journal called *Socialisme ou Barbarie*. He worked as an economist at the Organization for Economic Cooperation and Development from 1948 to 1970, and became its director of statistics, national accounts, and growth studies. Castoriadis was among the editors of *Textures* (1971-75) and *Libre* (1976-80) and has published in such North American journals as *Catalyst, Dissent, Salmagundi, Social Research*, and *Philosophy and Social Criticism*. Among his many books, *Crossroads in the Labyrinth* and *The Imaginary Institution of Society* are also available in English translation.

David Ames Curtis, translator, editor, writer, and activist, received his degree in philosophy from Harvard University. In the early 1980s he worked as a community organizer in the Carolinas with Carolina Action/ACORN and as a rank-and-file union organizer of clerical workers for the Federation of University Employees (Hotel Employees and Restaurant Employees International Union, AFL-CIO) at Yale University, where he was also the research director for the Black Periodical Fiction Project. He was a contributing researcher for *Anti-Slavery Newspapers and Periodicals* (edited by Mae G. Henderson and John Blassingame) and for the 1983 reprint edition of *Our Nig*, the recently rediscovered first novel by a black American woman (edited by Henry Louis Gates, Jr.), as well as coeditor of the forthcoming *Collected Works of John Jea* (the first black male poet to be published in book form), and has also published articles and translations in *Philosophy and Social Criticism* and *Free Associations*. Curtis currently lives in Paris, where he is working on a book about the French student and worker protests of 1968 and 1986.